XML

BY EXAMPLE

Second Edition

201 West 103rd Street
Indianapolis, Indiana 46290

Benoît Marchal

XML by Example, Second Edition

Copyright © *2002* by *Que*

International Standard Book Number: 0-7897-2504-5

Library of Congress Catalog Card Number: 00-111682

Printed in the United States of America

First Printing: September 2001

04   03   02   01   4   3   2   1

Trademarks

Warning and Disclaimer

Associate Publisher
Dean Miller

Acquisitions Editor
Todd Green

Development Editor
Sean Dixon

Managing Editor
Thomas F. Hayes

Senior Editor
Susan Ross Moore

Copy Editors
Geneil Breeze
Kay Hoskin

Indexer
Chris Barrick

Proofreader
Maribeth Echard

Technical Editor
Jeff McMahon

Team Coordinator
Cindy Teeters

Media Developer
Michael Hunter

Interior Designer
Karen Ruggles

Cover Designer
Rader Design

Page Layout
Steve Geiselman
Susan Geiselman

Contents at a Glance

Table of Contents

About the Author

Benoît Marchal is a writer and consultant based in Namur, Belgium. His company, Pineapplesoft, specializes in e-commerce with XML and Java. In 1997, he co-founded the XML/EDI Group, a think tank that promotes the use of XML in e-commerce applications.

He is the author of *Applied XML Solutions* (Sams), and a columnist for Gamelan and IBM developerWorks. You can reach him through his Web site at www.marchal.com or via e-mail at bmarchal@Pineapplesoft.com.

Dedication

To Pascale for her never-failing trust and patience.

Acknowledgments

Writing the first edition of this book was a challenge for my business and for my family. It turned out that revising it was equally challenging but this time I was particularly demanding on Que staff. Thank you for your understanding and patience.

Introduction

The *by Example* Series

How does the *by Example* series make you a better programmer? The *by Example* series teaches programming using the best method possible. After a concept is introduced, you'll see one or more examples of that concept in use. The text acts as a mentor by figuratively looking over your shoulder and showing you new ways to use the concepts you just learned. The examples are numerous. While the material is still fresh, you see example after example demonstrating the way you use the material you just learned.

The philosophy of the *by Example* series is simple: The best way to teach computer programming is using multiple examples. Command descriptions, format syntax, and language references are not enough to teach a newcomer a programming language. Only by looking at many examples in which new commands are immediately used and by running sample programs can programming students get more than just a feel for the language.

Who Should Use This Book

XML by Example is intended for programmers with some basic HTML coding experience. You don't need to be an expert, however. If you can write a simple HTML page and if you know the main tags (such as `<p>`, `<title>`, `<h1>`), you know enough HTML to understand this book.

Yet XML is mostly valuable in conjunction with a scripting or programming language. Some advanced techniques introduced in the second half of the book (starting with Chapter 5, "XSL Transformations," and even more so in Chapter 7, "The Parser and DOM" and later) require experience with scripting and JavaScript. You need to understand loops, variables, functions, and objects for these chapters. Remember, these are advanced techniques, so even if you are not a JavaScript wizard, you can pick up many valuable techniques in the book.

This book is for you if one of the following statements is true:

- You are an HTML whiz, have some experience in programming, and want to move to the next level in Internet publishing.

- You publish a large or dynamic document base on the Web, on CD-ROM, in print, or by using a combination of these media, and you have heard that XML can simplify your publishing efforts.

- You are a Web developer, so you know Java, JavaScript, or some other programming language inside out, and you have heard that XML is simple and enables you to do many cool things.

- You are active in electronic commerce or in EDI, and you want to learn what XML has to offer to your specialty.

- You use software from Microsoft, IBM, Oracle, Corel, Sun, or any of the other hundreds of companies that have added XML to their products, and you need to understand how to make the best of it.

This Book's Organization

This book teaches you about XML, the eXtensible Markup Language. XML is a new markup language developed to overcome limitations in HTML.

XML exists because HTML was successful. Therefore, XML incorporates many successful features of HTML. XML also exists because HTML could not live up to new demands. Therefore, XML breaks new ground when it is appropriate.

This book takes a hands-on approach to XML. Ideas and concepts are introduced through real-world examples so that you not only read about the concepts but also see them applied. With the examples, you immediately see the benefits and the costs associated with XML.

As you will see, there are two classes of applications for XML: publishing and data exchange (also known as application integration). Data exchange applications include most electronic commerce applications. This book draws most of its examples from data exchange applications because they are the most popular application of XML. However, it also includes a comprehensive example of Web site publishing.

I made some assumptions about you. I suppose that you are familiar with the Web, insofar as you can read, understand, and write basic HMTL pages as well as read and understand a simple JavaScript application. You don't have to be a master at HTML to learn XML. Nor do you need to be a guru of JavaScript, but you do need an understanding of both.

Most of the code in this book is based on XML and XML style sheets. When programming was required, I used JavaScript as often as possible. JavaScript, however, was not appropriate for the final example, so I turned to Java.

You don't need to know Java to understand this book, however, because very little Java is involved (again, most of the code in the final example is XML). Appendix A, "Crash Course on Java," will teach you just enough Java to understand the examples.

Conventions Used in This Book

Examples are identified by the icon shown at the left of this sentence:

Listing and code appears in monospace font, such as

```
<?xml version="1.0"?>
```

NOTE
Special notes augment the material you read in each chapter. These notes clarify concepts and procedures.

TIP
You'll find numerous tips offering shortcuts and solutions to common problems.

CAUTION
The cautions warn you about pitfalls that sometimes appear when programming in XML. Reading the caution sections will save you time and trouble.

What's Next

XML was introduced to overcome the limitations of HTML. Although the two will likely coexist in the foreseeable future, the importance of XML will only increase. It is important that you learn the benefits and limitations of XML so that you can prepare for the evolution.

Visit the *by Example* Web site or my own Web site for code examples or additional material associated with this book:

```
<http://www.quepublishing.com/series/by_example/>
```

```
<http://www.marchal.com>
```

While you are there, I encourage you to subscribe to my free monthly newsletter. It's the best solution to keep abreast of new developments in XML and Internet development.

Turn to the next page and begin learning XML by examples today!

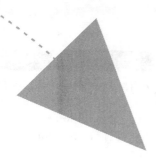

The XML Galaxy

This chapter introduces you to XML. It tells you the why and what: why was XML developed, and what is XML good at? Before we turn to how to use XML, which is the topic of the next 11 chapters, you need to understand where XML might be of use for you.

In this chapter, you will learn the essential concepts behind XML:

- Which problems XML solves; in other words, what XML is good at.

- What a markup language is and what the relationship between XML, HTML, and SGML is.

- How and why XML was developed.

- Typical applications of XML, with examples.

- The benefits of using XML when compared to HTML. When is XML better than HTML?

Introduction

XML stands for the eXtensible Markup Language. It was developed by the W3C (World Wide Web Consortium), primarily to overcome limitations in HTML. The W3C is the organization in charge of the development and maintenance of many Web standards, most notably HTML. For more information on the W3C, visit its Web site at www.w3.org.

Originally, the Web was a publishing tool for scientific documents. Today it has grown into a full-fledged medium, equal to print and TV. More importantly, the Web is an interactive medium because it supports applications such as online shops, electronic banking/trading, and discussion forums.

To accommodate this phenomenal popularity, HTML has been extended. Over the years, many new tags were introduced. The first version of HTML had a dozen tags; the latest version (HTML 4.0) has close to 100 tags (not counting browser-specific tags).

Furthermore, a large set of supporting technologies has been introduced: JavaScript, Java, Flash, CGI, ASP, JSP, servlet, EJB, streaming media, MP3, and more. Some of these technologies were developed by the W3C, whereas others were developed and introduced by vendors, such as Sun, Netscape, or Microsoft.

This incredible growth has turned HTML into an immensely popular language. According to some studies, there are 800 million Web pages, and they all are coded in HTML. HTML is supported by thousands of applications including browsers, editors, e-mail software, databases, contact managers, word processors, and more.

However, everything is not rosy with HTML. First, over the years, it has grown into a complex language. With almost 100 tags, it is definitively not a small language. The combinations of tags are almost endless, and the result of a particular combination of tags might be different from one browser to another.

Finally, despite this rich tag set, more are needed. For example, electronic commerce applications would need tags for product references, prices, names, addresses, and more. Streaming would need tags to control the flow of images and sound. Search engines would need more precise tags for keywords and descriptions. Security would need tags for signing.

When the W3C inquires on how to improve HTML, it faces a long list of developers clamoring for new HTML tags. Unfortunately, adding even more tags to HTML is not a satisfactory solution. The language is already on the verge of collapsing under its own weight, so why continue adding tags?

Worse, although many applications need more tags, some applications would benefit greatly from a reduction in the tag count! The W3C expects that by the year 2002, 75% of surfers won't be using a PC. Rather, they will access the Web from a personal digital assistant (PDA), such as the popular PalmPilot, or from so-called smart phones, such as the Japanese i-mode phones or European WAP phones.

PDAs and smart phones are not as powerful as PCs. They cannot process a complex language like HTML, much less an improved version of HTML that would offer even more tags.

Another, but related, problem is that it takes many tags to format a page. It is not uncommon to see Web pages that have more markup than content! These pages are slow to download and display, even on powerful PCs.

In conclusion, even though HTML is a popular and successful language, it has some major shortcomings, and it has turned into a maintenance nightmare for the W3C. XML was developed to address these shortcomings.

XML exists because HTML was successful. Therefore, XML incorporates many successful features of HTML. As you study XML, remember that it was not introduced for the sake of novelty. XML also exists because HTML could not live up to new demands. Therefore, XML breaks new ground only where it is appropriate.

It is difficult to change a successful technology like HTML; not surprisingly, XML has raised some level of controversy. More specifically, there have been many questions on the relationship between XML and HTML.

Let me be very clear: XML will not replace HTML in the near or medium-term. For the longer term, HTML will converge toward XML through the XHTML standard, a rewriting of HTML in XML.

Some areas where XML will be useful in the near-term include the following:

- Large Web site maintenance. XML would work behind the scenes (more specifically on the server) to simplify the maintenance of HTML documents.

- Exchange of information between organizations.

- Offloading and reloading of databases.

- Syndicated content, where content is being made available to different Web sites.

- Electronic commerce applications where different organizations collaborate to serve a customer.

- Scientific applications with new markup languages for mathematical and chemical formulas.

- Electronic books with new markup languages to express rights and ownership.

- Handheld devices and smartphones.with new markup languages optimized for these so-called "alternative" devices.

Where This Book Fits

This book takes a "hands-on" approach to XML. It teaches you how to deploy XML in your environment: how to decide where XML fits and how best to implement it. This book uses many real-world examples.

As you will see, there are two classes of applications for XML: publishing and data exchange. This book draws most of its examples from data exchange applications because they are currently the most popular. However, it also includes a comprehensive example of Web site publishing.

I make some assumptions about you. I assume that you are familiar with the Web, insofar that you can read, understand, and write basic HMTL pages as well as read and understand JavaScript applications. You don't have to be a master at HTML to learn XML, nor do you need to be JavaScript guru.

However, as we progress in the book, we'll build more sophisticated examples that require notions of programming. This is particularly true for the last two chapters. Again, you don't need to be an expert programmer. You may want to skip the code to concentrate on the concepts on first reading.

Most of the code in this book is based on XML and its companion standards. When programming was required, I used JavaScript as often as possible. JavaScript, however, was not appropriate for the final example, so I turned to Java.

You don't need to know Java to read this book. Very little Java is involved (again, most of the code in the final example is based on techniques that you learn in this book), and, if you already know another programming language, Appendix A, "Crash Course on Java," will teach you just enough Java to understand the examples.

The feedback I received from readers of the first edition is that they enjoyed the teaching by example and the no-nonsense approach. I tried to preserve these qualities for this edition.

You will find little hype and many practical examples of using XML.

A First Look at XML

The idea behind XML is deceptively simple. It aims at answering the conflicting demands that arrived at the W3C for the future of HTML.

As you have seen, on one hand, some applications need more tags, and these tags are increasingly specialized. For example, businessmen want tags for price and product reference. Mathematicians want tags for their formulas. Chemists also want tags for formulas, but they are not the same.

On the other hand, other applications want a simple language.

How can you provide both more tags and fewer tags in a single language? The W3C resolved this dilemma by making essentially two changes to HTML:

- It predefines no tags.

- It is stricter.

No Predefined Tags

EXAMPLE

Because there are no predefined tags in XML, you, the author, create the tags that you need. Do you need a tag for price? Do you need a tag for a bold hyperlink that floats on the right side of the screen? Make them

```
<price currency="usd">499.00</price>
<toc xlink:href="/newsletter">Pineapplesoft Link</toc>
```

The <price> tag has no equivalent in HTML although you could simulate the <toc> tag through a combination of table, hyperlink, and bold:

```
<table>
   <tr>
      <td><!-- main text here --></td>
      <td><a href="/newsletter"><b>Pineapplesoft Link</b></a></td>
   </tr>
</table>
```

This is the extensible aspect of XML (the X in XML). XML is extensible because it predefines no tags but lets the author create the tags needed for his or her application.

This looks like a good solution, but it opens many questions such as the following:

- How does the browser know that <toc> is equivalent to this combination of table, hyperlink, and bold?

- Can you compare different prices?

- What about the current and previous generations of browsers?
- How does this simplify Web site maintenance?

We will address these and many other questions in detail in the following chapters. Briefly the answers are

- The browsers or the Web servers use style sheets; see Chapter 5, "XSL Transformations," and Chapter 6, "XSL Formatting Objects and Cascading Style Sheets."
- You can compare prices; see Chapter 7, "The Parser and DOM," and Chapter 8, "Alternative API: SAX."
- XML can be made compatible with any browser; see Chapter 5.
- XML enables you to concentrate on more stable aspects of your document; see Chapter 5.

Stricter Syntax

HTML has a forgiving syntax. This is great for authors who can be as lazy as they want, but it also makes Web browsers more complex. According to some estimates, more than 50% of the code in a browser handles errors or sloppiness on the author's part.

However, authors increasingly use HMTL editors, so they don't really care how simple and forgiving the syntax is.

Yet browsers are growing in size and are becoming generally slower. The speed factor is a problem for every surfer. The size factor is a problem for owners of handheld devices who cannot afford to download 10MB browsers.

Therefore, it was decided that XML would adopt a strict syntax. A strict syntax results in smaller, faster, and lighter browsers.

EXAMPLE

For example, the following is acceptable in HTML:

```
<p>Welcome to our site!<img src=logo.jpg>
```

The equivalent code in XML would be

```
<p>Welcome to our site!<img src="logo.jpg"/></p>
```

Notice that the attribute value is quoted, and both the paragraph and image tags are terminated with the "/" character (the image tag uses a special form for so-called empty elements).

HTML is forgiving because it lets you ignore the quotes around the attribute in most cases. But XML accepts no such simplification, nor does it let you forget an ending tag.

If you are lost by the syntax, don't worry. We'll cover the details of the syntax in the next chapter. For now, just remember that XML syntax is strict.

A First Look on Document Structure

XML is all about document structure. This section looks into the issue of structured documents.

EXAMPLE

1. To illustrate document structure, I will use the fictitious memo in Listing 1.1 as an example.

Listing 1.1: memo.txt

```
INTERNAL MEMO

From:      John Doe
To:        Jack Smith
Regarding: XML at WhizBang

Have you heard of this new technology, XML? It looks promising.
It is similar to HTML but it is extensible. All the big names
(Microsoft, IBM, Oracle, Sun) are backing it.

We could use XML to launch new e-commerce services. It is also
useful for the web site: you complained it was a lot of work,
apparently XML can simplify the maintenance.

Check this web site <http://www.w3.org/XML> for more information.
Also visit Que <http://www.quepublishing.com>. They have just released
"XML by Example, 2nd Edition" by Benoît Marchal
<http://www.marchal.com> with lots of useful information and some
great examples. I have already ordered two copies!

John
```

The structure of this memo is not a monolithic entity. The memo is made of at least three distinct elements:

- The title

- The header, including sender and recipient names as well as the subject

- The body text

These elements are organized in relation to each other, following a structure. For example, the title indicates that this is a memo. The title is followed by the header.

Examine the memo more closely, and you find that the body text itself can be further broken down this way:

- Three paragraphs

- Several URLs

- A signature

You could continue this decomposition process and recognize smaller elements such as sentences, words, or even characters. However, these smaller elements usually add little information on the structure of the document.

EXAMPLE

2. The structure we have just identified is independent from the appearance of the memo. For example, the memo could have been written in HTML. It would have resulted in a nicer-looking document, as illustrated in Figure 1.1, but would have the same structure.

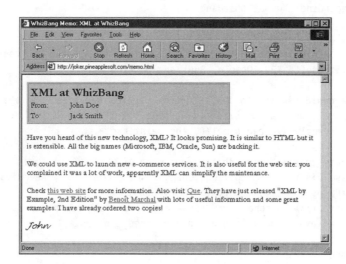

Figure 1.1: *The memo is nicely formatted in HTML.*

Figure 1.1 is just one possible presentation. The same memo could have been formatted completely differently, as illustrated by Figure 1.2.

It is important to notice that the memo presentation may be completely different and yet it still follows the same structure: The appearance has no impact on the structure. In other words, whether the subject, sender, and recipient are enclosed in a frame or as a bulleted list does not impact the structure.

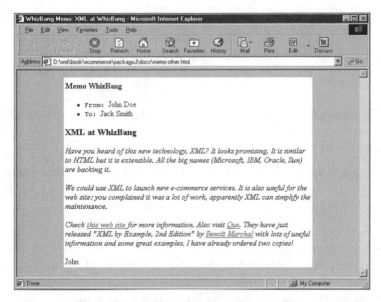

Figure 1.2: *A different presentation.*

In Listing 1.1, Figure 1.1, and Figure 1.2, the memo consists of the following:

- A title
- A header made of
    - The sender
    - The recipient
    - A subject
- The body text made of
    - Three paragraphs
    - Several URLs
    - A signature

And the relationship between those elements remains unchanged.

Does it mean that structure and appearance are totally unrelated? Not at all! Ideally, a text is formatted to expose its structure to the reader. Indeed, it is more pleasant to read the HTML versions of the memo rather than the text because the frame and bold characters make it easier to distinguish the header from the body.

For the same reasons, it is common practice to print chapter titles and other headings in bold. When you read, you come to rely on those typographic conventions: They help you build a mental image of the document structure. Also, they are particularly valuable when leafing through a document.

Likewise, magazines and newspapers try to build a visual style. They select a set of fonts and apply them consistently over the years so that you should be able to recognize your favorite magazine only by its typesetting choices.

It gives comfort to the regular reader and helps differentiate the magazine from the competition. For similar reasons, companies tend to enforce a corporate style with logos and common letterheads.

The moral of this section, and the key to understanding XML, is that the structure of a document is the foundation from which the appearance is deduced. Although I have illustrated it with only a memo, this holds true for all sorts of documents including technical documentation, books, letters, e-mails, reports, magazines, Web pages, and more.

Most file formats concentrate on the actual appearance of a document; they take great pain to ensure almost identical display on various platforms.

XML uses a different approach and records the structure of documents from which the formatting is automatically deduced. The difference might seem trivial, but it has far-reaching implications.

CAUTION

Don't be confused by the vocabulary: XML is not just a solution to publishing Web pages.

XML clearly has its roots in publishing: technical documentation, books, letters, Web pages, and more, and it shows in the vocabulary. For example, an XML file is referred to as an *XML document*. Likewise, to manipulate an XML document, you are likely to apply a *style sheet*, even when you're importing data from a database. Relationships between documents are expressed through *links*, even though they might not be hyperlinks.

The reliance on publishing terms in the XML jargon is the source of much confusion because it appears restrictive. This is unfortunate because it has turned off many people. So, I urge you to keep an open mind; as you will see in this book, XML documents are word-processing documents.

Markup Language History

HTML stands for Hypertext Markup Language; XML is the eXtensible Markup Language. That's two markup languages already. Another standard is called SGML, the Standard Generalized Markup Language. Do you see the pattern here?

All three languages are markup languages. What exactly is a markup language? What problem does it solve?

The easiest way to understand markup languages in general, and XML in particular, is probably a historical study of electronic markup—that is, the progression from procedural markup to generalized markup through generic coding.

This requires a brief discussion of SGML, the international standard underlying HTML and XML. I promise that I will limit references to SGML in this book. However, I cannot completely hide the relationship between XML and SGML.

Before we rush into the hows and whys, let me define markup. In an electronic document, the markup is the codes, embedded with the document text, which store the information required for electronic processing, such as font name, boldness, or, in the case of XML, the document structure. This is not specific to XML; every electronic document standard uses some sort of markup.

Mark-Up

Mark-up originates in the publishing industry. In traditional publishing, the manuscript is annotated with layout instructions for the typesetter. These handwritten annotations are called *mark-up*.

Procedural Markup

Similarly, word processing requires the user to specify the appearance of the text. For example, the user selects a typeface and its boldness. The user also can place a piece of text at a given position on the page and more. This information is called *markup* and is stored as special codes with the text.

NOTE

Electronic markup is spelled as one word to distinguish it from traditional handwritten mark-up.

Practically, the user selects commands in menus to add formatting instructions to the text. The formatting instructions tell the printer whether to print in bold or when to use another typeface.

To select the formatting instructions, the user implicitly analyses the structure of the document—that is, he identifies each separate meaningful element.

He then determines the commands that need to be applied to produce the format desired for that type of element, and he selects the appropriate commands.

Note that, once again, the document structure is the starting point from which actual formatting is deduced. However, this is an unconscious process.

This process is often referred to as *procedural markup* because the markup is effectively some procedure for the output device. It closely parallels the traditional mark-up activity. The main difference is that markup is stored electronically.

EXAMPLE

The Rich Text Format (RTF), developed by Microsoft but supported by most word processors, is a procedural markup. Listing 1.2 is the memo in RTF. You need not worry about all the codes used in this document, but it is clear that instructions (markup) have been added to the text to describe how it should be formatted.

For example, you'll recognize code to select special fonts:

```
{\f0\froman\fprq2\fcharset0 Garamond;}
```

Listing 1.2: memo.rtf

```
{\rtf1\ansi\ansicpg1252\deff0\deflang1033\deflangfe1033{\fonttbl
{\f0\froman\fprq2\fcharset0 Garamond;}{\f1\froman\fprq2\fcharset0
Times New Roman;}{\f2\fscript\fprq2\fcharset0 Lucida Handwriting;
}}{\colortbl ;\red0\green0\blue255;}
\viewkind4\uc1\pard\nowidctlpar\sb100\sa100\lang3081\b\f0\fs36
XML at WhizBang\b0\fs24\par From:\tab John Doe\line To:\tab Jack
Smith\par Have you heard of this new technology, XML? It looks
promising. It is similar to HTML but it is extensible. All the
big names (Microsoft, IBM, Oracle, Sun) are backing it.\f1\par
\f0 We could use XML to launch new e-commerce services. It is
also useful for the web site: you complained it was a lot of
work, apparently XML can simplify the maintenance.\par
Check \cf1\ul this web site <http://www.w3.org/XML>\cf0\ulnone
for more information. Also visit \cf1\ul Que
<http://www.quepublishing.com/>\cf0\ulnone . They have just released "XML
by Example, 2nd Edition" by \cf1\ul Beno\'eet Marchal
<http://www.marchal.com/>\cf0\ulnone with lots of useful
information and some great examples. I have already ordered
two copies!\par\i\f2 John\i0\f1\par}
```

OUTPUT

Figure 1.3 shows the RTF memo loaded in a word processor.

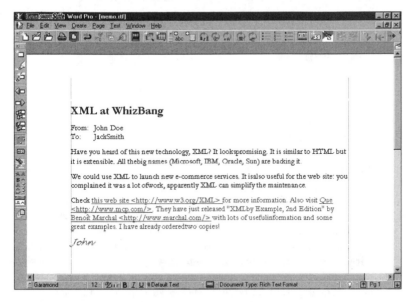

Figure 1.3: The RTF memo in a word processor.

This approach has three major problems:

- It does not record the structure of the document. The author deduces the document appearance from its structure, but it only records the result of the process. Therefore, information about the structure is lost.

- It is inflexible. Any change to the formatting rules implies manually changing the document. Also, the markup is more or less system dependent, which reduces portability. For example, relying on the availability of a particular typeface or on the output device being a certain printer reduces portability.

- It is an inherently slow process. It is also error-prone: It is easy to get confused and incorrectly format a document.

Generic Coding

Markup evolved into generic coding with the introduction of macros. Macros replace the controls with calls to external formatting procedures. A generic identifier (GI) or tag is attached to each text element, and formatting rules are further associated with tags. A formatter processes the text and produces a document in the format of the output device.

EXAMPLE

T_eX is a good example of generic coding. Listing 1.3 is the memo in T_eX. As you can see, it uses neutral tags, such as \par to identify logical constructs, like the paragraph. As always, don't worry about the T_eX syntax; we are only concerned with the concepts here.

Listing 1.3: memo.tex

```
% memo.tex
\nopagenumbers

\noindent John Doe\par
\noindent Jack Smith\par
\noindent XML at WhizBang\par
\smallskip

Have you heard of this new technology, XML? It looks promising.
It is similar to HTML but it is extensible. All the big names
(Microsoft, IBM, Oracle, Sun) are backing it.\par
We could use XML to launch new e-commerce services. It is also
useful for the web site: you complained it was a lot of work,
apparently XML can simplify the maintenance.\par
Check this web site {\url http://www.w3.org/XML} for more
information. Also visit Que {\url http://www.quepublishing.com}. They have
just released "XML by Example, 2nd Edition" by Benoît Marchal
{\url http://www.marchal.com} with lots of useful information and
some great examples. I have already ordered two copies!\par
John\par
\bye
```

The benefits of generic coding over procedural markup are twofold:

- It achieves higher portability and is more flexible. To change the appearance of the document, it suffices to adapt the macro. By editing one macro, the change is automatically reported throughout the document. In particular, it does not require reencoding the markup, which is a time-consuming and error-prone activity.

- The markup is closer to describing the structure.

Users tend to give significant names to the tags; for example, "Heading" is preferred to "X12," clearly recognizing the predominance of the structure over the formatting.

The good news is that it is now possible to automatically process the document—for example, it would be possible to compile an index of URLs.

Standard Generalized Markup Language

The Standard Generalized Markup Language (SGML) extends generic coding. Furthermore, it is an international standard published by the ISO (International Standards Organization). It is based on early work done within IBM in a research team led by Charles Goldfarb.

NOTE

The G, M, and L in SGML stand for Goldfarb, Mosher, and Lorie, the three inventors of SGML.

SGML is similar to generic coding in that the markup describes the document's structure, not its appearance, but it adds one new characteristic: The markup conforms to a model, which is similar to a database model. This means that the document can be processed by software or stored in a database.

SGML is not a standard structure that every document needs to follow. In other words, it does not define what a title or a paragraph is. In fact, it is unrealistic to believe that a single document structure can satisfy the needs of all authors. Technical documentation, books, letters, dictionaries, Web pages, timetables, and memos, to name only a few, are too different to fit in a single canvas without putting unacceptable constraints on the authors.

The SGML approach is not to impose a structure or a set of tags but to propose a language for authors to describe the structure of their documents and mark them accordingly. This is the major difference between generic coding and SGML: the author can not only mark up his document but also describe the structure of the document.

SGML is an enabling standard, not a complete document architecture. The strength of SGML is that it is a language to describe documents—in many respects similar to programming languages. It is therefore open to new applications and flexible.

The document structure is written in a *Document Type Definition* (DTD) sometimes also referred to as *SGML application*. A DTD specifies a set of elements, their relationships, and the tag set to mark the document. This is another difference between generic coding and SGML: The markup follows a model.

EXAMPLE

Listing 1.4 is the document in SGML. You will recognize the syntax (the angle brackets) because it is similar to HTML. However, the tags are not. As you will see, HTML is an application of SGML; therefore, it shares the SGML syntax. The tags, however, are specific to the structure of this document.

The first few lines of the document are the DTD (the document model); they describe the tags that will appear in the rest of the document.

Listing 1.4: `memo.sgml`

```
<!DOCTYPE memo [
<!ELEMENT memo       - - (header,body)>
<!ELEMENT header     - O ((from & to) & subject?)>
<!ELEMENT body       - O (para*, signature)>
<!ELEMENT from       - O (#PCDATA)>
<!ELEMENT to         - O (#PCDATA)>
<!ELEMENT subject    - O (#PCDATA)>
<!ELEMENT para       - O ((#PCDATA | link)*)>
<!ELEMENT link       - - (#PCDATA)>
<!ATTLIST link      url  CDATA #REQUIRED>
<!ELEMENT signature - O (#PCDATA)>]>
<memo>
<header>
<from>John Doe
<to>Jack Smith
<subject>XML at WhizBang
<body>
<para>Have you heard of this new technology, XML? It looks
promising. It is similar to HTML but it is extensible. All the
big names (Microsoft, IBM, Oracle, Sun) are backing it.
<para>We could use XML to launch new e-commerce services. It is
also useful for the web site: you complained it was a lot of
work, apparently XML can simplify the maintenance.
<para>Check <link url="http://www.w3.org/XML">this web
site</link> for more information. Also visit <link
url="http://www.quepublishing.com">Que</link>. They have just released
XML by Example, 2nd Edition" by <link
url="http://www.marchal.com">Benoît Marchal</link> with lots of
useful information and some great examples. I have already
ordered two copies!
<signature>John
</memo>
```

Although SGML does not impose a structure on documents, standard committees, industry groups, and others have built on SGML. They have defined standard DTDs for specific applications.

Some famous examples are

- HTML, the well-known markup language for Web documents. Although few HTML authors know about SGML, HTML has been defined as an SGML DTD.

- CALS standard MIL-M-28001B. CALS (Continuous Acquisition and Life-cycle Support) is a DoD (U.S. Department of Defense) initiative to promote electronic document interchange. MIL-M-28001B specifies DTDs for technical manuals in the format required for submission to the DoD.

- DocBook was developed by OASIS (Organization for the Advancement of Structured Information Standards) for technical books and articles.

Hypertext Markup Language

Without a doubt, the most popular application of SGML is HTML. Formally, HTML is an application of SGML. In other words, HTML is one set of tags that follows the rules of SGML. The set of tags defined by HTML is adapted to the structure of hypertext documents.

EXAMPLE

1. Listing 1.5 is the memo in HTML.

Listing 1.5: memo.html

```
<!DOCTYPE html PUBLIC "-//W3C//DTD HTML 4.0 Transitional//EN">
<html>
<head><title>WhizBang Memo: XML at WhizBang</title></head>
<body>
<table bgcolor="lightgrey" border="1" width="70%"><tr><td>
<table>
<tr><td colspan="2">
<font size="+2" face="Garamond"><b>XML at WhizBang</b></font>
</td></tr>
<tr>
<td><font face="Garamond">From:</font></td>
<td><font face="Garamond">John Doe</font></td>
</tr>
<tr>
<td><font face="Garamond">To:</font></td>
<td><font face="Garamond">Jack Smith</font></td>
</tr>
</table>
</td></tr></table>
<p><font face="Garamond">Have you heard of this new technology,
XML? It looks promising. It is similar to HTML but it is
extensible. All the big names (Microsoft, IBM, Oracle, Sun)
are backing it.</font></p>
<p><font face="Garamond">We could use XML to launch new
e-commerce services. It is also useful for the web site: you
complained it was a lot of work, apparently XML can simplify the
maintenance.</font></p>
<p><font face="Garamond">Check <a href="http://www.w3.org/XML">
this web site</a> for more information. Also visit
```

Listing 1.5: continued

```
<a href="http://www.quepublishing.com">Que</a>. They have just released
"XML by Example, 2nd Edition" by
<a href="http://www.marchal.com">Beno&icirc;t Marchal</a>
with lots of useful information and some great examples. I have
already ordered two copies!</font></p>
<p><font face="Lucida Handwriting"><i>John</i></font></p>
</body>
</html>
```

As you can see in Listing 1.5, HTML does not enforce a strict structure; in fact, HTML enforces very little structure. Incidentally, that's the irony of HTML: Although it is based on the structure-rich SGML, HTML has few options for organizing data.

HTML has evolved in two contradictory directions. First, many formatting tags have been introduced so that HTML is now partly a procedural markup language.

Tags in this category include <center> and <font>. Listing 1.5 clearly shows that the tags are used to express presentation, not only structure.

EXAMPLE

2. At the same time, the class attribute and style sheets were added to HTML. This turns HTML into a generic coding language! Listing 1.6 illustrates the use of class.

Listing 1.6: memocss.html

```
<!DOCTYPE html PUBLIC "-//W3C//DTD HTML 4.0 Transitional//EN">
<html>
<head><title>WhizBang Memo: XML at WhizBang</title>
<style>
.header {
    background-color: lightgrey;
}
.subject {
    font-family: Garamond;
    font-weight: bold;
    font-size: larger;
}
.to, .from  {
    font-family: Garamond;
}
.para { font-family: Garamond; }
.signature {
    font-family: "Lucida Handwriting";
    font-style: italic;
}
```

Listing 1.6: continued

```
</style>
</head>
<body>
<table class="header" border="1" width="70%"><tr><td>
<table>
<tr><td colspan="2" class="subject">XML at WhizBang</td></tr>
<tr>
<td class="from">From:</td>
<td class="from">John Doe</td>
</tr>
<tr>
<td class="to">To:</td>
<td class="to">Jack Smith</td>
</tr>
</table>
</td></tr></table>
<p class="para">Have you heard of this new technology, XML? It
looks promising. It is similar to HTML but it is extensible. All
the big names (Microsoft, IBM, Oracle, Sun) are backing it.</p>
<p class="para">We could use XML to launch new e-commerce
services. It is also useful for the web site: you complained it
was a lot of work, apparently XML can simplify the
maintenance.</p>
<p class="para">Check <a href="http://www.w3.org/XML"> this web
site</a> for more information. Also visit
<a href="http://www.quepublishing.com">Que</a>. They have just released
"XML by Example, 2nd Edition" by
<a href="http://www.marchal.com">Beno&icirc;t Marchal</a>
with lots of useful information and some great examples. I have
already ordered two copies!</p>
<p class="signature">John</p>
</body>
</html>
```

OUTPUT

Figure 1.4 shows the document loaded in a browser. Note that it looks
exactly like Figure 1.1 because Figure 1.1 was the document in Listing 1.5.
So, procedural markup and generic coding achieve identical pages.

Without going into the details of Listing 1.6, the classes are associated with
formatting instructions. For example, the class "para" is associated with

```
.para { font-family: Garamond; }
```

This says that the typeface must be "Garamond." In effect

```
<p class="para">...</p>
```

achieves the same result as

```
<p><font face="Garamond">...</font></p>
```

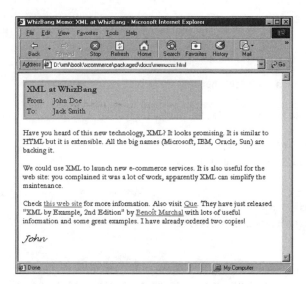

Figure 1.4: *A document with classes in a browser.*

However, the class offers generic coding, whereas the `<font>` tag is a procedural coding. Practically, it means that it is possible to change the appearance of all the paragraphs by changing only the formatting instructions associated with the para. That's one line to change as opposed to many `<font>` tags to update with a procedural markup.

EXAMPLE

3. Listing 1.7 illustrates this. It associates different formatting instructions to the paragraph. Figure 1.5 shows the result in a browser.

Listing 1.7: `memocss2.html`

```
<!DOCTYPE html PUBLIC "-//W3C//DTD HTML 4.0 Transitional//EN">
<html>
<head><title>WhizBang Memo: XML at WhizBang</title>
<style>
.header {
    background-color: #ffcc33;
}
.subject {
    font-family: Garamond;
    font-weight: bold;
    font-size: larger;
}
.to, .from  {
```

Listing 1.7: continued

```
   font-family: Garamond;
}
.para {
   font-family: "Letter Gothic MT";
   font-size: 16px;
 }
.signature {
   font-family: "Lucida Handwriting";
   font-style: italic;
}
</style>
</head>
<body>
<table class="header" border="1" width="70%"><tr><td>
<table>
<tr><td colspan="2" class="subject">XML at WhizBang</td></tr>
<tr>
<td class="from">From:</td>
<td class="from">John Doe</td>
</tr>
<tr>
<td class="to">To:</td>
<td class="to">Jack Smith</td>
</tr>
</table>
</td></tr></table>
<p class="para">Have you heard of this new technology, XML? It
looks promising. It is similar to HTML but it is extensible. All
the big names (Microsoft, IBM, Oracle, Sun) are backing it.</p>
<p class="para">We could use XML to launch new e-commerce
services. It is also useful for the web site: you complained it
was a lot of work, apparently XML can simplify the
maintenance.</p>
<p class="para">Check <a href="http://www.w3.org/XML"> this web
site</a> for more information. Also visit
<a href="http://www.quepublishing.com">Que</a>. They have just released
"XML by Example, 2nd Edition" by
<a href="http://www.marchal.com">Beno&icirc;t Marchal</a>
with lots of useful information and some great examples. I have
already ordered two copies!</p>
<p class="signature">John</p>
</body>
</html>
```

OUTPUT

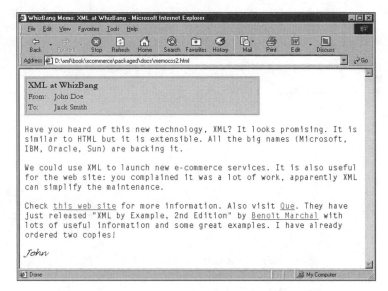

Figure 1.5: The new style in a browser.

eXtensible Markup Language

This conflicting evolution of HTML, partly toward procedural markup, partly toward generic coding, is illustrative of the forces at play behind HTML.

On one hand, the Web has evolved into a media in its own right, similar to printed magazines and television. Therefore, people need a lot of control over the formatting so that they can produce visually appealing Web sites.

Yet Web sites also have grown in size, and it is increasingly difficult to maintain them. For most organizations, publishing a Web site has gone through the following steps:

- The first 20 pages are produced with enthusiasm.

- Somebody (usually from the marketing department) realizes that the Web site looks terrible.

- A design agency is contracted to redo the appearance of the site; they manually edit the 20 pages. The site is now three times slower, but it looks great.

- Another 50 pages are added with enthusiasm. They more or less follow the new appearance. As time passes, they tend to diverge from the original style.

- Another design agency is contracted to redo the site. It would be too expensive to edit the whole site, so 30 pages are deleted (resulting in the dreaded "404 Page Not Found" error message). The remaining 40 pages are manually edited.

Hopefully somebody realizes it is a costly process before another 50 pages are added. If not, the process repeats.

Generic coding (the class attribute) was added to HTML to help alleviate this problem. However, although it is popular with Webmasters, class is limited. For example, it is not possible to redesign the navigation system of a site via this method.

This problem also was one of the motivations for the development of XML. It was felt that HTML was increasingly inefficient and a more flexible mechanism was needed.

One option could have been to turn to SGML. In fact, it was envisioned at one point. However, it rapidly became evident that SGML was too complex for the Web. Many facilities in SGML are useless in a Web environment.

The W3C eventually decided to simplify SGML. XML removes all the options that are not absolutely required in SGML. However, it retains the key principle that markup needs to describe the structure of the document and that a model may be associated with the document.

The result is a simple standard that is almost as powerful as SGML while being as simple to use as HTML. In fact, simplicity was paramount during the development of XML. Indeed, it was felt that the original simplicity of HTML had been a major element in its early success.

As already stated, it is unlikely that HTML will disappear in the predictable future. Rather HTML will evolve toward XML—for example, as XHTML.

EXAMPLE

Listing 1.8 is the memo in XML. Notice that it is similar to SGML, but every element has an end tag and the DTD has disappeared (it is optional in XML). Do not worry about XML syntax now. We will cover the syntax in greater detail in the next two chapters.

Listing 1.8: memo.xml

```
<?xml version="1.0"?>
<memo>
<header>
<from>John Doe</from>
<to>Jack Smith</to>
<subject>XML at WhizBang</subject>
```

Listing 1.8: continued

```
</header>
<body>
<para>Have you heard of this new technology, XML? It looks
promising. It is similar to HTML but it is extensible. All the
big names (Microsoft, IBM, Oracle, Sun) are backing it.</para>
<para>We could use XML to launch new e-commerce services. It is
also useful for the web site: you complained it was a lot of
work, apparently XML can simplify the maintenance.</para>
<para>Check <link url="http://www.w3.org/XML">this web
site</link> for more information. Also visit <link
url="http://www.quepublishing.com">Que</link>. They have just released
XML by Example, 2nd Edition" by <link
url="http://www.marchal.com">Beno&#238;t Marchal</link> with lots
of useful information and some great examples. I have already
ordered two copies!</para>
<signature>John</signature>
</body>
</memo>
```

Application of XML

Although I have mentioned in passing that XML is not just for Web site publishing, all the examples given so far are more or less related to publishing. This section discusses some of the most popular applications for XML.

Applications of XML are always of one of the following two types:

- Document applications manipulate information primarily intended for human consumption.

- Data applications manipulate information primarily intended for software consumption.

The difference between the two types of applications is a qualitative one. It is the same XML standard; it is implemented by using the same tools, but it serves different goals. This diversity of application is good for you because it means that you can reuse tools and experience across a large set of applications.

Document Applications

The first application of XML would be document publishing. The main advantage of XML in this arena is that XML concentrates on the structure of the document, and this makes it independent of the delivery medium (see Figure 1.6).

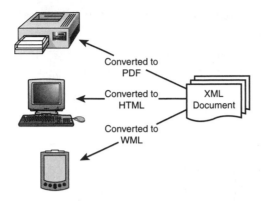

Figure 1.6: *XML is independent from the medium.*

Therefore, it is possible to edit and maintain documents in XML and automatically publish them on different media. The operative word here is "automatically."

The capability to target multiple media is becoming increasingly important because many publications are available online and in print. Also the Web is changing rapidly. What is fashionable this year will be *passé* next year, so you need to reformat your site regularly.

Finally, new markup languages are being introduced that target specific devices such as WML, the Wireless Markup Language, for smart phones. Practically, it means that a publisher has to maintain two or more versions of the same site: one generic version and one optimized for some users. If done manually, this is costly.

For all these reasons, it makes sense to write the documents in XML and to automatically convert them into publishing formats such as HTML, WML, PostScript, PDF, and more.

Of course, the more media we need to support and the larger the document, the more important it is that publishing be automated.

✔ You'll learn the tools for document conversion in Chapters 5 and 6 **pages 137** and **175**.

Data Applications

One of the original goals of SGML was to give document management access to the software similar to that used to manage other datasets, such as databases.

With XML, the loop has come to a full circle because XML brings a publishing kind of distribution to data. This leads to the concept of "the application as the document" where, ultimately, there is no difference between documents and applications.

Indeed, if the structure of a document can be expressed in XML, as illustrated in Figure 1.7, so can the structure of a database, as illustrated in Figure 1.8.

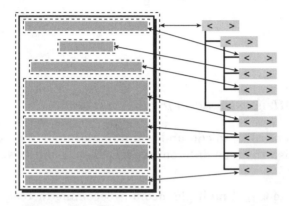

Figure 1.7: *The structure of a document in XML.*

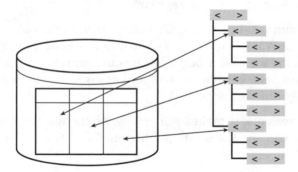

Figure 1.8: *The structure of a database in XML.*

EXAMPLE

For example, consider Table 1.1, which lists products and prices as they would be stored in a relational database. Listing 1.9 is the same list of products in XML.

Table 1.1: A List of Products in a Relational Database

Identifier	Name	Price
p1	XML Editor	$499.00
p2	DTD Editor	$199.00
p3	XML Book	$29.99
p4	XML Training	$699.00

Listing 1.9: A List of Products in XML

```xml
<?xml version="1.0"?>
<products>
   <product id="p1">
      <name>XML Editor</name>
      <price>499.00</price>
   </product>
   <product id="p2">
      <name>DTD Editor</name>
      <price>199.00</price>
   </product>
   <product id="p3">
      <name>XML Book</name>
      <price>29.99</price>
   </product>
   <product id="p4">
      <name>XML Training</name>
      <price>699.00</price>
   </product>
</products>
```

In this context, XML is used to exchange information between organizations. The XML Web is a large database that applications can tap (see Figure 1.9).

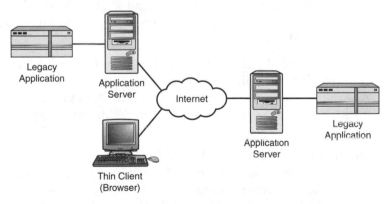

Figure 1.9: Applications exchanging data over the Web.

This can be viewed as an extension for extranets. The idea behind an extranet is that one organization publishes some of its data on the Web for its partners.

For example, an organization publishes its price list on its Web site. In the electronics industry, the price list is dynamic. Prices can change several times during a month. If the information is available on a Web site, customers can always access the latest, most up-to-date information.

Before HTML, the price list would have been published in HTML—that is, intended for viewing by a human. This is acceptable if you have few providers with few products, but as soon as you have many providers or many products, you want a more automated solution.

With XML, software can automatically visit the price list, extract the price, and update the information in your own database. This is shown in the top half of Figure 1.9. It requires a markup language that does not concentrate on appearance but on structure.

✔Chapter 11, "N-Tiered Architecture and XML," and Chapter 12, "Putting It All Together: An e-Commerce Example," **pages 365** and **391**, build an extensive example.

Companion Standards

The value of XML is not that it is a markup language, but that it is a standard markup language. It wouldn't be difficult to create your own markup language using your own conventions (for example, parentheses instead of angle brackets). However, by adopting XML, you buy into a growing community supported by a large range of standards and products.

This means that it will be easier to find support in the form of books, articles, and services, as well as software to create, manipulate, store, and exchange XML documents.

There is a sort of positive loop at play here: Because XML is a standard, more vendors are willing to support it. This leads more people to adopt it. A growing market means that even more vendors propose XML tools. This, in turn, attracts even more users, which, again, attracts new vendors. And so on, and so on.

The title for this chapter, "The XML Galaxy," reflects my view that XML is more than a markup language. It is a whole range of tools that you can put to work in your environment.

In particular, the W3C has developed a number of standards that complement XML. These standards are often referred to as *XML companion standards*.

It is not my intention in this chapter to introduce these standards comprehensively (that's the topic for the next 11 chapters), but I do want to give you a feeling for what they have to offer. Therefore, I will point to some of the major companion standards.

This is not a complete list. New standards are being introduced regularly.

XML Namespace

XML namespace is often an overlooked companion standard although it is second to none in importance. Namespace places elements within a global naming system.

The concept of namespace is similar to the scope of variables in programming languages. If you declare an i variable in a function computeAverage(), the scope of i is the computeAverage() function.

If another function, say computeMax() also declares an i variable, there is no conflict. For the compiler, the two variables are different because they are defined in different functions. They have different scopes.

Namespace is somewhat similar. Namespace makes it possible to define elements specific to a given application of XML. If another application defines elements with the same name but in a different namespace, there is no conflict.

✔XML namespaces are covered in more detail in Chapter 3, "XML Namespaces," **page 71**.

EXAMPLE

Listing 1.10 is a list of names in XML. As you can see, it includes two table elements: xbe:table and html:table. The latter you're familiar with because it's an XHTML table element, and it is defined like the HTML table.

The first one, however, is specific to this document, and it describes a table in a database. Namespaces are used to distinguish between the two table elements. Again, we'll look at the details of the syntax in another chapter.

Listing 1.10: list.xml

```xml
<?xml version="1.0"?>
<xbe:list xmlns:html="http://www.w3.org/1999/xhtml"
          xmlns:xbe="http://www.psol.com/xbe2/listing1.9">
<xbe:table>
<xbe:name>persons</xbe:name>
<xbe:column>first-name</xbe:column>
<xbe:column>last-name</xbe:column>
</xbe:table>
<html:table>
<html:tr>
<html:td>Sean</html:td><html:td>Dixon</html:td>
</html:tr>
<html:tr>
<html:td>Todd</html:td><html:td>Green</html:td>
</html:tr>
```

Listing 1.10: continued

```
<html:tr>
<html:td>Beno&#238;t</html:td><html:td>Marchal</html:td>
</html:tr>
</html:table>
</xbe:list>
```

Style Sheets

XML is supported by two style sheet languages: XSL (XML Stylesheet Language) and CSS (Cascading Style Sheets). Style sheets are probably the most widely discussed companion standards. They specify how XML documents should be rendered onscreen, on paper, or in an editor. XSL is more powerful, but CSS is widely implemented.

✔Listing 1.11 is an example of an XSL style sheet to render an XML article. Style sheets are covered in more detail in Chapters 5 and 6, **pages 137** and **175.**

EXAMPLE

Listing 1.11: basic.xsl

```
<?xml version="1.0"?>
<xsl:stylesheet
    xmlns:xsl="http://www.w3.org/1999/XSL/Transform"
    version="1.0">

<xsl:output method="html"/>

<xsl:template match="/">
<html>
    <head>
        <title><xsl:value-of
            select="article/articleinfo/title"/></title>
    </head>
    <xsl:apply-templates/>
</html>
</xsl:template>

<xsl:template match="article">
<body>
    <xsl:apply-templates/>
</body>
</xsl:template>

<xsl:template match="articleinfo/title">
    <h1><xsl:apply-templates/></h1>
</xsl:template>
```

Listing 1.11: continued

```
<xsl:template match="sect1/title">
    <h2><xsl:apply-templates/></h2>
</xsl:template>

<xsl:template match="ulink">
    <a href="{@url}"><xsl:apply-templates/></a>
</xsl:template>

<xsl:template match="emphasis">
    <b><xsl:apply-templates/></b>
</xsl:template>

<xsl:template match="para">
    <p><xsl:apply-templates/></p>
</xsl:template>

<xsl:template match="author">
    <p>by <xsl:value-of select="firstname"/>
    <xsl:text> </xsl:text>
    <xsl:value-of select="surname"/></p>
</xsl:template>

</xsl:stylesheet>
```

DOM and SAX

DOM (Document Object Model) and SAX (Simple API for XML) are APIs to access XML documents. They allow applications to read XML documents without having to worry about the syntax. They are complementary: DOM is best suited for browsers and editors; SAX is best for all the rest.

✔ DOM and SAX are covered in Chapters 7 and 8, **pages 211** and **253**. Chapter 9, "Writing XML," **page 287** discusses how to create XML documents.

XLink and XPointer

XLink and XPointer are two parts of one standard currently under development to provide a mechanism to establish relationships and hyperlinks between documents.

Listing 1.12 demonstrates how a set of links can be maintained in XML.

EXAMPLE

Listing 1.12: resources.xml

```
<?xml version="1.0"?>
<resources xmlns:xlink="http://www.w3.org/1999/xlink">
    <entry xlink:type="simple" xlink:show="replace"
```

Listing 1.12: continued

```
        xlink:href="http://www.mcp.com">Que</entry>
 <entry xlink:type="simple" xlink:show="replace"
        xlink:href="http://www.marchal.com">marchal.com</entry>
 <entry xlink:type="simple" xlink:show="replace"
        xlink:href="http://www.informit.com">InformIT</entry>
 <entry xlink:type="simple" xlink:show="replace"
        xlink:href="http://www.pineapplesoft.com/newsletter">
            Pineapplesoft Link</entry>
</resources>
```

✔ XLink is discussed in Chapter 10, "Important XML Models," **page 325**.

XML Software

As explained in the previous section, XML popularity means that many vendors are supporting it. This, in turn, means that many applications are available to manipulate XML documents.

This section lists some of the most commonly used XML applications. Again, this is not a complete list. We will discuss these products in more detail in the following chapters.

XML Browser

An XML browser is the first application you would think of because it is so close to the familiar HTML browser. An XML browser is used to view and print XML documents. At the time of writing, there are not many high-quality XML browsers.

Microsoft Internet Explorer has supported XML since version 4.0. Internet Explorer 5.0 has greatly enhanced the XML support. Unfortunately, the support is based on early versions of the standards, and, for example, the support for style sheets is almost unusable. It you opt for Internet Explorer 5.0, I strongly recommend you download the XML upgrade from msdn.microsoft.com/xml.

Netscape has added support for XML in release 6. Netscape 6 supports XHTML, Xlink, and CSS. Unfortunately, it does not support XSL.

In most cases, you will find it more convenient to ignore the browser and apply style sheets on the Web server to generate HTML documents.

XML Editors

As an XML programmer, you will need at least one XML editor. Different products have different characteristics, and you should evaluate them until you find the one that suits you.

Be aware that there are two approaches to XML editors:

- Programmer's editors, such as XML Spy (www.xmlspy.com) or XML Pro (www.vervet.com), let you manipulate the XML code directly. They are powerful, but you have to know XML to use them.

- WYSIWYG editors, such as XMetaL (www.xmetal.com), simulate word processors. Tools in this category are ideal for end users who may not be familiar with the XML (and may not want to be).

Figure 1.10 shows how to edit an XML document with XML Spy. The tabular view makes the structure of the document apparent. It shows clearly how elements nest. In contrast, XMetaL, in Figure 1.11, hides the XML code entirely. XMetaL is ideal for markup-challenged users—or simply when you want to concentrate on writing and not on the markup.

Both category of tools are useful but not for the same purpose and not at the same time. I like XML Spy for style sheet editing and other technical tasks, but I love the WYSIWYG view of XMetaL when authoring new documents.

Figure 1.10: *XML Spy appeals to developers.*

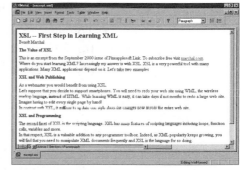

Figure 1.11: *XMetaL is suitable for clerical staff.*

XML Parsers

If you are writing your own XML applications, you won't want to fool around with the XML syntax. Parsers will shield you from the XML syntax and let you concentrate on your application.

Many XML parsers are available on the Internet. One of the most popular parsers is Apache's Xerces for Java, C++, and Perl (xml.apache.org).

✔Parsers are discussed in Chapters 7 and 8, **pages 211** and **253**.

XSL Processor

In many cases, you want to use XML "behind the scenes." You want to take advantage of XML internally, but you don't want to force your users to upgrade to an XML-compliant browser (especially because, as you have seen, the two most popular browsers differ in their support of XML).

The solution is to use XSL. With XSL, it is possible to create classic HTML that works with current and former-generation browsers (and older, too) from XML documents. XSL lets you have the cake (the strong structure of XML documents) and eat it, too (because it's compatible with HTML browsers).

To apply the magic of XSL, you use an XSL processor. Several XSL processors are available, and one of the most popular is Apache's Xalan (xml.apache.org).

✔XSL processors are discussed in Chapter 5, **page 137**.

What's Next

The book is organized as follows:

- The next three chapters teach you the XML syntax, including the syntax for DTDs, schemas, and namespaces.

- Chapters 5 and 6 teach you how to use style sheets to publish documents.

- Chapters 7, 8, and 9 teach you how to manipulate XML documents from your applications.

- Chapter 10 discusses how to create models for XML documents. You have seen in this introduction how structure is important for XML. Modeling is the process of creating the structure.

- Chapters 11 and 12 wrap it up with a realistic electronic commerce application. This application exercises most, if not all, the techniques introduced in the previous chapters.

- Appendix A teaches you just enough Java to be able to follow the examples in Chapters 8 and 12. It also discusses when you should use JavaScript and when you should turn to Java.

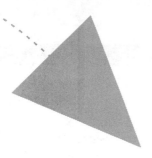

XML Syntax

In this chapter you learn the syntax for XML documents. More specifically you learn

- How to write and read XML documents

- How XML structures documents

- How and where XML can be used

If you are curious, the latest version of the official recommendation is always available from www.w3.org/TR/REC-xml. XML version 1.0 (the version used in this book) is available from www.w3.org/TR/2000/REC-xml-20001006.

A First Look at the XML Syntax

If I had to summarize XML in one sentence, it would be something like, "a set of standards to exchange and publish information in a structured manner." The emphasis on structure cannot be underestimated.

XML is a language used to describe and manipulate documents that follow a structure. XML documents are not limited to books, articles, or Web sites. They could be used with objects from a client/server application.

XML defines a syntax or a file format that is useful for books, articles, client/server applications and more. This is possible because the XML format does not dictate or enforce a particular structure. It limits itself to rules that you can use to write a tree data structure on disk.

Getting Started with XML Markup

EXAMPLE

Listing 2.1 is a (small) address book in XML. It has only two entries: John Doe and Jack Smith. Study it because you will use it throughout most of this chapter and Chapter 4, "XML Models."

Listing 2.1: abook.xml

```
<?xml version="1.0"?>
<!-- Download from www.marchal.com or www.mcp.com -->
<address-book>
   <entry>
      <name>John Doe</name>
      <address>
         <street>34 Fountain Square Plaza</street>
         <region>OH</region>
         <postal-code>45202</postal-code>
         <locality>Cincinnati</locality>
         <country>US</country>
      </address>
      <tel preferred="true">513-744-8889</tel>
      <tel>513-744-7098</tel>
      <email href="mailto:john@emailaholic.com"/>
   </entry>
   <entry>
      <name>Jack Smith</name>
      <tel>513-744-3465</tel>
      <email href="mailto:jack@emailaholic.com"/>
      <comments>Never leave messages on his answering
      machine. <b>Email instead.</b></comments>
   </entry>
</address-book>
```

NOTE

You can download the listings from www.marchal.com or www.quepublishing.com.

As you can see, an XML document is a text. XML-wise, the document consists of *character data* and *markup*. Both are represented as text in the document.

Ultimately it's the character data we are interested in because that is the information. However, the markup is also important because it records the structure of the document.

As you will see, there are several markup constructs in XML, but you can always recognize them by the angle brackets. Markup is always enclosed in angle brackets. Anything outside angle brackets is character data.

Obviously, it's the markup that differentiates an XML document from plain text. Listing 2.2 is the same address book in plain text (in other words, with no markup and only character data).

EXAMPLE

Listing 2.2: abook.txt

```
John Doe
34 Fountain Square Plaza
Cincinnati, OH 45202
US
513-744-8889 (preferred)
513-744-7098
jdoe@emailaholic.com
Jack Smith
513-744-3465
jsmith@emailaholic.com
Never leave messages on his answering machine. Email instead.
```

Listing 2.2 helps illustrate the benefits of a markup language. Listings 2.1 and 2.2 carry exactly the same information. Yet, because Listing 2.2 has no markup, there is no structure information.

In both cases, it is easy to recognize the names, the phone numbers, the email addresses, and so on. If anything, you might find Listing 2.2 more readable because it lacks the codes.

For a software application, however, it's exactly the opposite. The software is dumb and it needs to be told precisely which is what. It needs to be told where the name is, where the address is, and so on. That's what the markup is all about; it breaks the text into its constituents to make it easier for software.

For all its stupidity, software has one major advantage over humans—speed. It can do dumb things but it is fast at being dumb. Although it would take you a long time to sort through a long list containing a thousand addresses, software will plunge through the same list in less than a minute.

However, before it can start, it needs to have the information in a preset format. This book concentrates on XML as a preset format.

The reward comes in Chapter 5, "XSL Transformations," and subsequent chapters where we write small programs (called style sheets) to have the computer do something useful with XML documents.

Element's Start and End Tags

The building block of XML is the *element*. Each element has a name and a content.

```
<tel>513-744-7098</tel>
```

EXAMPLE

The content of an element is delimited by special markups known as a *start tag* and *end tag*. The tagging mechanism is similar to HTML, which is logical because both HTML and XML inherited their tagging mechanism from SGML.

The start tag is the element name (tel in the example) in angle brackets; the end tag adds an extra slash character before the name.

Unlike HTML, both start and end tags are required. The following is not correct in XML:

```
<tel>513-744-7098
```

Before you ask, who defined tel as an XML element? Me! It can't be stressed enough that XML does not list or define elements. Nowhere in the XML recommendation will you find the address book of Listing 2.1 or the tel element.

XML limits itself to defining what an element is and how to mark up an element with tags. It provides a syntax to store information according to a structure but, unlike HTML, it does not define what the structure is.

In XML, it is the document author who creates the elements. In other words, the author extends the markup language with the elements it needs—therefore, the name eXtensible Markup Language.

In this respect, I liken XML to SQL. SQL is the language you use to program relational databases such as Oracle, SQL Server, or DB2. SQL provides a common language to create and manage relational databases. However, SQL does not specify what you should store in the database or which tables you should use.

In other words, SQL does not define a product table. It is up to you, the programmer, to create a product table if you need one.

Still, the availability of a common language has led to the development of a lively industry. SQL vendors provide databases, modeling and development tools, magazines, seminars, conferences, training, books, and more.

Admittedly, the XML industry is not yet as large as the SQL industry, but it's catching up fast. By moving your data to XML rather than to an esoteric format, you can tap the growing XML industry for support.

Names in XML

Element names must follow certain rules. Specifically they must start with either a letter or the underscore character ("_"). The rest of the name consists of letters, digits, the underscore character, the dot (".") or a hyphen ("-"). Spaces are not allowed in names.

Finally, names cannot start with the string "xml", which is reserved for the XML specification itself.

NOTE

There is one more character you can use in names—It Is the colon (:). However, the colon is reserved for namespaces and it will be introduced in Chapter 3, "XML Namespaces."

EXAMPLE

The following are examples of valid element names in XML.

```
<copyright-information>
<p>
<base64>
<décompte.client>
<firstname>
```

The following are examples of invalid element names. You could not use these names in XML:

```
<123>
<first name>
<tom&jerry>
```

Unlike HTML, names are case sensitive in XML. So, the following names are all different:

```
<address>
<ADDRESS>
<Address>
```

There are two popular conventions for XML elements:

- Write the name entirely in lowercase. When a name consists of several words, the words are separated by a hyphen, as in address-book.

- Capitalize the first letter of each word and use no separation character as in AddressBook. This convention is called "camel case."

NOTE

Let me stress again that XML does not dictate element names. If you don't like these conventions, feel free to adopt others (for instance, all uppercase words as in ADDRESS_BOOK).

EXAMPLE

There are other conventions but these two are the most popular. Choose the convention that works best for you but try to be consistent. It is difficult to work with documents that mix conventions, as Listing 2.3 illustrates.

Listing 2.3: poorstyle.xml

```
<?xml version="1.0"?>
<address-book>
    <ENTRY>
        <name>John Doe</name>
        <Address>
            <street>34 Fountain Square Plaza</street>
            <Region>OH</Region>
            <PostalCode>45202</PostalCode>
            <locality>Cincinnati</locality>
            <country>US</country>
        </Address>
        <TEL PREFERRED="true">513-744-8889</TEL>
        <TEL>513-744-7098</TEL>
        <email href="mailto:jdoe@emailaholic.com"/>
    </ENTRY>
</address-book>
```

Although the document in Listing 2.3 is well formed (it respects the XML syntax), it is difficult to work with it because you never know how to write the next element. Is it Address or address or ADDRESS? Mixing case is cumbersome and considered a poor style.

NOTE

As you will see in the "Unicode" section, XML supports characters from most spoken languages. You can use letters from any alphabet in names, including letters from the Greek, Japanese, or Cyrillic alphabets.

Attributes

It is possible to attach additional information to elements in the form of *attributes*. Attributes have a name and a value. The names follow the same rules as element names.

Again, the syntax is similar to HTML. Elements can have zero, one, or more attributes in the start tag. The name of the attribute is separated from the value by the equal character. The value of the attribute is enclosed in double or single quotation marks.

For example, the `tel` element can have a `preferred` attribute (for example, to indicate which phone number you should try first):

```
<tel preferred="true">513-744-8889</tel>
```

EXAMPLE

Unlike HTML, XML insists on the quotation marks. An XML parser would reject the following:

```
<tel preferred=true>513-744 8880</tel>
```

Quotation marks can be either single or double quotes. This is convenient if you need to insert single or double quotes in an attribute value.

```
<confidentiality level="I don't know">
This document is not confidential.
</confidentiality>
```

EXAMPLE

or

```
<confidentiality level='approved "for your eyes only"'>
This document is top-secret
</confidentiality>
```

CAUTION

Attributes are not part of the element name. In the following example

```
<tel preferred="true">513-744-8889</tel>
```

the element's name is tel, not tel preferred="true". Indeed, the end tag is tel.

Empty Element

Elements that have no content are known as *empty elements*. Usually (although it is not required), they have attributes.

There is a shorthand notation for empty elements: The start and end tags merge and the slash from the end tag is added at the end of the opening tag.

For XML, the following two empty elements are identical:

```
<email href="mailto:jdoe@emailaholic.com"/>
<email href="mailto:jdoe@emailaholic.com"></email>
```

Nesting of Elements

As Listing 2.1 illustrated earlier, elements can contain text (name), other elements (entry), or a combination of text and elements (comments).

The underlying data structure for XML document is the tree of elements. The depth of the tree has no limit, and elements can repeat. Figure 2.1 is the tree of Listing 2.1.

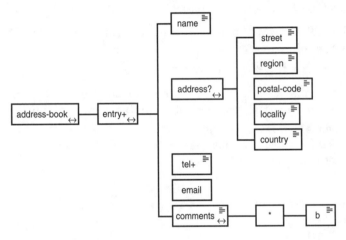

Figure 2.1: *Tree of the address book.*

An element that is enclosed in another element is called a *child*. The element it is enclosed into is its *parent*. In the following example, the entry element has four children: name, tel, email, and comments.

```
<entry>
    <name>Jack Smith</name>
    <tel>513-744-3465</tel>
    <email href="mailto:jack@emailaholic.com"/>
    <comments>Never leave messages on his answering
    machine. <b>Email instead.</b></comments>
</entry>
```

Start and end tags must always be balanced and children are always completely contained in their parents. In other words, it is not possible that the end tag of a child appears after the end tag of its parent. The following is invalid:

```
<entry>
   <name>Jack Smith</tel>
   <tel>513-744-3465</name>
   <email href="mailto:jack@emailaholic.com"/>
   <comments>Never leave messages on his answering
   machine. <b>Email instead.</entry></comments>
</b>
```

NOTE

It is not an accident if XML documents are trees. Trees are flexible, simple, and powerful data structures.

In particular, any other data structure can be represented as a tree. For example, it is easy to turn an array into a tree.

Root

EXAMPLE

At the root of the document there must be one and only one element. In other words, all the elements in the document must be the children of a single element. The following example is invalid because the two entry elements are not enclosed in a top-level element:

```
<?xml version="1.0"?>
<entry>
   <name>John Doe</name>
   <email href="mailto:jdoe@emailaholic.com"/>
</entry>
<entry>
   <name>JackSmith</name>
   <email href="mailto:jsmith@emailaholic.com"/>
</entry>
```

EXAMPLE

It is easy to fix the previous example by introducing a new root element, such as address-book:

```
<?xml version="1.0"?>
<address-book>
   <entry>
      <name>John Doe</name>
      <email href="mailto:jdoe@emailaholic.com"/>
   </entry>
   <entry>
      <name>JackSmith</name>
      <email href="mailto:jsmith@emailaholic.com"/>
   </entry>
</address-book>
```

EXAMPLE

There is no rule to impose address-book as the root of a document. If there were only one entry, it might be the root:

```
<?xml version="1.0"?>
<entry>
   <name>John Doe</name>
   <email href="mailto:jdoe@emailaholic.com"/>
</entry>
```

XML Declaration

EXAMPLE

The *XML declaration* is the first line of the document. The declaration identifies the document as an XML document. The declaration also lists the version of XML used in the document. For the time being, it's 1.0.

```
<?xml version="1.0"?>
```

An XML parser can reject documents with another version number. If the W3C ever releases a second version of XML, I would imagine that the declaration would become mandatory.

NOTE

There has been some confusion on a possible second version of XML. Let me try to clarify. At the time of writing, there is only one version of XML (1.0) and no upgrade is in the making.

However, the W3C has published a second edition (not version) of XML version 1.0 to fix errors and typos in the original edition.

The declaration can contain other attributes to support special features such as character-set encoding. These attributes will be introduced alongside the feature they support in the remainder of this chapter and in Chapter 4.

EXAMPLE

The XML declaration is optional. The following document is valid even though it doesn't have a declaration:

```
<address-book>
   <entry>
      <name>John Doe</name>
      <email href="mailto:jdoe@emailaholic.com"/>
   </entry>
   <entry>
      <name>JackSmith</name>
      <email href="mailto:jsmith@emailaholic.com"/>
   </entry>
</address-book>
```

If the declaration is included, however, it must start on the first character of the first line of the document. The XML recommendation suggests you include the declaration in every XML document.

Advanced Topics

As you can see, the core of the XML syntax is not difficult. Furthermore, if you already know HTML, it is familiar. The two major differences between HTML and XML are

- XML does not define elements but it provides a mechanism to create your own. With HTML, the W3C had defined elements for paragraphs (<p>), bold (<b>), section titles (<h1>-<h6>) and more. In XML, it's up to you, the author of the document, to create meaningful elements.

- XML is very strict. For example, every element must have a start and end tag (unless they are empty elements, but then they must follow a special rule).

One of the design goals of XML was to develop a simple markup language that would be easy to use and would remain human-readable. I think that goal has been achieved.

This section covers more advanced features of XML. You might not use them in every document, but they are often useful.

Comments

EXAMPLE

To insert comments in a document, enclose them between "<!--" and "-->". Comments are intended for the human reader and the XML parser ignores them. In the following example, a comment reminds you that you can download the listings from www.marchal.com or www.quepublishing.com. The parser does nothing with this comment but it may be useful information for you.

```
<!-- Download from www.marchal.com or www.quepublishing.com -->
```

EXAMPLE

Comments cannot be inserted in the markup. They must appear before or after the markup. The following is invalid:

```
<name <!-- a comment in the markup, invalid -->>JackSmith</name>
```

Unicode

Characters in XML documents follow the *Unicode standard*. Unicode is a major extension to the familiar ASCII character set. It is published by the Unicode Consortium (www.unicode.org). The same standard is published by the ISO as ISO/IEC 10646.

Unicode supports all spoken languages (on Earth) as well as mathematical and other symbols. It supports English, Western European languages, Cyrillic, Japanese, Chinese, and so on.

We are used to character sets, such as Latin-1 (Windows' default character set), that need only 8 bits per character. However, 8 bits is limited to 256 characters—not enough for Japanese, not to mention Chinese, English, Greek, Norwegian, and others.

Unicode, to accommodate all those characters, needs 16 bits per character. Unicode characters are twice as large as their Latin-1 counterparts; that's the price to pay for international support.

Logically, XML documents should be twice as large as normal text files. Fortunately, there is a workaround. In most cases, you don't need 16 bits and you can encode XML documents with an 8-bit character set.

An encoding is a representation of Unicode's characters as combinations of bytes. XML parsers recognize at least two encodings: UTF-8 and UTF-16. As the name implies, UTF-8 uses 8 bits for English characters and 16 or 24 for other characters, whereas UTF-16 uses 16 bits for every character.

Most parsers support other encodings. In particular, for Western European languages, they support ISO 8859-1 (also known as Latin-1, the character set of Windows).

Documents that use encoding other than UTF-8 or UTF-16 must start with an XML declaration. The declaration must have an encoding attribute to announce the encoding used.

EXAMPLE

For example, a document written in Latin-1 (with Windows Notepad) needs the following XML declaration:

```
<?xml version="1.0" encoding="ISO-8859-1"?>
<entrée>
   <nom>José Dupont</nom>
   <email href="mailto:jdupont@emailaholic.com"/>
</entrée>
```

NOTE

You might wonder how the XML parser reads the encoding parameter. Indeed, to reach the parameter, the parser must read the declaration. However, to read the declaration, the parser needs to know which encoding is being used.

This looks like a dog running after its tail until you realize that the first character in the document is always <, no matter which encoding is used. The parser tests whether < is encoded in 8 or 16 bits and it knows enough to read the declaration.

Entities

The document in Listing 2.1, shown earlier in this chapter, is self-contained: The document is complete and can be stored in just one file. Complex documents are often split among several files: the text, the accompanying graphics, and so on.

XML, however, does not reason in terms of files. Instead, it organizes documents physically in *entities*. In some cases, entities are equivalent to files; in others they are not.

XML entities is a complex topic that we will revisit in Chapter 4, "XML Models," when we will see how to declare these entities. In this chapter, we will concentrate on using entities.

EXAMPLE

Entities are inserted in the document through *entity references*. An entity reference is the name of the entity between an ampersand character and a semicolon.

The XML parser replaces the entity reference with its value. If we assume we have defined an entity "us" with the value "United States" (we'll see how in chapter 4), the following two lines are strictly equivalent:

```
<country>&us;</country>
<country>United States</country>
```

XML predefines entities for its delimiters (angle brackets, quotes, and so on). These entities are used to escape the delimiters in elements or attributes content. The predefined entities are

- < left-angle bracket "<" must be escaped with <

- & ampersand "&" must be escaped with &

- > right-angle bracket ">" must be escaped with > in the combination]]> in CDATA sections (see the following CDATA section)

- ' single quote "'" can be escaped with ' essentially in attribute value

- " double quote "″" can be escaped with " essentially in attribute value

The following is not valid because the ampersand would confuse the XML processor:

```
<company>Marks & Spencer</company>
```

Instead, it must be rewritten to escape the ampersand bracket with an & entity:

```
<company>Marks &amp; Spencer</company>
```

XML also supports *character references* where a letter is replaced by its Unicode character code. For example, if your keyboard does not support accented letters, you can still write my name in XML as

```
<name>Beno&#238;t Marchal</name>
```

In Unicode, the î character has the code 238.

Character references that start with &#x use a hexadecimal representation of the character code. Character references that start with &# use a decimal representation of the character code.

TIP

Under Windows, to find the character code of most characters, use the Character Map. The character code appears in the status bar; see Figure 2.2.

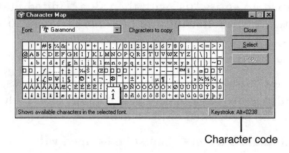

Character code

Figure 2.2: *The character code in Character Map.*

Special Attributes

XML defines two attributes:

- xml:space: Like Web browsers, most XML applications discard duplicated spaces. Yet, sometimes spaces are meaningful. HTML has a special element (<PRE>) to preserve spaces. This attribute tells the application what to do with spaces. If set to preserve, the application should preserve all spaces. If set to default, the application can ignore duplicate spaces.

The following example asks the application to preserve spaces in a `listing` element:

```
<listing xml:space="preserve">for(String line = reader.readLine();
     null != line;
     line = reader.readLine())
   writer.println(line);
</listing>
```

EXAMPLE

- `xml:lang:`.... It is often desirable to know in which language the content is written. This attribute records the language. For example:

```
<p xml:lang="en-GB">What colour is it?</p>
<p xml:lang="en-US">What color is it?</p>
```

Processing Instructions

Processing instructions (abbreviated *PI*) is a mechanism to insert non-XML statements, such as scripts, in the document.

At first sight, the existence of processing instructions is at odds with the XML concept that structure comes first. As we saw in the first chapter, XML processing is derived from the structure of the document, not from instructions inserted in the document.

That's the theory, at least. In practice, there are cases where it is simpler to insert instructions rather than define complex structures. Processing instructions are a concession to reality by the standard developers.

EXAMPLE

You are already familiar with processing instructions because the xml declaration is a processing instruction:

```
<?xml version="1.0" encoding="ISO-8859-1"?>
```

Processing instructions are enclosed in <? and ?>. The first word is the *target*. It identifies the application or the device to which the instruction is directed. The remainder is in a format specific to the target and it does not have to be XML.

EXAMPLE

✔In Chapter 5, you will see how to use processing instructions to attach style sheets to documents (**page 137**).

```
<?xml-stylesheet href="simple-ie5.xsl" type="text/xsl"?>
```

EXAMPLE

Finally, processing instructions are used by some applications. For example, XMetaL (an XML editor) uses them to create templates. This processing instruction is specific to XMetaL:

```
<?xm-replace_text {Click here to type the name}?>
```

CDATA Sections

As you have seen, markup delimiters (left-angle bracket and ampersand) that appear in the content of an element must be escaped with an entity.

For some applications, it is difficult to escape markup characters, if only because there are too many of them. Mathematical equations can use many left-angle brackets. It is difficult to include a scripting language in a document and to escape the angle brackets and ampersands. Also, it is difficult to include an XML document in an XML document.

CDATA sections were introduced for those cases. CDATA sections are delimited by "<![CDATA[" and "]]>". The XML parser ignores delimiters within the CDATA section, except for]]> (which means it is not possible to include a CDATA section in another CDATA section).

EXAMPLE

The following example uses a CDATA section to insert an XML example into an XML document.

```
<?xml version="1.0"?>
<example>
<![CDATA[
<?xml version="1.0"?>
<entry>
   <name>John Doe</name>
   <email href="mailto:jdoe@emailaholic.com"/>
</entry>]]>
</example>
```

NOTE

CDATA stands for character data. In the first section of this chapter, I explained that XML documents include markup and character data. That was a simplification. Strictly speaking, I should have discussed *parsed character data* (which contains no markup delimiters such as <), *character data* (which may contain markup delimiters) and *markup*.

The difference between parsed character data and character data is seldom relevant. In most cases, you would call all the text in the document character data—as I did in the first section.

Frequently Asked Questions About XML

This completes our study of the XML syntax. The only aspect of the XML recommendation we haven't studied yet is the DTD (and the more recent schema). The DTD is introduced in Chapter 4, "XML Models" In the next chapter, we'll study XML namespaces, a complement to the core syntax introduced in this chapter.

Before moving to namespaces and schemas, however, I'd like to answer three common questions on XML documents.

Code Indenting

Listing 2.1, shown earlier, is indented to make the tree more apparent. Although, it is not required for the XML parser, it makes the code more readable as you can see immediately where an element starts and ends.

This raises the question of what the parser does with the indenting. Is it ignored? The answer is a qualified no.

EXAMPLE

Strictly speaking, the XML parser does not ignore white spaces. In the following example, it sees the content of `entry` as a line break, three spaces, `name`, another line break, three more spaces, `tel`, and a line break.

```
<entry>
   <name>Jack Smith</name>
   <tel>513-744-3465</tel>
</entry>
```

EXAMPLE

In the following example, it sees the content of `entry` as just `name` and `tel`. No line breaks, and no spaces.

```
<entry><name>Jack Smith</name><tel>513-744-3465</tel></entry>
```

The two examples are therefore different for the parser. However, it is easy to filter unwanted white spaces and most applications do it. For example, XSL (XML Stylesheet Language) ignores what it recognizes as indenting.

Likewise, most XML editors give you the option of indenting source code automatically. If they indent the code, they will ignore most spaces in the document.

If whitespaces are important for your application, you should use the `xml:space` attribute that was introduced earlier.

Why the End Tag?

At first, the need to terminate each element with an end tag is annoying. It is required because XML is extensible.

An HTML browser can determine when an element has no closing tags because it knows the structure of the document—it knows which elements are allowed where and it can deduce where each element should end.

EXAMPLE

Indeed, if the following is an HTML fragment, a browser does not need end tags for paragraphs, nor does it need an empty tag for the break (see Listing 2.4).

Listing 2.4: abook.html

```
<html><body>
<p><b>John Doe</b>
<p>34 Fountain Square Plaza<br>
Cincinnati, OH 45202<br>
US
<p>Tel: 513-744-8889
<p>Tel: 513-744-7098
<p>Email: jdoe@emailaholic.com
```

The browser can deduce where the paragraphs end because it knows that paragraphs cannot nest. Therefore, the beginning of a new paragraph must coincide with the end of the previous one. Likewise, the browser knows that the break is an empty element. Because of all this a priori knowledge, the browser knows the document must be interpreted as

```
<html><body>
<p><b>John Doe</b></p>
<p>34 Fountain Square Plaza<br>
Cincinnati, OH 45202<br>
US</p>
<p>Tel: 513-744-8889</p>
<p>Tel: 513-744-7098</p>
<p>Email: jdoe@emailaholic.com</p>
</body></html>
```

However, an XML parser does not know the structure of the document because it does not know which elements are empty and which elements nest. So, an XML processor does not know that p elements (it does not know they are paragraphs, either) cannot nest. If Listing 2.4 shown earlier were XML, the processor could interpret it as

```
<html><body>
<p><b>John Doe</b>
   <p>34 Fountain Square Plaza
      <br>Cincinnati, OH 45202</br>
      <br>US</br>
      <p>Tel: 513-744-8889
         <p>Tel: 513-744-7098
            <p>Email: jdoe@emailaholic.com</p>
         </p>
      </p>
   </p>
</p></body></html>
```

or as:

```
<html><body>
<p><b>John Doe</b></p>
```

```
<p>34 Fountain Square Plaza
   <br>Cincinnati, OH 45202</br>
   <br/>US
   <p>Tel: 513-744-8889</p>
   <p>Tel: 513-744-7098</p>
</p>
<p>Email: jdoe@emailaholic.com</p>
</body></html>
```

There are many other possibilities and that's precisely the problem. The parser wouldn't know which one to pick so the markup has to be unambiguous.

TIP

In Chapter 4, you will see how to declare the structure of documents with schemas. Theoretically, the XML parser could use the schema to resolve ambiguities in the markup. Indeed, that's how SGML processors work. However, you will also learn that a category of XML parsers ignores schemas.

XML and Semantic

It is important to realize that XML alone does not define the meaning (the semantic) of the document. The element names are meaningful only to humans. They are meaningless for the XML parser.

EXAMPLE

The parser does not know what a name is. And it does not know the difference between a name and an address, apart from the fact that an address element has more children than a name element. For the XML processor, Listing 2.5, where the element names are totally mixed up, is as sensible (or rather, as meaningless) as Listing 2.1.

Listing 2.5: mixedup.xml

```
<?xml version="1.0"?>
<name>
   <tel>
      <street>John Doe</street>
      <country>
         <email>34 Fountain Square Plaza</email>
         <locality>OH</locality>
         <comments>45202</comments>
         <postal-code>Cincinnati</postal-code>
         <address>US</address>
      </country>
      <address-book preferred="true">513-744-8889</address-book>
      <address-book>513-744-7098</address-book>
      <entry href="mailto:jdoe@emailaholic.com"/>
```

Listing 2.5: continued

```
   </tel>
   <tel>
      <street>Jack Smith</street>
      <address-book>513-744-3465</address-book>
      <entry href="mailto:jsmith@emailaholic.com"/>
      <b>Never leave messages on his answering
      machine. <region>Email instead.</region></b>
   </tel>
</name>
```

The semantic of an XML document is provided by the application. As we will see in Chapter 5, "XSL Transformations," and later, some XML companion standards deal with some aspects of semantic.

For example, XSL describes how to format documents. XLink and RDF (Resource Definition Framework) can be used to describe the relationships between documents.

Four Common Errors

As you have seen, the XML syntax is very strict: Elements must have both a start and end tag, or they must use the special empty-element tag; attribute values must be fully quoted; there can be only one top-level element, and so on.

A strict syntax was a design goal for XML. The browser vendors asked for it. HTML is very lenient, and HTML browsers accept anything that looks vaguely like HTML. It might have helped with the early adoption of HTML, but now it is a problem.

Studies estimate that more than 50% of the code in a browser deals with errors or the sloppiness of HTML authors. Consequently, an HTML browser is difficult to write, it has slowed competition, and it makes for mega-downloads.

It is expected that in the future, people will increasingly rely on PDAs (Personal Digital Assistants like the PalmPilot) or smartphones to access the Web. These devices don't have the resources to accommodate a complex syntax or megabyte browsers.

In short, making XML stricter meant simplifying the work of the programmers, which translates into more competition, more tools, and more efficient tools that fit in smaller devices.

Yet, it means that you have to be very careful about what you write. This is particularly true if you are used to writing HTML documents. In this section, you will review the four most common errors in writing XML code.

Forgetting End Tags

EXAMPLE

For reasons explained previously, end tags are mandatory (except for empty elements). The XML processor would reject the following because street and country have no end tags:

```
<address>
    <street>34 Fountain Square Plaza
    <region>OH</region>
    <postal-code>45202</postal-code>
    <locality>Cincinnati</locality>
    <country>US
</address>
```

Forgetting That XML Is Case Sensitive

EXAMPLE

XML names are case sensitive. The following two elements are different for XML. The first one is a tel element whereas the second one is a TEL element

```
<tel>513-744-7098</tel>
<TEL>513-744-7098</TEL>
```

EXAMPLE

A popular variation on this error is to use a different case in the opening and closing tags:

```
<tel>513-744-7098</TEL>
```

Introducing Spaces in the Name of the Element

EXAMPLE

It is incorrect to introduce spaces in the name of elements. The XML parser interprets spaces as the beginning of an attribute. The following example is not valid because address book has a space in it:

```
<address book>
    <entry>
        <name>John Doe</name>
        <email href="mailto:jdoe@emailaholic.com"/>
    </entry>
</address book>
```

Forgetting the Quotes for the Attribute Value

EXAMPLE

Unlike HTML, XML forces you to quote attributes. The following is not acceptable:

```
<tel preferred=true>513-744-8889</tel>
```

A popular variation on this error is to forget the closing quote. The XML processor assumes that the content of the element is part of the attribute, which is guaranteed to produce funny results! The following is incorrect because the attribute has no closing quote:

```
<tel preferred="true>513-744-8889</tel>
```

Two Applications of XML

Another design goal for XML was to develop a language to suit a large variety of applications. In this respect, XML has probably exceeded its creators' wildest dreams.

In this section, you are introduced to two applications of XML. As you will see throughout the book, many more applications benefit from XML but this section gives you some early ideas of what XML is used for.

Publishing

XML roots are in publishing, it's no wonder the standard is well adapted to publishing. XML is being used by an increasing number of online publishers (such as www.developer.com) as the format for documents. The XML standard itself was published with XML.

EXAMPLE

Listing 2.6 is an XML document for a monthly newsletter. As you can see, it has XML elements for the title, paragraphs, section, and other concepts common in publishing.

Listing 2.6: excerpt.xml

```
<?xml version="1.0"?>
<article>
<articleinfo>
 <title>XSL -- First Step in Learning XML</title>
 <author><firstname>Beno&#238;t</firstname>
  <surname>Marchal</surname></author>
</articleinfo>
<sect1><title>The Value of XSL</title>
 <para>This is an excerpt from the September 2000 issue of
  Pineapplesoft Link. To subscribe free visit
   <ulink url="http://www.marchal.com">marchal.com</ulink>.</para>
 <para>Where do you start learning XML? Increasingly my answer
  is with XSL. XSL is a very powerful tool with many
  applications. Many XML applications depend on it. Let's take
  two examples.</para>
</sect1>
<sect1>
 <title>XSL and Web Publishing</title>
```

Listing 2.6: continued

```
 <para>As a webmaster you would benefit from using XSL.</para>
 <para>Let's suppose that you decide to support smartphones.
  You will need to redo your web site using WML, the
  <emphasis>wireless markup language</emphasis>, instead of
  HTML. While learning WML is easy, it can take days if not
  months to redo a large web site. Imagine having to edit every
  single page by hand!</para>
 <para>In contrast with XSL, it suffices to update one style
  sheet the changes flow across the entire web site.</para>
</sect1>
<sect1>
 <title>XSL and Programming</title>
 <para>The second facet of XSL is the scripting language. XSL
  has many features of scripting languages including loops,
  function calls, variables and more.</para>
 <para>In that respect, XSL is a valuable addition to any
  programmer toolbox. Indeed, as XML popularity keeps growing,
  you will find that you need to manipulate XML documents
  frequently and XSL is the language for so doing.</para>
</sect1>
<sect1>
 <title>Conclusion</title>
 <para>If you're serious about learning XML, learn XSL. XSL is
  a tool to manipulate XML documents for web publishing or
  programming.</para>
</sect1>
</article>
```

The main advantages of using XML for publishing are

- The capability to convert XML documents to different media: the Web, print, and more

- For large document sets, the ability to enforce a common structure that simplifies editing

- The emphasis on structure means that XML documents are better equipped to withstand the test of time, because structure is more stable than formatting (as anybody who publishes a Web site knows, fashion changes every year but the content need not be rewritten that often)

✔Turn to Chapter 5, "XSL Transformations," **page 137** and Chapter 6, "XSL Formatting Objects and Cascading Style Sheets," **page 175** for a more complete discussion of how to use XML for publishing.

Electronic Commerce

EXAMPLE

XML is not limited to publishing, it is also very popular for business-to-business e-commerce.

The XML elements are price, product descriptions, and so on. Listing 2.7 is a book order in XML.

Listing 2.7: order.xml

```
<?xml version="1.0"?>
<Order confirm="true">
   <Date>2000-03-10</Date>
   <Reference>AGL153</Reference>
   <DeliverBy>2000-04-10</DeliverBy>
   <Buyer>
      <Name>Playfield Books</Name>
      <Address>
         <Street>34 Fountain Square Plaza</Street>
         <Locality>Cincinnati</Locality>
         <PostalCode>45202</PostalCode>
         <Region>OH</Region>
         <Country>US</Country>
      </Address>
   </Buyer>
   <Seller>
      <Name>Macmillan Publishing</Name>
      <Address>
         <Street>201 West 103RD Street</Street>
         <Locality>Indianapolis</Locality>
         <PostalCode>46290</PostalCode>
         <Region>IN</Region>
         <Country>US</Country>
      </Address>
   </Seller>
   <Lines>
      <Product>
         <Code type="ISBN">0789725045</Code>
         <Description>XML by Example</Description>
         <Quantity>15</Quantity>
         <Price>29.99</Price>
      </Product>
      <Product>
         <Code type="ISBN">0672320541</Code>
         <Description>Applied XML Solutions</Description>
         <Quantity>5</Quantity>
         <Price>44.99</Price>
      </Product>
   </Lines>
</Order>
```

When you buy something (say, a book) from a store, that's a business-to-consumer transaction. Everything that happens behind the scene to deliver this product to you is known as business-to-business transactions. As an example, imagine the bookstore orders the book from a book distributor, which, in turn, orders it from the publisher. The publisher had the book manufactured by a printer, which had to buy paper and ink to print it. Did I mention express delivery? To serve you, many businesses had to collaborate, which led to many business-to-business transactions.

Electronic storefronts, such as `stores.yahoo.com` or `www.mivamerchant.com`, are adequate for business-to-consumer, but they are ill fitted for business-to-business e-commerce.

Why? Without going into all the details, storefronts cover only the selling function and they offer little room for automation. HTML, which is ideal for storefronts, is inadequate for business-to-business because it requires a clerk who sits in front of the computer and clicks his or her way through the ordering system.

Because business-to-business transactions are frequent, it is advantageous to automate them entirely. Ideally, one would like to replace some or all of the paperwork with electronic documents: the purchase order, the invoice, the delivery notification, shipping documents, and the check.

If the electronic documents are written in XML, the markup matches the structure of the document. E-commerce applications can scan the invoice in Listing 2.7 and recognize the product codes and the quantity ordered.

For years this was the realm of EDI technologies (*EDI* stands for *Electronic Data Interchange*). The core of EDI is a major effort to standardize every commercial and administrative document (order, invoice, tax declaration, payment, catalog, and more).

EDI, however, has traditionally focused on reducing costs. The idea was to replace the most human-intensive operations with computer systems.

With XML and the Internet, the focus is not merely on reducing costs but increasingly on opening new markets. Companies such as CommerceOne (`www.commerceone.com`) and Ariba (`www.ariba.com`) have built so-called electronic marketplaces. They provide new opportunities for buyers and sellers to meet and conduct business.

✔You will revisit this topic in Chapter 11, "N-Tiered Architecture and XML," and Chapter 12, "Putting It All Together: An e-Commerce Example."

XML Editors

If you are like me, you will soon hate writing XML with a text editor. It's not that the syntax is difficult, but it is annoying to have to remember to close every element and to escape left angle brackets.

Fortunately, there are several XML editors on the market to make your life easier. XML Spy (www.xmlspy.com) is popular with developers because it offers many shortcuts.

XML Spy displays the XML code in different modes. In Figure 2.3, Listing 2.1 is edited in grid view, where a collapsible grid replaces the markup. Grid view is ideal to navigate through a document.

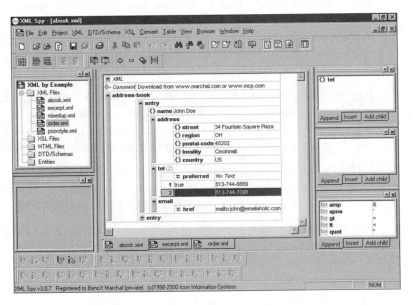

Figure 2.3: *XML Spy in Grid View.*

In Figure 2.4, an XML style sheet is created (see Chapter 5 for more on style sheets) in text view. The editor completes the instructions as they are typed.

XML Spy is appropriate for developers; however, for authors or clerical staff, you might want to hide the XML markup. Turn to XMetaL from SoftQuad (www.xmetal.com), an editor that behaves like a word processor. In Figure 2.5, I have edited Listing 2.6 with XMetaL. As you can see, there's not a tag to be seen. XMetaL is almost WYSIWYG: titles are in bold, the URL is underlined, and the paragraphs wrap nicely.

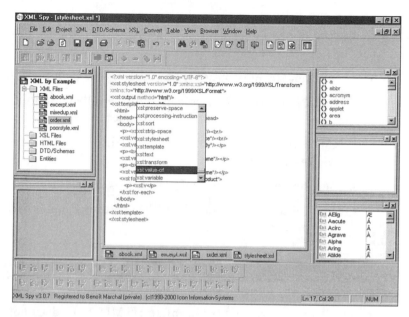

Figure 2.4: XML Spy in Text View.

✔For a more comprehensive discussion of what you should look for when shopping for an XML editor, turn to the section "CSS and XML Editors" in Chapter 6 **(page 175)**.

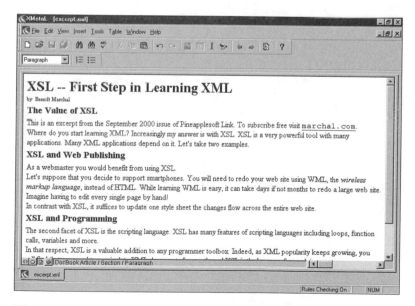

Figure 2.5: XMetaL is as friendly as a word processor.

XML Spy and XMetaL represent two categories of XML editors, respectively: the programmer's editor (for authors knowledgeable in XML) and the author's editor (for the others).

These are not the only options, however. Other popular editors include:

- XML Notepad from Microsoft is a free (albeit limited) programmer's editor. It is available at `msdn.microsoft.com`.

- XML Pro is another programmer's editor available from `www.vervet.com`.

- Morphon was written in Java. It is available from `www.morphon.com`.

- Epic Editor is a pseudo-WYSIWYG editor from Arbortext (`www.arbortext.com`).

What's Next

In this chapter you learned enough XML syntax to read or write XML documents. You also learned that, unlike HTML, XML does not define elements. The document author has to create the elements it needs.

In the next chapter, you will learn an important extension to XML: the XML namespaces. Namespaces are useful to organize elements in a document.

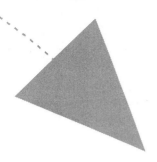

XML Namespaces

The previous chapter introduced the syntax for XML documents. You learned what an XML document is and what it can be used for. You also have seen how to write XML documents.

This chapter complements the previous chapter with a discussion on *XML namespaces*. You will learn

- How namespaces complement XML extensibility
- How to use namespaces in documents
- How the W3C uses namespaces in its own recommendations

The Problem Namespaces Solves

XML is extensible. So it says in the name: eXtensible Markup Language. The problem is that extensibility does not come free. Misused, it could be a source of problems. In a networked environment, such as the Web, extensibility must be managed to avoid conflicts. Namespaces is a solution to help manage XML extensibility.

XML namespace is a mechanism to identify XML elements. It places the name of the elements in a more global context—the namespace.

The namespace recommendation is available at www.w3.org/TR/REC-xml-names.

It is relatively thin. As you will see, the concepts are not difficult, either. Unfortunately, this means that namespaces are often overlooked! Don't make that mistake; namespaces are an essential component of XML.

EXAMPLE

Let's suppose you decide to publish your bookmarks in some sort of a portal site (there is heavy competition from Yahoo! but let's ignore this for a moment). Listing 3.1 shows what it might look like in XML. As a stand-alone document, Listing 3.1 works perfectly.

Listing 3.1: resources.xml

```
<?xml version="1.0"?>
<bookmarks>
   <site href="http://www.marchal.com">
      <title>Beno&#238;t marchal</title></site>
   <site href="http://www.pineapplesoft.com/newsletter">
      <title>Pineapplesoft Link</title></site>
   <site href="http://www.mcp.com">
      <title>Macmillan Publishing</title></site>
   <site href="http://www.xml.com">
      <title>XML.com</title></site>
   <site href="http://xml.apache.org">
      <title>Apache XML</title></site>
   <site href="http://www.abcnews.com">
      <title>ABC News</title></site>
</bookmarks>
```

✔ Chapter 5, "XSL Transformations," **page 137** will show you how to publish this document on a Web site.

EXAMPLE

In practice, however, documents are seldom standalone. In a collaborative environment such as the Web, people build on one another's work. Somebody might take your list and rate it. The result would be similar to Listing 3.2 (admittedly, I'm biased in the ratings).

Listing 3.2: `ratings.xml`

```
<?xml version="1.0"?>
<bookmarks>
    <site href="http://www.marchal.com">
       <title>Beno&#238;t marchal</title>
       <rating>5 stars</rating></site>
    <site href="http://www.pineapplesoft.com/newsletter">
       <title>Pineapplesoft Link</title>
       <rating>5 stars</rating></site>
    <site href="http://www.mcp.com">
       <title>Macmillan Publishing</title>
       <rating>5 stars</rating></site>
    <site href="http://www.xml.com">
       <title>XML.com</title>
       <rating>4 stars</rating></site>
    <site href="http://xml.apache.org">
       <title>Apache XML</title>
       <rating>4 stars</rating></site>
    <site href="http://www.abcnews.com">
       <title>ABC News</title>
       <rating>3 stars</rating></site>
</bookmarks>
```

Listing 3.2 is the same document with one new element: `rating`. It is often desirable to extend documents to convey new information instead of designing new ones from scratch.

EXAMPLE

Problems occur, however, if extensions are not properly managed. Suppose somebody else decides to rate the list, but instead of quality, it rates against family criteria. Listing 3.3 shows the result (ABC News might report on violence, hence its PG rating).

Listing 3.3: `pgratings.xml`

```
<?xml version="1.0"?>
<bookmarks>
    <site href="http://www.marchal.com">
       <title>Beno&#238;t marchal</title>
       <rating>G</rating></site>
    <site href="http://www.pineapplesoft.com/newsletter">
       <title>Pineapplesoft Link</title>
       <rating>G</rating></site>
    <site href="http://www.mcp.com">
       <title>Macmillan Publishing</title>
       <rating>G</rating></site>
    <site href="http://www.xml.com">
       <title>XML.com</title>
```

Listing 3.3: continued

```
    <rating>G</rating></site>
  <site href="http://xml.apache.org">
    <title>Apache XML</title>
    <rating>G</rating></site>
  <site href="http://www.abcnews.com">
    <title>ABC News</title>
    <rating>PG</rating></site>
</bookmarks>
```

This is problematic. Listing 3.3 also is an extension to Listing 3.1 but it creates incompatibilities between Listing 3.2 and Listing 3.3, because both introduce a `rating` element. This is a very common problem: Two groups extend the same document in incompatible ways.

EXAMPLE

Things get really out of hand when trying to combine both ratings in a listing. After all, when building a portal, you want to present the visitor with both quality rating and parental guidance. The result would look like Listing 3.4, in which the conflict between the two `rating` elements is obvious.

Listing 3.4: combinedratings.xml

```
<?xml version="1.0"?>
<bookmarks>
    <site href="http://www.marchal.com">
      <title>Beno&#238;t marchal</title>
      <rating>5 stars</rating>
      <rating>G</rating></site>
    <site href="http://www.pineapplesoft.com/newsletter">
      <title>Pineapplesoft Link</title>
      <rating>5 stars</rating>
      <rating>G</rating></site>
    <site href="http://www.mcp.com">
      <title>Macmillan Publishing</title>
      <rating>5 stars</rating>
      <rating>G</rating></site>
    <site href="http://www.xml.com">
      <title>XML.com</title>
      <rating>4 stars</rating>
      <rating>G</rating></site>
    <site href="http://xml.apache.org">
      <title>Apache XML</title>
      <rating>4 stars</rating>
      <rating>G</rating></site>
    <site href="http://www.abcnews.com">
```

Listing 3.4: continued

```
      <title>ABC News</title>
      <rating>3 stars</rating>
      <rating>PG</rating></site>
</bookmarks>
```

The problem with Listing 3.4 is that software designed to operate with Listing 3.3 (for example, to filter offensive links) would be completely lost. It wouldn't know what to do with the "4 stars" rating. The software should simply ignore quality rating tags but how can it recognize them because they are in a rating element?

EXAMPLE

The solution is obvious: Use different element names for each concept. In Listing 3.4, we have two concepts: quality rating and parental guidance. They should have different tags. Listing 3.5 renames the "quality" element as qa-rating and the "parental" element as pa-rating.

Listing 3.5: prefixratings.xml

```xml
<?xml version="1.0"?>
<bookmarks>
   <site href="http://www.marchal.com">
      <title>Beno&#238;t marchal</title>
      <qa-rating>5 stars</qa-rating>
      <pg-rating>G</pg-rating></site>
   <site href="http://www.pineapplesoft.com/newsletter">
      <title>Pineapplesoft Link</title>
      <qa-rating>5 stars</qa-rating>
      <pg-rating>G</pg-rating></site>
   <site href="http://www.mcp.com">
      <title>Macmillan Publishing</title>
      <qa-rating>5 stars</qa-rating>
      <pg-rating>G</pg-rating></site>
   <site href="http://www.xml.com">
      <title>XML.com</title>
      <qa-rating>4 stars</qa-rating>
      <pg-rating>G</pg-rating></site>
   <site href="http://xml.apache.org">
      <title>Apache XML</title>
      <qa-rating>4 stars</qa-rating>
      <pg-rating>G</pg-rating></site>
   <site href="http://www.abcnews.com">
      <title>ABC News</title>
      <qa-rating>3 stars</qa-rating>
      <pg-rating>PG</pg-rating></site>
</bookmarks>
```

Namespaces

The problem outlined in the previous example is the extensible character of XML. There is no way to prevent somebody from extending a document in a way that is incompatible with other works. That's the nature of extensibility. Because anybody can create tags, there is a huge risk of conflicts.

Coming up with prefixes, as we did in Listing 3.5, is possible only if we are aware of the conflict in advance.

What's the best way to handle this problem? The W3C could establish a global registry of tags in use. When creating a new document, you would have to validate your tag names against a global dictionary. "Sorry Sir, but you can't name this element rating. Somebody else is already using it." It would, however, severely limit XML's flexibility and friendliness.

Nobody wants to limit XML's flexibility. Flexibility was a major goal in the design of XML. The namespaces proposal addresses the same problem but with a more elegant approach: It does not limit extensibility, but instead introduces a mechanism to manage it.

EXAMPLE

Listing 3.6 is equivalent to Listing 3.5, but it uses namespaces to prevent naming clashes.

Listing 3.6: nsratings.xml

```
<?xml version="1.0"?>
<bookmarks xmlns:pg="http://www.playfield.com/parental/en/1.0"
           xmlns:qa="http://www.writeit.com/quality"
           xmlns="http://www.pineapplesoft.com/2001/bookmark">
   <site href="http://www.marchal.com">
      <title>Beno&#238;t marchal</title>
      <qa:rating>5 stars</qa:rating>
      <pg:rating>G</pg:rating></site>
   <site href="http://www.pineapplesoft.com/newsletter">
      <title>Pineapplesoft Link</title>
      <qa:rating>5 stars</qa:rating>
      <pg:rating>G</pg:rating></site>
   <site href="http://www.mcp.com">
      <title>Macmillan Publishing</title>
      <qa:rating>5 stars</qa:rating>
      <pg:rating>G</pg:rating></site>
   <site href="http://www.xml.com">
      <title>XML.com</title>
      <qa:rating>4 stars</qa:rating>
      <pg:rating>G</pg:rating></site>
   <site href="http://xml.apache.org">
      <title>Apache XML</title>
```

Listing 3.6: continued

```
    <qa:rating>4 stars</qa:rating>
    <pg:rating>G</pg:rating></site>
  <site href="http://www.abcnews.com">
    <title>ABC News</title>
    <qa:rating>3 stars</qa:rating>
    <pg:rating>PG</pg:rating></site>
</bookmarks>
```

At first sight, Listing 3.6 is similar to Listing 3.5: It declares two different names for the ratings—pg:rating and qa-rating.

The major difference is the form of the names. In Listing 3.6, a colon separates the name from its prefix:

```
<qa:rating>5 stars</qa:rating>
```

The prefix unambiguously identifies the type of rating within this document. However, prefixes alone do not solve problems because anybody can create prefixes. Therefore, different people can create incompatible prefixes and you are back to step one except that you have moved the risk of conflicts from element names to prefixes. To avoid conflicts in prefixes, prefixes are declared:

```
<bookmarks xmlns:pg="http://www.playfield.com/parental/en/1.0"
           xmlns:qa="http://www.writeit.com/quality"
           xmlns="http://www.pineapplesoft.com/2001/bookmark">
```

The declaration associates a URI (Uniform Resource Identifier) with a prefix. This is the crux of the namespaces proposal because URIs, unlike element names or prefixes, can be made unique.

In practice, most URIs are in fact URLs (Uniform Resource Locators) but, as you will see in a moment, URNs (Uniform Resource Names) are also acceptable. URLs are guaranteed to be unique because they are based on domain names, which are registered to prevent conflicts.

A namespace declaration is introduced in an attribute, starting with xmlns followed by the prefix (note that, for the declaration, the prefix comes at the end of the attribute; when used, the prefix comes first). In Listing 3.6, two prefixes are declared: qa and pa.

The attribute xmlns, without a following prefix, declares the default namespace—that is, the namespace for those elements that have no attributes. In Listing 3.6, a default namespace is also declared.

A namespace is valid for the element on which it is declared and its content (including elements contained within the element), unless overridden by another namespace declaration with the same prefix.

In summary, XML namespaces is a mechanism to unambiguously identify who has developed which element. It's not much, but it is an essential service.

The Namespace Name

The namespace name is the URI, not the prefix. In other words, when comparing two elements, the parser uses the URIs, not the prefixes to recognize their namespaces.

Therefore, in Listing 3.7 `bk:title` and `site:title` are in the same namespace and are considered identical even though they have different prefixes. Both are in the `http://www.pineapplesoft.com/2001/bookmark` namespace.

EXAMPLE

Listing 3.7: 2prefixes.xml

```
<?xml version="1.0"?>
<bk:bookmarks
    xmlns:bk="http://www.pineapplesoft.com/2001/bookmark">
    <bk:site href="http://www.marchal.com">
       <bk:title>Beno&#238;t marchal</bk:title></bk:site>
    <site:site href="http://www.pineapplesoft.com/newsletter"
          xmlns:site="http://www.pineapplesoft.com/2001/bookmark">
       <site:title>Pineapplesoft Link</site:title></site:site>
</bk:bookmarks>
```

URIs

The namespace declaration associates a global name (the URI) with the name of the element. There's lots of confusion surrounding the use of URIs in XML namespaces. Let me try to clear some of the confusion.

Requirements on URIs

First and foremost, the URI is only used as an identifier. As far as XML namespaces are concerned, it need not be valid. In other words, it might not point to anything. Indeed, if you point your browser to `http://www.pineapplesoft.com/2001/bookmark`, you will be greeted with a "404-File not found" error.

This is confusing. Logically, you would expect the URI to be used for something. For example, you would expect the URI to point to a definition of the bookmark element. That might be what you're expecting, but that's not what XML namespace mandates.

Why? There are many reasons, but they boil down to this: You must be able to process XML documents without a connection to the Internet.

Here are two examples. In electronic commerce, some XML applications run on secured computers that are not connected to the Internet. It would be difficult to process XML namespaces if they had to resolve URIs.

Another example is what happens if the company who owns the URI goes out of business. Let's suppose Pineapplesoft goes under (not that I want it to happen but, for the sake of discussion, suppose it does), how could you process Listing 3.6 if the Pineapplesoft site is no longer accessible?

The solution made by the namespace team is sensible: Use URIs to guarantee uniqueness through domain names, but place no restrictions on the URIs. In particular, the URIs do not need be valid—they do not need to point to a resource.

CAUTION

Because URIs need not be valid, XML namespaces treats them as a string. In particular, comparisons are done character-by-character. According to this definition, the following two URIs are not identical, even though they point to the same document:

```
http://www.marchal.com
http://marchal.com
```

Even differences in case are interpreted as different URIs. For XML namespaces, the following two URIs are different:

```
http://www.marchal.com
http://www.MARCHAL.com
```

This raises the mirror question: Do URIs have to be invalid? Not at all! The XML namespace recommendation places no special constraints on URIs but, if you're going to set up a Web site anyway, it's a good idea to make it accessible through the namespace URI.

For example, if I ever decide to build a Web site to describe the bookmark application, I would be wise to install it at `http://www.pineapplesoft.com/2001/bookmark`. Document authors would see the URL anyway.

And now for the philosophical question, "If XML namespaces treats URIs as strings, why bother? Why not use words as a namespace identifier?"

The answer is to avoid conflicts of names. Remember that namespaces exist to prevent two organizations from giving the same name to different concepts. If you could use any name as an URI identifier, we wouldn't have solved any problems.

EXAMPLE

The following example illustrates the problem. It is unsafe because the namespace identifier is simply "bookmarks." The risk of somebody else declaring a bookmarks namespace is huge. In fact, this solves no problems at all:

```
<?xml version="1.0"?>
<!-- this namespace is invalid -->
<bk:bookmarks xmlns:bk="bookmarks">
   <bk:site href="http://www.marchal.com">
     <bk:title>Beno&#238;t marchal</bk:title></bk:site>
   <bk:site href="http://www.pineapplesoft.com/newsletter">
     <bk:title>Pineapplesoft Link</bk:title></bk:site>
</bk:bookmarks>
```

URLs, on the other hand, incorporate a domain name that has been registered to guarantee uniqueness.

URLs and URNs

Most URIs are URLs or Internet addresses. They might point to a file on a machine (`http://www.marchal.com`), a user mailbox (`mailto:bmarchal@pineapplesoft.com`), or a newsgroup (`news:comp.text.xml`).

The *IETF (Internet Engineering Task Force)* is working on other forms of URIs, more specifically *URN (Uniform Resource Name)*.

The difference is that, with an address, if the document moves, the address becomes invalid—the dreadful "404 - File not found" error message. URNs are not addresses. They are independent of the location of the document. This should eliminate the "404" errors.

As you have seen, it is not a problem for XML namespaces (because the URI can be invalid) but it might be inconvenient for the users who expect to find some information at the URI.

EXAMPLE

URNs are constructed from the `urn:` prefix, followed by a prefix to identify the URN type and, finally, the value.

ISBN numbers (the number at the back of the book, on top of the bar code) are good candidates for URNs. An ISBN number identifies a book, irrespective of where the book is currently located. You can use the ISBN number to order the book from a bookstore or to borrow it from a library. The URN for my other book, *Applied XML Solutions*, is

```
urn:ISBN:0-672-32054-1
```

Another approach is to use PURLs (Permanent URLs). Unlike regular URLs, *PURLs* are registered to avoid "404" errors. The registration process is the key. If the document moves, it suffices to update the registry. The PURL remains unchanged. You can find more information on PURLs (and create your first PURL) at `www.purl.org`.

What's in a Name?

Because most namespace URIs are URLs, it's worth studying them in more detail.

EXAMPLE

URLs are of the form:

```
http://www.marchal.com
http://www.pineapplesoft.com/newsletter
ftp://ftp.mcp.com
news :comp.text.xml
mailto:bmarchal@pineapplesoft.com
```

For namespaces, the http: URLs are most convenient because

- They can be made unique because they include a domain name that has been registered. No two organizations have the same domain name. A news: URL, for example, would not guarantee uniqueness.

- They are very flexible because you can create an infinite number of namespaces from a simple root: `http://www.marchal.com`, `http://www.marchal.com/2001/xbe2`, `http://www.marchal.com/2001/xbe2/mynamespace`, and more.

- It is easy to set up a Web site, if the need arises to provide information on the namespace. A mailto: URL, for example, would be less flexible.

Although the recommendation gives no hints as to what constitutes a good URL for namespaces, experience shows that the best URLs strike a balance between brevity and descriptiveness—an URL such as `http://www.pineapplesoft.com/bookmark-for-xml-by-example-2nd-edition-chapter-3` is inconvenient.

Beware of your co-workers! In medium-to-large organizations, it is easy to have two people using an URL. Most organizations solve the problem by creating special subdirectories on their server. For example, the W3C includes the year the URL was allocated, as in

```
http://www.w3.org/1999/XSL/Transform
http://www.w3.org/2000/09/xmldsig
```

Other organizations include a one-word description of the project. For example, I could have used the string xbe2 (XML by Example, 2nd) in namespaces created for this book:

```
http://www.marchal.com/xbe2/bookmark
```

Registering a Domain Name

If you are serious about XML development and you currently don't have a domain name, you might want to register one.

Remember, to guarantee uniqueness, you should never use somebody else's domain name in your namespaces. Domain names are so cheap that I would advise you to register one.

At the time of writing, a .com domain costs between $12 and $35 per year. Your ISP can register a domain name for you or you can turn to Register.com (www.register.com), WorldNIC (www.worldnic.com), or MyDomain (www.mydomain.com). These organizations (and many others) offer *domain parking*, that is, they keep the domain until you create a Web site.

After you register a domain name, provided you are listed as the administrative contact and you pay the yearly fee, it's yours. You are free to move to another ISP and still retain the domain name.

TIP

If you register a domain name specifically for namespaces, opt for a short name. Over time, it will save you a lot of typing!

I did not worry about domain length when I founded Pineapplesoft—I was happy with pineapplesoft.com. However, after one year of intensive coding, I registered psol.com (short for Pineapplesoft Object Library) to use in Java packages. It's a small saving (8 letters against 17) but I felt it was worth it! I use the same domain for some XML namespaces.

Scoping

EXAMPLE

The namespace is valid for the element where it is declared and all the elements within its content, as illustrated in Listing 3.8. In programming circles, this is referred to as *scoping*.

Listing 3.8: `scoping.xml`

```
<?xml version="1.0"?>
<bk:bookmarks
    xmlns:bk="http://www.pineapplesoft.com/2001/bookmark">
    <bk:site href="http://www.marchal.com">
        <bk:title>Beno&#238;t marchal</bk:title>
        <ns:rating
         xmlns:ns="http://www.playfield.com/parental/en/1.0">G
        </ns:rating>
        <ns:rating
```

Listing 3.8: continued

```
      xmlns:ns="http://www.writeit.com/quality">5 stars
   </ns:rating>
  </bk:site>
</bk:bookmarks>
```

Again, there are three namespaces declared in Listing 3.7. bk is declared on the top-level element and is therefore valid for all the elements. ns is declared twice for the two rating elements, but with different URIs (corresponding to different namespaces).

EXAMPLE

So far, the attributes are not associated with any namespace but, as Listing 3.9 illustrates, they could be. In Listing 3.9, a new sponsored attribute has been added to identify those links that have been paid for. The sponsored attribute is in its own namespace.

Listing 3.9: sponsored.xml

```
<?xml version="1.0"?>
<bookmarks
   xmlns="http://www.pineapplesoft.com/2001/bookmark"
   xmlns:acc="http://www.pineapplesoft.com/2001/accounting">
   <site href="http://www.marchal.com"
       acc:sponsored-"false">
     <title>Beno&#238;t marchal</title>
   </site>
   <site href="http://www.pineapplesoft.com/newsletter"
       acc:sponsored="true">
     <title>Pineapplesoft Link</title></site>
</bookmarks>
```

NOTE

The xml prefix introduced in the previous chapter with the xml:space and xml:lang is bound to http://www.w3.org/XML/1998/namespace. There is no need to declare the xml prefix.

Digital Signature: An Example of Namespaces

XML namespacesare a small extension to XML that places names (elements or attributes) in a more global context. It's not much but it enables reuse in document creation.

Initially, XML documents were developed in isolation. One would develop a vocabulary for a specific application, such as a magazine, an order, or a Web site—as we saw in the last chapter. The XML elements would be specific to that application. There is little reuse of elements except, perhaps, by cutting and pasting old documents into new ones. In so doing, you have to be careful not to introduce name conflicts.

Thanks to namespaces, it is possible to develop *reusable elements*, that is, elements that can be reused in multiple documents.

Increasingly, the W3C and other groups work on such reusable elements. This is illustrated by a forthcoming W3C recommendation: Digital Signatures.

For e-commerce and other applications, it is useful to digitally sign XML documents. A digital signature warrants that the document has not been tampered with. The W3C and the IETF have developed a standard for signing XML documents.

EXAMPLE

Listing 3.10 is an example of a signed XML document. Toward the bottom of this document, you find the familiar bookmarks in the `http://www.pineapplesoft.com/2001/bookmark` namespace.

The bookmark is wrapped in a signature element in the `http://www.w3.org/2000/09/xmldsig` namespace. Signature is defined by the W3C. Figure 3.1 illustrates the document's organization: It starts with the digital

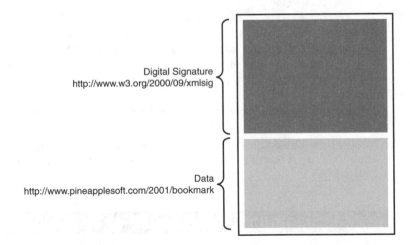

Digital Signature
http://www.w3.org/2000/09/xmlsig

Data
http://www.pineapplesoft.com/2001/bookmark

signature and is followed by the data itself.

Figure 3.1: *Signature and data are identified by their namespace.*

What makes it attractive is that a digital signature toolkit (such as IBM's

XML Security Suite) recognizes the digital signature through its namespace and it can verify that the document has been signed properly, even though it does not recognize the bookmarks element. Conversely, the portal would ignore the digital signature (based on its namespace) and processes the bookmarks only.

Listing 3.10 shows how you can combine elements defined in different namespaces. Each application will look for elements in namespaces it recognizes and ignore the rest.

CAUTION

This example is based on a draft version of XML Signatures. The final recommendation may be different. Please visit www.w3.org/Signature for the latest version of the XML signature.

Listing 3.10: `signed.xml`

```
<?xml version='1.0' encoding='UTF-8'?>
<Signature xmlns="http://www.w3.org/2000/09/xmldsig#">
  <SignedInfo>
    <CanonicalizationMethod
➥Algorithm="http://www.w3.org/TR/2000/WD-xml-c14n-20000119"/>
    <SignatureMethod
➥Algorithm="http://www.w3.org/2000/09/xmldsig#dsa-sha1"/>
    <Reference URI="#Res0">
      <Transforms>
        <Transform
➥Algorithm="http://www.w3.org/TR/2000/WD-xml-c14n-20000119"/>
      </Transforms>
      <DigestMethod
➥Algorithm="http://www.w3.org/2000/09/xmldsig#sha1"/>
      <DigestValue>bFiC6tyFSqBToSGiDCnjmCH5T5c=</DigestValue>
    </Reference>
  </SignedInfo>
  <SignatureValue>
    f8pJgbAwONSlrqz0rwb9ErGa0zAxTyPMjJbUnLv/OEITYYSolNN9Rw==
  </SignatureValue>
  <KeyInfo>
    <KeyValue>
      <DSAKeyValue>
        <P>
          /X9TgR11EilS30qcLuzk5/YRt1I870QAwx4/gLZRJmlFXUAiU
➥ftZPY1Y+r/F9bow9s
          ubVWzXgTuAHTRv8mZgt2uZUKWkn5/oBHsQIsJPu6nX/rfGG/g
➥7V+fGqKYVDwT7g/bT
          xR7DAjVUE1oWkTL2df0uK2HXKu/yIgMZndFIAcc=
```

Listing 3.10: continued

```
        </P>
        <Q>l2BQjxUjC8yykrmCouuEC/BYHPU=</Q>
        <G>
            9+GghdabPd7LvKtcNrhXuXmUr7v6OuqC+VdMCz0HgmdRWVeOu
➥tRZT+ZxBxCBgLRJFn
            Ej6EwoFhO3zwkyjMim4TwWeotUfI0o4KOuHiuzpnWRbqN/C/o
➥hNWLx+2J6ASQ7zKTx
            vqhRkImog9/hWuWfBpKLZl6Ae1UlZAFMO/7PSSo=
        </G>
        <Y>
            x9m0mL5NoU5BUx9MzH0Edmdlkrvi5mXplMAy60ctuk1ObjNvi
➥N/cQbdHJXfAUMfx6Y
            7Krv514ZXo85GD1ynawTqKhg3DgGe1nFQ2mcDuanAIrF3aLGJ
➥atUlWZWZeRP/TN/1d
            ZOqzana2pk/uJb2IoankoSf4EbM880aosorQgjw=
        </Y>
    </DSAKeyValue>
  </KeyValue>
  <X509Data>
    <X509SubjectName>CN=Beno&#238;t Marchal, O=Pineapplesoft,
➥L=Namur, C=BE</X509SubjectName>
    <X509Certificate>
MIIC0TCCAo8CBDora0YwCwYHKoZIzjgEAwUAME4xCzAJBgNVBAYTAkJFMQ4
➥wDAYDVQQHEwVOYW11
cjEWMBQGA1UEChMNUG1uZWFwcGxlc29mdDEXMBUGA1UEAxMOQmVub+50IE1
➥hcmNoYWwwHhcNMDAx
MjA0MTAwMDM0WhcNMDEwMzA0MTAwMDM4WjBOMQswCQYDVQQGEwJCRTEOMAw
➥GA1UEBxMFTmFtdXIx
FjAUBgNVBAoTDVBpbmVhcHBsZXNvZnQxFzAVBgNVBAMTDkJlbm/udCBNYXJ
➥jaGFsMIIBuDCCASwG
ByqGSM44BAEwggEfAoGBAP1/U4EddRIpUt9KnC7s5Of2EbdSPO9EAMMeP4C
➥2USZpRV1AIlH7WT2N
WPq/xfW6MPbLm1Vs14E7gB00b/JmYLdrmVClpJ+f6AR7ECLCT7up1/63xhv
➥4O1fnxqimFQ8E+4P2
08UewwI1VBNaFpEy9nXzrith1yrv8iIDGZ3RSAHHAhUAl2BQjxUjC8yykrm
➥CouuEC/BYHPUCgYEA
9+GghdabPd7LvKtcNrhXuXmUr7v6OuqC+VdMCz0HgmdRWVeOutRZT+ZxBxC
➥BgLRJFnEj6EwoFhO3
zwkyjMim4TwWeotUfI0o4KOuHiuzpnWRbqN/C/ohNWLx+2J6ASQ7zKTxvqh
➥RkImog9/hWuWfBpKL
Zl6Ae1UlZAFMO/7PSSoDgYUAAoGBAMfZtJi+TaFOQVMfTMx9BHZnZZK74uZ
➥l6ZTAMutHLbpNTm4z
b4jf3EG3RyV3wFDH8emOyq7+deGV6PORg9cp2sE6ioYNw4BntZxUNpnA7mp
➥wCKxd2ixiWrVJVmVm
XkT/0zf9XWTqs2p2tqZP7iW9iKGp5KEn+BGzPPNGqLKK0II8MAsGByqGSM4
```

Listing 3.10: continued

```
➥4BAMFAAMvADAsAhQY
dG0QePo5D6uqUq/m/n5lbeAMJQIUN8lkH9tW/m122xxBizxVC3eVpUU=
      </X509Certificate>
    </X509Data>
  </KeyInfo>
  <dsig:Object Id="Res0" xmlns=""
➥xmlns:dsig="http://www.w3.org/2000/09/xmldsig#"><bk:bookmarks
➥xmlns:bk="http://www.pineapplesoft.com/2001/bookmark">
    <bk:site href="http://www.marchal.com">
      <bk:title>Beno&238;t marchal</bk:title></bk:site>
    <bk:site href="http://www.pineapplesoft.com/newsletter">
      <bk:title>Pineapplesoft Link</bk:title></bk:site>
    <bk:site href="http://www.mcp.com">
      <bk:title>Macmillan Publishing</bk:title></bk:site>
    <bk:site href="http://www.xml.com">
      <bk:title>XML.com</bk:title></bk:site>
    <bk:site href="http://xml.apache.org">
      <bk:title>Apache XML</bk:title></bk:site>
    <bk:site href="http://www.abcnews.com">
      <bk:title>ABC News</bk:title></bk:site>
</bk:bookmarks></dsig:Object>
</Signature>
```

What's Next

The next chapter is dedicated to XML Schemas. With schemas, you will learn how to model XML documents. You will also learn how to validate documents against their model.

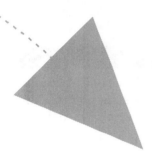

XML Models

In Chapter 2, "XML Syntax," you learned how to write and read XML documents. More importantly, you learned that XML emphasizes the structure of documents over their appearance.

This chapter further develops that theme by looking at XML models. You'll learn about two mechanisms to describe the structure of documents. The two mechanisms are the DTD, short for *Document Type Definition* and the more recent XML Schema recommendation. The fact that there are two solutions to serve the same need is a source of confusion. So, before going any further, let's clarify the differences.

More specifically, you will learn how to

- Model XML documents

- Express these models in DTDs or XML Schemas

- Validate documents against the model

Note, however, that XML Schemas have so many options that it's impossible to cover them completely in less than a book. In this chapter, you'll learn the most useful concepts only.

DTDs and XML Schemas

It is important to understand that DTDs and XML Schemas ultimately serve the same objective. Both let you describe the structure of XML documents. Both are used to validate documents against their models.

The DTD dates back to SGML. It is a proven solution, and, as you will see, it is easy to use. Yet DTDs are not perfect. In particular, they were found lacking on three issues:

- DTDs are based on 20-year-old modeling concepts. They have no support for modern design, such as object-oriented modeling.

- DTDs were designed for publishing. They are ill-suited to more recent applications of XML, in particular, data exchange and application integration.

- DTDs have their own syntax, which is incompatible with XML documents. Therefore, it is not possible to use XML tools (for example, XML editors or style sheets—see Chapter 5, "XSL Transformations") with DTDs. Not a good omen for what should be a universal syntax.

This has led to some frustration. In answer, the W3C has launched an effort to develop a replacement called XML Schema. Schemas support more modern modeling concepts, are better suited for data exchange and application integration, and, last but not least, are written as XML documents.

The price to pay is increased complexity, as you'll see in the remainder of this chapter. Note that both DTDs and XML Schemas are complex, abstract issues. You might want to temporarily skip the advanced sections in this chapter and revisit them after you have read through the remainder of the book.

NOTE

As explained previously, the W3C developed XML Schemas to answer criticisms against DTDs. Unfortunately, the resulting standard is so complex that many feel XML Schemas do not adequately solve the problem.

Opponents to schemas launched an alternative effort, RELAX NG, under the auspice of OASIS (www.oasis-open.org/committees/relax-ng). It aims to offer the same benefits as XML Schemas but be easier to use and cleaner.

The DTD Syntax

EXAMPLE

Let's start with DTDs. As already hinted at, the syntax for DTDs is different from the syntax of XML documents. Listing 4.1 is the address book introduced in Chapter 2 but with one difference: It has a new `<!DOCTYPE>` statement that links the document file to its DTD.

Listing 4.1: `abook-dtd.xml`

```
<?xml version="1.0"?>
<!DOCTYPE address-book SYSTEM "abook-dtd.dtd">
<address-book>
    <entry>
        <name>John Doe</name>
        <address>
            <street>34 Fountain Square Plaza</street>
            <region>OH</region>
            <postal-code>45202</postal-code>
            <locality>Cincinnati</locality>
            <country>US</country>
        </address>
        <tel preferred="true">513-744-8889</tel>
        <tel>513-744-7098</tel>
        <email href="mailto:john@emailaholic.com"/>
    </entry>
    <entry>
        <name>Jack Smith</name>
        <tel>513-744-3465</tel>
        <email href="mailto:jack@emailaholic.com"/>
        <comments>Never leave messages on his answering
        machine. <b>Email instead.</b></comments>
    </entry>
```

The `<!DOCTYPE>` statement is known as the *Document Type Declaration* (not to be confused with the DTD).

The `<!DOCTYPE>` contains the root of the document (`address-book`) and the filename (or a URI) for the DTD itself (`SYSTEM "abook-dtd.dtd"`). As Listing 4.1 illustrates, if present, the document type declaration appears immediately after the XML declaration

```
<!DOCTYPE address-book SYSTEM "abook-dtd.dtd">
```

Why include the root element? As you will see, the DTD declares a list of elements but does not specify which one is the root. It's up to the document to select a root.

CAUTION

Do not forget to include the root element of the document in the <!DOCTYPE> statement.

EXAMPLE

The DTD itself is in Listing 4.2.

NOTE

Incidentally, as you would have guessed having read Chapters 2 and 3, DTDs are optional.

XML recognizes two classes of documents: *well-formed* and *valid*. The documents introduced so far were well-formed, which in XML jargon means that they follow the XML syntax.

In practice, well-formed documents have the right mix of start and end tags, attributes are properly quoted, and character sets are properly used, but they have no DTD. The XML parser only checks that they follow the rules of the syntax.

Valid documents are more strict. They follow the syntax rules, and they have a DTD or a schema to describe their structure. Of course, they respect the structure.

Listing 4.2: `abook-dtd.dtd`

```
<!ELEMENT address-book (entry+)>
<!ELEMENT entry         (name,address*,tel*,fax*,email*,comments?)>
<!ELEMENT name          (#PCDATA)>
<!ELEMENT address       (street,region?,postal-code,
                         locality,country)>
<!ATTLIST address       preferred (true | false)  "false">
<!ELEMENT street        (#PCDATA)>
<!ELEMENT region        (#PCDATA)>
<!ELEMENT postal-code   (#PCDATA)>
<!ELEMENT locality      (#PCDATA)>
<!ELEMENT country       (#PCDATA)>
<!ELEMENT tel           (#PCDATA)>
<!ATTLIST tel           preferred (true | false)  "false">
<!ELEMENT fax           (#PCDATA)>
<!ATTLIST fax           preferred (true | false)  "false">
<!ELEMENT email         EMPTY>
<!ATTLIST email         href  CDATA               #REQUIRED
                        preferred (true | false)  "false">
<!ELEMENT comments      (#PCDATA | b)*>
<!ELEMENT b             (#PCDATA)>
```

Element Declaration

The DTD uses a special syntax to declare every object (elements, attributes, and so on) that can appear in XML documents. Let's start with element declarations.

EXAMPLE

Element declarations take the form of an <!ELEMENT statement and contain the element name (entry) and its *content model* ((name,address*,tel*,fax*,email*,comments?)). The content model simply lists the possible children of the element:

```
<!ELEMENT entry (name,address*,tel*,fax*,email*,comments?)>
```

In the previous example, an entry element consists of a sequence of name, address, tel, fax, email, and comments elements.

You will recall from Chapter 2 that XML names must follow certain rules and, in particular, cannot contain spaces. Those rules remain valid with DTDs.

The Secret of Plus, Star, and Question Mark

The plus ("+"), star ("*"), and question mark ("?")in the content model are known as *occurrence indicators*. They indicate whether and how elements repeat.

- An element followed by no occurrence indicator must appear once and only once.

- An element followed by a "+" character must appear one or several times. In other words, it can repeat.

- An element followed by a "*" character can appear zero or more times. The element is optional but, if it is included, it can repeat.

- An element followed by a "?" character can appear once or not at all. It indicates that the element is optional and, if included, cannot repeat.

EXAMPLE

The content model for entry uses occurrence indicators. They enforce the repetitiveness of children: Except for name, the children are optional, and all but name and comments can appear several times in the document:

```
<!ELEMENT entry (name,address*,tel*,fax*,email*,comments?)>
```

The Secret of Comma and Vertical Bar

EXAMPLE

The comma (",") and vertical bar ("|") characters are *connectors*. They indicate the order in which the children can appear:

- The "," character indicates that both elements (on the right and the left of the comma) must appear in the same order in the document.

- The "|" character indicates that only one of the two elements on the left or right of the vertical bar can appear in the document.

Note that parentheses can be used to group elements on the left and right of connectors.

EXAMPLE

If we were to change the declaration of entry into

```
<!ELEMENT entry (name,(address* | tel* | fax* | email*),comments?)>
```

only one of address, tel, fax or email could appear after the name. So, an entry could have several addresses or several phone numbers but not both.

Keywords

In addition to elements, the following keywords can appear in content models:

- #PCDATA means that the element can contain text. #PCDATA stands for parsed character data.

- EMPTY means that the element is an empty element.

- ANY means that the element can contain any element provided that it was declared elsewhere in the DTD. ANY is used mostly during the development of a DTD, until a more precise content has been developed.

EXAMPLE

In Listing 4.2, tel is declared as text, whereas email is an empty element:

```
<!ELEMENT tel    (#PCDATA)>
<!ELEMENT email EMPTY>
```

Note that CDATA sections can appear within #PCDATA as well. They need not be declared explicitly.

MIXED CONTENT

EXAMPLE

Element contents that include both elements and #PCDATA are said to be *mixed content*. Those that contain only elements are said to be *element content*. In Listing 4.2, comments has mixed content:

```
<!ELEMENT comments (#PCDATA | b)*>
```

The elements and #PCDATA in mixed content must always be separated by a "|" and the whole model must always repeat. The following definition would be incorrect:

```
<!ELEMENT comments (#PCDATA, b) >
```

Nonambiguous Model

There's one additional rule: The content model must be *deterministic* or unambiguous. In plain English, it must be possible to validate a document by reading it one element at a time. DTDs hate suspense.

EXAMPLE

For example, the following model is not acceptable:

```
<!ELEMENT cover ((title, author) | (title, subtitle))>
```

because when reading

```
<cover><title>XML by Example</title>
➡<author>Beno&#238;t Marchal</author></cover>
```

it is not possible to decide whether the title element is part of (title, author) or of (title, subtitle) by looking at title only (one element at a time). You have to know that title is followed by author.

It is often possible to remove the ambiguity, as in

```
<!ELEMENT cover (title, (author | subtitle))>
```

Now you do not need to read further than title to know that it fits the model.

Attributes

EXAMPLE

Attributes too must be declared in the DTD. The <!ATTLIST> declaration fits the bill, for example:

```
<!ATTLIST email  href       CDATA          #REQUIRED
                 preferred (true | false)  "false">
```

The declaration starts with the element name (email) followed by one or more attribute declarations. In this example, two attributes have been declared (href and preferred). The declaration includes their type (CDATA or (true | false)) and a default value (#REQUIRED or "false").

Attribute declaration can appear anywhere in the DTD. For readability, it is best to list attributes immediately after their corresponding element.

EXAMPLE

The DTD provides more control over attributes than over elements. They are broadly divided into three categories:

- String attributes contain text, for example:
  ```
  <!ATTLIST email  href CDATA #REQUIRED>
  ```

- Tokenized attributes limit the content of the attribute, for example:
  ```
  <!ATTLIST entry id ID #IMPLIED>
  ```

- Enumerated type attributes lists acceptable value, for example:
  ```
  <!ATTLIST entry preferred (true | false)  "false">
  ```

See Appendix B, "DTD and XML Schema Simple Types," for the complete descriptions of types supported by DTDs.

CAUTION

The DTD predates XML namespaces, and, therefore, it does not recognize them. If your document uses namespaces, you need to declare the `xmlns` attributes and the element prefixes explicitly, as in

```
<!ELEMENT xbe2:name (#PCDATA)>
<!ATTLIST xbe2:name xmlns:xbe2 CDATA
#FIXED "http://www.psol.com/xbe2/listing4.2">
```

Relationship Between the DTD and the Document

So that it's not overlooked, let me stress the relationship between the DTD (the model) and its document. In a nutshell, the DTD specifies which elements are allowed where in the document.

For example, the document in Listing 4.1 is valid because it respects its DTD. Practically, it means that, among other things, the `entry` elements are enclosed in an `address-book`; that they each contain a `name`; and that the `address`, `tel`, and `email` appear in the order specified in the DTD. Only the second `entry` has a `comment` element, but that is not a problem because `comment` is optional.

EXAMPLE

Listing 4.3 is also valid. Granted, it contains only one `entry`, but the `<!DOCTYPE>` statement has been adapted to reflect it. Surprised? As explained, the DTD defines a list of elements, but it does not specify the root. That is left to the document. A document can select a different root and still conform to the same DTD.

Listing 4.3: entry-dtd.xml

```
<?xml version="1.0"?>
<!DOCTYPE entry SYSTEM "abook-dtd.dtd">
<entry>
   <name>Jack Smith</name>
   <tel>513-744-3465</tel>
   <email href="mailto:jack@emailaholic.com"/>
   <comments>Never leave messages on his answering
   machine. <b>Email instead.</b></comments>
</entry>
```

EXAMPLE

In contrast, Listing 4.4 is invalid for two reasons:

- It does not respect the definition of `entry` because `email` and `tel` are in the wrong order, and it contains an undefined element: `note`.

- It does not respect the definition of `name` because the `name` includes a `b` element that cannot appear there.

A parser would reject Listing 4.4, which illustrates that the DTD is not an abstract definition. To the contrary, it's a concrete definition of the elements that can appear in XML documents.

Listing 4.4: `entry-invalid-dtd.xml`

```
<?xml version="1.0"?>
<!DOCTYPE entry SYSTEM "abook-dtd.dtd">
<!-- invalid -->
<entry>
   <name>Jack <b>Smith</b></name>
   <email href="mailto:jack@emailaholic.com"/>
   <tel>513-744-3465</tel>
   <note>Never leave messages on his answering machine.</note>
</entry>
```

Validating the Document

To validate XML documents, you need a *validating parser*, such as those from Microsoft (`www.microsoft.com`), Oracle (`www.oracle.com`), or Apache (`xml.apache.org`). We'll use Xerces, which was originally developed by IBM and later donated to the Apache Foundation. It also incorporates code from Sun.

Xerces comes with a command-line interface, but, for your convenience, you can download a graphical user interface from `www.marchal.com` or `www.quepublishing.com`.

It suffices to select the input XML document (for example, `abook-dtd.xml`, Listing 4.1), make sure that Validate Against Grammar, in the Tools menu, is checked, and click the Parse button (see Figure 4.1). You can either enter the filename directly or use the Browse buttons.

NOTE

If you don't check Validate Against Grammar, you'll be using a nonvalidating version of Xerces. A nonvalidating parser enforces the XML syntax (for example, opening and closing tags) but not the structure.

Why Use DTDs?

Why use DTDs? Suppose that you work in an editorial department, and you want to make sure that all the writers follow the same set of editorial rules.

You can prepare a DTD to enforce those rules (for example, every chapter must include a summary or sidebars can only appear at section level). Next, to ensure that the editorial rules have been followed, it suffices to validate the documents.

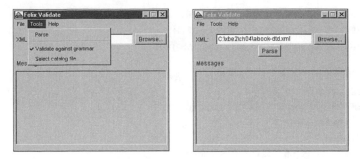

Figure 4.1: *Validating XML documents.*

To make everybody's life easier, you can turn to an XML editor that will validate the document as you type (see Figure 4.2).

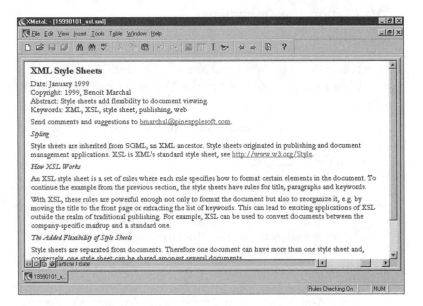

Figure 4.2: *An XML editor enforces the DTD as you write.*

Obviously, DTDs are not limited to editorial departments. Whenever you need to enforce the structure of XML documents, you want to turn to DTDs (or XML Schemas).

Advanced DTD Concepts

This section introduces the more advanced DTD concepts, as always, through examples.

Internal and External Subsets

The DTD you have worked with so far was contained in a different file from the documents. This is useful to share a DTD across several documents. In the previous editorial department example, you would have only one DTD, and all the documents would point to it. Among other things, it makes it easier to maintain the DTD because changes need to be applied only once.

It is also possible to include the DTD in the documents themselves or use a combination where some elements are declared in a separate file whereas others are declared in the document.

When a DTD is included in a document, it is known as the *internal subset.* Otherwise, the DTD is part of the external subset. There are important differences between the two subsets, which we'll cover in the "General and Parameter Entities" section later in the chapter.

EXAMPLE

Listing 4.5 is a document with an internal and an external subset. The external subset is referred to as a file, as usual, whereas the internal subset is stored between square brackets.

From an XML standpoint, the two DTDs (internal and external) are combined before the document is validated. So, it is possible to reuse elements defined in the external subset in the internal subset. Listing 4.5 illustrates this. The internal subset defines a new element (card) in terms of elements defined in Listing 4.2 (the external subset).

Listing 4.5: card.xml

```
<?xml version="1.0"?>
<!DOCTYPE card SYSTEM "abook-dtd.dtd" [
<!ELEMENT card (name,tel,email?)>
<!ATTLIST card type (personal | business) #IMPLIED>
]>
<card type="business">
   <name>Jack Smith</name>
   <tel>513-744-3465</tel>
   <email href="mailto:jack@emailaholic.com"/>
</card>
```

Public Identifier

Although most <!DOCTYPE> statements point to a file or an URL, there is another option known as *public identifiers.* A public identifier takes the form

-//Company Name//Document Description//Language

where *Company Name* is your company name, *Document Description* is a description of the DTD, and *Language* is the language used in preparing the DTD (EN for English).

EXAMPLE

Using the keyword PUBLIC, instead of SYSTEM in the <!DOCTYPE> points to a public identifier. The public identifier must always be followed by a system identifier (a filename or an URL), as in

```
<!DOCTYPE address-book PUBLIC "-//Pineapplesoft//Address Book//EN"
➥"abook-dtd.dtd">
```

When a parser hits a public identifier, it searches a catalog file to translate it into a regular file or an URL. If it fails to translate the public identifier, it uses the system one.

TIP

You can think of public identifiers as precursors to URLs. They are inherited from SGML but are seldom used today, although some XML applications (such as WAP phones) require them.

Standalone Documents

We have looked at the DTD solely as a mechanism to describe documents. There's another side to DTDs; they can change the documents, too.

For example, default and fixed attributes actually add information to the document. Likewise, declaring entities (entities are covered in the next section) modifies the document.

If all the declarations that could influence the document are in the internal subset of the DTD, the document is said to be *standalone*. In lay terms, it means that the parser need not download or access additional files to interpret the document.

TIP

A standalone document may have an external subset as long as it does not declare entities or default attributes, for example.

EXAMPLE

Obviously, a standalone document is more efficient for communication over a network because only one file needs to be downloaded. The XML declaration has an attribute, standalone, that declares whether the document is standalone. It accepts only two values: yes and no. The default is no.

```
<?xml version="1.0" standalone="yes"?>
```

Entities

As already mentioned in the Chapter 2, strictly speaking, XML doesn't work with files but with entities. Entities are the physical representation of XML documents. Although entities usually are stored as files, they need not be.

In XML, the document, its DTD, and the various files it references (images, stock-phrases, and so on) are entities. The document has a special status because it is the starting point for the parser; it is known as the *document entity*.

TIP

In Chapter 8, "Alternative API: SAX," you'll learn about `EntityResolver`, which enables the application to retrieve entities from databases or other sources.

XML has many types of entities, classified according to three criteria: *general* or *parameter entities*, *internal* or *external entities*, and *parsed* or *unparsed*.

General and Parameter Entities

In a nutshell, general entities are for the document; parameter entities are for the DTD. Both entities are macros or shorthands for a string of text.

EXAMPLE

Entities are declared in the DTD with the `<!ENTITY>` statements, which consist of the entity name and its definition. As you saw in Chapter 2, entity references appear in the document as `&entity;`.

In the following example, an entity `icirc` is declared as a shorthand for character î. The entity is then used in the document in place of `&#238;`:

```
<?xml version="1.0"?>
<!DOCTYPE name [
<!ENTITY icirc "&#238;">
]>
<name>Beno&icirc;t Marchal</name>
```

TIP

The previous example illustrates both a common application of entities (define shorthand for accentuated and other exotic characters) and a common application for an internal subset of DTDs (define general entities used in the document).

As you saw in Chapter 2, the following entities are predefined in XML: "`&lt;`", "`&amp;`", "`&gt;`", "`&apos;`", and "`&quot;`".

Parameter entities are similar, but they can appear only in the DTD. They are declared with an extra % character, which also replaces the & in the entity reference, as in

```
<!ENTITY % boolean   "(true | false) 'false'">
<!ELEMENT tel        (#PCDATA)>
<!ATTLIST tel        preferred %boolean;>
```

Parameter entities are handy for frequently used definitions, such as the definition of boolean in the preceding example.

CAUTION

The previous example is valid only in the external subset of a DTD. In the internal sub-set, parameter entities can appear only where a complete declaration can appear (that is, they cannot appear within a statement).

Internal and External Entities

XML also distinguishes between internal and external entities. Like inter-nal and external subsets, internal entities are declared in the document, whereas external entities point to a file, an URL or a public identifier.

The examples in the previous section declared internal entities because their value was given in the DTD, as part of the entity definition. To declare external entities, simply replace the definition by a SYSTEM or PUB-LIC identifier.

External entities are particularly useful to include an external DTD. Suppose that we have created a list of general entities for every U.S. state and Canadian province, as in Listing 4.6.

Listing 4.6: states-provinces.ent

```
<!-- download the listing from www.marchal.com
     or www.quepublishing.com for the complete list     -->
<!ENTITY OH "Ohio">
<!ENTITY OK "Oklahoma">
<!ENTITY ON "Ontario">
<!ENTITY OR "Oregon">
```

Creating such a list takes time, and we want to reuse it in several docu-ments. The construct illustrated by Listing 4.7 pulls the list states-provinces.ent into an external parameter entity. Next, it immediately references the entity. The reference copies the content of the entity (the con-tent of states-provinces.ent in this case) in the internal subset of the DTD. This effectively includes the content of the other file in the current document.

CAUTION

Given the limitation on parameter entities in the internal subset of the DTD, this is the only sensible application of parameter entities in the internal subset.

Listing 4.7: `entry-entity.xml`

```
<?xml version="1.0"?>
<!DOCTYPE entry SYSTEM "abook-dtd.dtd" [
<!ENTITY % states-provinces SYSTEM "states-provinces.ent">
%states-provinces;
]>
<entry>
    <name>John Doe</name>
    <address>
        <street>34 Fountain Square Plaza</street>
        <region>&OH;</region>
        <postal-code>45202</postal-code>
        <locality>Cincinnati</locality>
        <country>US</country>
    </address>
    <tel preferred="true">513-744-8889</tel>
    <tel>513-744-7098</tel>
    <email href="mailto:john@emailaholic.com"/>
</entry>
```

TIP

External entities (and DTDs for that matter) might start with an XML declaration. This is helpful when working with non-ASCII character sets because it lets you declare an encoding.

```
    <?xml version="1.0" encoding="ISO-8859-1"?>
<!ENTITY icirc "î">
```

Parsed, Unparsed Entities, and Notation

External general entities can contain non-XML content, such as images, sound, movies, and so on. They are said to be unparsed entities (as opposed to parsed entities that contain XML markup).

EXAMPLE

Most modern applications use XLink (introduced in Chapter 10, "Important XML Models") instead of unparsed entities. Still you might encounter the following:

```
<!NOTATION GIF89a PUBLIC "-//CompuServe//NOTATION Graphics
➥ Interchange Format 89a//EN" "image/gif">
<!ENTITY logo SYSTEM "logo.gif" NDATA GIF>
```

The first line declares a notation. In a nutshell, notations identify the type of a document, such as GIF or JPEG. The unparsed entity specifies the notation after the NDATA keyword. The parser uses the notation to decide how to process unparsed external general entities.

Conditional Sections

The last DTD feature is the *conditional section*. Conditional section easily can be included or excluded from the DTD when combined with parameter entities.

EXAMPLE

Listing 4.8 shows how to use conditional sections. It defines two parameter entities: strict resolves to INCLUDE, whereas lenient resolves to IGNORE. The DTD uses only the INCLUDE section or, in this case, the section marked as %strict;.

Listing 4.8: Using Conditional Sections

```
<!ENTITY % strict  'INCLUDE'>
<!ENTITY % lenient 'IGNORE' >
<!-- a name is a first name and a last name -->
<![%strict;[
<!ELEMENT name  (fname, lname)>
<!ELEMENT fname (#PCDATA)     >
<!ELEMENT lname (#PCDATA)     >
]]>
<!-- a name is string              -->
<![%lenient;[
<!ELEMENT name  (#PCDATA)>
]]>
```

However, to revert to the lenient definition of name, it suffices to invert the parameter entity declarations:

```
<!ENTITY % strict  'IGNORE' >
<!ENTITY % lenient 'INCLUDE'>
```

The Schema Syntax

Schemas improve DTDs by supporting more data types and XML namespaces and adopting the familiar syntax of XML documents for the model itself. The concept, however, remains the same: A schema describes XML documents so that parsers can validate them. In this chapter, you will learn the most useful constructs for Schemas.

EXAMPLE

Listing 4.9 is an XML Schema for the address we used so far. It is not strictly identical to the DTD, however, because it makes good use of advanced DTD features.

Notice that the schema is an XML document; no more special syntax. The root element is predictably called schema, and the entire schema is in the http://www.w3.org/2001/XMLSchema namespace. It lists a number of type definitions, and at least one element declaration.

CAUTION

One of the most visible differences between DTDs and XML Schemas is that schemas are regular XML documents. Unlike DTDs, they don't rely on a special syntax.

As you study Listing 4.9, keep in mind that it is an XML document that describes other XML documents!

Listing 4.9: abook-wo-ns.xsd

```xml
<xsd:schema xmlns:xsd="http://www.w3.org/2001/XMLSchema">
   <xsd:simpleType name="states-provinces">
      <xsd:restriction base="xsd:string">
         <!-- download the listing from www.marchal.com
              or www.quepublishing.com for the complete list    -->
         <xsd:enumeration value="OH"/>
         <xsd:enumeration value="OK"/>
         <xsd:enumeration value="ON"/>
         <xsd:enumeration value="OR"/>
      </xsd:restriction>
   </xsd:simpleType>

   <xsd:complexType name="address-details">
      <xsd:sequence>
         <xsd:element name="street"      type="xsd:string"/>
         <xsd:element name="region"      type="states-provinces"
                      minOccurs="0"/>
         <xsd:element name="postal-code" type="xsd:string"/>
         <xsd:element name="locality"    type="xsd:string"/>
         <xsd:element name="country"     type="xsd:string"/>
      </xsd:sequence>
      <xsd:attribute name="preferred" type="xsd:boolean"
                     default="true"/>
   </xsd:complexType>

   <xsd:complexType name="preferable">
      <xsd:simpleContent>
         <xsd:extension base="xsd:string">
            <xsd:attribute name="preferred"
                           type="xsd:boolean"
                           default="false"/>
         </xsd:extension>
      </xsd:simpleContent>
```

Listing 4.9: continued

```xsd
    </xsd:complexType>

    <xsd:complexType name="uri">
      <xsd:complexContent>
        <xsd:restriction base="xsd:anyType">
          <xsd:attribute name="href"
                         type="xsd:anyURI"/>
          <xsd:attribute name="preferred"
                         type="xsd:boolean"
                         default="false"/>
        </xsd:restriction>
      </xsd:complexContent>
    </xsd:complexType>

    <xsd:complexType name="boldable" mixed="true">
      <xsd:sequence>
        <xsd:element name="b" type="xsd:string"/>
      </xsd:sequence>
    </xsd:complexType>

    <xsd:complexType name="entry-details">
      <xsd:sequence>
        <xsd:element name="name"     type="xsd:string"/>
        <xsd:element name="address"  type="address-details"
                     minOccurs="0"   maxOccurs="unbounded"/>
        <xsd:element name="tel"      type="preferable"
                     minOccurs="0"   maxOccurs="unbounded"/>
        <xsd:element name="fax"      type="preferable"
                     minOccurs="0"   maxOccurs="unbounded"/>
        <xsd:element name="email"    type="uri"
                     minOccurs="0"   maxOccurs="unbounded"/>
        <xsd:element name="comments" type="boldable"
                     minOccurs="0"/>
      </xsd:sequence>
    </xsd:complexType>

    <xsd:element name="address-book">
      <xsd:complexType>
        <xsd:sequence>
          <xsd:element name="entry" type="entry-details"
                       maxOccurs="unbounded"/>
        </xsd:sequence>
      </xsd:complexType>
    </xsd:element>
</xsd:schema>
```

Before studying the details of schemas, let's see how to associate them with documents. Unlike DTDs, you don't use the `<!DOCTYPE>` statement. Instead, add a `noNamespaceSchemaLocation` attribute in the `http://www.w3.org/2001/XMLSchema-instance` namespace to the root element of the document, as illustrated in Listing 4.10.

Note that you can validate a document, such as Listing 4.10, against a schema, using Xerces. Follow the steps in the "Validating the Document" section earlier in the chapter. From that standpoint, it makes no differences whether you use DTDs or XML Schemas.

Listing 4.10: `abook-wo-ns.xml`

```
<?xml version="1.0"?>
<address-book
    xmlns:xsi="http://www.w3.org/2001/XMLSchema-instance"
    xsi:noNamespaceSchemaLocation="abook-wo-ns.xsd">
    <entry>
        <name>John Doe</name>
        <address>
            <street>34 Fountain Square Plaza</street>
            <region>OH</region>
            <postal-code>45202</postal-code>
            <locality>Cincinnati</locality>
            <country>US</country>
        </address>
        <tel preferred="true">513-744-8889</tel>
        <tel>513-744-7098</tel>
        <email href="mailto:john@emailaholic.com"/>
    </entry>
    <entry>
        <name>Jack Smith</name>
        <tel>513-744-3465</tel>
        <email href="mailto:jack@emailaholic.com"/>
        <comments>Never leave messages on his answering
        machine. <b>Email instead.</b></comments>
    </entry>
</address-book>
```

Simple Type Definitions

Schemas support *simple* and *complex types*. Simple types are atomic (string, integer, boolean, and more), whereas complex types aggregate simple types.

Simple type definitions (written as `simpleType` elements) restrict or augment the built-in simple types. As the name implies, the `restriction` element limits the values of a simple type. The original type is referenced in the base attribute.

The following example restricts string to a set of values. Therefore, the user-defined type states-provinces is limited to the standard codes for U.S. states or Canadian provinces.

```
<xsd:simpleType name="states-provinces">
   <xsd:restriction base="xsd:string">
      <!-- download the listing from www.marchal.com
           or www.quepublishing.com for the complete list    -->

      <xsd:enumeration value="OH"/>
      <xsd:enumeration value="OK"/>
      <xsd:enumeration value="ON"/>
      <xsd:enumeration value="OR"/>
   </xsd:restriction>
</xsd:simpleType>
```

There is a mirror element, extension, which, as the name implies, extends simple types.

Complex Type Definitions

Complex type definitions take the form of a complexType element. A complex type can be a sequence of elements, attributes, simple or complex content (more on this later), and more.

EXAMPLE

The following example defines address-details as a sequence of elements and a preferred boolean attribute. The sequence element indicates that its constituents must appear in the same order in the document; it is similar to the comma in DTDs, but bear in mind that this is a type definition, not an element declaration (the difference will become clearer as you proceed).

```
<xsd:complexType name="address-details">
   <xsd:sequence>
      <xsd:element name="street"      type="xsd:string"/>
      <xsd:element name="region"      type="states-provinces"
                   minOccurs="0"/>
      <xsd:element name="postal-code" type="xsd:string"/>
      <xsd:element name="locality"    type="xsd:string"/>
      <xsd:element name="country"     type="xsd:string"/>
   </xsd:sequence>
      <xsd:attribute name="preferred" type="xsd:boolean"
                     default="true"/>
</xsd:complexType>
```

Although Listing 4.9 does not illustrate it, there is also a choice element, which works like sequence but indicates that one of its constituents can appear in the document. choice replaces the vertical bar from DTDs.

A third option is `all`, which is similar to `sequence`, but it does not impose an order. Like `sequence`, `all` forces the use of all its constituents, but it does not define the order of their appearance. There are some limitations on `all`, though: It can only appear at the topmost position in a content model, and its constituents must be elements. There is no DTD equivalent—yet another example of schemas being more powerful.

Elements are declared in the sequence with the `element` tag. They are given a name and a type. In this example, most types are built-in types, but `region` uses the type `states-provinces`, defined in the previous section. Incidentally, it's another illustration of the power of schemas: You have more control over the content of elements.

To control repetitiveness, use the (`minOccurs` and `maxOccurs` attributes (they work not only on element declarations but also on `sequence`, `choice`, and `all`). The default value for both is 1, meaning that the element must appear exactly once, but any integer is acceptable. Again schemas prove more powerful than DTDs because you control precisely how often an element appears in the document. In the following example, `selection` must appear at least three times but fewer than ten times:

```
<xsd:element name="selection" type="xsd:string"
        minOccurs="3" maxOccurs="10"/>
```

When `minOccurs` is `0`, the element is optional. When `maxOccurs` is the keyword `"unbounded"`, the element can repeat infinitely. The equivalent of the DTD asterisk is thus:

```
<xsd:element name="address"  type="address-details"
            minOccurs="0"    maxOccurs="unbounded"/>
```

Simple and Complex Content

Complex type definitions may contain `simpleContent` and `complexContent`. I find the concept murky, but it is useful to define complex types as restrictions or extensions of simple ones.

EXAMPLE

For example, the `preferable` type is defined by extending a string with a preferred attribute:

```
<xsd:complexType name="preferable">
   <xsd:simpleContent>
      <xsd:extension base="xsd:string">
         <xsd:attribute name="preferred"
                        type="xsd:boolean"
                        default="false"/>
      </xsd:extension>
   </xsd:simpleContent>
</xsd:complexType>
```

Empty elements are declared as a restriction on the built-in anyType. anyType could be anything, but the following restricts it to a set of attributes. Because the element is only a set of attributes, it is empty:

```
<xsd:complexType name="uri">
   <xsd:complexContent>
      <xsd:restriction base="xsd:anyType">
         <xsd:attribute name="href"
                           type="xsd:anyURI"/>
         <xsd:attribute name="preferred"
                           type="xsd:boolean"
                           default="false"/>
      </xsd:restriction>
   </xsd:complexContent>
</xsd:complexType>
```

Mixed Content

Mixed content is declared as a complex type with the mixed attribute, as in the following:

```
<xsd:complexType name="boldable" mixed="true">
   <xsd:sequence>
      <xsd:element name="b" type="xsd:string"/>
   </xsd:sequence>
</xsd:complexType>
```

Global Element Declaration

Element declarations you have seen so far were *local* because they were contained within a complex type. A schema must contain at least one *global* declaration, which appears directly under the schema element (at the level of type declarations):

```
<xsd:element name="address-book">
   <xsd:complexType>
      <xsd:sequence>
         <xsd:element name="entry" type="entry-details"
                        maxOccurs="unbounded"/>
      </xsd:sequence>
   </xsd:complexType>
</xsd:element>
```

Only globally declared elements can become roots of documents so, unlike DTDs, a schema can control which elements make suitable roots. As you will see shortly, global and local elements handle namespaces differently as well.

The preceding example also illustrates *anonymous* type definition. Look at the complexType element for an example of this. Unlike other instances of complexType in this schema, it does not have a name.

Anonymous definitions can only appear in other definitions or in element declarations (as in this example). They can appear wherever a type is expected.

Of course, you do not have to use anonymous definitions. The declaration of address-book could be rewritten using a name type and a reference to the type:

```
<xsd:complexType name="address-book-type">
   <xsd:sequence>
      <xsd:element name="entry" type="entry-details"
                   maxOccurs="unbounded"/>
   </xsd:sequence>
</xsd:complexType>

<xsd:element name="address-book" type="address-book-type"/>
```

Namespaces and Other Advanced Schema Concepts

You have learned two important schema concepts so far:

- Unlike DTDs, XML Schemas use the regular XML document syntax. As you have seen, there are XML elements to declare elements and complex and simple types.

- XML Schemas offer a rich set of types.

In this section, you'll learn the third important concept: support for XML namespaces.

EXAMPLE

Listing 4.11 is a schema that declares a namespace. Most of this schema is similar to Listing 4.9 but for four new attributes:

- xmlns:xbe2 associates the xbe2 prefix with the http://www.psol.com/xbe2/listing4.11 namespace, using the syntax introduced in Chapter 3, "XML Namespaces."

- targetNamespace is the namespace used for this schema. Note that this attribute plays a different role than xmlns:xbe2, which associates a prefix to the namespace.

- elementFormDefault and attributeFormDefault control whether respectively local elements and attributes need to be qualified by a namespace prefix. Acceptable values are unqualified (local elements cannot be qualified by a namespace prefix) and qualified (local elements must be qualified by a namespace prefix). We'll revisit this issue in a moment.

Listing 4.11: `abook-wt-ns.xsd`

```
<xsd:schema
    xmlns:xsd="http://www.w3.org/2001/XMLSchema"
    xmlns:xbe2="http://www.psol.com/xbe2/listing4.11"
    targetNamespace="http://www.psol.com/xbe2/listing4.11"
    elementFormDefault="unqualified"
    attributeFormDefault="unqualified">
    <xsd:simpleType name="states-provinces">
        <xsd:restriction base="xsd:string">
            <xsd:annotation>
                <xsd:documentation xml:lang="en">
                    download the listing from www.marchal.com
                    or www.quepublishing.com for the complete list

                </xsd:documentation>
            </xsd:annotation>
            <xsd:enumeration value="OH"/>
            <xsd:enumeration value="OK"/>
            <xsd:enumeration value="ON"/>
            <xsd:enumeration value="OR"/>
        </xsd:restriction>
    </xsd:simpleType>

    <xsd:complexType name="address-details">
        <xsd:sequence>
            <xsd:element name="street"      type="xsd:string"/>
            <xsd:element name="region"      minOccurs="0"
                         type="xbe2:states-provinces"/>
            <xsd:element name="postal-code" type="xsd:string"/>
            <xsd:element name="locality"    type="xsd:string"/>
            <xsd:element name="country"     type="xsd:string"/>
        </xsd:sequence>
        <xsd:attribute name="preferred" type="xsd:boolean"
                       default="true"/>
    </xsd:complexType>

    <xsd:complexType name="preferable">
        <xsd:simpleContent>
            <xsd:extension base="xsd:string">
                <xsd:attribute name="preferred"
                               type="xsd:boolean"
                               default="false"/>
            </xsd:extension>
```

Listing 4.11: continued

```
      </xsd:simpleContent>
   </xsd:complexType>

   <xsd:complexType name="uri">
      <xsd:complexContent>
         <xsd:restriction base="xsd:anyType">
            <xsd:attribute name="href"
                           type="xsd:anyURI"/>
            <xsd:attribute name="preferred"
                           type="xsd:boolean"
                           default="false"/>
         </xsd:restriction>
      </xsd:complexContent>
   </xsd:complexType>

   <xsd:complexType name="boldable" mixed="true">
      <xsd:sequence>
         <xsd:element name="b" type="xsd:string"/>
      </xsd:sequence>
   </xsd:complexType>

   <xsd:element name="entry">
      <xsd:annotation>
        <xsd:documentation xml:lang="en">
           entry is a global element, it needs a namespace prefix
        </xsd:documentation>
      </xsd:annotation>
      <xsd:complexType>
        <xsd:sequence>
           <xsd:element name="name"     type="xsd:string"/>
           <xsd:element name="address"  minOccurs="0"
                        type="xbe2:address-details"
                        maxOccurs="unbounded"/>
           <xsd:element name="tel"      type="xbe2:preferable"
                        minOccurs="0"   maxOccurs="unbounded"/>
           <xsd:element name="fax"      type="xbe2:preferable"
                        minOccurs="0"   maxOccurs="unbounded"/>
           <xsd:element name="email"    type="xbe2:uri"
                        minOccurs="0"   maxOccurs="unbounded"/>
           <xsd:element name="comments" type="xbe2:boldable"
                        minOccurs="0"/>
        </xsd:sequence>
      </xsd:complexType>
   </xsd:element>
```

Listing 4.11: continued

```
   <xsd:element name="address-book">
      <xsd:complexType>
         <xsd:sequence>
            <xsd:element ref="xbe2:entry" maxOccurs="unbounded"/>
         </xsd:sequence>
      </xsd:complexType>
   </xsd:element>
</xsd:schema>
```

After a namespace is used, references to global elements and named types must include it. For example, states-provinces is now defined in the namespace, and references to it in address-details must be qualified with a namespace prefix (xbe2:states-provinces). Compare the following with Listing 4.9:

```
<xsd:complexType name="address-details">
   <xsd:sequence>
      <xsd:element name="street"      type="xsd:string"/>
      <xsd:element name="region"      minOccurs="0"
                      type="xbe2:states-provinces"/>
      <xsd:element name="postal-code" type="xsd:string"/>
      <xsd:element name="locality"    type="xsd:string"/>
      <xsd:element name="country"     type="xsd:string"/>
   </xsd:sequence>
   <xsd:attribute name="preferred" type="xsd:boolean"
                   default="true"/>
</xsd:complexType>
```

References to Global Elements

Listing 4.11 also introduces references to global elements. As explained previously, XML Schema introduces the notion of global and local elements, which have no equivalent in DTDs.

EXAMPLE

Listing 4.9 declared only one global element, address-book. For pedagogical reasons, Listing 4.11 declares two global elements: address-book and entry (you can ignore the annotation element for the time being).

```
<xsd:element name="entry">
   <xsd:annotation>
     <xsd:documentation xml:lang="en">
        entry is a global element, it needs a namespace prefix
     </xsd:documentation>
   </xsd:annotation>
   <xsd:complexType>
      <xsd:sequence>
         <xsd:element name="name"      type="xsd:string"/>
```

```
        <xsd:element name="address"  minOccurs="0"
                     type="xbe2:address-details"
                     maxOccurs="unbounded"/>
        <xsd:element name="tel"       type="xbe2:preferable"
                     minOccurs="0"    maxOccurs="unbounded"/>
        <xsd:element name="fax"       type="xbe2:preferable"
                     minOccurs="0"    maxOccurs="unbounded"/>
        <xsd:element name="email"     type="xbe2:uri"
                     minOccurs="0"    maxOccurs="unbounded"/>
        <xsd:element name="comments" type="xbe2:boldable"
                     minOccurs="0"/>
      </xsd:sequence>
    </xsd:complexType>
</xsd:element>

<xsd:element name="address-book">
    <xsd:complexType>
      <xsd:sequence>
         <xsd:element ref="xbe2:entry" maxOccurs="unbounded"/>
      </xsd:sequence>
    </xsd:complexType>
</xsd:element>
```

The declaration of address-book includes a reference to the entry element in the ref attribute. Compare this with Listing 4.9 where entry was defined as a type.

CAUTION

The rules are simple, but, unless you understand that there's a difference between types and elements, it's easy to be confused.

Type definitions take the form of complexType or simpleType tags. Elements are declared with element tags.

To include types or elements in other definitions or declarations, you use the type attribute for types and the ref attribute for elements.

Namespaces and the Document

When it comes to namespaces, XML Schemas treat local elements differently from global ones. The rules follow:

- Global elements must always be qualified with a namespace prefix.

- Local elements may or may not be qualified with a namespace prefix depending on the value of the elementFormDefault attribute.

Because Listing 4.11 sets `elementFormDefault` to unqualified, local elements cannot be qualified in documents that follow this schema. Yet `address-book` and `entry`, being global elements, must be qualified, as shown in Listing 4.12 (pay attention to `xbe2` prefixes).

TIP

If you want authors to qualify all the elements in a document, you can either set `elementFormDefault` to qualified or use global elements exclusively.

Listing 4.12: `abook-wt-ns.xml`

```xml
<?xml version="1.0"?>
<xbe2:address-book
    xmlns:xsi="http://www.w3.org/2001/XMLSchema-instance"
    xmlns:xbe2="http://www.psol.com/xbe2/listing4.11"
    xsi:schemaLocation="http://www.psol.com/xbe2/listing4.11 abook-wt-ns.xsd">
    <xbe2:entry>
        <name>John Doe</name>
        <address>
            <street>34 Fountain Square Plaza</street>
            <region>OH</region>
            <postal-code>45202</postal-code>
            <locality>Cincinnati</locality>
            <country>US</country>
        </address>
        <tel preferred="true">513-744-8889</tel>
        <tel>513-744-7098</tel>
        <email href="mailto:john@emailaholic.com"/>
    </xbe2:entry>
    <xbe2:entry>
        <name>Jack Smith</name>
        <tel>513-744-3465</tel>
        <email href="mailto:jack@emailaholic.com"/>
        <comments>Never leave messages on his answering
        machine. <b>Email instead.</b></comments>
    </xbe2:entry>
</xbe2:address-book>
```

Notice that Listing 4.12 uses the `schemaLocation` attribute instead of `noNamespaceSchemaLocation`. `schemaLocation` contains one or more pairs of XML namespaces and schema location.

The parser selects the right schema based on the namespace of the element.

For example, if a document contained elements from two namespaces, you would write

```
schemaLocation="http://www.psol.com/xbe2/listing4.11 abook-wt-ns.xsd
➥ http://www.psol.com/xbe2/etc etc.xsd"
```

CAUTION

Remember that, although namespaces are URIs, they are used strictly as identifiers. Specifically, they do not contain the location of the schema, which is why you have to associate a namespace with an actual file.

Annotations

EXAMPLE

The definition of states-provinces and the declaration of entry include annotation elements. Annotation typically replaces comments with a documentation element. It is recommended that documentation include an xml:lang attribute (introduced in Chapter 2) for the comment's language:

```
<xsd:simpleType name="states-provinces">
    <xsd:restriction base="xsd:string">
        <xsd:annotation>
            <xsd:documentation xml:lang="en">
                download the listing from www.marchal.com
                or www.quepublishing.com for the complete list
            </xsd:documentation>
        </xsd:annotation>
        <xsd:enumeration value="OH"/>
        <xsd:enumeration value="OK"/>
        <xsd:enumeration value="ON"/>
        <xsd:enumeration value="OR"/>
    </xsd:restriction>
</xsd:simpleType>
```

Annotation may also contain appInfo elements, which are intended for machine-readable comments. For example, appInfo may pass information to style sheets (style sheets are introduced in Chapter 5).

TIP

Why use annotation instead of plain XML comments? Unlike annotation, plain comments are ignored by parsers.

One motivation for schemas was to use XML document syntax such that one could edit schemas with regular XML tools. Obviously, if comments are lost to those tools, it makes more sense to use annotation elements.

More on Global and Local Elements

Because it is brand new, let's review the notion of global and local elements one more time. To summarize, global elements can become root of XML documents but local elements cannot.

EXAMPLE

Listing 4.11 declares `address-book` and `entry` as global elements. The following document, which contains only one entry, is therefore valid:

```
<?xml version="1.0"?>
<xbe2:entry
    xmlns:xsi="http://www.w3.org/2001/XMLSchema-instance"
    xmlns:xbe2="http://www.psol.com/xbe2/listing4.11"
    xsi:schemaLocation="http://www.psol.com/xbe2/listing4.11 abook-wt-ns.xsd">
    <name>Jack Smith</name>
    <tel>513-744-3465</tel>
    <email href="mailto:jack@emailaholic.com"/>
    <comments>Never leave messages on his answering
    machine. <b>Email instead.</b></comments>
</xbe2:entry>
```

But the following document, which attempts to use a local element (comments) as its root, is invalid:

```
<?xml version="1.0"?>
<!-- invalid document -->
<comments
    xmlns:xsi="http://www.w3.org/2001/XMLSchema-instance"
    xmlns:xbe2="http://www.psol.com/xbe2/listing4.11"
    xsi:schemaLocation="http://www.psol.com/xbe2/listing4.11 abook-wt-ns.xsd">
Never leave messages on his answering machine.
<b>Email instead.</b>
</comments>
```

And it remains so even with a namespace prefix:

```
<?xml version="1.0"?>
<!-- invalid document -->
<xbe2:comments
    xmlns:xsi="http://www.w3.org/2001/XMLSchema-instance"
    xmlns:xbe2="http://www.psol.com/xbe2/listing4.11"
    xsi:schemaLocation="http://www.psol.com/xbe2/listing4.11 abook-wt-ns.xsd">
Never leave messages on his answering machine.
<b>Email instead.</b>
</xbe2:comments>
```

Name Groups

For completeness, this section studies groups. There are two forms of groups: element groups (marked with group) and attribute groups (marked with `attributeGroup`). Essentially, a group is a substitute for a number of elements or attributes. Groups are declared with a `name` attribute and are accessed through a `ref` attribute.

EXAMPLE

In Listing 4.11, we could have used groups in the definitions of `address-type` and `uri`, as illustrated here:

```
<xsd:attributeGroup name="uri-attributes">
   <xsd:attribute name="href"
                  type="xsd:anyURI"/>
   <xsd:attribute name="preferred"
                  type="xsd:boolean"
                  default="false"/>
</xsd:attributeGroup>

<xsd:group name="address-elements">
   <xsd:sequence>
      <xsd:element name="street"      type="xsd:string"/>
      <xsd:element name="region"      minOccurs="0"
                   type="xbe2:states-provinces"/>
      <xsd:element name="postal-code" type="xsd:string"/>
      <xsd:element name="locality"    type="xsd:string"/>
      <xsd:element name="country"     type="xsd:string"/>
   </xsd:sequence>
</xsd:group>

<xsd:complexType name="address-details">
   <xsd:group ref="xbe2:address-elements"/>
   <xsd:attribute name="preferred" type="xsd:boolean"
                  default="true"/>
</xsd:complexType>

<xsd:complexType name="uri">
   <xsd:complexContent>
      <xsd:restriction base="xsd:anyType">
         <xsd:attributeGroup ref="xbe2:uri-attributes"/>
      </xsd:restriction>
   </xsd:complexContent>
</xsd:complexType>
```

Modeling XML Documents

Now that you understand what models are for and how to use them, it is time to look at the process of modeling itself. Document modeling is a creative, fun, and rewarding activity.

It is not be possible, in this section, to cover every aspect of document modeling. Books have been devoted to that topic. Use this section as guidance to get you started and remember that practice makes proficient.

Avoid Modeling If You Can

Many XML DTDs and schemas are available already, and it seems more are being released every day. With so many existing models, you might wonder whether it's worth designing your own.

It's a fair question. I will argue that you should refrain from reinventing the wheel and, whenever possible, use existing models. Using models developed by others results in many savings. Not only do you save the time spent modeling, but also you don't have to maintain or update the model.

Furthermore, there's more to XML programming than modeling. As you will learn in upcoming chapters, you might also have to design style sheets, customize tools such as editors, and/or write special code using a parser.

This adds up to a lot of work. And it follows what I call the "oh, oh" rule of project planning (for "oh, oh it took more work than I thought it would.") The moral? Unless you can raise a following, it often pays to reuse somebody else's models.

If you're in publishing, make sure that you have reviewed the following models before launching your own effort: XHTML (www.w3.org/MarkUp), DocBook (www.oasis-open.org/docbook), XMLNews-Story (www.xmlnews.org/XMLNews), RSS (www.purl.org/rss).

If you're in electronic commerce or application integration, ebXML (www.ebxml.org), RosettaNet (www.rosettanet.org), XML Signature (www.w3.org/Signature), SOAP (www.w3.org/TR/SOAP) and BizTalk (www.biztalk.org) are worth reviewing.

If you're in multimedia, you may find that SMIL (www.w3.org/AudioVideo) or SVG (www.w3.org/Graphics/SVG) holds the answer you are looking for.

The first step in a new XML project should be to search the Internet for similar applications—and their XML models. I suggest that you start at xml.coverpages.org. The site, maintained by Robin Cover, is the most comprehensive list of XML links.

In practice, you are likely to find models that almost fit your needs but aren't exactly what you are looking for. It's okay because XML is extensible. Take the model that almost works and extend it (in a namespace of your own).

Modeling Documents from an Object Model

This section demonstrates two examples of document modeling. In the first example, we will start from an object model. This is the easiest solution because you can reuse the objects defined in the model, but it means that you or somebody else has spent time creating the object model. We will use XML Schemas for this example.

In the second example, we will create a new model from scratch. We will use a DTD for this example.

EXAMPLE

Increasingly, object models are made available in the Unified Modeling Language (UML—yes, there is an "ML" that does not stand for "markup language"). UML is typically used for designing applications written in object-oriented programming languages, such as Java or C++, but the same models can be used with XML.

An object model is often available when XML-enabling an existing Java or C++ application. Figure 4.3 is a (simplified) object model for bank accounts. It identifies the following objects:

- Account—An abstract class with two properties: the balance and a list of transactions.

- Savings—Specializes (inherits from) Account for savings accounts. It adds one property (interest).

- Checking—Specializes Account for checking accounts. It defines a fee property.

- Owner—The account owner. An Account can have more than one Owner, and an Owner can own more than one Account. Owner has a name property.

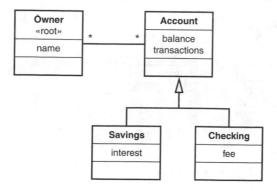

Figure 4.3: *The banking account object model.*

CAUTION

There is an official representation of XML models in UML, and it is very different from Figure 4.3. This is because Figure 4.3 is a high-level, abstract view of a data model, whereas the UML representation for XML model is a low-level, implementation-specific view of XML documents.

To translate this model in XML, we have to decide on the root element. XML documents are hierarchical, and a well-chosen root simplifies navigating the document. Conversely, a poorly chosen root complicates data extraction.

Some object models have natural roots; others (such as Figure 4.3) don't. In the latter case, we have to choose a root based on the application. For the sake of this example, let's suppose that we want to give the owner access to account information. That makes Account the best root in this case. A root stereotype on the Account object documents this decision.

Note that the choice of a root element depends on the application. Had we been working on a financial application, examining accounts, it would have been more sensible to use a list of owners (the bank customers) as the root element.

At this stage, it is time to draw a tree of the document model under development. You can use a piece of paper, flipchart, whiteboard, or whatever works for you (I prefer flipcharts).

In drawing the tree, simply create an element for every object in the model. Element nesting is used to model object relationships.

Figure 4.4 is a first shot at converting the object model into a hierarchy model. Every object in the original model is now an element. However, as it turns out, this is both incorrect and suboptimal.

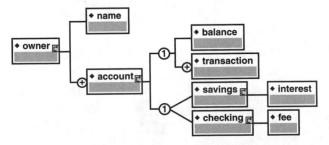

Figure 4.4: *A first tree for the object model.*

On closer examination, the tree in Figure 4.4 is incorrect because, in the object model, an account can have more than one owner. Yet we cannot add the owner element into the account because this would lead to infinite recursion where an account includes its owner, which itself includes the account, which includes the owner, which…. You get the picture.

One possible solution is to introduce a new coowners element. Accounts can now have zero, one, or more coowners in addition to their owner.

In so doing, we realize that the document really is a list of accounts owned by one person. To express this, we rename the root element as accountsList and rename the name element as owner (otherwise, name would be understood as the name of the list, which does not make any sense).

In so doing, we effectively change the definition of the owner element. Renaming is not uncommon when modeling. It shows that you have refined your understanding of the document. Make sure that those changes are properly documented, though, or you'll quickly get lost.

EXAMPLE

The solution in Figure 4.5 is a correct implementation of the object model. To evaluate how good it is, we'll create a few sample documents, such as Listing 4.13.

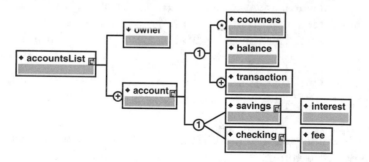

Figure 4.5: *The corrected tree.*

Listing 4.13: account-samples.xml

```xml
<?xml version = "1.0"?>
<accountsList>
   <owner>John Doe</owner>
   <account>
      <balance>534.00</balance>
      <transaction>-231.00</transaction>
      <transaction>-17.00</transaction>
      <checking>
         <fee>4.00</fee>
      </checking>
   </account>
   <account>
```

Listing 4.13: continued

```
        <coowners>Mary Doe</coowners>
        <balance>3502.00</balance>
        <transaction>+17.00</transaction>
        <transaction>+24.00</transaction>
        <transaction>+100.00</transaction>
        <savings>
            <interest>5.50</interest>
        </savings>
    </account>
</accountsList>
```

This works, but it is inefficient. More specifically, the fee and interest elements are completely redundant with the checking and savings element. It is more efficient to create a type for account and extend this type in checking and savings accounts—in effect, mimicking in XML the inheritance relationship found in the UML model.

Furthermore, this document contains a number of what I call *freestanding repeating elements*. Look at transaction for an example. The problem is that are several transaction elements, so you might think of the list of transactions as a group. Yet no XML element exists for the group as such. Elements exist for the individual elements in the group (the transactions) only.

From a syntactical point of view, this is correct (in XML lingo, the document is valid), but, in practice, it makes it more difficult to manipulate the document.

You have not manipulated XML documents yet (you'll start in the next chapter), so you may see why this is a problem. But trust me; as your understanding of XML grows, you will understand that it is easier to add an extra element to group the transactions—likewise for coowners.

What about the list of account itself? Isn't it freestanding when compared to the owner element? Strictly speaking, it is; but, because there's only one owner, it's unlikely to ever be a problem, so do not worry about it.

The final version appears in Figure 4.6. In addition to an account type (which is not visible in Figure 4.6), it introduces two new elements: transactionsList and name. Again, I chose to change the definition of an element—coowners in this case.

EXAMPLE

Listing 4.14 is a sample document. Again, it's useful to write a few sample documents to spot problems with the model. The only problem I could find was the lack of a namespace, so I added one (http://www.psol.com/xbe2/listing4.14). Granted, the namespace is not immediately useful, but it gives me room to grow this model in the future.

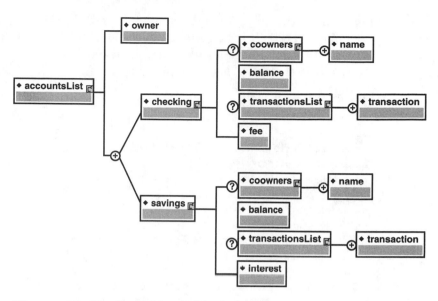

Figure 4.6: *The final hierarchical model.*

Listing 4.14: accounts.xml

```
<?xml version = "1.0"?>
<accountsList xmlns="http://www.psol.com/xbe2/listing4.14">
   <owner>John Doe</owner>
   <checking>
      <balance>534.00</balance>
      <transactionsList>
         <transaction>-231.00</transaction>
         <transaction>-17.00</transaction>
      </transactionsList>
      <fee>4.00</fee>
   </checking>
   <savings>
      <coowners>
         <name>Mary Doe</name>
      </coowners>
      <balance>3502.00</balance>
      <transactionsList>
         <transaction>+17.00</transaction>
         <transaction>+24.00</transaction>
         <transaction>+100.00</transaction>
      </transactionsList>
      <interest>5.50</interest>
   </savings>
</accountsList>
```

Having built the model on a flipchart, it is trivial to turn it into an XML Schema or a DTD. It suffices to list every element in the tree and declare its content model. Special attention is required for types, such as account. The result is shown in Listing 4.15.

Listing 4.15: `accounts.xsd`

```
<?xml version="1.0"?>
<xsd:schema
    xmlns:xsd="http://www.w3.org/2001/XMLSchema"
    xmlns:xbe2="http://www.psol.com/xbe2/listing4.14"
    targetNamespace="http://www.psol.com/xbe2/listing4.14"
    elementFormDefault="qualified">
<xsd:complexType name="account">
    <xsd:sequence>
        <xsd:element name="coowners" minOccurs="0">
            <xsd:complexType>
                <xsd:sequence>
                    <xsd:element name="name" type="xsd:string"
                                 maxOccurs="unbounded"/>
                </xsd:sequence>
            </xsd:complexType>
        </xsd:element>
        <xsd:element name="balance" type="xsd:decimal"/>
        <xsd:element name="transactionsList" minOccurs="0">
            <xsd:complexType>
                <xsd:sequence>
                    <xsd:element name="transaction"
                                 type="xsd:decimal"
                                 maxOccurs="unbounded"/>
                </xsd:sequence>
            </xsd:complexType>
        </xsd:element>
    </xsd:sequence>
</xsd:complexType>

<xsd:complexType name="checking-type">
    <xsd:complexContent>
        <xsd:extension base="xbe2:account">
            <xsd:sequence>
                <xsd:element name="fee" type="xsd:decimal"/>
            </xsd:sequence>
        </xsd:extension>
    </xsd:complexContent>
</xsd:complexType>

<xsd:complexType name="savings-type">
```

Listing 4.15: continued

```
      <xsd:complexContent>
        <xsd:extension base="xbe2:account">
          <xsd:sequence>
            <xsd:element name="interest" type="xsd:decimal"/>
          </xsd:sequence>
        </xsd:extension>
      </xsd:complexContent>
    </xsd:complexType>

    <xsd:element name="accountsList">
      <xsd:complexType>
        <xsd:sequence>
          <xsd:element name="owner" type="xsd:string"/>
          <xsd:choice maxOccurs="unbounded">
            <xsd:element name="checking"
                         type="xbe2:checking-type"/>
            <xsd:element name="savings"
                         type="xbe2:savings-type"/>
          </xsd:choice>
        </xsd:sequence>
      </xsd:complexType>
    </xsd:element>
</xsd:schema>
```

Listing 4.15 used `elementFormDefault="qualified"` so that even local elements are qualified in the XML document (in Listing 4.14, they are qualified by the default prefix).

This example demonstrates how to model an XML document from an object model. This works well because XML's hierarchical structure is a natural fit for objects.

On Elements Versus Attributes

As you have seen, you have many choices when modeling XML documents. One of the hottest debates among XML modelers is about the merits of elements versus attributes. We will revisit this topic in Chapter 10, "Important XML Models," but here are some guidelines:

- The main argument for attributes is that DTDs offer more controls over the type of attributes. XML Schema has made this argument redundant, however.

- The main argument for elements is that it is easier to edit and view them in a document. XML editors and browsers in general have more intuitive handling of elements than of attributes.

I try to be pragmatic. In most cases, I use elements for "major" properties of an object. I define major properties as all the properties that you manipulate regularly.

I reserve attributes for ancillary properties or properties related to a major property. For example, I might include a currency indicator as an attribute to the balance.

TIP

Why does XML support both elements and attributes? Aren't elements enough?

Yes, they are, but XML was originally used in publishing. Elements were used for the text (what should be printed) and attributes for anything else.

On DTDs Versus Schemas

Another worthy question is whether you should model documents using DTDs or schemas. Again, I try to take a pragmatic view.

The only reason you use models is so that tools, such as XML parsers, can validate documents. For example, e-commerce servers can automatically validate documents for which they know the model.

Therefore, the most sensible choice between DTDs and schemas depends on your tools. If the tools you are using expect DTDs, you have to use them. On the contrary, if your tools work best with schemas, use schemas.

Modeling from Scratch

Modeling an XML document without an object model is more work. The object model provides a ready-made analysis of the problem that you just have to convert in XML. For example, the objects, their properties, and their relationships have already been identified.

If you create a model from scratch, you have to do that analysis as well.

An interesting variant is to modify an existing XML model. Typically, the underlying model does not support all your content (you need to add new elements/attributes) or is too complex for your application (you need to remove elements/attributes).

This is somewhat similar to designing a new model from scratch in the sense that you will have to create sample documents and analyze them to understand how to adapt the proposed model. Incidentally, when you add elements to an existing model, it's a good idea to use a different namespace.

On Flexibility

When designing your own models, you want to prepare for evolution. We'll revisit this topic in Chapter 10, but it is important that you build a model flexible enough to accommodate extensions as new content becomes available.

The worst case is to develop a model, create a few hundred or a few thousand documents, and realize that you are missing a key piece of information but that you can't change your model to accommodate it. It's bad because it means that you have to edit all your documents.

To avoid that trap, you want to provide as much structural information as possible but not too much. The difficulty is in striking the right balance between enough and too much.

You want to provide enough structural information because it is easy to degrade information but difficult to clean degraded information.

Compare it with a clean, neatly sorted stack of cards on your desk. It takes half a minute to knock it down and shuffle it. Yet it will take the best of one day to sort the cards again.

The same is true with electronic documents. It is easy to lose structural information when you create the document. And if you lose structural information, it will be difficult to retrieve it later.

EXAMPLE

Compare Listing 4.1, the address book we used throughout this chapter, with Listing 4.16—a text that contains the same document but without markup.

In Listing 4.1, the information is highly structured—for example, the address is broken down into smaller components: street, region, and so on.

But in Listing 4.16, the structure is lost, and, unfortunately, it will be difficult to restore it automatically. "Automatically" is the operative word here. You would need sophisticated software to retrieve the entry boundaries or break the address into its components.

Listing 4.16: The Address Book in Plain Text

```
John Doe
34 Fountain Square Plaza
45202 Cincinnati, OH
US
513-744-8889 (preferred)
513-744-7098
john@emailaholic.com
Jack Smith
513-744-3465
```

Listing 4.16: continued

```
jack@emailaholic.com
Never leave messages on his answering machine. Email instead.
```

However, as you design your structure, be careful not to fall for the reverse problem and make sure that your model remains usable. Structures that are too complex or too strict will actually lower the quality of your document because it encourages users to cheat.

Consider electronic commerce Web sites that want a region, province, county, or state in the buyer address. Yet many countries don't have the notion of region, province, county, or state, or, at least, don't use it for their addresses.

Forcing people to enter information they don't have is asking them to cheat.

Keep in mind the number one rule of professional modeling: Changes will come from where you least expect them. Chances are that, if your application is successful, people will want to include data you had never even considered. How often did I provide room for "future extensions" that were never used? Yet users came and asked for totally unexpected things.

There is no silver bullet in modeling. There is no foolproof solution to strike the right balance between extensibility, flexibility, and usability. As you grow more experienced with XML and DTDs, you will improve your modeling skills.

In the meantime, a workable solution is to define a model rich enough for your application but not richer. Still, it is a good idea to leave hooks in the models—places where it would be easy to add a new element, if required.

Modeling an XML Document

EXAMPLE

The first step in modeling XML documents is to create documents. Because we are modeling an address book, I took a number of business cards and created documents with them. You can see one such sample in Listing 4.17 (names have been changed).

Listing 4.17: Sample Address Book

```
<address-book>
   <entry>
      <name><fname>John</fname><lname>Doe</lname></name>
      <address>
         <street>34 Fountain Square Plaza</street>
         <state>OH</state>
         <zip>45202</zip>
         <locality>Cincinnati</locality>
```

Listing 4.17: continued

```
            <country>US</country>
        </address>
        <tel>513-744-8889</tel>
        <email href="mailto:jdoe@emailaholic.com"/>
    </entry>
    <entry>
        <name><fname>Jean</fname><lname>Dupont</lname></name>
        <address>
            <street>Rue du Lombard 345</street>
            <postal-code>5000</postal-code>
            <locality>Namur</locality>
            <country>Belgium</country>
        </address>
        <email href="mailto:jdupont@emailaholic.com"/>
    </entry>
    <entry>
        <name><fname>Olivier</fname><lname>Rame</lname></name>
        <email href="mailto:orame@emailaholic.com"/>
    </entry>
</address-book>
```

As you can see, I decided early on to break the address into smaller components. In making these documents, I tried to reuse elements. Early in the project, it was clear that there would be a name element, an address element, and more.

Also I decided that addresses, phone numbers, and so on would be conditional. I have incomplete entries in my address book, and the XML version must be able to handle it as well.

I looked at commonalties and found I could group postal code and zip under one element. Although they have different names, they are the same concepts.

This is the creative part of modeling when you list all possible elements, group them, and reorganize them until you achieve something that makes sense. Gradually, a structure appears.

Producing a rough model from this example is easy. Back to the flipchart, I first draw a hierarchy with all the elements introduced in the document so far and their relationships. It is clear that some elements, such as state, are optional. Figure 4.7 shows the result.

This was fast to develop because the underlying model is simple and well-known. For a more complex application, you would want to spend more time drafting documents and understanding the model.

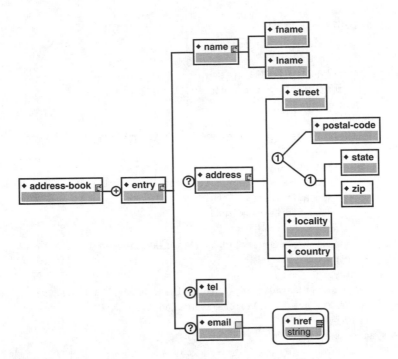

Figure 4.7: *The updated tree.*

At this stage, it is a good idea to compare my work with similar works. In this case, I choose to compare with the vCard standard (RFC 2426). vCard (now in its third version) is a standard for electronic business cards.

vCard is an extensive standard that lists all the fields required in an electronic business card. vCard, however, is too complicated for my needs, so I don't want to simply duplicate that work.

By comparing the vCard structure with my structure, I realized that names are not always easily broken into first and last name, particularly foreign names. I reasoned that I never need the breakdown, so I took it out entirely (an alternative would have been to create a more flexible model).

I also realized that address, phone number, fax number, and e-mail address might repeat. Indeed, it didn't show up in my sample of business cards, but many people have several phone numbers or e-mail addresses (and I should have known about multiple e-mail addresses from personal experience). I introduced a repetition for these as well as an attribute to mark the preferred address. The attribute has a default value of `false`.

In the process, I picked the name "region" for the state element. For some reason, I find region is more generic and, therefore, more appealing.

Comparing my model with vCard gave me the confidence that the simple address book can cope with most addresses used. Figure 4.8 is the final result.

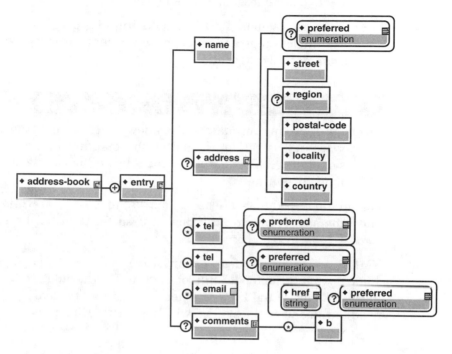

Figure 4.8: *The model for an address book.*

Again, converting the model into a DTD or a schema is trivial. You have already seen the result in Listing 4.2 or Listing 4.9.

Naming Elements

You need to be imaginative and keep an open mind during the process of modeling. Modeling also implies making decisions on the naming of elements and attributes.

As you can see, I like to use meaningful names for XML elements. Others prefer to use meaningless names or acronyms. Again, as so frequent in modeling, there are several schools of thought, and all have convincing arguments. Use what works best for you, but try to be consistent.

In general, meaningful names

- Are easier to debug
- Provide some level of document for the DTD

However, a case can be made for acronyms:

- Acronyms are shorter and, therefore, more efficient.

- Acronyms are less language-dependent.

- Name choice should not be a substitute for proper documentation; meaningless tags and acronyms might not encourage you to properly document the application.

A Tool to Help

Although I love my flipchart, I also know that drawing models on paper is an exercise in frustration. No matter how careful you are, after a few rounds of editing, the result is unreadable, and modeling often requires several rounds of editing!

Fortunately, good tools are on the market to assist you while writing DTDs and Schemas. To prepare this book, I used XML Authority from Tibco (`www.extensibility.com`).

XML Authority is not nearly as intuitive as a piece of paper, but even after 1,000 changes, the model still looks good. Furthermore, to convert the model into an actual DTD or schema, it suffices to save it. There's also no need to remember the syntax, which is another big plus.

EXAMPLE

Figure 4.9 shows XML Authority.

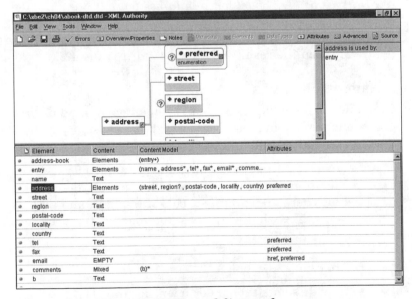

Figure 4.9: *Using an XML modeling tool.*

What's Next

This chapter concludes the background introduction to XML. The next chapters will teach you how to use XML in your environment. We will start by looking at how XML can simplify Web site development.

In particular, the following two chapters look at style sheets. Style sheets are used to render XML onscreen or on paper.

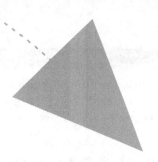

XSL Transformations

In the last three chapters, you learned the basics of XML. Specifically, you learned the XML syntax, how to read and write documents, how to organize and structure XML documents with models and schemas, and how to organize schemas through namespaces.

This chapter is more practical. It shows you how to manipulate XML documents. In this and the following chapter, you will look at *styling*—how to display a document with a browser or an editor.

In this chapter, you will learn how to use XSL, the eXtensible Stylesheet Language, to

- Convert XML documents to HTML or another XML markup

- Publish a large set of documents

- Reorganize XML documents to create table of contents or other information

Why Styling?

XML concentrates on the structure of the information and not its appearance. However, to view XML documents you need to decide on the presentation. Obviously, the presentation or styling instructions are directly related to and derived from the structure of the document.

In practice, styling instructions are organized in style sheets; before viewing a document, you apply the appropriate style sheet to it.

The W3C has published two recommendations for style sheets: CSS, short for *Cascading Style Sheets* and XSL, short for *eXtensible Stylesheet Language*.

EXAMPLE

CSS

CSS was originally developed for HTML, but it was extended for XML. With CSS, a style sheet is a set of rules that tells the browser which font, style, and margin to use to display the text, as shown in the following example:

```
sect1 title
{
  font-family: Palatino;
  font-size: 10pt;
  display: block;
}
```

✔ CSS is the topic of Chapter 6, "XSL Formatting Objects and Cascading Style Sheets," **page 175**.

EXAMPLE

XSL

XSL is more ambitious than CSS because it includes a scripting language (XSLT) specifically designed to manipulate XML documents. With XSL, it is possible to create a table of contents, compile an index, and much more. XSL style sheets are themselves written in XML:

```
<xsl:template match="sect1/title">
   <fo:block font-family="Palatino" font-size="10pt">
      <xsl:apply-templates/>
   </fo:block>
</xsl:template>
```

XSL

XSL, the W3C recommendation, is organized into two parts: XSLT, short for *XSL Transformations*, and FO, short for *Formatting Objects*. This chapter concentrates on XSLT. The next chapter discusses FO as well as CSS. As you will see, FO and CSS are very similar in scope.

Xalan

To run the examples in this chapter, you need an *XSLT processor*. An XSLT processor is simply a software component that implements the XSLT standard.

There are several XSLT processors on the market including those from Microsoft (www.microsoft.com), Oracle (www.oracle.com), and Apache (xml.apache.org). James Clark, the editor of the XSLT standard, has also released an XSLT processor (www.jclark.com and www.4xt.org).

In this chapter, you'll use Xalan, an open-source processor by the Apache foundation. Xalan was originally developed by Lotus/IBM and later donated to the Apache Foundation. Like most XML tools, Xalan is written in Java.

Xalan comes with a command-line interface but, for your convenience, a graphical user interface is wrapped around it. You can download it from www.marchal.com or www.mcp.com.

Concepts of XSLT

You should think of XSLT as a simple scripting language to manipulate XML documents. More specifically, XSLT is a language to specify transformations on XML documents. It takes an XML document (input or source document) and transforms it into another XML document (result or output document), as illustrated by Figure 5.1.

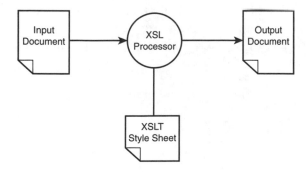

Figure 5.1: *Using XSL to transform XML documents.*

Because it's a small scripting language, XSLT is not limited to rendering documents for viewing. In fact, many applications need to transform XML documents, even in a nonvisual context, and XSLT is the appropriate solution. Some possible applications of XSLT include

- Add elements specifically for viewing, such as add the logo or the address of the sender to an XML invoice.

- Create new content from existing content, such as create a table of contents.

- Extract information from an XML document. This can be useful to present the reader with the right level of details. For example, by using a style sheet to present only high-level information to a managerial person, while using another style sheet to present more detailed technical information to the staff.

- Convert between different XML vocabularies or models, such as convert a company-specific document to an industry standard.

- Transform XML documents into HTML for backward compatibility with existing browsers.

The last case is very common. The XSLT recommendation considers HTML conversion as a special case of XML transformation. This also is one of the solutions supported by Microsoft Internet Explorer 4.0, 5.0, and 5.5.

Basic XSLT

I maintain several Web sites (most notably, www.marchal.com and www.pineapplesoft.com) and I use XML and XSL extensively for Web site maintenance. Why? I write the documents in XML and use XSLT style sheets to automatically format the documents.

Because style sheets create the HTML document, it is easy to change the layout of the sites: I just update one style sheet, press a button and it re-creates all my pages. Because Web fashion keeps changing, this is a major advantage.

Furthermore, I use style sheets for my monthly e-zine, Pineapplesoft Link. Every month, I need to email the e-zine to subscribers and post a copy on my Web site. That's two formats to support: text and HTML. Two style sheets generate the two versions automatically.

Viewing XML in a Browser

EXAMPLE

Listing 5.1 is an abbreviated version of the September 2000 article on XML style sheets. The structure of the document, borrowed from DocBook, is illustrated in Figure 5.2. Essentially, an article contains a title followed by a number of paragraphs organized in sections, called sect1 in DocBook. Figures 5.3 and 5.4 show how the document looks in Internet Explorer 5.

Listing 5.1: `excerpt.xml`

```
<?xml version="1.0"?>
<article>
<articleinfo>
 <title>XSL -- First Step in Learning XML</title>
 <author><firstname>Beno&#238;t</firstname>
  <surname>Marchal</surname></author>
</articleinfo>
<sect1><title>The Value of XSL</title>
 <para>This is an excerpt from the September 2000 issue of
  Pineapplesoft Link. To subscribe free visit
   <ulink url="http://www.marchal.com">marchal.com</ulink>.</para>
 <para>Where do you start learning XML? Increasingly my answer
  is with XSL. XSL is a very powerful tool with many
  applications. Many XML applications depend on it. Let's take
  two examples.</para>
</sect1>
<sect1>
 <title>XSL and Web Publishing</title>
 <para>As a webmaster you would benefit from using XSL.</para>
 <para>Let's suppose that you decide to support smartphones.
  You will need to redo your web site using WML, the
   <emphasis>wireless markup language</emphasis>, instead of
  HTML. While learning WML is easy, it can take days if not
```

Listing 5.1: continued

```
months to redo a large web site. Imagine having to edit every
single page by hand!</para>
<para>In contrast with XSL, it suffices to update one style
sheet the changes flow across the entire web site.</para>
</sect1>
<sect1>
<title>XSL and Programming</title>
<para>The second facet of XSL is the scripting language. XSL
has many features of scripting languages including loops,
function calls, variables and more.</para>
<para>In that respect, XSL is a valuable addition to any
programmer toolbox. Indeed, as XML popularity keeps growing,
you will find that you need to manipulate XML documents
frequently and XSL is the language for so doing.</para>
</sect1>
<sect1>
<title>Conclusion</title>
<para>If you're serious about learning XML, learn XSL. XSL is
a tool to manipulate XML documents for web publishing or
programming.</para>
</sect1>
</article>
```

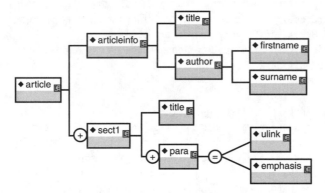

Figure 5.2: *The structure of the article.*

Figure 5.3 and Figure 5.4: *Viewing the XML document in Internet Explorer 5.*

DOCBOOK

DocBook is an XML vocabulary developed and maintained by OASIS, the Organization for the Advancement of Structured Information Standards.

The DocBook vocabulary was designed for technical documents and, more specifically, documents related to computer software and hardware. It is easier to adopt the DocBook standard rather than develop your own vocabulary because DocBook is rich and well documented.

Furthermore, because it is an industry standard, it is well known and several tools are available to edit and otherwise manipulate DocBook documents.

Note that DocBook was originally developed for SGML but an XML variant—which I use in this book—was later released. For the official standard, turn to `www.oasis-open.org/docbook`.

By default, Internet Explorer presents the document as collapsible elements—clicking the minus or plus symbol next to an element will extend or collapse it. Indeed, in Figure 5.4, the first two sections are collapsed. It is possible to override the default behavior with style sheets.

✔ Chapter 6, "XSL Formatting Objects and Cascading Style Sheets," discusses more formatting options.

A Simple Style Sheet

Let's start by writing a style sheet to convert the XML document into HTML. Listing 5.2 is such a style sheet.

EXAMPLE

Listing 5.2: `basic.xsl`

```xml
<?xml version="1.0"?>
<xsl:stylesheet
   xmlns:xsl="http://www.w3.org/1999/XSL/Transform"
   version="1.0">

<xsl:output method="html"/>

<xsl:template match="/">
<html>
   <head>
      <title><xsl:value-of
         select="article/articleinfo/title"/></title>
   </head>
   <xsl:apply-templates/>
</html>
</xsl:template>
```

Listing 5.2 continued

```xsl
<xsl:template match="article">
<body>
   <xsl:apply-templates/>
</body>
</xsl:template>

<xsl:template match="articleinfo/title">
   <h1><xsl:apply-templates/></h1>
</xsl:template>

<xsl:template match="sect1/title">
   <h2><xsl:apply-templates/></h2>
</xsl:template>

<xsl:template match="ulink">
   <a href="{@url}"><xsl:apply-templates/></a>
</xsl:template>

<xsl:template match="emphasis">
   <b><xsl:apply-templates/></b>
</xsl:template>

<xsl:template match="para">
   <p><xsl:apply-templates/></p>
</xsl:template>

<xsl:template match="author">
   <p>by <xsl:value-of select="firstname"/>
   <xsl:text> </xsl:text>
   <xsl:value-of select="surname"/></p>
</xsl:template>

</xsl:stylesheet>
```

To apply the style sheet, use Xalan. If you have downloaded the graphical interface from www.marchal.com or www.mcp.com, it suffices to select the input XML document (excerpt.xml, Listing 5.1), the style sheet (basic.xsl, Listing 5.2) and a filename for the output HTML document (see Figure 5.5). You can either enter the names directly or use the Browse buttons.

Hit the Transform button and Xalan applies the style sheet to your XML document. In so doing, it creates an HTML document.

NOTE

Although I hope you'll find it useful, you don't have to use the graphical interface. The official Xalan download from `xml.apache.org` offers a command-line interface that is more powerful (for example, you can use the command-line interface to include Xalan in batch files), but also more complex to use. Consult the Xalan documentation for more information.

Finally, some XML editors include an XSLT processor. For example, XML Spy (`www.xmlspy.com`) enables you to apply XSLT style sheets via a menu.

Figure 5.5: *Applying the XSLT style sheet to create an HTML document.*

If everything goes well, Xalan will create a new HTML file, `basic.html`. Listing 5.3 is `basic.html` (I reformatted the code so it prints better). Figure 5.6 views it in a browser.

There is confusion on how browsers support XML. Some people think that you need XML-compatible browsers to view XML documents. That is simply untrue if you use XSLT. The style sheet creates HTML documents, which any browser can load (unless you use browser-specific tags in the style sheet, of course). Thanks to XSLT, the browser does not know or even need to know that the document was once written in XML.

In practice, this guarantees compatibility with every browser, including the very old ones. Thanks to XSLT, XML is not limited to the latest generation of browsers.

OUTPUT

Listing 5.3: `basic.html`

```
<html>
    <head>
        <title>XSL -- First Step in Learning XML</title>
    </head>
    <body>
```

Listing 5.3: continued

```
<h1>XSL -- First Step in Learning XML</h1>
<p>by Beno&icirc;t Marchal</p>
<h2>The Value of XSL</h2>
<p>This is an excerpt from the September 2000 issue of
 Pineapplesoft Link. To subscribe free visit
 <a href="http://www.marchal.com">marchal.com</a>.</p>
<p>Where do you start learning XML? Increasingly my answer
 is with XSL. XSL is a very powerful tool with many
 applications. Many XML applications depend on it. Let's take
 two examples.</p>
<h2>XSL and Web Publishing</h2>
<p>As a webmaster you would benefit from using XSL.</p>
<p>Let's suppose that you decide to support smartphones.
 You will need to redo your web site using WML, the
 <b>wireless markup language</b>, instead of
 HTML. While learning WML is easy, it can take days if not
 months to redo a large web site. Imagine having to edit every
 single page by hand!</p>
<p>In contrast with XSL, it suffices to update one style
 sheet the changes flow across the entire web site.</p>
<h2>XSL and Programming</h2>
<p>The second facet of XSL is the scripting language. XSL
 has many features of scripting languages including loops,
 function calls, variables and more.</p>
<p>In that respect, XSL is a valuable addition to any
 programmer toolbox. Indeed, as XML popularity keeps growing,
 you will find that you need to manipulate XML documents
 frequently and XSL is the language for so doing.</p>
<h2>Conclusion</h2>
<p>If you're serious about learning XML, learn XSL. XSL is
 a tool to manipulate XML documents for web publishing or
 programming.</p>
</body>
</html>
```

The following sections examine the style sheet in more detail.

The stylesheet Element

The style sheet is a well-formed XML document (XSL designers thought that XML was the best syntax for a style sheet). The root element is stylesheet as shown in the example:

EXAMPLE

```
<xsl:stylesheet
    xmlns:xsl="http://www.w3.org/1999/XSL/Transform"
    version="1.0">
```

OUTPUT

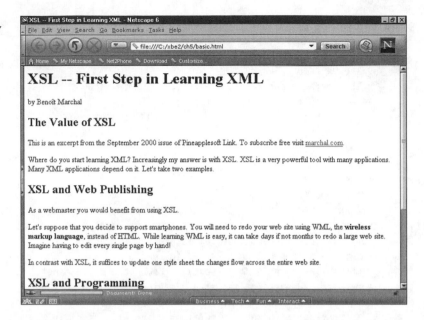

Figure 5.6: *Viewing the result with Netscape 6.*

Because the style sheet contains elements from at least three different documents (input, output, and the style sheet language itself), it relies on namespaces to organize the elements. These namespaces are

- The xsl prefix is used for the XSL vocabulary. The URI for the namespace must be http://www.w3.org/1999/XSL/Transform.

- If the input or output documents had their own namespaces, they would be declared on the stylesheet element as well. However, in this case, neither DocBook nor HTML uses namespaces.

The version attribute is mandatory and its value must be 1.0. At the time of writing, the W3C is working on a new version of XSLT, version 1.1. XSLT 1.1 defines a few extensions to XSLT 1.0 and changes the version number.

EXAMPLE

The output Element

Immediately after stylesheet comes the output element. It controls how the XSLT processor writes the output document.

```
<xsl:output method="html"/>
```

The following are the most important attributes:

- `method` accepts three values: `html`, `xml`, and `text`. It controls how the XSLT processor writes the output document. It mostly affects empty elements, which are written as `<br>` in HTML and `<br/>` in XML. Note that although there's a text option, text support is very limited. In text mode, the processor simply skips the markup.

- `indent` controls whether the processor indents the XML markup (aligns tags, depending on how deep they are in the document) or not. Acceptable values are `yes` and `no`.

- `encoding` selects a specific character encoding. By default, the processor writes XML documents in UTF-8.

- `doctype-public` and `doctype-system` create a doctype statement (to select a DTD) in the output document.

Template Elements

EXAMPLE

The bulk of the style sheet is a list of *templates*. The following example transforms the title of a section in an HTML heading:

```
<xsl:template match="sect1/title">
   <h2><xsl:apply-templates/></h2>
</xsl:template>
```

OUTPUT

which creates the following line in the output document:

```
<h2>The Value of XSL</h2>
```

A template has two parts:

- The `match` parameter is a path to the elements in the input document to which the template applies.

- The content of the template lists the elements to create in the output document when the template matches.

XPaths

The syntax for XML paths, called *XPaths*, is similar to file paths. XML paths start from the root of the document and list all the elements along the way. Elements are separated by the "/" character.

EXAMPLE

The following path matches the title of the article (`<title>XSL -- First Step in Learning XML</title>`):

```
/article/articleinfo/title
```

while this path points to the section titles (`<title>`The Value of XSL`</title>`, `<title>`XSL and Web Publishing`</title>`, and the like):

`/article/sect1/title`

The following path matches the author information (`<author><firstname>`Benoît`</firstname><surname>`Marchal`</surname></author>`). Note that this path matches several elements:

`/article/articleinfo/author`

TIP

Note that "/" points to the immediate children of a node.

To select all the descendants from a node, use the "//" sequence. `/article//title` selects all the titles in the article. It selects the main title and the section titles.

As in a file system, XPaths can be either relative or absolute. Absolute paths start with the "/" character at the beginning of the document.

In a style sheet, most paths are relative to the current element. Again, this is similar to the file system. Double-clicking the `accessories` folder in the `c:\program files` folder moves to `c:\program files\accessories` folder, not to `c:\accessories`.

If the current element is `articleinfo` then `title` matches `/article/articleinfo/title` but if the current article is `sect1`, `title` matches one of the `/article/sect1/title`.

To match any element, use the wildcard character "*". The path `/article/*` matches any direct descendant from article: `articleinfo` and `sect1`.

It is possible to combine paths in a match with the "|" character, such as `title | para` matches `title` or `para` elements.

EXAMPLE

Matching on Attributes

Paths can match attributes, too. The following path selects the `url` attribute from the `ulink` element (`url="http://www.marchal.com"`):

`/article/sect1/para/url/@url`

As you can see, the "@" character indicates that `url` is an attribute name, not an element.

EXAMPLE

Matching with a Condition

XPaths can also include conditions, in which case they match only if the condition is true. Conditions are added in angle brackets after the element to which the condition applies. For example, the following XPath selects paragraphs (para in DocBook) that contain a hyperlink (ulink in DocBook):

```
/article/sect1/para[ulink]
```

EXAMPLE

Matching Text and Functions

Functions can further restrict XPaths to specific elements. The following path selects the title of the second section. It uses the position() function that returns the position of the element and is particularly useful with conditions:

```
/article/sect1[position()=2]/title
```

Table 5.1 lists some of the most common functions. Most functions can also take a path as an argument. For example, the following function returns the number of title elements in the document:

```
count(//title)
```

Table 5.1: The Most Common XSL Functions

XSL Function	Description
position()	Returns the position of the current node in the node set
text()	Returns the text (the content) of an element
last()	Returns the position of the last node in the current node set
count()	Returns the number of nodes in the current node set
not()	Negates the argument
contains()	Returns true if the first argument contains the second argument
starts-with()	Returns true if the first argument starts with the second argument

TIP

There's a shorthand notation to select the position of an element. Simply add the position in angle brackets as in

```
/article/sect1[2]/title
```

Following the Processor

After loading the style sheet, the XSL processor loads the source document. Next, it walks through the source document from root to leaf nodes. At each step, it attempts to match the current node against a template.

Let's follow the XSL processor for the first few templates in the style sheet. After loading the style sheet and the source document, the processor positions itself at the root of the input document. It looks for a template that matches the root and it immediately finds

```
<xsl:template match="/">
<html>
   <head>
      <title><xsl:value-of
         select="article/articleinfo/title"/></title>
   </head>
   <xsl:apply-templates/>
</html>
</xsl:template>
```

This template, which matches the root of the XML document, is ideal to create root elements in the output document: the html element and its head.

The XSLT value-of element is a query. It takes an XPath in its select attribute and returns its value. In practice, this template copies the article title from XML to HTML.

The XPath for value-of is a relative XPath. Because the current element is the root, it is equivalent to

```
/article/articleinfo/title
```

One of the most important XSLT elements is apply-templates. When it encounters apply-templates, the processor moves to the children of the current node and repeats the process—that is, it attempts to match them against a template.

In other words, apply-templates is a recursive call to the style sheet. If you have a programming background, you might have recognized a depth-first search walking of a tree.

In this case, the processor encounters apply-templates after creating the head. Because the current node is the root, it has only one child: article. The processor makes article the current node and repeats the process; that is, it tries to match article with a template and it finds

```
<xsl:template match="article">
<body>
   <xsl:apply-templates/>
</body>
</xsl:template>
```

Note that the processor matches on a relative path because the current node is /article. The processor creates the HTML body. apply-templates repeats the process by loading article's first child: articleinfo.

The style sheet defines no templates for articleinfo. Does that stop the processor? Fortunately not. If no template in the style sheet matches, the processor tries *built-in templates*. Built-in templates are predefined by the processor. They need not appear in the style sheet. In this case, the following built-in rule matches articleinfo:

```
<xsl:template match="* | /">
   <xsl:apply-templates/>
</xsl:template>
```

NOTE

The built-in template does not modify the resulting tree (it does not create elements) but it recursively calls the current element's children.

Without the default template, there would be no rules to trigger the recursive matching process and the processor would stop.

It is possible to override the built-in template, for example, to stop processing for elements not explicitly defined elsewhere:

```
<xsl:template match="* | /"/>
```

The built-in template forces the processor to load the first children of articleinfo—that is, the title element. The following template matches:

```
<xsl:template match="articleinfo/title">
   <h1><xsl:apply-templates/></h1>
</xsl:template>
```

Again, the processor matches on a relative path because the current node is title. This template does not match every title, only those titles enclosed in articleinfo. More specifically, it does not match sect1/title. The template creates an h1 HTML element and, through apply-templates, moves on to title's child.

The only child for title is its content, the title's text. Again no rules in the style sheet match the text and the processor resorts to a built-in template. The built-in template copies the text in the output document:

```
<xsl:template match="text()">
   <xsl:value-of select="."/>
</xsl:template>
```

The built-in template does not include apply-templates so the processor has completely processed the title element (in any case, because the text has no children, it has to stop). The processor backtracks to the articleinfo element and moves to the next child, the author element, which matches

```
<xsl:template match="author">
   <p>by <xsl:value-of select="firstname"/>
   <xsl:text> </xsl:text>
   <xsl:value-of select="surname"/></p>
</xsl:template>
```

This template is mostly familiar. It creates an HTML paragraph with the first and last name. Notice that it does not use `apply-templates` but directly extracts relevant information from the input document with `value-of`.

Why? Besides the obvious pedagogical interest, `value-of` gives more control over the placement of information. In this template, it is easier to insert a space between the first and last names using `value-of` than `apply-templates`.

The template also introduces one new element: `text`. As the name implies, `text` creates a text node in the output document.

In most cases, to insert text in the output document, you can just type it where needed. However, the XSLT processor may strip spaces, line returns, tabs, and other special characters. `text` gives you more control because it tells the XSLT processor to use the text verbatim. It is particularly handy to insert a single space, as in this template.

The processor has completed `articleinfo` so it backtracks again to `article` and works on its other children—the four `sect1` element. In so doing, it processes `sect1` children (`para`) and their children's children (`ulink` and `emphasis`) until the end of the document. I will spare you the details.

The remainder of the style sheet should be familiar with the exception of

```
<xsl:template match="ulink">
    <a href="{@url}"><xsl:apply-templates/></a>
</xsl:template>
```

This template matches the `ulink` element and turns it into an HTML element. The URL must go in the `href` attribute, but how do you use an XPath in an attribute? As the template illustrates, you simply wrap the XPath in curly brackets. You can think of curly brackets as the correct replacement for the following construct (which is not valid XML because it includes a tag in an attribute):

```
<xsl:template match="ulink">
    <a href="<xsl:value-of select='@url'>"><xsl:apply-templates/></a>
</xsl:template>
```

CAUTION

Curly brackets can be used only to wrap XPaths within an attribute.

Supporting Different Markup Languages

Currently, whether they are using a Windows PC, a Macintosh, or a Unix workstation, most people access the Web through a browser, which is typically Internet Explorer or Netscape. This will change in the future as more people turn to specialized devices, the so-called Net Appliances. Already WebTV has achieved some success with a browser in a TV set.

Mobile phones and PDAs, such as the popular PalmPilot, will be increasingly used for Web browsing. Ever tried surfing on a PalmPilot? It works surprisingly well but, on the small screen, many Web sites are not readable.

To address the specific limitations of this new range of devices, new markup languages are being developed.

The most vocal group is the WAP Forum, a consortium of mobile phone vendors. They developed WML (Wireless Markup Language) as a simple markup language specifically designed to accommodate small phone screens and slow connections. WML is available in the U.S. and in Europe. You can find more information at www.wapforum.org.

In Japan, DoCoMo, the country's largest mobile phone operator, has achieved enormous success with its i-mode phones. The phones recognize cHTML (Compact HTML), a cut-down version of HTML.

Another proprietary language is WebClip from Palm, manufacturer of the popular PalmPilot. WebClip is also a subset of HTML but, unfortunately, it is not directly compatible with cHTML. You can find more information at www.palmos.com.

In an attempt to reconcile these standards, the W3C has produced XHTML, an XML version of HTML. It would appear that supporting XHTML is trivial (after all, it's almost HTML) but it may not be so. In fact, XHTML has been broken down into a multitude of modules and most devices will implement a subset of these modules. Read more at www.w3.org.

Did I mention portals and search engines, some of which would like you to adopt RSS (Rich Site Summary), to help them provide more relevant information to their users? RSS is yet another XML-based markup language designed specifically to list Web sites on portals.

For completeness, I should also mention the Open eBook Publication Structure. eBooks are like specialized PDAs that let you download books and read them on the road. The benefit is that a small eBook reader can carry a whole library. Open owners of information-rich Web sites may also decide to publish the Web sites as eBooks or Electronic books. eBooks use yet another markup language, called OEB (Open eBook). More information about this is available at www.openebook.org.

Obviously, not all these formats are relevant to you. Likewise, not all these formats will survive long enough to become relevant, but new markup languages will probably be introduced in the future and this is one of the challenges that Webmasters will need to address.

XSLT to the rescue! XSLT enables Webmasters to manage the diversity of browsers and platforms by maintaining the document source in XML and converting to the appropriate markup language when needed. Figure 5.7 illustrates how this works.

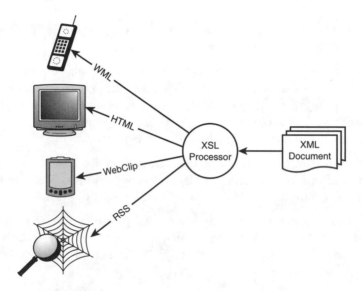

Figure 5.7: *Maintain one XML document and convert it to the appropriate markup language.*

EXAMPLE

WML Conversion

As an illustration, we'll create a style sheet for WML (see Listing 5.4). The style sheet is very similar to the previous style sheet except that it inserts WML markup instead of HTML.

Listing 5.4: smartphone.xsl

```
<?xml version="1.0"?>
<xsl:stylesheet
    xmlns:xsl="http://www.w3.org/1999/XSL/Transform"
    version="1.0">

<xsl:output
    method="xml"
```

Listing 5.4: continued

```
        doctype-public="-//WAPFORUM//DTD WML 1.1//EN"
        doctype-system="http://www.wapforum.org/DTD/wml_1.1.xml"/>

<xsl:template match="/">
<wml>
    <xsl:apply-templates/>
</wml>
</xsl:template>

<xsl:template match="article">
<card title="{articleinfo/title}">
    <xsl:apply-templates/>
</card>
</xsl:template>

<xsl:template match="articleinfo"/>

<xsl:template match="title">
    <p align="center"><b>Today's News</b></p>
</xsl:template>

<xsl:template match="ulink">
    <anchor><xsl:apply-templates/><go href="{@url}"/></anchor>
</xsl:template>

<xsl:template match="emphasis">
    <i><xsl:apply-templates/></i>
</xsl:template>

<xsl:template match="para">
    <p><xsl:apply-templates/></p>
</xsl:template>

</xsl:stylesheet>
```

OUTPUT

When you apply this style sheet, you create a WML document. Typically to render WML documents, you'll need a WAP-enabled smartphone. If you're happy with your current phone, you can download a phone emulator from forum.nokia.com or use the Opera browser. Opera is a regular HTML browser but also does WML. Figure 5.8 shows the document loaded in Opera. You can download Opera from www.opera.com.

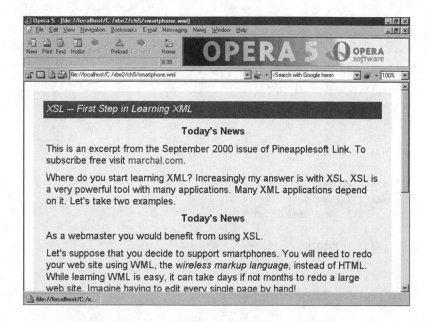

Figure 5.8: *Loading a WML document in Opera.*

Most of this style sheet should be familiar. The most notable difference is the output element. The method attribute has an xml value, meaning that we create an XML document (as opposed to HTML). Indeed, WML is an XML-based language:

```
<xsl:output
   method="xml"
   doctype-public="-//WAPFORUM//DTD WML 1.1//EN"
   doctype-system="http://www.wapforum.org/DTD/wml_1.1.xml"/>
```

The style sheet also uses the doctype-public and doctype-system attribute to create the following doctype statement in the WML document (WML documents must be valid—that is, include a DTD):

```
<!DOCTYPE wml PUBLIC "-//WAPFORUM//DTD WML 1.1//EN"
                     "http://www.wapforum.org/DTD/wml_1.1.xml">
```

OUTPUT

Also, to accommodate a smaller screen, the style sheet ignores the articleinfo element through an empty template:

```
<xsl:template match="articleinfo"/>
```

The other differences are because this style sheet is designed for a WML document. If you know HTML, WML is a breeze to learn. Some of the most important differences are that the root element is called `wml` instead of `html`:

```
<xsl:template match="/">
<wml>
    <xsl:apply-templates/>
</wml>
```

There is no `head` or `body`. Instead, use the `card` element. Interestingly enough, WML enables you to define more than one card element per document, although this style sheet does not demonstrate it. In HTML, `head` contains a `title` element, whereas in WML, `card` has a `title` attribute:

```
<xsl:template match="article">
<card title="{articleinfo/title}">
    <xsl:apply-templates/>
</card>
</xsl:template>
```

Hyperlinks use a combination of `anchor` and `go` elements instead of the a:

```
<xsl:template match="ulink">
    <anchor><xsl:apply-templates/><go href="{@url}"/></anchor>
</xsl:template>
```

Most other elements, such as p, were borrowed from HTML:

```
<xsl:template match="para">
    <p><xsl:apply-templates/></p>
</xsl:template>
```

When and Where to Use Style Sheets

So far, we converted the XML documents before publishing them. The browser never saw XML—it manipulated HTML or WML. At the time of writing, it is the only safe option.

Why? Internet Explorer is the only popular browser with XSLT support. However, there are serious compatibility issues between versions of Internet Explorer in their support of XSLT. Furthermore, all versions of Internet Explorer currently available ship with an outdated XSLT processor that does not respect the standard!

If you want to explore XSLT with Internet Explorer, I recommend you update the XSLT processor to the latest version. You can download the update from `msdn.microsoft.com/xml`.

Of course, keeping these incompatibilities in mind, I strongly advise against applying XSLT style sheets on the browser. It is safer to convert XML documents to HTML before publishing.

Figure 5.9 contrasts the two options: In the first case, XML documents are converted to HTML (or WML) before publishing. This is the safer option, and it guarantees total compatibility with all visitors. In the second case, the XML document and the style sheet are sent to the browser, which uses its own XSLT processor to apply we the style sheet and renders the result.

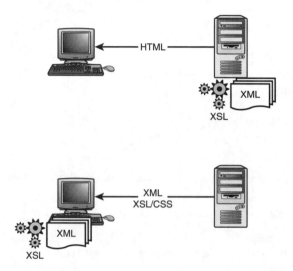

Figure 5.9: *Style sheets on the server or on the client.*

Special Note—Internet Explorer 5.0

CAUTION

Lest it's overlooked, for compatibility reasons explained previously, I strongly advise that you convert to HTML before publishing. This section was introduced as a glimpse into a possible future where browsers will fully implement XSLT. Use this material with care.

How do we you apply a style sheet in the browser? The first problem is to tell the browser which style sheet to apply.

EXAMPLE

The solution comes from the xml-stylesheet processing instruction. It associates a style sheet with the current document through two attributes: an href to the style sheet and the type of the style sheet (text/xsl, in this case).

```
<?xml-stylesheet href="ie5.xsl" type="text/xsl"?>
```

Unfortunately, as explained previously, Internet Explorer 5 ships with an old XSLT processor. This processor is not compatible with the XSLT recommendation and, therefore, you must modify the style sheets.

Listing 5.5 is the XML document with the appropriate processing instruction for Internet Explorer 5. With the exception of the processing instruction, this remains unchanged.

Listing 5.5: `ie5.xml`

```
<?xml version="1.0"?>
<?xml-stylesheet href="ie5.xsl" type="text/xsl"?>
<article>
<articleinfo>
 <title>XSL -- First Step in Learning XML</title>
 <author><firstname>Beno&#238;t</firstname>
  <surname>Marchal</surname></author>
</articleinfo>
<sect1><title>The Value of XSL</title>
 <para>This is an excerpt from the September 2000 issue of
  Pineapplesoft Link. To subscribe free visit
   <ulink url="http://www.marchal.com">marchal.com</ulink>.</para>
 <para>Where do you start learning XML? Increasingly my answer
  is with XSL. XSL is a very powerful tool with many
  applications. Many XML applications depend on it. Let's take
  two examples.</para>
</sect1>
<sect1>
 <title>XSL and Web Publishing</title>
 <para>As a webmaster you would benefit from using XSL.</para>
 <para>Let's suppose that you decide to support smartphones.
  You will need to redo your web site using WML, the
  <emphasis>wireless markup language</emphasis>, instead of
  HTML. While learning WML is easy, it can take days if not
  months to redo a large web site. Imagine having to edit every
  single page by hand!</para>
 <para>In contrast with XSL, it suffices to update one style
  sheet the changes flow across the entire web site.</para>
</sect1>
<sect1>
 <title>XSL and Programming</title>
 <para>The second facet of XSL is the scripting language. XSL
  has many features of scripting languages including loops,
  function calls, variables and more.</para>
 <para>In that respect, XSL is a valuable addition to any
```

Listing 5.5: continued

```
programmer toolbox. Indeed, as XML popularity keeps growing,
you will find that you need to manipulate XML documents
frequently and XSL is the language for so doing.</para>
</sect1>
<sect1>
 <title>Conclusion</title>
 <para>If you're serious about learning XML, learn XSL. XSL is
 a tool to manipulate XML documents for web publishing or
 programming.</para>
</sect1>
</article>
```

By contrast, the style sheet in Listing 5.6 has been adapted to the peculiar version of XSLT that Internet Explorer supports. Figure 5.10 shows the result in Internet Explorer.

Listing 5.6 ie5.xsl

```
<?xml version="1.0"?>
<xsl:stylesheet
    xmlns:xsl="http://www.w3.org/TR/WD-xsl"
    xmlns="http://www.w3.org/TR/REC-html40"
    result-ns="">

<xsl:template match="*">
    <xsl:apply-templates/>
</xsl:template>

<xsl:template match="text()">
    <xsl:value-of select="."/>
</xsl:template>

<xsl:template match="/">
<html>
    <head>
        <title><xsl:value-of
            select="article/articleinfo/title"/></title>
    </head>
    <xsl:apply-templates/>
</html>
</xsl:template>

<xsl:template match="article">
<body>
    <xsl:apply-templates/>
</body>
```

Listing 5.6: continued

```
</xsl:template>

<xsl:template match="articleinfo/title">
   <h1><xsl:apply-templates/></h1>
</xsl:template>

<xsl:template match="sect1/title">
   <h2><xsl:apply-templates/></h2>
</xsl:template>

<xsl:template match="ulink">
   <a href="{@url}"><xsl:apply-templates/></a>
</xsl:template>

<xsl:template match="emphasis">
   <b><xsl:apply-templates/></b>
</xsl:template>

<xsl:template match="para">
   <p><xsl:apply-templates/></p>
</xsl:template>

<xsl:template match="author">
   <p>by <xsl:value-of select="firstname"/> <xsl:value-of
      select="surname"/></p>
</xsl:template>

</xsl:stylesheet>
```

Changes to the Style Sheet

The style sheet had to be adapted in three places. First, there is no output element; it is replaced by a namespace for HTML on the stylesheet element. Speaking of which, the XSL namespace points to an earlier version of XSL. Finally, an empty result-ns argument has been added:

```
<xsl:stylesheet
   xmlns:xsl="http://www.w3.org/TR/WD-xsl"
   xmlns="http://www.w3.org/TR/REC-html40"
   result-ns="">
```

Second, Internet Explorer has no built-in templates. They must be declared explicitly in the style sheet:

```
<xsl:template match="*">
   <xsl:apply-templates/>
</xsl:template>
```

```
<xsl:template match="text()">
   <xsl:value-of select="."/>
</xsl:template>
```

OUTPUT

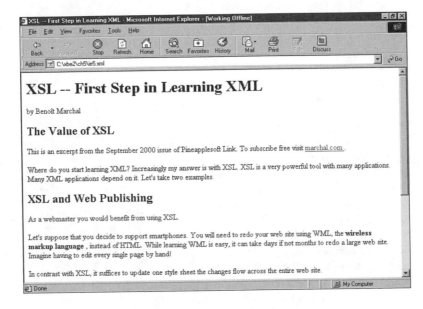

Figure 5.10: *Internet Explorer 5.0 renders XML.*

CAUTION

Internet Explorer 5 does not use the standard priority rules. Therefore, the default templates must appear at the top of the style sheet; otherwise, they would have higher priority than the rules.

Finally, Internet Explorer does not recognize the text element, so the author template has been adapted:

```
<xsl:template match="author">
   <p>by <xsl:value-of select="firstname"/> <xsl:value-of
      select="surname"/></p>
</xsl:template>
```

Advanced XSLT

XSLT is a powerful transformation mechanism. So far, we have only used a subset of it. The structure of the document created is close to the structure of the original document.

Yet, it is often useful to reorganize the source document more completely, up to the point that you might create documents that bear little resemblance to the original one. In most cases, you will limit yourself to creating new content from an existing one; for example, you might want to create a table of contents at the beginning of the document.

The following style sheet demonstrates two things:

- The flexibility of XSLT for Webmasters. You can change the style sheet at any time and it creates a different HTML document. Thanks to style sheets, it is possible to redo a large Web site in minutes.

- Advanced techniques that give you more control on the styling.

EXAMPLE

Listing 5.7 is a more sophisticated style sheet that, among other things, creates a table of contents.

Listing 5.7: `fun.xsl`

```
<?xml version="1.0"?>
<xsl:stylesheet
   xmlns:xsl="http://www.w3.org/1999/XSL/Transform"
   version="1.0">

<xsl:output method="html" indent="yes"/>

<xsl:param name="title" select="/article/articleinfo/title"/>

<xsl:template match="/">
<html>
   <head>
      <script language="JavaScript"><xsl:comment><xsl:text
         disable-output-escaping="yes"><![CDATA[
function GetCookie(name)
{
   var arg = name + "=",
      alen = arg.length,
      clen = document.cookie.length,
      i = 0;
   while(i < clen)
   {
      var j = i + alen;
      if(document.cookie.substring(i,j) == arg)
         return "found";
      i = document.cookie.indexOf(" ",i) + 1;
      if(i==0)
            break;
```

Listing 5.7: continued

```
      }
      return null;
   }
   var cookie = "XBE220010130";
   if(GetCookie(cookie) == null)
   {
      newwin = open("pslink.jpg","dispwin",
                    "width=200,height=115,menubar=no");
      document.cookie = cookie + "=found; " +
                        "expires=Thu 01-01-2005 00:00:00 GMT;";
   }  //]]></xsl:text></xsl:comment></script>
         <title><xsl:value-of select="$title"/></title>
      </head>
      <body bgcolor="#ffcc33">
         <xsl:apply-templates/>
      </body>
</html>
</xsl:template>

<xsl:template match="article">
<table bgcolor="#ffffff" width="80%" align="center"><tr><td>
   <xsl:apply-templates select="articleinfo"/>
   <p><xsl:for-each select="sect1/title">
      <a href="#{generate-id()}"><xsl:value-of
         select="."/></a><br/>
   </xsl:for-each></p>
   <xsl:apply-templates select="sect1"/>
</td></tr></table>
</xsl:template>

<xsl:template match="articleinfo/title">
   <h1><xsl:apply-templates/></h1>
</xsl:template>

<xsl:template match="title">
   <h2><a name="{generate-id()}"><xsl:apply-templates/></a></h2>
</xsl:template>

<xsl:template match="sect1[not(position() mod 2 = 1)]/title">
   <h2 align="right"><a name="{generate-id()}"><xsl:apply-templates/></a></h2>
</xsl:template>

<xsl:template match="ulink">
   <a href="{@url}"><xsl:apply-templates/></a>
</xsl:template>
```

Listing 5.7: continued

```
<xsl:template match="emphasis">
   <b><xsl:apply-templates/></b>
</xsl:template>


<xsl:template match="para">
   <p><xsl:apply-templates/></p>
</xsl:template>


<xsl:template match="sect1[not(position() mod 2 = 1)]/para">
   <p align="right"><xsl:apply-templates/></p>
</xsl:template>


<xsl:template match="author">
   <p>by <xsl:value-of select="firstname"/>
   <xsl:text> </xsl:text>
   <xsl:value-of select="surname"/></p>
</xsl:template>


</xsl:stylesheet>
```

OUTPUT

Using Xalan apply this style sheet to Listing 5.1. Figure 5.11 shows the result in the browser. The style sheet demonstrates a number of new XSLT techniques and you will review them in the next sections.

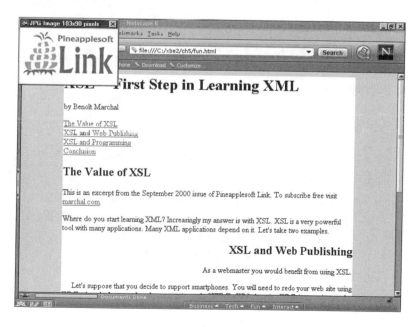

Figure 5.11: The resulting HTML document in a browser.

The indent Parameter

The style sheet uses yet another option for output: indent. The indent attribute asks the processor to indent the markup in the output document (align the start tags). In most cases, you would want to set indent to no, because it results in smaller files that download faster. Here, indenting is enabled to improve readability.

```
<xsl:output method="html" indent="yes"/>
```

Using Parameters

The style sheet is made more customizable through a param element. It takes a style sheet parameter that acts like a function parameter—that is, you can change its value before calling the style sheet.

The parameter takes an optional default value through either a select attribute or through the content of the param element itself:

```
<xsl:param name="title" select="/article/articleinfo/title"/>
```

To use the parameter's value anywhere in the style sheet, prefix its name with a dollar character as in the root template:

```
<title><xsl:value-of select="$title"/></title>
```

Now it is easy to change the title of your document. You can set parameters by using Set Style Sheet Parameters... in the Tools menu (see Figure 5.12).

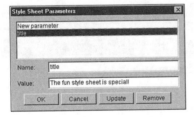

Figure 5.12: *Set the parameter's value in the interface.*

Creating Special Nodes in the Output Document

The root template demonstrates how to insert special code in the output document. The style sheet creates a small JavaScript function. Note that the JavaScript is generated in the HTML document and, therefore, will be executed by the browser. As far as the style sheet is concerned, there is no difference between JavaScript code and other text.

However, this is easier said than done. Indeed, JavaScript may use illegal XML characters such as "<". What is the solution? Insert the JavaScript in a CDATA section.

However, CDATA solves only one half of the problem. How can you make sure the XSLT processor does not escape the "<" in the output document? The trick is to use the text element which, you will remember, enables you to control how text is rendered. In this case, the `disable-output-escaping="yes"` attribute preserves angle brackets:

TIP

If you're confused by this rule, always remember that a style sheet is an XML document. It is interpreted according to XML rules. The processor only sees the result of the parsing where CDATA sections and entities (<) have been resolved.

NOTE

If you're curious about the JavaScript code, It's a classic use of cookies. The script opens a window if, and only if, this is your first visit. To remember you have already visited the page, it creates a cookie.

```
<xsl:template match="/">
<html>
  <head>
    <script language="JavaScript"><xsl:comment><xsl:text
      disable-output-escaping="yes"><![CDATA[
function GetCookie(name)
{
   var arg = name + "=",
       alen = arg.length,
       clen = document.cookie.length,
       i = 0;
   while(i < clen)
   {
      var j = i + alen;
      if(document.cookie.substring(i,j) == arg)
         return "found";
      i = document.cookie.indexOf(" ",i) + 1;
      if(i==0)
              break;
   }
   return null;
}
var cookie = "XBE220010130";
if(GetCookie(cookie) == null)
```

```
{
    newwin = open("pslink.jpg","dispwin",
                   "width=200,height=115,menubar=no");
    document.cookie = cookie + "=found; " +
                      "expires=Thu 01-01-2005 00:00:00 GMT;";
}   //]]></xsl:text></xsl:comment></script>
      <title><xsl:value-of select="$title"/></title>
    </head>
    <body bgcolor="#ffcc33">
      <xsl:apply-templates/>
    </body>
</html>
</xsl:template>
```

NOTE

value-of also supports the disable-output-escaping attribute.

Besides text, the template also uses the comment element to insert a comment in HTML. comment, like text, is one of several XSLT elements that create nodes in the output document. Table 5.2 lists them all.

Table 5.2: XSL Elements to Create New Objects

XSL Element	Description
xsl:element	Create element with a computed name
xsl:attribute	Create attribute with a computed value
xsl:attribute-set	Conveniently combine several xsl:attributes
xsl:text	Create a text node
xsl:processing-instruction	Create a processing instruction
xsl:comment	Create a comment
xsl:copy	Copy the current node
xsl:value-of	Compute text by extracting from the source tree or inserting a variable
xsl:if	Instantiate its content if the expression is true
xsl:choose	Select elements to instantiate among possible alternatives
xsl:number	Create formatted number

Creating a Table of Contents

EXAMPLE

The article template creates a table of contents. It uses the for-each element to loop over a set of elements. for-each is very effective when the output document has a very strict structure, as is the case for a table of contents:

```
<xsl:template match="article">
<table bgcolor="#ffffff" width="80%" align="center"><tr><td>
  <xsl:apply-templates select="articleinfo"/>
```

```
<p><xsl:for-each select="sect1/title">
   <a href="#{generate-id()}"><xsl:value-of
      select="."/></a><br/>
 </xsl:for-each></p>
 <xsl:apply-templates select="sect1"/>
</td></tr></table>
</xsl:template>
```

CAUTION

Note that the style sheet is being written in XML; you must write empty elements the XML way. The <br> element is written <br/>. The XSLT processor automatically converts to <br> based on the value of the output element.

The template also uses the generate-id() function. The function assigns a unique identifier to each node in the input document. This is useful to create local references in a document:

OUTPUT

```
<p>
   <a href="#N11">The Value of XSL</a><br/>
   <a href="#N22">XSL and Web Publishing</a><br/>
   <a href="#N34">XSL and Programming</a><br/>
   <a href="#N40">Conclusion</a><br/>
</p>
```

Note that the apply-templates element accepts a select attribute, like the value-of and for-each elements.

In many cases, you can achieve similar results using apply-templates or for-each/value-of. To decide which works better, remember that apply-templates is a recursive walking of the input document. In practice, it means the processor is guided by the structure of the input document. It is well suited when the input format is flexible.

On the contrary, for-each/value-of is built on the structure of the output document and is well suited when the output format is rigid.

Of course, as Listing 5.7 illustrates, it is often a good idea to combine the two.

CAUTION

Because select points to any element in the source tree, paths tend to be longer than for the match attribute. It is common to spell out a complete path from the root to an element.

EXAMPLE

It is not uncommon to find style sheets built around one or more for-each elements. This is particularly handy when the output document is a list or another rigid format. For example, Listing 5.8 compiles a list of titles. The output format is fixed and the style sheet has only one template:

Listing 5.8: `rigid.xsl`

```
<?xml version="1.0"?>
<xsl:stylesheet
    xmlns:xsl="http://www.w3.org/1999/XSL/Transform"
    version="1.0">

<xsl:output method="html"/>

<xsl:template match="/">
<html>
    <head><title>List of titles</title></head>
    <body>
        <xsl:for-each select="//title">
            <p><xsl:value-of select="."/></p>
        </xsl:for-each>
    </body>
</html>
</xsl:template>

</xsl:stylesheet>
```

Priority

EXAMPLE

There are rules to prioritize templates. Without going into too many details, templates with more specific paths take precedence over less specific templates. In the following example, the first template and the third template have a higher priority than the second template, because they match an element more specifically.

```
<xsl:template match="articleinfo/title">
    <h1><xsl:apply-templates/></h1>
</xsl:template>

<xsl:template match="title">
    <h2><a name="{generate-id()}"><xsl:apply-templates/></a></h2>
</xsl:template>

<xsl:template match="sect1[not(position() mod 2 = 1)]/title">
    <h2 align="right"><a name="{generate-id()}"><xsl:apply-templates/></a></h2>
</xsl:template>
```

If there is a conflict between two templates of equivalent priority, the XSL processor can either report an error or choose the template that appears last in the style sheet.

What's Next

In this chapter, you learned how to use XSLT, the transformation half of XSL. The next chapter is dedicated to more styling experiences with FO and CSS.

The combination of XSLT, FO, and CSS gives you total control over how your document is displayed.

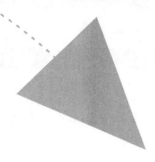

XSL Formatting Objects and Cascading Style Sheets

The previous chapter introduced the most common solution for viewing and styling XML documents. You learned how to use XSLT to convert XML documents to HTML.

This chapter looks at the second half of XSL: the Formatting Objects (FO). Although we have concentrated on XSLT, XSL really is the combination of XSLT and FO. In this chapter, we'll also discuss Cascading Style Sheets (CSS), because conceptually, FO and CSS are similar.

Specifically, in this chapter, you will learn

- How to display XML without converting it to HTML

- How to convert XML to PDF (Portable Document Format, the Adobe Acrobat file format)

- How to customize an XML editor for author comfort

This chapter builds on the previous one. You should not read it unless you are familiar with XSLT.

Rendering XML Without HTML

HTML is a fixed markup and HTML browsers are hard-coded to render it onscreen. More specifically, HTML browsers know that the title element will appear in the title bar; they know that hyperlinks are blue and underlined. They need not be told how to style elements.

XML, on the contrary, has no predefined set of elements. It is up to you, the author, to define elements. Consequently, an XML browser cannot be hard-coded. It needs to be told how to style the elements you defined.

In the previous chapter, you worked around the difficulty by converting XML to HTML. Ultimately, the browser you used was a standard HTML browser rendering regular HTML documents. This is ideal for backward compatibility but it also limits what you can do with XML documents.

You can think of FO as a more sophisticated replacement for HTML. Using FO is similar to what you did in the previous chapter. You still need to convert XML documents but, this time, you convert them to FO not HTML. Like HTML, FO is a fixed set of elements. However, FO gives you significantly greater control over the presentation than HTML and is better suited for printing.

CSS follows yet a different approach. With CSS, no conversion is required. CSS describes how to render the elements directly onscreen or on paper. CSS deals with fonts, colors, text indentation, and so on. Figure 6.1 illustrates the difference between rendering to HTML, to FO, or to CSS.

EXAMPLE

For example, to render a section title with XSLT, you used the following template:

```
<xsl:template match="sect1/title">
    <h2><xsl:apply-templates/></h2>
</xsl:template>
```

The equivalent with XSL (the combination of XSLT and FO) would be

```
<xsl:template match="sect1/title">
    <fo:block font-family="Helvetica" font-weight="bold"
        space-after="5pt">
      <xsl:apply-templates/>
    </fo:block>
</xsl:template>
```

And with CSS, it would be

```
sect1 title
{
  display: block;
  font-style: italic;
}
```

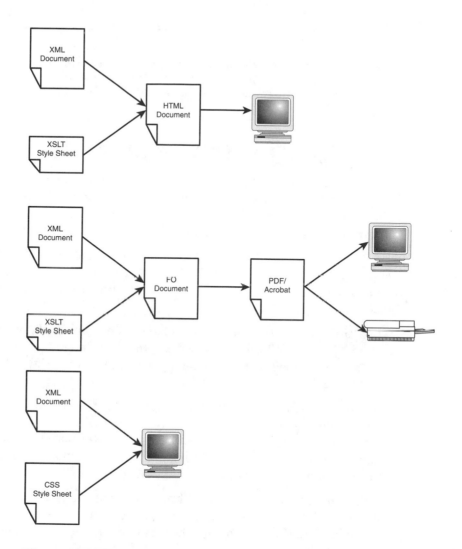

Figure 6.1: *How XSL differs from CSS.*

Let's compare the three options. In the first example, an XSLT style sheet converts the XML title element in two HTML elements: paragraph and italicized text. A regular browser displays the HTML document.

In the second example, another XSLT style sheet converts the XML title element in one FO block element with specific font and spacing. An FO processor renders it to PDF which Adobe Acrobat can display or print.

The CSS style sheet gives information on how to display the title element directly (unlike the other two examples, no conversion is required): It states that the title is an independent block of italicized text.

TIP

If we were to compare XML style sheets with word processor commands, XSLT is similar to the Export or the Save as... commands that save the current document in a different format. CSS is closer to commands in the Format menu and FO borrows from both.

The Basics of CSS and FO

Style sheets on the Web date back to the CSS recommendation, which was originally drafted for HTML. Over the last few years, the complexity of HTML has grown dramatically and many elements, such as <center> or <font>, have given designers more control over the appearance of pages.

However, it was not practical to keep adding elements to HTML. The bigger HTML got, the more complex Web pages became. They proved more difficult to read, more difficult to maintain, and unnecessarily slow to download.

The definitive solution came, as we have seen, from XML, but before working on XML, the W3C had devised a style sheet language for HTML: *CSS*, the *Cascading Style Sheet* language. Although it was originally designed for HTML, CSS also works with XML.

Two versions of CSS have been released so far, CSS1 and CSS2, and a third is under development, CSS3. CSS2 builds on CSS1. It improves XML support, adds new styling options, and supports alternative media such as paper printing and aural rendering (for blind persons). The latest revision of the standard is available from www.w3.org/Style/CSS.

At the time of this writing, most browsers implement at least some support for CSS1. Unfortunately, they are not consistent in the features they support. Browsers that support a subset of CSS2 are appearing on the market.

Microsoft Internet Explorer 5.0 and 5.5 support CSS1. Netscape 6.0 has decent support for CSS2. Opera 5.0 also supports CSS2.

If you are curious, Web Review tests the major browsers for CSS compatibility. The updated results are at webreview.com/wr/pub/guides/style/lboard.html.

After XML was released, it appeared it needed a more powerful style sheet language. CSS is appropriate for simple needs but it lacks the ability to reorganize text (for example, create a table of contents) and its support for printing is limited.

The W3C developed XSL as a style sheet language optimized for XML. It broke it down into two parts: XSLT, with which you are now familiar, and FO, the formatting objects introduced in this chapter.

Simple CSS

EXAMPLE

Listing 6.1 is a simple CSS to render the document you used throughout Chapter 5, "XSL Transformations."

Listing 6.1 `basic.css`

```css
/* a simple style sheet */

article
{
  font-family: Palatino, Garamond, "Times New Roman", serif;
  font-size: 10pt;
  margin: 5px;
}

article, para, title
{
  display: block;
  margin-bottom: 10px;
}

ulink
{
  text-decoration: underline;
  color: blue;
}

articleinfo title
{
  font-size: larger;
  font-weight: bold;
}

sect1 title
{
  font-style: italic;
}

author
{
  display: none;
}
```

As you can see, unlike XSLT, the syntax is distinctively not XML. A CSS style sheet is a list of *rules* (similar to XSL templates). Each rule starts with a *selector* (similar to XSL path) to which *properties* are associated. As the name implies, the selector selects to which element the properties apply.

Figure 6.2 shows the document from Listing 6.2 loaded in Internet Explorer 5.0. To attach the style sheet to a document, you use the familiar xml-style sheet processing instruction (second line in Listing 6.2). The type attribute is text/css. Unlike XSLT, there is no special processor for CSS. The browser is the processor.

Listing 6.2: excerpt.xml

```
<?xml version="1.0"?>
<?xml-stylesheet href="basic.css" type="text/css"?>
<article>
<articleinfo>
 <title>XSL -- First Step in Learning XML</title>
 <author><firstname>Beno&#238;t</firstname>
  <surname>Marchal</surname></author>
</articleinfo>
<sect1><title>The Value of XSL</title>
 <para>This is an excerpt from the September 2000 issue of
  Pineapplesoft Link. To subscribe free visit
   <ulink url="http://www.marchal.com">marchal.com</ulink>.</para>
 <para>Where do you start learning XML? Increasingly my answer
  is with XSL. XSL is a very powerful tool with many
  applications. Many XML applications depend on it. Let's take
  two examples.</para>
 </sect1>
 <sect1>
  <title>XSL and Web Publishing</title>
  <para>As a webmaster you would benefit from using XSL.</para>
  <para>Let's suppose that you decide to support smartphones.
   You will need to redo your web site using WML, the
   <emphasis>wireless markup language</emphasis>, instead of
   HTML. While learning WML is easy, it can take days if not
   months to redo a large web site. Imagine having to edit every
   single page by hand!</para>
  <para>In contrast with XSL, it suffices to update one style
   sheet the changes flow across the entire web site.</para>
 </sect1>
 <sect1>
  <title>XSL and Programming</title>
  <para>The second facet of XSL is the scripting language. XSL
```

Listing 6.2: continued

```
  has many features of scripting languages including loops,
  function calls, variables and more.</para>
 <para>In that respect, XSL is a valuable addition to any
  programmer toolbox. Indeed, as XML popularity keeps growing,
  you will find that you need to manipulate XML documents
  frequently and XSL is the language for so doing.</para>
</sect1>
<sect1>
 <title>Conclusion</title>
 <para>If you're serious about learning XML, learn XSL. XSL is
  a tool to manipulate XML documents for web publishing or
  programming.</para>
</sect1>
</article>
```

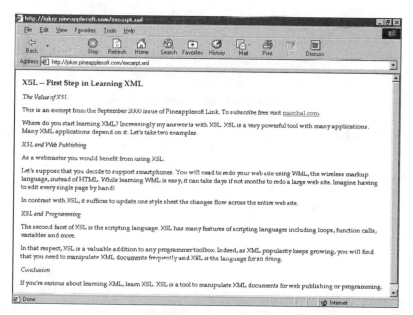

Figure 6.2: *The XML document loaded into a browser.*

CAUTION

The URL (http://www.marchal.com) is not recognized as a hyperlink, although it appears as underlined blue text.

The next sections examine the style sheet in more detail.

Comments

Comments are enclosed in `/*` and `*/`, like in C. They are ignored by the browser; they are intended for human readers only. For example, you can write

```
/* a simple style sheet */
```

Selector

CSS rules are associated with elements through selectors. Unfortunately, selectors use a different syntax than XPaths, even though they are logically similar!

The selector for an element is the element's name. The following example applies a rule to the `article` element:

```
article {
    font-family: Palatino, Garamond, "Times New Roman", serif;
    font-size: 10pt;
    margin: 5px;
}
```

TIP

The `*` character used as a selector matches any elements.

To select several elements, separate them with commas. The following example applies to the `article`, `para`, and `title` elements. It is equivalent to `article | para | title` in XSLT. Notice that there are two rules for the `article` element (this one and the previous one); their contents are simply merged.

```
article, para, title {
    display: block;
    margin-bottom: 10px;
}
```

To select an element depending on its ancestor, list the two elements separated by spaces. The following example selects every `title` with an `articleinfo` ancestor but it ignores a title within a `sect1`. Beware that the selector applies to all descendants from `articleinfo`. In other words, it is equivalent to the `articleinfo//title` XPath, not `articleinfo/title`.

```
articleinfo title {
    font-size: larger;
    font-weight: bold;
}
```

CSS Properties

EXAMPLE

The list of properties is enclosed in curly brackets, after the selector. Each property has a name followed by a colon and one or more values (separated by comas). A semicolon terminates each property.

```
article {
    font-family: Palatino, Garamond, "Times New Roman", serif;
    font-size: 10pt;
    margin: 5px;
}
```

Most properties are readable. The `font-family` selects the font, `margin` sets the margins, `font-size` is the font size, and so on. You will study the properties in more detail in the second half of this chapter.

The `display` property may be the most confusing. `display` controls how the element is being displayed. The options are `block`, `inline`, `list-item`, and `none`. `block` treats the element as a paragraph, with a line break before and after it. `inline` inserts no breaks whereas `none` hides the element. Lists are outside the scope of this chapter.

Simple FO

CSS is a simple and efficient styling mechanism. However, it cannot reorganize the document being styled, which is a serious limitation for XML documents. For example, unlike XSLT, it is not possible to build a table of contents or compile an index. What are the benefits of using semantic-rich markup if you don't take advantage of it?

However, XSLT is just a transformation mechanism. You need a target language that describes how to format the document. Today, the target language is often HTML, but HTML may be too limited for complex designs. Also, what HTML offers is not suitable for printing.

In practice, it would be impossible to create a book with the combination of XSLT and HTML. FO was introduced as a richer, better target language than HTML. FO has rich graphic primitives and is ideally suited for printing.

CAUTION

At the time of writing, FO is still under development. Although I don't anticipate major changes, you might want to visit www.w3.org/Style/XSL for the official recommendation. If required, I will post updates at www.marchal.com and www.mcp.com.

FO Elements

At first sight, FO appears as a rewriting of CSS properties in XML markup. There are elements and attributes for all CSS properties. FO improves on CSS by offering more options, such as hyperlinks and proper page management.

Listing 6.3 is a simple XSL style sheet that combines XSLT and FO. Figure 6.3 shows the result in Adobe Acrobat. The next section explains how to create the Acrobat file.

Listing 6.3: `basic.xsl`

```
<?xml version="1.0"?>
<xsl:stylesheet
    xmlns:xsl="http://www.w3.org/1999/XSL/Transform"
    xmlns:fo="http://www.w3.org/1999/XSL/Format"
    version="1.0">

<xsl:output method="xml" indent="yes"/>

<xsl:template match="/">
    <fo:root>
        <fo:layout-master-set>
            <fo:simple-page-master master-name="basic"
                margin-right="1in" margin-left="1in"
                margin-bottom="1in" margin-top="1in"
                page-width="8.5in" page-height="11in">
                <fo:region-body/>
            </fo:simple-page-master>
        </fo:layout-master-set>
        <xsl:apply-templates/>
    </fo:root>
</xsl:template>

<xsl:template match="article">
    <fo:page-sequence master-name="basic">
        <fo:flow flow-name="xsl-region-body">
            <fo:block font-family="Times Roman" font-size="11pt">
                <xsl:apply-templates/>
            </fo:block>
        </fo:flow>
    </fo:page-sequence>
</xsl:template>

<xsl:template match="articleinfo/title">
    <fo:block font-family="Helvetica" font-weight="bold" font-size="18pt"
        space-after="9pt">
```

Listing 6.3: continued

```
        <xsl:apply-templates/>
    </fo:block>
</xsl:template>

<xsl:template match="sect1/title">
    <fo:block font-family="Helvetica" font-weight="bold" space-after="5pt">
        <xsl:apply-templates/>
    </fo:block>
</xsl:template>

<xsl:template match="ulink">
    <fo:basic-link external-destination="{@url}" color="blue">
    <xsl:apply-templates/></fo:basic-link>
</xsl:template>

<xsl:template match="emphasis">
    <fo:inline font-weight="bold"><xsl:apply-templates/></fo:inline>
</xsl:template>

<xsl:template match="para">
    <fo:block space-after="5pt">
        <xsl:apply-templates/>
    </fo:block>
</xsl:template>

<xsl:template match="author">
    <fo:block font-style="italic" space-after="5pt">by <xsl:apply-
templates/></fo:block>
</xsl:template>

</xsl:stylesheet>
```

The style sheet is a list of XSLT templates. The templates transform the original XML document into a new XML document with FO markup.

If you compare Listings 6.1 and 6.3, you will recognize many properties. For example, the `display: block` CSS property becomes the `fo:block` element in FO. The `font-family` CSS property has a matching `font-family` FO attribute.

Applying the Style Sheet

Applying the XSL style sheet is a two-step process. First, use the XSLT processor with Listing 6.3. It creates an XML document similar to Listing 6.4. Notice that Listing 6.4 has the same text as Listing 6.2, but the markup is now FO.

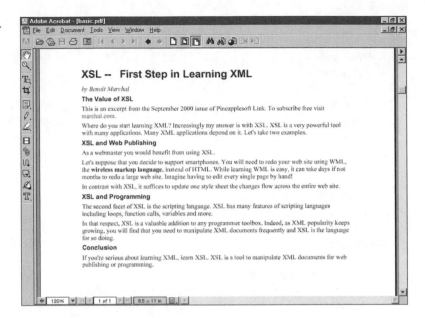

Figure 6.3: *Rendering an XML document to PDF.*

✔ Refer to Chapter 5, "XSL Transformations," for instructions on how to apply XSLT style sheets.

Listing 6.4: `basic.fo`

```
<?xml version="1.0" encoding="UTF-8"?>
<fo:root xmlns:fo="http://www.w3.org/1999/XSL/Format">
    <fo:layout-master-set>
        <fo:simple-page-master page-height="11in"
            page-width="8.5in" margin-top="1in"
            margin-bottom="1in" margin-left="1in"
            margin-right="1in" master-name="basic">
            <fo:region-body/>
        </fo:simple-page-master>
    </fo:layout-master-set>
    <fo:page-sequence master-name="basic">
        <fo:flow flow-name="xsl-region-body">
            <fo:block font-size="11pt"
                    font-family="Times Roman">

<fo:block space-after="9pt" font-size="18pt" font-weight="bold"
    font-family="Helvetica">XSL -- First Step in Learning XML</fo:block>
<fo:block space-after="5pt" font-style="italic">by Benoît
 Marchal</fo:block>
```

Listing 6.4: continued

```
<fo:block space-after="5pt" font-weight="bold"
    font-family="Helvetica">The Value of XSL</fo:block>
 <fo:block space-after="5pt">This is an excerpt from the
    September 2000 issue of Pineapplesoft Link. To subscribe
    free visit <fo:basic-link color="blue"
    external-destination="http://www.marchal.com">marchal.com
    </fo:basic-link>.</fo:block>
<fo:block space-after="5pt">Where do you start learning XML?
    Increasingly my answer is with XSL. XSL is a very powerful
    tool with many applications. Many XML applications depend
    on it. Let's take two examples.</fo:block>


<fo:block space-after="5pt" font-weight="bold"
    font-family="Helvetica">XSL and Web Publishing</fo:block>
<fo:block space-after="5pt">As a webmaster you would benefit
    from using XSL.</fo:block>
<fo:block space-after="5pt">Let's suppose that you decide to
    support smartphones. You will need to redo your web site
    using WML, the <fo:inline font-weight="bold">wireless
    markup language</fo:inline>, instead of HTML. While
    learning WML is easy, it can take days if not months to
    redo a large web site. Imagine having to edit every
    single page by hand!</fo:block>
<fo:block space-after="5pt">In contrast with XSL, it suffices
    to update one style sheet the changes flow across the
    entire web site.</fo:block>


<fo:block space-after="5pt" font-weight="bold"
    font-family="Helvetica">XSL and Programming</fo:block>
<fo:block space-after="5pt">The second facet of XSL is the
    scripting language. XSL has many features of scripting
    languages including loops, function calls, variables and
    more.</fo:block>
<fo:block space-after="5pt">In that respect, XSL is a valuable
    addition to any programmer toolbox. Indeed, as XML
    popularity keeps growing, you will find that you need to
    manipulate XML documents frequently and XSL is the language
    for so doing.</fo:block>


<fo:block space-after="5pt" font-weight="bold"
    font-family="Helvetica">Conclusion</fo:block>
```

Listing 6.4: continued

```
<fo:block space-after="5pt">If you're serious about learning
   XML, learn XSL. XSL is a tool to manipulate XML documents
   for web publishing or programming.</fo:block>

</fo:block>
       </fo:flow>
   </fo:page-sequence>
</fo:root>
```

The first step is very similar to what we did in the previous chapter. The second step is new. You need to convert the FO (Listing 6.4) in Adobe Acrobat's PDF format using an FO processor.

More specifically, you will be using FOP—an FO processor developed by the Apache project. A commercial FO processor is available from www.renderx.com.

CAUTION

At the time of this writing, FOP supports a subset of FO. Consult the FOP documentation for more details.

NOTE

Although, at the time of this writing, most FO processors generate PDF documents, this is not a W3C requirement. The XSL recommendation describes formatting in abstract terms.

Most FO implementers choose PDF because it is available on many platforms, is well documented, and prints well. Indeed PDF was developed by Adobe and incorporates many PostScript features.

Incidentally, the latest version of FOP has a print-preview option that bypasses PDF entirely.

You can download the latest version of FOP from xml.apache.org. By default, it ships with a command-line interface. To make your life easier, I've wrapped a graphical user interface around it. You can download it from www.marchal.com and www.mcp.com.

You also will need the free Acrobat reader available from www.adobe.com/acrobat. By default, Adobe points to the commercial version of Acrobat. Look under related products for the free reader.

The interface to FOP, Format, is similar to Transform from Chapter 5: browse for the FO file, the output PDF, and then hit the Format button (see Figure 6.4). Make sure you select Listing 6.4, the output from Transform, and not Listing 6.3, the style sheet itself.

CAUTION

You will get a fatal error message similar to `c:\xbe2\ch6\boxes.pdf` (The process cannot access the file because it is being used by another process) if the PDF file is opened in Adobe Acrobat. Simply close it and try again.

TIP

Because it is a two-step process, you need to transform and format if you update the style sheet or the document.

If you are comfortable with the DOS command line, FOP comes with a tool that applies the two steps in one go. See the FOP user guide for more information.

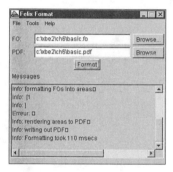

Figure 6.4: *Using FOP to create PDF.*

FO Style Sheet Overview

FO is defined in the `http://www.w3.org/1999/XSL/Format` namespace. The style sheet declares the namespace and associates it with the `fo` prefix:

`xmlns:fo="http://www.w3.org/1999/XSL/Format"`

The output method is set to `xml`; indeed, FO is an XML vocabulary:

`<xsl:output method="xml" indent="yes"/>`

An FO document is enclosed in an element called `root`. The first element must be a `layout master-set` that includes one or more page master elements. As seen earlier in Listing 6.3, there is one `simple page-master` element that defines the page size. It is given a name (its `master-name` attribute) because, as you will see, some documents have more than one page master.

`simple-page-master` declares the page width and height (respectively, `page-width` and `page-height` attributes) as well as the page margins (through the various `margin-...` attributes).

The page master contains one or more region elements. Again, in Listing 6.3, there is only one region-body element. The region-body indicates where the main text will appear. You'll learn how to insert headers and footers as regions at the end of this chapter.

Following the layout-master-set is the document itself. Earlier in Listing 6.3, the familiar XSLT apply-templates element calls the remainder of the style sheet (everything you learned about XSLT in the previous chapter is still valid).

```
<xsl:template match="/">
   <fo:root>
      <fo:layout-master-set>
         <fo:simple-page-master master-name="basic"
             margin-right="1in" margin-left="1in"
             margin-bottom="1in" margin-top="1in"
             page-width="8.5in" page-height="11in">
            <fo:region-body/>
         </fo:simple-page-master>
      </fo:layout-master-set>
      <xsl:apply-templates/>
   </fo:root>
</xsl:template>
```

Following the layout-master-set is a page-sequence, which is generated in the article template. The page-sequence contains the text. The FO processor will insert page breaks as needed. The page-sequence, through its master-name attribute, selects the page master defined previously.

Within the page sequence is one or more flow elements. Each flow matches one region (through the flow-name attribute) defined in the page master. In this case, the page master defines only one "body" region; therefore, there is only one flow-name element. It selects the "body" region as xsl-region-body.

The document content is one or more block element. A block element creates a paragraph (line break after the element), as the CSS display:block property.

```
<xsl:template match="article">
   <fo:page-sequence master-name="basic">
      <fo:flow flow-name="xsl-region-body">
         <fo:block font-family="Times Roman" font-size="11pt">
            <xsl:apply-templates/>
         </fo:block>
      </fo:flow>
   </fo:page-sequence>
</xsl:template>
```

The `block` has various attributes to control the presentation: `font-family`, `font-size`, and more. The attributes are similar to corresponding CSS properties.

TIP

There is no equivalent to CSS's `display:none` but you can achieve the same result by writing an empty XSLT template:

```
<xsl:template match="author"/>
```

Two more templates are worth studying, the `ulink` template, which uses the `basic-link` element to create a hyperlink. Unlike CSS, FO supports hyperlinks. Indeed, if you click on the URL in the PDF document, it works.

```
<xsl:template match="ulink">
  <fo:basic-link external-destination="{@url}" color="blue">
  <xsl:apply-templates/></fo:basic-link>
</xsl:template>
```

The `emphasis` template has an `inline` element which works like CSS `display:inline`. It contains text with no line breaks.

```
<xsl:template match="emphasis">
  <fo:inline font-weight="bold"><xsl:apply-templates/></fo:inline>
</xsl:template>
```

Flow Objects and Areas

It's time to drill down into the list of CSS properties and formatting objects. Although there are some differences in how CSS and FO work, they are remarkably coherent, so most of what you'll learn in this section applies to both CSS and FO.

Flow Objects

To render the screen or print a page, the processor uses *flow objects*. The concept is very simple: The document flows from the top to the bottom of the page or screen. Anything in the flow (characters, words, paragraphs, images) is a flow object.

Style sheets associate properties to flow objects. Through selectors, CSS can address most flow objects from the element upward. The recommendation even specifies how to associate properties to characters or words but browsers don't implement it, yet. As we have seen, FO takes a different road and defines specific XML elements for the flow objects (such as `block`, `inline`, or `basic-link`).

Properties Inheritance

Flow objects inherit most of their properties from their parents.

Look at Listing 6.4 again. The content is enclosed in a block with specific font information. This takes advantage of inheritance: The block specifies default font. Because the other blocks in the document are enclosed within it, they inherit the default information. Some blocks choose to override the inherited properties.

```
<fo:block font-size="11pt"
    font-family="Times Roman">
    <fo:block space-after="9pt" font-size="18pt" font-weight="bold"
        font-family="Helvetica">XSL -- First Step in Learning XML</fo:block>
    <!-- ... -->
</fo:block>
```

In practice, it means that sections inherit their properties from the article, because sections are included in the article. Paragraphs in turn inherit their properties from sections.

However, if a rule is attached to paragraphs, it overrides some of the properties inherited from sections. The hyperlink inherits its properties from its ancestor, the paragraph, including overridden properties. Figure 6.5 illustrates the inheritance.

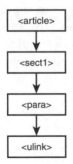

Figure 6.5: *Inheriting properties.*

Most properties are inherited. Turn your attention to the few properties not inherited in the following discussion.

Rectangular Areas or Boxes

On the screen or on paper, flow objects are rendered as rectangular areas (FO jargon) or boxes (CSS jargon). Typically, you don't see the rectangles but Listing 6.5 makes most of them visible (through the border-width property). Figure 6.6 shows the result in Adobe Acrobat.

Listing 6.5: boxes.xsl

```xml
<?xml version="1.0"?>
<xsl:stylesheet
    xmlns:xsl="http://www.w3.org/1999/XSL/Transform"
    xmlns:fo="http://www.w3.org/1999/XSL/Format"
    version="1.0">

<xsl:output method="xml" indent="yes"/>

<xsl:template match="/">
   <fo:root>
      <fo:layout-master-set>
         <fo:simple-page-master master-name="basic"
             margin-right="1in" margin-left="1in"
             margin-bottom="1in" margin-top="1in"
             page-width="8.5in" page-height="11in">
            <fo:region-body/>
         </fo:simple-page-master>
      </fo:layout-master-set>
      <xsl:apply-templates/>
   </fo:root>
</xsl:template>

<xsl:template match="article">
   <fo:page-sequence master-name="basic">
      <fo:flow flow-name="xsl-region-body">
         <fo:block font-family="Times Roman" font-size="11pt">
            <xsl:apply-templates/>
         </fo:block>
      </fo:flow>
   </fo:page-sequence>
</xsl:template>

<xsl:template match="ulink | emphasis | firstname | surname">
   <xsl:apply-templates/>
</xsl:template>

<xsl:template match="*">
   <fo:block border-style="solid" border-width="1pt"
                             space-after="7pt">
      <xsl:apply-templates/>
   </fo:block>
</xsl:template>

</xsl:stylesheet>
```

OUTPUT

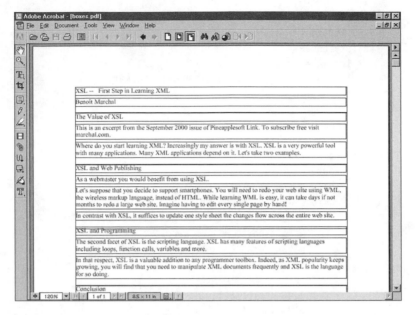

Figure 6.6: *Making the rectangles visible.*

FO and CSS support several types of rectangles. The important ones are

- *Block area*, which has a line break before and after it. It is the most important element in organizing a document onscreen. In the examples, paragraphs are rendered as blocks.

- *Inline area*, which appears in a single line within a block box. There are no line breaks before or after it. In the examples, the link is rendered with an inline box.

The processor may also create anonymous areas. For example, when a paragraph spans two pages, the processor creates two rectangular areas (one on each page), even though the style sheet treats the whole paragraph as one area.

Figure 6.7 illustrates the major properties of rectangular areas:

- *Margin*, the space between the border and the edges.

- *Border*, a rectangle around the box.

- *Padding*, the space between the text and the border.

- *Element*, the content.

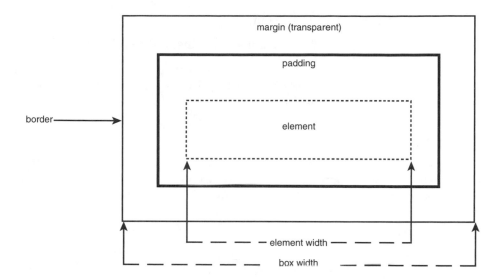

Figure 6.7: *Rectangular area properties.*

Property Values

The CSS and FO properties commonly use three values: length, percentage, and color. Before going into the specifics of properties, let's first review these values.

EXAMPLE

Length

Lengths are used for widths, heights, and sizes. A *length* is a number followed by a unit with no spaces between them. For example, the following two FO properties define a font size of 18 points and a space after the element of 0.5em (half a line), respectively:

```
font-size="18pt"
space-after="0.5em"
```

Units are represented by two-letter abbreviations:

- px: pixels
- in: inches
- cm: centimeters
- mm: millimeters
- pt: points, where a point is 1/72 inch

- pc: picas, where a pica is 12 points

- em: ems, the height of the element's font, this unit is relative to the element's font

- ex: x-height, the height of the "x" letter, this unit is relative to the element's font and is defined only for CSS

EXAMPLE

Percentage

Percentages are used for width, height, and position. A *percentage* is a number followed by the percent sign "%". There are no spaces between the number and the sign. For example, the following CSS rule defines a line height, which is twice the text:

```
line-height: 200%
```

EXAMPLE

Color

Many properties accept a color value. There are three solutions to represent a color. The first one (borrowed from HTML) has the form: `#00ffe1`; that is, an RGB value in hexadecimal. This CSS example selects a green background:

```
background-color: #00ff00
```

NOTE

With RGB, three numbers represent the proportion of red, green, and blue in the color. The three numbers are represented in hexadecimal and their value goes from 0 to ff.

Therefore #ff0000 is pure red (maximum red, no green or blue) whereas #000022 is light blue (no red or green, some blue).

Shades of gray have the same amount of red, green, and blue. The following are all shades of gray: #222222, #555555, and #cccccc.

Most graphics programs can tell you the amount of red, green, and blue in a color.

EXAMPLE

If, like me, you prefer readable colors to RGB values, you will turn to the second solution: color keywords. Acceptable values are `black`, `maroon`, `green`, `navy`, `silver`, `red`, `lime`, `blue`, `gray`, `purple`, `olive`, `teal`, `white`, `fuchsia`, `yellow`, and `aqua`. The following FO example selects the blue color:

```
color="blue"
```

The last option is to use functions. CSS defines only one function: `rgb()` which takes three integer values (from 0 to 255). FO also supports the `system-color()` and `icc-color()` functions. The former selects a system-specific color whereas the latter uses colors defined by the International

Color Consortium (www.color.org). The CSS following example selects blue text:

```
color: rgb(0,0,255)
```

Box Properties

It is futile to try to cover every property in this chapter. There are so many properties that I could fill a book with them. Instead, I will concentrate on the most frequently used properties. We will start with the properties associated with boxes.

For more information on specific properties, consult the recommendations themselves at www.w3.org/Style.

EXAMPLE

Margin Properties

CSS has four properties to control the margins of a box. margin-top, margin-right, margin-bottom, and margin-left apply to each side of the margin, as in the following FO example:

```
margin-top="10px"
```

Acceptable values include an absolute length, a percentage relative to the parent's width, or the value auto. As the name implies, auto deduces the length from the size of the content.

EXAMPLE

Having four properties may require too much writing. Fortunately, there is a shorthand: Margin property sets the four sides in one pass. It takes either one value if the four margins have the same length or four values in the order top, right, bottom, and left. The following FO example sets the margin to 10 pixels wide in every direction:

```
margin="10px"
```

EXAMPLE

Padding Properties

Padding is defined exactly like margins with the properties padding-top, padding-right, padding-bottom, padding-left, and padding, except that auto is not an acceptable value. The following CSS example sets a padding of 0.2 inch:

```
padding: 0.2in;
```

EXAMPLE

Spacing Properties

FO defines one additional set of properties: space-before and space-after. They control the amount of space before and after the block, respectively. The following example adds a space of 5 points after the block:

```
space-after="5pt"
```

CAUTION

At the time of this writing, FOP does not recognize the margin and padding properties. Use spacing properties instead.

EXAMPLE

Border Style Properties

The `border-left-style`, `border-right-style`, `border-top-style`, `border-bottom-style`, and `border-style` properties set the style of the border to `none`, `hidden`, `dotted`, `dashed`, `solid`, `double`, `groove`, `ridge`, `inset`, or `outset`. The following FO example paints a solid border around the element:

```
border-style="solid"
```

TIP

The border of an element is not visible until the `border-style` property is set. By default, `border-style` is set to none.

EXAMPLE

Border Width Properties

The `border-top-width`, `border-right-width`, `border-bottom-width`, and `border-left-width` properties control the width of each border independently. Acceptable values are `thin`, `medium`, `thick`, or an absolute length.

It is easier to set the four values at once, with the `border-width` property, as in the following CSS example:

```
border-width: thin;
```

Text and Font Properties

After box properties, text and font properties are the most commonly used ones.

EXAMPLE

Font Name

The `font-family` property selects the name of the font. It is a good idea to list several font names in case the preferred font is not available. The following CSS example attempts to select a serif font. The list goes from more specific font (Palatino) to more common ones (Times New Roman). The list ends with a generic family name for maximal safety:

```
font-family: Palatino, Garamond, "Times New Roman", serif;
```

Generic names (`serif`, `sans-serif`, `cursive`, `fantasy`, and `monospace`) select a typical font for the family. They are useful safeguards.Figure 6.8 shows the generic fonts installed on my computer.

serif

sans-serif

cursive

FANTASY

`monospace`

Figure 6.8: *Font samples on my machine.*

EXAMPLE

Font Size

As the name implies, the `font-size` property selects the size of characters. The `font-size` value can be a length or `xx-small`, `x-small`, `small`, `medium`, `large`, `x-large`, and `xx-large`. Finally, it is possible to use values relative to the inherited size: `larger` and `smaller`.

The medium size font is around 10 points so the following two FO examples should be identical:

```
font-size="medium"
font-size="10pt"
```

EXAMPLE

Font Style and Weight

The `font-style` and `font-weight` properties indicate whether the font is italicized or bold, respectively. The following CSS example sets the font to bold and italic.

```
font-weight: bold;
font-style: italic;
```

`font-style` accepts only three values: `normal`, `italic`, and `oblique`. Italic and oblique are similar but italic uses a special font drawn for italic, whereas oblique is the original font bent.

`font-weight` accepts the following values: `normal`, `bold`, `bolder`, `lighter`, `100`, `200`, `300`, `400`, `500`, `600`, `700`, `800`, `900`.

`normal` and `bold` are self-explanatory. `bolder` and `lighter` are relative to the inherited weight value. `normal` is equivalent to `400` and bold is `700`.

Text Decoration

The `text-decoration` property controls the appearance of the text. It takes the following values: `none`, `underline`, `no-underline`, `overline`, `no-overline`, `line-through`, `no-line-through`, `blink`, or `no-blink`. The following CSS example creates underlined text.

```
text-decoration: underline;
```

Text Alignment

There are two properties to control text alignment: `text-align` controls alignment against the left and right margins, whereas `vertical-align` specifies vertical alignment. Use vertical alignment to write x^2. The following example prints the text in superscript justified against the right margin.

```
text-align="right" vertical-align="super"
```

`text-align` accepts the `start`, `end`, `inside`, `outside`, `left`, `right`, `center`, and `justify`. `vertical-align` accepts `baseline`, `sub`, `super`, `top`, `text-top`, `middle`, `bottom`, `text-bottom`, or a percentage.

Text Indent and Line Height

The `text-indent` and `line-height` properties define, respectively, the indentation of the first line and the spacing between adjacent lines. The following example indents the element by 0.5 inch. It also defines the line height as being 120% of the font size.

```
text-indent: 0.5in;
line-height: 120%;
```

`text-ident` accepts a percentage (relative to the parent's element) or a length. `line-height` defines the spacing between adjacent lines as `normal`, as a length, as a percentage (relative to the font size), or as a number. If the value is a number, the line height is equal to the font size times the number.

Some Advanced Features

We've barely scratched the surface of CSS and FO, but you have learned enough properties to produce good-looking documents. In this section, we'll look at some additional features that help create better-looking documents.

Listing 6.6 demonstrates some advanced concepts for smart-looking documents. With these advanced concepts you create documents that look as good as word processor documents. Figure 6.9 loads the result in Adobe Acrobat.

Listing 6.6: `smart.xsl`

```xml
<?xml version="1.0"?>
<xsl:stylesheet
    xmlns:xsl="http://www.w3.org/1999/XSL/Transform"
    xmlns:fo="http://www.w3.org/1999/XSL/Format"
    version="1.0">

<xsl:output method="xml" indent="yes"/>

<xsl:param name="font-family-title">Helvetica</xsl:param>
<xsl:param name="font-family-normal">Times Roman</xsl:param>
<xsl:param name="logo">/xbe2/chr6/listings/pslink.jpg</xsl:param>

<xsl:template match="/">
    <fo:root>
        <fo:layout-master-set>
            <fo:simple-page-master master-name="first"
                margin-right="1in" margin-left="1in"
                margin-bottom="1in" margin-top="1in"
                page-width="8.5in" page-height="11in">
                <fo:region-body margin-bottom="0.5in"/>
                <fo:region-after extent="0.2in"/>
            </fo:simple-page-master>
            <fo:simple-page-master master-name="rest"
                margin-right="1in" margin-left="1in"
                margin-bottom="0.5in" margin-top="0.5in"
                page-width="8.5in" page-height="11in">
                <fo:region-before extent="0.5in"/>
                <fo:region-body margin-top="0.5in"
                    margin-bottom="0.5in"/>
                <fo:region-after extent="0.2in"/>
            </fo:simple-page-master>
            <fo:page-sequence-master master-name="smart">
                <fo:repeatable-page-master-alternatives>
                    <fo:conditional-page-master-reference
                        master-name="first"
                        page-position="first"/>
                    <fo:conditional-page-master-reference
                        master-name="rest"/>
                </fo:repeatable-page-master-alternatives>
            </fo:page-sequence-master>
        </fo:layout-master-set>
        <xsl:apply-templates/>
    </fo:root>
</xsl:template>
```

Listing 6.6: continued

```
<xsl:template match="article">
    <fo:page-sequence master-name="smart">
        <fo:static-content flow-name="xsl-region-before">
            <fo:block text-align="end"
                      font-size="11pt"
                      font-family="{$font-family-title}">
                <xsl:value-of select="articleinfo/title"/>
            </fo:block>
        </fo:static-content>
        <fo:flow flow-name="xsl-region-body">
            <fo:block font-family="{$font-family-normal}"
                 font-size="11pt">
                <xsl:apply-templates/>
            </fo:block>
        </fo:flow>
        <fo:static-content flow-name="xsl-region-after">
            <fo:block text-align="end"
                      font-size="11pt"
                      font-family="{$font-family-title}">
                Page <fo:page-number/> of <fo:page-number-citation
                                              ref-id="lastPage"/>
            </fo:block>
        </fo:static-content>
    </fo:page-sequence>
</xsl:template>

<xsl:template match="articleinfo">
    <xsl:apply-templates/>
    <fo:block font-family="{$font-family-title}"
         font-weight="bold" space-after="0.5em">Content</fo:block>
    <fo:table space-after="0.5em">
        <fo:table-column column-width="3in"/>
        <fo:table-column column-width="1in"/>
        <fo:table-body>
            <xsl:for-each select="/article/sect1/title">
                <fo:table-row>
                    <fo:table-cell>
                        <fo:block>
                            <fo:basic-link
                                internal-destination="{generate-id()}"
                                color="blue"><xsl:value-of select="."/>
                            </fo:basic-link>
                        </fo:block>
                    </fo:table-cell>
                    <fo:table-cell>
```

Listing 6.6: continued

```
                    <fo:block text-align="end">
                        <fo:page-number-citation
                            ref-id="{generate-id()}"/>
                    </fo:block>
                </fo:table-cell>
            </fo:table-row>
        </xsl:for-each>
      </fo:table-body>
    </fo:table>
</xsl:template>

<xsl:template match="articleinfo/title">
    <fo:block space-after="1em">
        <fo:external-graphic
            src="{$logo}"/>
    </fo:block>
    <fo:block font-family="{$font-family-title}"
        font-weight="bold" font-size="18pt" space-after="0.5em">
        <xsl:apply-templates/>
    </fo:block>
</xsl:template>

<xsl:template match="author">
    <fo:block font-family="{$font-family-title}"
        font-style="italic" space-after="0.5em">
        <xsl:text>by </xsl:text>
        <xsl:apply-templates/>
    </fo:block>
</xsl:template>

<xsl:template match="sect1/title">
    <fo:block id="{generate-id()}"
        font-family="{$font-family-title}" font-weight="bold"
        space-after="0.5em"><xsl:apply-templates/></fo:block>
</xsl:template>

<xsl:template match="ulink">
    <fo:basic-link external-destination="{@url}"
        color="blue"><xsl:apply-templates/></fo:basic-link>
</xsl:template>

<xsl:template match="emphasis">
    <fo:inline
        font-weight="bold"><xsl:apply-templates/></fo:inline>
</xsl:template>
```

Listing 6.6: continued

```
<xsl:template match="para">
   <fo:block space-after="0.5em">
      <xsl:apply-templates/>
   </fo:block>
</xsl:template>

<xsl:template
   match="sect1[position()=last()]/para[position()=last()]">
   <fo:block>
      <xsl:apply-templates/>
      <fo:inline id="lastPage"
         font-family="ZapfDingbats"> &#167;</fo:inline>
   </fo:block>
</xsl:template>

</xsl:stylesheet>
```

OUTPUT

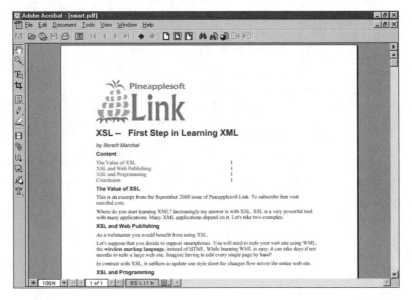

Figure 6.9: Better formatting in Adobe Acrobat.

CAUTION

This style sheet inserts a JPEG image and FOP is very sensitive to filenames. If it seems to hang, double-check that the filename (in the "logo" parameter) is correct on your machine. Update the style sheet if required and reapply both Transform and Format.

The style sheet starts by defining a few parameters. This is not required by FO but it makes it easier to maintain. For example, to change the font title, it suffices to change the value of one parameter. Also, the filename for the logo is defined as a parameter because it may be different on your system:

```
<xsl:param name="font-family-title">Helvetica</xsl:param>
<xsl:param name="font-family-normal">Times Roman</xsl:param>
<xsl:param name="logo">/xbe2/ch6/listings/pslink.jpg</xsl:param>
```

More interestingly, this style sheet defines two page masters (named first and rest). They include up to three regions: the main body (region-body), header (region-before), and footer (region-after). Notice that the first page master does not define a header.

```
<fo:simple-page-master master-name="first"
   margin-right="1in" margin-left="1in"
   margin-bottom="1in" margin-top="1in"
   page-width="8.5in" page-height="11in">
   <fo:region-body margin-bottom="0.5in"/>
   <fo:region-after extent="0.2in"/>
</fo:simple-page-master>
<fo:simple-page-master master-name="rest"
   margin-right="1in" margin-left="1in"
   margin-bottom="0.5in" margin-top="0.5in"
   page-width="8.5in" page-height="11in">
   <fo:region-before extent="0.5in"/>
   <fo:region-body margin-top="0.5in"
       margin-bottom="0.5in"/>
   <fo:region-after extent="0.2in"/>
</fo:simple-page-master>
```

We want the first page to follow the first page master and the rest of the document to follow the rest of the page master. In other words, we don't want a header on the first page.

We can achieve this through a page-sequence master element. It contains conditional-page-master-alternatives elements pointing to the page masters defined previously. The page-position attribute acts as a selector. The first page master applies to the first page, the other master applies to the remainder of the document.

```
<fo:page-sequence-master master-name="smart">
    <fo:repeatable-page-master-alternatives>
       <fo:conditional-page-master-reference
           master-name="first"
           page-position="first"/>
         <fo:conditional-page-master-reference
           master-name="rest"/>
```

```
        </fo:repeatable-page-master-alternatives>
</fo:page-sequence-master>
```

The page-sequence-master is itself a page master so we can select it through the master-name attribute in page-sequence:

```
<fo:page-sequence master-name="smart">
```

The header and the footer are generated through static-content (such as fixed content) with a flow-name attribute matching the regions we've just defined (xsl-region-after matches the region-after element—the footer).

Pay special attention to the footer. It uses the page-number and page-number-citation elements to insert page numbering.

```
<fo:static-content flow-name="xsl-region-after">
   <fo:block text-align="end"
             font-size="11pt"
             font-family="{$font-family-title}">
      Page <fo:page-number/> of <fo:page-number-citation
                                    ref-id="lastPage"/>
   </fo:block>
</fo:static-content>
```

page-number is the current page number, whereas page-number-citation points to an element on another page. The trick is to point to an element on the last page. We achieve this through a special template that matches the last paragraph of the last section. I also choose to insert a dingbat, but you could have used an empty inline element. What matters is the id attribute to which the page-number-citation points.

```
<xsl:template
    match="sect1[position()=last()]/para[position()=last()]">
   <fo:block>
      <xsl:apply-templates/>
      <fo:inline id="lastPage"
          font-family="ZapfDingbats"> &#167;</fo:inline>
   </fo:block>
</xsl:template>
```

A good document should include a table of contents, and the style sheet creates it as a table.

The table model in FO is similar to HTML tables. The table is a table element. New rows start with the table-row element (tr in HTML); new cells start with the table-cell element (td in HTML).

At the time of writing, FOP cannot compute a column width so you need to insert a table-column element with a column-width attribute for each column in the table (two in this case).

The table of contents itself uses the now familiar page-number-citation element. It also creates hyperlinks, but note the use of an internal-destination attribute to indicate that those links are internal to the document.

```
<fo:table space-after="0.5em">
   <fo:table-column column-width="3in"/>
   <fo:table-column column-width="1in"/>
   <fo:table-body>
      <xsl:for-each select="/article/sect1/title">
         <fo:table-row>
            <fo:table-cell>
               <fo:block>
                  <fo:basic-link
                     internal-destination="{generate-id()}"
                     color="blue"><xsl:value-of select="."/>
                  </fo:basic-link>
               </fo:block>
            </fo:table-cell>
            <fo:table-cell>
               <fo:block text-align="end">
                  <fo:page-number-citation
                     ref-id="{generate-id()}"/>
               </fo:block>
            </fo:table-cell>
         </fo:table-row>
      </xsl:for-each>
   </fo:table-body>
</fo:table>
```

The style sheet also inserts a JPEG image with the external-graphic element. As I have already indicated, FOP is very sensitive to filenames so double-check it in case of problems with this style sheet.

```
<fo:external-graphic src="{$logo}"/>
```

When Should You Use Which

You have learned three styling options for XML:

- XSLT, transforming the document to HTML;
- FO, ultimately transforming the document to PDF;
- CSS, displaying the document unmodified.

Which one should you use? The tools you use will guide your decision. If you are publishing a Web site, XSLT is the best approach, because it creates HTML documents that you can upload on the Web site. This guarantees compatibility with all browsers.

If you need to print documents, your best bet is probably FO.

EXAMPLE

CSS is particularly popular with XML editors. High-end XML editors, such as XMetaL from SoftQuad (`www.softquad.com`) offer a pseudo-WYSIWYG mode based on CSS.

A WYSIWYG editor aims at making XML completely transparent and as easy to use as a word processor. In practice, it means clerical staff familiar with word processor experience quickly learn how to create XML documents.

Figure 6.10 shows XMetaL. It uses CSS to offer a pseudo-WYSIWYG editor which completely hides the tags.

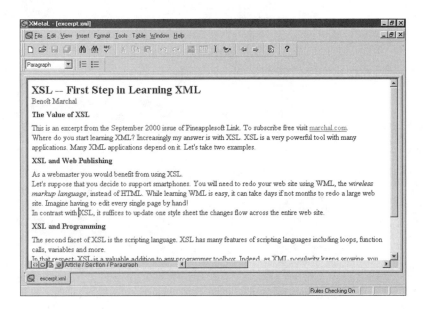

Figure 6.10: *XMetaL, a pseudo-WYSIWYG editor.*

Thankfully, it is not an exclusive choice. You don't have to adopt, say CSS, and forgo the benefits of XSLT. Far from it.

For example, I write my Web site in XML with XMetaL. I use an XSLT style sheet to publish it in HTML. I have another set of FO style sheets to create PDFs for reprints. In practice, the three modes complement one other.

What's Next

Now that you know how to create and view XML documents, the next three chapters will take you one step further and teach you how to manipulate and create XML documents from a scripting or programming language.

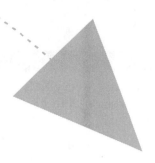

The Parser and DOM

The previous chapters showed how to view and transform XML documents. Style sheets are a powerful technology but are limited to viewing and transforming. When you have more specific needs, turn to programming. This chapter introduces the best way to read XML documents from JavaScript or Java.

In this chapter, you learn

- What an XML parser is
- How to interface a parser with an application
- What DOM, the Document Object Model, is
- How to write JavaScript applications that use DOM
- How to write Java applications that use DOM
- Which other applications use DOM

What Is a Parser?

A *parser* is the most basic yet most important XML tool. Every XML application includes a parser. For example, the XSL processors (Xalan and FOP) from the last chapters were based on the Xerces parser.

A parser is a software component that sits between the application and XML files. Its goal is to shield the developer from the intricacies of the XML syntax.

Parsers are confusing because they have received a lot of publicity: There are dozens of parsers freely available on the Internet. When Microsoft shipped Internet Explorer 4.0 as the first browser with XML support, they really meant they had bundled two XML parsers with it.

Yet, if you ask for a demo of a parser, you won't see much. The parser is a low-level tool that is almost invisible to everybody but programmers. The confusion arises because the tool that has so much visibility in the marketplace turns out to be a very low-level library.

Parsers

Why do you need parsers? Imagine you are given an XML file with product descriptions, including prices. Your job is to write an application to convert the prices from dollars to euros.

It looks like a simple assignment: Loop through the price list and multiply each price by the exchange rate. How long would that take? A quarter of a day's work, including tests.

Yet, remember the prices are in an XML file. To loop through the prices means to read and interpret the XML syntax. It doesn't look difficult—basically, elements are in angle brackets. Let's say the quarter-of-a-day assignment is now a one-day assignment.

Do you remember entities? The XML syntax is not just about angle brackets. There might be entities in the price list. Therefore, the application must read and interpret the DTD to be able to resolve entities. While it's reading the DTD, it might as well read element definitions and validate the document.

✔ For more information on how the DTD influences the document, see the section "Standalone Documents" in Chapter 4 (**page 100**).

What about other XML features: character encodings, namespaces, parameter entities? And did you consider errors? How does your software recover from a missing closing tag?

The XML syntax is simple. Yet it's an extensible syntax so XML applications have to be ready to cope with many options. As it turns out, writing a software library to decode XML files is a one-month assignment. If you were to write such a library, after one month, you would have written your own parser.

Is it productive to spend one month writing a parser library when you need only a quarter of a day's work to process the data? Of course not. It is more sensible to download a parser from the Internet or use one that ships with your favorite development tool.

Admittedly, this example is oversimplified, but it illustrates the definition of a parser: an off-the-shelf component that isolates programmers from the specifics of the XML syntax.

If you are not convinced yet or if you would rather write your own XML parser, consider this: No programmer in his or her right mind (except those working for Oracle, Sybase, Informix, and the like) would write low-level database drivers. It makes more sense to use the drivers that ship with the database.

Likewise, no programmer should spend time decoding XML files—it makes more sense to turn to existing parsers.

NOTE

The word parser comes from compilers. In a compiler, a parser is the module that reads and interprets the source code.

In a compiler, the parser creates a parse tree, which is an in-memory representation of the source code.

The second half of the compiler, known as the *backend*, uses parse trees to generate object files (compiled modules).

Validating and Nonvalidating Parsers

You will remember that XML documents can be either well formed or valid. Well-formed documents respect the syntactic rules. Valid documents not only respect the syntactic rules but also conform to a structure as described in a DTD or a schema.

Likewise, there are validating and nonvalidating parsers. Both parsers enforce syntactic rules but only validating parsers know how to validate documents against their DTDs or schemas.

Lest there be any confusion, there is no direct mapping between well-formed and nonvalidating parsers. Nonvalidating parsers can read valid documents (that is, a document with a DTD or a schema) but they won't validate them. To a nonvalidating parser, every document is a well-formed document.

Similarly, some validating parsers accept well-formed documents (others consider it an error not to have a DTD or a schema). Of course, when working on well-formed documents, they behave like nonvalidating parsers.

As a programmer, you will like the combination of validating parsers and valid documents. The parser catches most of the structural errors for you. And you don't have to write a single line of code to benefit from the service: The parser figures it out by reading the DTD or the schema. In short, it means less work for you.

The Parser and the Application

This section shows you how to integrate the parser in your applications. It discusses the various interfaces available to the programmer.

The Architecture of an XML Program

Figure 7.1 illustrates the architecture of XML programs. As you can see, it is divided into two parts:

- The parser deals with the XML file.

- The application consumes the content of the file through the parser.

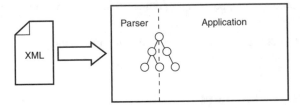

Figure 7.1: *Architecture of an XML program.*

Note that the application can be very simple (such as printing information on the screen) or quite complex (such as a browser, an editor, or an XSL processor).

This chapter and the next one concentrate on the dotted line between the two elements. This is the API (application programming interface) or the communication path between the parser and the application.

The parser and the application must share a common model for XML data. In practice, the common model is always some variation on a tree in memory that matches the tree in the XML document.

The parser reads the XML document and populates the tree in memory. This tree built by the parser is an exact match of the tree in the XML document. The application manipulates it as if it were the XML document. In fact, for the application, it is the XML document.

Object-Based Interface

There are two basic ways to interface a parser with an application: using object-based APIs and using event-based APIs. In practice, the two approaches are more complementary than competitive.

Using an object-based interface, the parser explicitly builds a tree of objects that contains all the elements in the XML document.

This is probably the most natural interface for the application because it is handed a tree in memory that exactly matches the file on disk.

Obviously, it's more convenient for the application to work with the tree in memory, if only because it doesn't have to worry about the XML syntax. Furthermore, if using a validating parser, the tree may have been validated against a DTD or a schema.

Listing 7.1 is a list of products, with their prices in U.S. dollars, presented in an XML document. The structure for this document is shown in Figure 7.2.

EXAMPLE

Listing 7.1: `products.xml`

```
<?xml version="1.0"?>
<xbe:products xmlns:xbe="http://www.psol.com/xbe2/listing7.1">
    <xbe:product price="499.00">XML Editor</xbe:product>
    <xbe:product price="199.00">DTD Editor</xbe:product>
    <xbe:product price="29.99">XML Book</xbe:product>
    <xbe:product price="699.00">XML Training</xbe:product>
</xbe:products>
```

The parser reads this document and gradually builds a tree of objects that matches the document. Figure 7.3 illustrates how the tree is being built.

When the XML parser reads the document in Listing 7.1, it recognizes that the top-level element is named products. Therefore, it constructs an object to represent the products element.

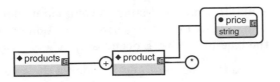

Figure 7.2: *The structure of the price list.*

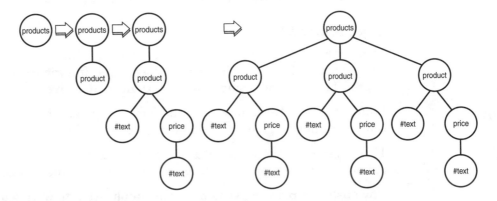

Figure 7.3: *Building the tree of objects.*

The next element is a product. The parser creates another object to represent the product element. Because this is a tree, it attaches the product object to the products object.

The next step is to recognize the price attribute. Again, the parser creates an object for the price and adds it to the tree being built.

In the product, there is some text that the parser translates in another object, a text node, in the tree.

The parser then moves to another product element, which also contains a price attribute and a text node. This results in more objects in the tree.

The process continues until the document has been completely read. By the time the parser reaches the end of the document, it has built a tree of objects in memory that matches the tree of the document

Event-Based Interface

The second approach to interfacing the parser and the application is through events. An event-based interface is natural for the parser but it is more complex for the application. Yet, with some practice, event-based interfaces prove very powerful. More programmers (and more parsers) are turning to event-based APIs for this reason.

EXAMPLE

With an event-based interface, the parser does not explicitly build a tree of objects. Instead, it reads the file and generates events as it finds elements, attributes, or text in the file. There are events for element starts, element ends, attributes, text content, entities, and so on. Figure 7.4 illustrates how it works.

At first sight, this solution is less natural for the application because it is not given an explicit tree that matches the file. Instead, the application has to listen to events and determine which tree is being described.

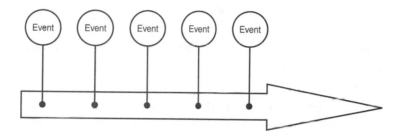

Figure 7.4: *An event-based API.*

In practice, both forms of interfaces are helpful, but they serve different goals. Object-based interfaces are ideal for applications that manipulate XML documents such as browsers, editors, XSL processors, and so on.

Event-based interfaces are geared toward applications that maintain their own data structure. For example, event-based interfaces are well adapted to applications that import XML documents in databases. These applications have their own data structure and they map directly from the XML structure to their structure.

An event-based interface is therefore more efficient because it does not explicitly build the XML tree in memory. Fewer objects are required and less memory is being used.

✔ Chapter 8 discusses event-based interfaces in greater detail ("Alternative API: SAX," **page 253**).

The Need for Standards

Ideally, the interface between the parser and the application should be standardized. A standard interface allows you to write software using one parser and to deploy the software with another parser.

Again, there is a similarity with databases. Relational databases use SQL as their standard interface. Because they all share the same interface, developers can write software with one database and later move to another database (for price reasons, availability, and so on) without changing the application.

That's the theory, at least. In practice, small differences, vendor extensions, and other issues mean that moving from one product to another requires more work than just recompiling the application. At the minimum, even if they follow the same standards, vendors tend to differ on bugs.

But even if different vendors are not 100% compatible with one another, standards are a good thing.

For one thing, it is still easier to adapt an application from a vendor-tainted version of the standard to another vendor-tainted version of the same standard than to port the application between vendors that use completely different APIs.

Furthermore, standards make it easier to learn new tools. It is easier to learn a new interface when 90% of it is similar to the interface of another product.

Obviously, the two different approaches for interfaces translate into two different standards. The standard for object-based interfaces is DOM, Document Object Model, published by the W3C (www.w3.org/TR/ DOM-Level-2-Core).

The standard for event-based interface is SAX, Simple API, developed collaboratively by members of the XML-DEV mailing list and edited by David Megginson (www.megginson.com/SAX

The two standards are not really in opposition because they serve different needs. Sun has integrated DOM and SAX in the Java API.

This chapter concentrates on DOM. The next chapter discusses SAX. Chapter 9, "Writing XML," looks at how to create XML documents.

Document Object Model

Originally, the W3C developed DOM for browsers. DOM grew out of an attempt to unify the object models of Netscape Navigator 3 and Internet Explorer 3. The DOM recommendation supports both XML and HTML documents.

The current recommendation is DOM level 2, but most browsers still support only level 1. Level 1 supports well-formed documents. DOM level 2 builds on level 1; it adds support for styling, events, document traversal and, most importantly, XML namespaces. Level 3 is under development at the time of this writing.

DOM's status as the official recommendation from the W3C means that most parsers support it. DOM is also implemented in browsers, meaning that you can write DOM applications with a browser and JavaScript.

As you can imagine, DOM has defined classes of objects to represent every element in an XML file. There are objects for elements, attributes, entities, text, and so on. Figure 7.5 shows the most important objects in the DOM hierarchy.

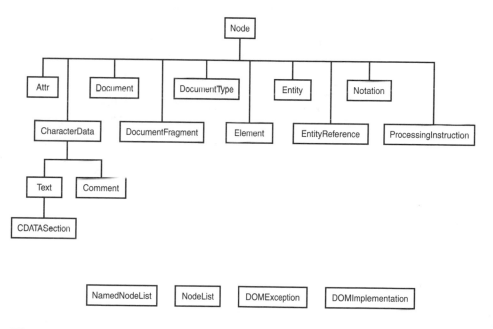

Figure 7.5: *The hierarchy in DOM.*

Getting Started with DOM

Let's see, through examples, how to use a DOM parser. DOM is implemented in Web browsers so these examples run in a browser. At the time of this writing, Internet Explorer and Netscape have differences in how they implement DOM.

This is partly due to the fact that DOM level 2 does not specify how to load XML documents! Loading of documents is planned for DOM level 3 only. Therefore, to run these examples, make sure you use the correct browser, as indicated before the listing.

A DOM Application

Listing 7.2 is an HTML page for a JavaScript application to convert prices from U.S. dollars to euros. The price list is an XML document. The application demonstrates how to use DOM.

A slightly modified version of this page (essentially, better looking) could be used on an electronic shop. International shoppers could access product prices in their local currency.

CAUTION

By default, Internet Explorer supports a draft version of DOM, not the official recommendation.

Most differences are for namespace-related properties or functions. For example, DOM defines a property called `localName` but Internet Explorer implements `baseName`.

You can upgrade Internet Explorer to full standard conformance by downloading the latest Microsoft XML parser from `msdn.microsoft.com/xml`. If doing so, you would need to adapt the listings in this chapter.

Listing 7.2: `conversion-ie5.html`

```
<html>
<head>
<title>Currency Conversion</title>
<script language="JavaScript">
function convert(form,document)
{
  var output = form.output,
      rate = form.rate.value,
      root = document.documentElement;
  output.value = "";
  searchPrice(root,output,rate);
}

function searchPrice(node,output,rate)
{
  if(node.nodeType == 1)
  {
    // with DOM Level 2, it would be localName
    if(node.baseName == "product" &&
       node.namespaceURI== "http://www.psol.com/xbe2/listing7.1")
    {
      // with DOM Level 2, it would be getAttributeNS()
      var price = node.attributes.getQualifiedItem("price","");
      output.value += getText(node) + ": ";
      output.value += (price.value * rate) + "\r";
```

Listing 7.2: continued

```
      }
      var children,
          i;
      children = node.childNodes;
      for(i = 0;i < children.length;i++)
          searchPrice(children.item(i),output,rate);
   }
}

function getText(node)
{
   var children = node.childNodes,
       text = "";
   for(i = 0;i < children.length;i++)
   {
      var n = children.item(i);
      if(n.nodeType == 3)
          text += n.data;
   }
   return text;
}
</script>
</head>
<body>
<center>
<form id="controls">
Rate: <input type="text" name="rate" value="1.0622" size="4"><br>
<input type="button" value="Convert"
       onclick="convert(controls,products)">
<input type="button" value="Clear" onclick="output.value=''"><br>
<!-- make sure there is one character in the text area -->
<textarea name="output" rows="10" cols="50" readonly> </textarea>
</form>
</center>
<xml id="products">
<xbe:products xmlns:xbe="http://www.psol.com/xbe2/listing7.1">
   <xbe:product price="499.00">XML Editor</xbe:product>
   <xbe:product price="199.00">DTD Editor</xbe:product>
   <xbe:product price="29.99">XML Book</xbe:product>
   <xbe:product price="699.00">XML Training</xbe:product>
</xbe:products>
</xml>
</body>
</html>
```

This page contains the XML document, the conversion routine in JavaScript, as well as an HTML form. Figure 7.6 shows the result in the browser.

OUTPUT

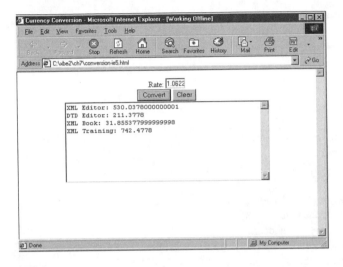

Figure 7.6: *Running the script in a browser.*

The page defines a form with one field for the exchange rate (you can find the current exchange rate on any financial Web site):

```
Rate: <input type="text" name="rate" value="1.0622" size="4"><br>
```

It also defines a read-only text area that serves as output:

```
<textarea name="output" rows="10" cols="50" readonly> </textarea>
```

Finally, it defines an XML island. XML islands is a proprietary extension to HTML from Microsoft to insert XML documents within HTML documents. In this case, XML islands are used to access Internet Explorer's XML parser. The price list is loaded into the island:

```
<xml id="products">
<xbe:products xmlns:xbe="http://www.psol.com/xbe2/listing7.1">
   <xbe:product price="499.00">XML Editor</xbe:product>
   <xbe:product price="199.00">DTD Editor</xbe:product>
   <xbe:product price="29.99">XML Book</xbe:product>
   <xbe:product price="699.00">XML Training</xbe:product>
</xbe:products>
</xml>
```

NOTE

XML island is specific to Internet Explorer. It will not work with another browser. You will see why you have to use browser-specific code in a moment.

The "Convert" button in the HTML file calls the JavaScript function convert(), which is the conversion routine. convert() accepts two parameters—the form and the XML island:

```
<input type="button" value="Convert"
    onclick="convert(controls,products)">
```

The script retrieves the exchange rate from the form. It walks through the document (see the next section for the details). It communicates with the XML parser through the XML island.

DOM Node

Remember that DOM defines a set of objects that the parser uses to represent an XML document. Because XML documents are hierarchical, it stands to reason that DOM defines objects to build hierarchies or, as they are known to programmers, trees.

The core object in DOM is the Node. Nodes are generic objects in the tree and most DOM objects are derived from nodes. There are specialized versions of nodes for elements, attributes, entities, text, and so on.

Node defines several properties to help you walk through the tree. The following are the most important ones:

- nodeType is a code representing the type of the object. The list of codes is shown in Table 7.1.

- parentNode is the parent (if any) of current Node object.

- childNodes is the list of children for the current Node object. childNodes is of type NodeList.

- firstChild is the Node's first child.

- lastChild is the Node's last child.

- previousSibling is the Node immediately preceding the current one.

- nextSibling is the Node immediately following the current one.

- attributes is the list of attributes, if the current Node has any. The property is a NamedNodeMap.

In addition, Node defines four properties to manipulate the underlying object:

- nodeName is the name of the Node (for an element, it's the tag name). The nodeName includes the namespace prefix, if any (for example, xbe:product).

- localName/baseName is the local part of name—that is, the name without the namespace prefix such as product. The official DOM recommendation specifies localName but, by default, Internet Explorer uses baseName. You can upgrade Internet Explorer to full DOM support by downloading the latest parser from msdn.microsoft.com/xml.

- namespaceURI is, as the name implies, the namespace's URI (for example, http://www.psol.com/xbe2/listing7.1).

- prefix is the namespace prefix (for example, xbe).

- nodeValue is the value of the Node (for a text node, it's the text).

✔ DOM also defines functions that will be introduced in Chapter 9, "Writing XML."

Table 7.1: **nodeType** *Code*

Type	Code
Element	1
Attribute	2
Text	3
CDATA section	4
Entity reference	5
Entity	6
Processing instruction	7
Comment	8
Document	9
Document type	10
Document fragment	11
Notation	12

EXAMPLE

In the example, the function searchPrice() tests whether the current node is an element:

```
if(node.nodeType == 1)
{
   // with DOM Level 2, it would be node.localName
   if(node.baseName == "product" &&
      node.namespaceURI== "http://www.psol.com/xbe2/listing7.1")
   {
      // with DOM Level 2, it would be node.getAttributeNodeNS()
```

```
          var price = node.attributes.getQualifiedItem("price","");
          output.value += getText(node) + ": ";
          output.value += (price.value * rate) + "\r";
      }
      var children,
          i;
      children = node.childNodes;
      for(i = 0;i < children.length;i++)
          searchPrice(children.item(i),output,rate);
}
```

NodeList

NodeList is a DOM object that contains a list of Node objects. It has only two properties:

- length, the number of nodes in the list.

- item(i), a method to access node i in the list.

NamedNodeMap

The searchPrice() function also accesses the price attribute. Element objects expose their attributes in the attributes property. The attributes property is a NamedNodeMap object.

A NamedNodeMap is a list of nodes with a name attached to them. It supports the same properties and methods as NodeList—length and item(i)—but, it also has special methods to access nodes by name:

- getNamedItem()/getNamedItemNS()/getQualifiedItem()returns the node with the given name. getNamedItem() uses the element's tag, getNamedItemNS() uses its namespace URI and local name. getQualifiedItem() is the older form of getNamedItemNS(); it is not part of the official DOM standard, but it is the method required for Internet Explorer.

- setNamedItem()/setNamedItemNS()sets the node with the given name. As seen previously, setNamedItemNS() uses the namespace.

- removeNamedItem()/removeNamedItemNS()removes the node with the given name.

searchPrice() illustrates how to use attributes to retrieve the price attribute.

```
// with DOM Level 2, it would be node.getAttributeNodeNS()
var price = node.attributes.getQualifiedItem("price","");
```

EXAMPLE

CAUTION

Bear in mind that, by default, Internet Explorer 5.0 and 5.5 recognize an obsolete version of DOM. However, if you have upgraded them to the latest Microsoft parser, you will need to use the official DOM constructs.

Document Object

The topmost element in a DOM tree is Document. Document inherits from Node so it can be inserted in a tree. Document inherits most properties from Node and adds only three new properties:

- documentElement is the root from the document.

- implementation is a special object that defines methods that work without a document (such as createDocument(), which creates new documents).

- doctype is the Document Type Definition.

Note that the Document object sits one step before the root element. Indeed the root element is in the documentElement property.

To return a tree, the parser returns a Document object. From the Document object, it is possible to access the complete document tree.

CAUTION

Unfortunately, the DOM recommendation starts with the Document object, not with the parser itself. DOM level 3 defines new methods to load and save XML documents but, for the time being, one must use proprietary solutions such as Microsoft's XML island.

Element Object

Element is the descendant of Node that is used specifically to represent XML elements. In addition to the properties inherited from Node, Element defines the tagName property for its tag name.

Obviously, since Element is a Node, it inherits the attributes property from Node. The property is a NamedNodeMap with a list of Attr elements.

Element also defines methods to extract information (there are more methods to create documents and they are introduced in Chapter 9, "Writing XML"):

- getElementsByTagName()/getElementsByTagNamesNS() return a NodeList of all descendants of the element with a given tag name. The first method works with the element's tag, (xbe:product) whereas the second expects a namespace URI and local name (http://www.psol.com/xbe2/listing7.1 and product).

- getAttributeNode() and getAttributeNodeNS() return an attribute from its tag or the combination of its namespace URI and local name, respectively.

Attr

Attr objects represent the attributes. Attr is a Node descendant. In addition to the properties it inherits from Node, Attr defines the following properties:

- name is the name of the attribute.

- value is the value of the attribute.

- ownerElement is the Element this attribute is attached to.

- specified is true if the attribute was given a value in the document; it is false if the attribute has taken a default value from the DTD.

TIP

The W3C decided to call the attribute object Attr to avoid confusion with object properties. In some languages, object properties are called object attributes. An Attribute object would have been very confusing.

Text Object

As the name implies, Text objects represent text such as the textual content of an element.

In the listing, the function uses getText() to return the textual content of a node. For safety, the function iterates over the element's children looking for Text objects:

EXAMPLE

```
function getText(node)
{
   var children = node.childNodes,
      text = "";
   for(i = 0;i < children.length;i++)
   {
      var n = children.item(i);
      if(n.nodeType == 3)
         text += n.data;
   }
   return text;
}
```

Why bother iterating over text elements or, if we brush that topic, why bother with Text objects at all? Why can't the parser attach the text directly to the element? The problem is with mixed content where an element contains both text and other elements. The following <p> element contains two text objects and one element object (<img>).

```
<p>The element can contain text and other elements such as images
➥<img src="logo.gif"/> or other.</p>
```

The <img> element object splits the text into two text objects:

- The text before the <img> element, "The element can contain text and other elements such as images."

- The text after, "or other."

Walking the Element Tree

To extract information or otherwise manipulate the document, the application walks the document tree. You have already seen this happening with the XSL processor.

Essentially, the script visits every element in the tree. This is easy with a recursive algorithm. To visit a node:

- Do any node-specific processing, such as printing data.

- Visit all its children.

Given that children are nodes, to visit them means visiting their children, and the children of their children, and so on.

EXAMPLE

The function searchPrice() illustrates this process. It visits each node by recursively calling itself for all children of the current node. This is a deep-first search—as you saw with the XSL processor. Figure 7.7 illustrates how it works.

```
function searchPrice(node,output,rate)
{
  if(node.nodeType == 1)
  {
    // with DOM Level 2, it would be localName
    if(node.baseName == "product" &&
       node.namespaceURI== "http://www.psol.com/xbe2/listing7.1")
    {
      // with DOM Level 2, it would be getAttributeNS()
      var price = node.attributes.getQualifiedItem("price","");
      output.value += getText(node) + ": ";
      output.value += (price.value * rate) + "\r";
    }
```

```
  var children,
      i;
  children = node.childNodes;
  for(i = 0;i < children.length;i++)
     searchPrice(children.item(i),output,rate);
  }
}
```

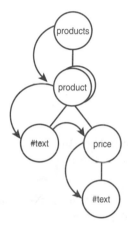

Figure 7.7: *Walking down the tree.*

There is a major simplification in searchPrice(): The function only examines nodes of type element (node.nodeType == 1). This is logical given that
the function is looking for product elements, so there is no point in examining other types of nodes such as text or entities. As you will see, more complex applications have to examine all the nodes.

At each step, the function tests whether the current node is a product. For
each product element, it extracts the price attribute, computes the price in
euros, and prints it.

NOTE

For the first time, in this listing, you're seeing how an application processes namespaces. It's not difficult, the application simply compares an element namespace with
a predefined value.

In effect, the application tests the element name by comparing both its local name and
its namespace:

```
if(node.baseName == "product" &&
   node.namespaceURI== "http://www.psol.com/xbe2/listing7.1")
```

Next, the function turns to the node's children. It loops through all the children and recursively calls itself for each child.

To walk through the node's children, the function accesses the `childNodes` property. `childNodes` contains a `NodeList`.

To get started, we just call `searchPrice()` passing it the root of the XML document, the exchange rate, and text area where it can write the result. The root is accessible through the `documentElement` property:

```
var output = form.output,
    rate = form.rate.value,
    root = document.documentElement;
output.value = "";
searchPrice(root,output,rate);
```

A More Standard Version

Internet Explorer is close to the DOM standard but not exactly there yet (unless you upgrade to the latest version of the parser or download from `msdn.microsoft.com/xml`).

As a comparison, we'll build a similar application in Netscape 6 which has more solid support for DOM. Netscape takes a different approach to supporting XML documents. Instead of using proprietary XML island, Netscape loads the XML document directly. To build the user interface, insert HTML elements (or, to be more precise, XHTML elements—HTML elements written with the XML syntax).

EXAMPLE

This approach has some advantages; most notably it frees us from using proprietary XML island because the whole document is an XML document. On the downside, it makes it difficult to load new XML documents. Furthermore, a bug prevents us from using text input fields. The application would look like Listings 7.3 and 7.4.

Listing 7.3: `conversion-ns6.xml`

```
<?xml version="1.0"?>
<?xml-stylesheet href="common.css" type="text/css"?>
<conversion xmlns:html="http://www.w3.org/1999/xhtml">
<html:script language="JavaScript"><![CDATA[
function convert()
{
  var rate = 1.06224,
      root = document.documentElement,
      products = root.getElementsByTagNameNS(
              "http://www.psol.com/xbe2/listing7.1","products"),
      outputs = root.getElementsByTagNameNS(
```

Listing 7.3: continued

```
                                  "http://www.w3.org/1999/xhtml","pre");
  if(outputs.length < 1 || products.length < 1)
    return;
  var output = outputs.item(0).firstChild;
  output.data = "";
  searchPrice(products.item(0),output,rate);
}

function searchPrice(node,output,rate)
{
  if(node.nodeType == 1)
  {
    if(node.localName == "product" &&
       node.namespaceURI== "http://www.psol.com/xbe2/listing7.1")
    {
      for(j = 0;j < node.attributes.length;j++)
      var price = node.getAttributeNodeNS("","price").value;
      output.data += getText(node) + ": ";
      output.data += (price * rate) + "\n";
    }
    var children,
        i;
    children = node.childNodes;
    for(i = 0;i < children.length;i++)
        searchPrice(children.item(i),output,rate);
  }
}

function getText(node)
{
   var children = node.childNodes,
       text = "";
   for(i = 0;i < children.length;i++)
   {
     var n = children.item(i);
     if(n.nodeType == 3)
        text += n.data;
   }
   return text;
}
]]></html:script>
<html:center>
<!-- make sure there is one character in the text area -->
<html:pre> </html:pre>
```

Listing 7.3: continued

```
<html:form id="controls">
<html:input type="button" value="Convert" onclick="convert()"/>
</html:form>
</html:center>
<xbe:products xmlns:xbe="http://www.psol.com/xbe2/listing7.1">
   <xbe:product price="499.00">XML Editor</xbe:product>
   <xbe:product price="199.00">DTD Editor</xbe:product>
   <xbe:product price="29.99">XML Book</xbe:product>
   <xbe:product price="699.00">XML Training</xbe:product>
</xbe:products>
</conversion>
```

Listing 7.4: common.css

```
product
{
   display: block;
   text-align: center;
}
```

Figure 7.8 illustrates the result in a browser.

OUTPUT

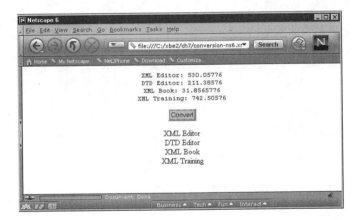

Figure 7.8: *Price conversions in Netscape 6.*

The document's root could be any element because it is not used anywhere else. It declares the xhtml namespace. The document also uses a CSS (from Listing 7.4):

```
<?xml-stylesheet href="common.css" type="text/css"?>
<conversion xmlns:html="http://www.w3.org/1999/xhtml">
```

Where needed, we can insert XHTML element for the script (html:script) or for a simple HTML form:

```
<html:center>
<!-- make sure there is one character in the text area -->
<html:pre> </html:pre>
<html:form id="controls">
<html:input type="button" value="Convert" onclick="convert()"/>
</html:form>
</html:center>
```

The XML price list is inserted directly in the XML document. It is recognizable through its own namespace:

```
<xbe:products xmlns:xbe="http://www.psol.com/xbe2/listing7.1">
   <xbe:product price="499.00">XML Editor</xbe:product>
   <xbe:product price="199.00">DTD Editor</xbe:product>
   <xbe:product price="29.99">XML Book</xbe:product>
   <xbe:product price="699.00">XML Training</xbe:product>
</xbe:products>
```

Unfortunately, a bug prevents us from using text input fields or text area in XHTML. The exchange rate must be stored as a variable in the script; to update the exchange rate, you need to update the script. A similar problem with text areas means that the script must write its output in a pre-element.

Because the entire document is an XML document, documentElement points to the conversion root. The script uses getElementsByTagNameNS() to retrieve the product list. Notice how the namespace helps pinpoint the right elements. The remainder of the script should be familiar because it calls searchPrice():

```
var rate = 1.06224,
    root = document.documentElement,
    products = root.getElementsByTagNameNS(
            "http://www.psol.com/xbe2/listing7.1","products"),
    outputs = root.getElementsByTagNameNS(
                      "http://www.w3.org/1999/xhtml","pre");
if(outputs.length < 1 || products.length < 1)
  return;
var output = outputs.item(0).firstChild;
output.data = "";
searchPrice(products.item(0),output,rate);
```

`searchPrice()` is nearly identical to Listing 7.2, except that it uses the standard DOM methods such as

```
if(node.localName == "product" &&
   node.namespaceURI== "http://www.psol.com/xbe2/listing7.1")
```

or

```
var price = node.getAttributeNodeNS("","price").value;
```

Managing the State

The previous example is very simple. The script walks through the tree looking for a specific element, `product`. At each step, the script considers only the current node.

In many cases, the processing is more complicated. Specifically, it is common to process different nodes differently, to collect information from several elements, or to process elements only if they are children of other elements.

With XSL, you can write paths such as `section/title` and combine information from several elements with `value-of`.

How do you do something similar with DOM? Essentially, the script must maintain state information. In other words, as it examines a node, the script must remember where it's coming from (the node ancestor) or what children it is expecting.

A DOM Application That Maintains the State

Listing 7.5 is a slightly different list of products. This time, the price and the name of the product are stored in elements below `product`.

Listing 7.5: `products2.xml`

```
<?xml version="1.0"?>
<xbe:products xmlns:xbe="http://www.psol.com/xbe2/listing7.5">
   <xbe:product>
      <xbe:name>XML Editor</xbe:name>
      <xbe:price>499.00</xbe:price>
   </xbe:product>
   <xbe:product>
      <xbe:name>DTD Editor</xbe:name>
      <xbe:price>199.00</xbe:price>
   </xbe:product>
   <xbe:product>
      <xbe:name>XML Book</xbe:name>
      <xbe:price>19.99</xbe:price>
   </xbe:product>
```

Listing 7.5: continued

```
    <xbe:product>
        <xbe:name>XML Training</xbe:name>
        <xbe:price>699.00</xbe:price>
    </xbe:product>
</xbe:products>
```

EXAMPLE

Unlike Listing 7.1, to print the converted price and the product name, the script needs to remember that it is within a name, below a product.

As Listing 7.6 illustrates, this is very easy to do with special functions. Figure 7.9 shows the result in a browser.

Listing 7.6: stateful.html

```
<html>
<head>
<title>Currency Conversion</title>
<script language="JavaScript">
var ns = "http://www.psol.com/xbe2/listing7.5";

function convert(form,xmlisland)
{
  var fname = form.fname.value,
      output = form.output,
      rate = form.rate.value;

  output.value = "";

  var document = loadIntoIsland(fname,xmlisland),
      root = document.documentElement;
  walkNode(root,output,rate)
}

function loadIntoIsland(fname,xmlisland)
{
  xmlisland.async = false;
  xmlisland.load(fname);

  if(xmlisland.parseError.errorCode != 0)
    alert(xmlisland.parseError.reason);

  return xmlisland;
}

function walkNode(node,output,rate)
{
  if(node.nodeType == 1)
```

Listing 7.6: continued

```
    {
      if(node.baseName == "product" && node.namespaceURI == ns)
        walkProduct(node,output,rate);
      else
          {
        var children,
            i;
        children = node.childNodes;
        for(i = 0;i < children.length;i++)
          walkNode(children.item(i),output,rate);
      }
    }
}

function walkProduct(node,output,rate)
{
  var children = node.childNodes,
      i;
  for(i = 0;i < children.length;i++)
  {
    var child = children.item(i);
    if(child.nodeType == 1)
    {
      if(child.baseName == "price" && child.namespaceURI == ns)
        walkPrice(child,output,rate);
      else if(child.baseName == "name" &&
              child.namespaceURI == ns)
        walkName(child,output);
    }
  }
  output.value += "\r";
}

function walkPrice(node,output,rate)
{
  var children = node.childNodes,
      price = "";
  for(i = 0;i < children.length;i++)
  {
    var child = children.item(i);
    if(child.nodeType == 3)
        price += child.data;
  }
  output.value += price * rate;
}

function walkName(node,output,rate)
```

Listing 7.6: continued

```
{
  var children = node.childNodes;
  for(i = 0;i < children.length;i++)
  {
    var child = children.item(i);
    if(child.nodeType == 3)
        output.value += child.data;
  }
  output.value += ": ";
}
</script>
</head>
<body>
<center>
<form id="controls">
File: <input type="text" name="fname" value="products2.xml">
Rate: <input type="text" name="rate" value="1.0622" size="6"><br>
<input type="button" value="Convert"
        onclick="convert(controls,xmlisland)">
<input type="button" value="Clear" onclick="output.value=''"><br>
<!-- make sure there is one character in the text area -->
<textarea name="output" rows="10" cols="50" readonly> </textarea>
</form>
</center>
<xml id="xmlisland"></xml>
</body>
</html>
```

OUTPUT

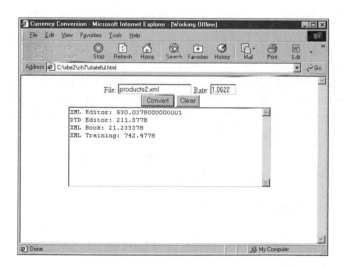

Figure 7.9: *Running the conversion utility.*

You recognize many elements from the previous listing. The novelty is in functions `walkNode()`, `walkProduct()`, `walkName()`, and `walkPrice()`.

`walkNode()` is very similar to `searchPrice()`. It walks down the tree looking for `product` elements. When it finds a `product`, it hands it to `walkProduct()`.

`walkProduct()` is a specialized function that processes only `product` elements. However, by virtue of being specialized, it knows that a `product` element contains a `name` element and a `price` element. It looks specifically for these two in the `product`'s children and hands them to other specialized functions: `walkName()` and `walkPrice()`. This illustrates how the function maintains state information: It knows it is in a product element and it expects the product to contain specific elements.

You might also be interested in `loadIntoIsland()`. This function loads the price list in the XML island from a file. Indeed, the XML island is now empty; it is just a placeholder for the XML parser:

```
<xml id="xmlisland"></xml>
```

`loadIntoIsland()` returns the `Document`. Most of the code in this function is Internet Explorer–specific because, as explained before, DOM currently does not specify how to load XML documents:

```
function loadIntoIsland(fname,xmlisland)
{
  xmlisland.async = false;
  xmlisland.load(fname);

  if(xmlisland.parseError.errorCode != 0)
    alert(xmlisland.parseError.reason);

  return xmlisland;
}
```

The function first set the `async` property to false. `async` is specific to Internet Explorer 5; it enables or disables background download. Next, it calls `load()`, which is also specific to Internet Explorer 5. As the name implies, `load()` loads the document.

Finally, it checks for errors while parsing. The `parseError` property holds information about parsing errors.

A Note on Structure

If you compare Listing 7.1 and Listing 7.5, it appears that the structure of the two listings is different. The first listing has few elements. Important information, such as the product's price, is stored in attributes. In practice, it means that when the parser has found a product, it has all the information it needs.

In contrast, the second listing has more elements and a hierarchy that goes three levels deep. When the script hits the product, it needs to search the next level for name and price.

Compare Listing 7.2 with Listing 7.6. As you can see, walking the attribute-oriented listing is easier because there is no need to maintain state information.

TIP

One of the major reasons programmers like to place data in attributes is to avoid having to maintain state when walking down an XML file.

Common Errors and How to Solve Them

In this chapter, you have learned how to use XML parsers, particularly DOM parsers, from JavaScript. A discussion of parsers would not be complete without a discussion of common parsing errors and how to solve them.

This section deals with debugging XML documents when the parser reports an error.

XML Parsers Are Strict

When debugging XML documents, it is important to remember that XML parsers are strict. They complain for errors that an HTML browser would silently ignore.

This was a design goal for the development of XML. It was decided that HTML had grown too difficult to implement because the browsers were too lenient. According to some estimate, more than 50% of the code in a browser deals with correcting errors.

That's a huge burden on the browser developers and it may explain why competition in the browser space is limited.

Furthermore, XML has been designed with a wide range of computing platforms in mind. This includes regular desktop machines as well as smaller devices (smartphones, PDAs such as the PalmPilot, and so on). These devices lack the memory and power to recover from complex errors.

To minimize the risk of errors in XML documents, I suggest you adopt a validating XML editor such as XMetaL (www.xmetal.com) or XMLSpy (www.xmlspy.com). Such an editor validates your code as you write.

Depending on the options, the validating editor may or may not enforce a DTD but it always enforces the XML syntax.

Error Messages

Parsers produce error messages that are often confusing. XML parsers are written with compiler technology. Consequently, error messages are similar to what you should expect from a compiler: helpful, but they rarely find the real error. Again, an XML editor may help. The best XML editors provide extra guidance about errors which makes it easier to fix them.

EXAMPLE

In the best case, the error message points to the problem. For example, given the following fragment:

```
<p>Send comments and suggestions to <url protocol="mailto">
➥bmarchal@pineapplesoft.com.</p>
```

OUTPUT

- The parser generates an error message similar to this (the exact message depends on your parser):

  ```
  </url> expected
  ```

  And it is right. The fragment misses a `</url>` closing tag.

EXAMPLE

- Unfortunately, the error message can be very confusing. Given the following fragment:

  ```
  <p>Send comments and suggestions to <url protocol="mailto>
  ➥bmarchal@pineapplesoft.com.</url></p>
  ```

the parser generates two error messages:

OUTPUT

```
attribute value must not contain '<'
"</p>" expected
```

However, these error messages are incorrect. The real problem is that the attribute has no closing quotation mark. The correct message should have been

```
" expected.
```

Instead, the parser thinks that the attribute continues until the end of the line. When it reaches the end of the line, the parser is confused and it misses the p closing tag.

As you can see, it's important to take error messages with a grain of salt.

XSLT Common Errors

EXAMPLE

When writing XSLT style sheets, it is very common to forget to close HTML elements. However, in XML, a p element must have an opening and a closing tag.

EXAMPLE

The following line is guaranteed to confuse the parser:

```
<xsl:template match="p">
    <p><xsl:apply-templates/>
</xsl:template>
```

Fortunately, the error message ("`</p>`" expected) is clear.

Similarly, `<br>` is an empty tag. In XML, empty tags have the format `<br/>`. Again, the error message ("`</BR>`" expected) is useful to pinpoint the problem.

EXAMPLE

- Another common error is to forget the attribute with `for-each`, `value-of`, or `if` elements. This is invalid XML coding and the parser will report an error:

  ```
  <xsl:value-of="title"/>
  ```

DOM and Java

DOM is not limited to browsers. Nor is it limited to JavaScript. DOM is a multiplatform, multilanguage API.

DOM and IDL

There are versions of DOM for JavaScript, Java, and C++. In fact, there are versions of DOM for most languages because the W3C adopted a clever trick: It specified DOM using the OMG IDL.

OMG IDL is a specification language for object interfaces. It is used to describe not what an object does but which methods and which properties it has. IDL, which stands for *Interface Definition Language*, was published by the OMG, the Object Management Group (www.omg.org).

The good thing about IDL is that it has been mapped to many object-oriented programming languages. There are mappings of IDL for Java, C++, Smalltalk, Ada, and even COBOL. By writing the DOM recommendation in IDL, the W3C benefits from this cross-language support. Essentially, DOM is available in all of these languages.

CAUTION

The fact that DOM is specified in IDL does not mean that parsers must be implemented as CORBA objects. In fact, to the best of my knowledge, there are no XML parsers implemented as CORBA objects. The W3C used only the multilanguage aspect of IDL and left out all the distribution aspects.

Java and JavaScript are privileged languages for XML development. Most XML tools are written in Java and have a Java version. Indeed, there are probably more Java parsers than parsers written in all other languages. Most of these parsers support the DOM interface.

✔ If you would like to learn how to write Java software for XML, read Appendix A, "Crash Course on Java," (**page 443**).

A Java Version of the DOM Application

EXAMPLE

Listing 7.7 is the conversion utility in Java. As you can see, it uses the same objects as the JavaScript listing. The objects have the same properties and methods. That's because it's the same DOM underneath.

Listing 7.7: Conversion.java

```java
package com.psol.xbe2;

import java.io.*;
import org.w3c.dom.*;
import org.xml.sax.*;
import javax.xml.parsers.*;
import org.apache.xerces.parsers.*;

public class Conversion
{
  public static void main(String[] args)
    throws Exception
  {
    if(args.length < 2)
    {
      System.out.print("java com.psol.xbe2.Conversion");
      System.out.println(" filename rate");
      return;
    }
    double rate = Double.parseDouble(args[1]);
    DocumentBuilderFactory factory =
       DocumentBuilderFactory.newInstance();
    factory.setNamespaceAware(true);
    factory.setValidating(false);
    DocumentBuilder builder = factory.newDocumentBuilder();
    Document document = builder.parse(new File(args[0]));
    Conversion conversion =
      new Conversion(document,rate);
  }

  public Conversion(Document document,double rate)
```

Listing 7.7: continued

```
  {
     searchPrice(document.getDocumentElement(),rate);
  }

  protected void searchPrice(Node node,double rate)
  {
    if(node.getNodeType() == Node.ELEMENT_NODE)
    {
      Element element = (Element)node;
      if(element.getLocalName().equals("product") &&
          element.getNamespaceURI().equals(
            "http://www.psol.com/xbe2/listing7.1"))
      {
        NamedNodeMap atts = element.getAttributes();
        Attr att = (Attr)atts.getNamedItemNS(null,"price");
        double price = att != null ?
                       Double.parseDouble(att.getValue()) : 0;
        System.out.print(getText(node) + ": ");
        System.out.println(price * rate);
      }
      NodeList children = node.getChildNodes();
      for(int i = 0;i < children.getLength();i++)
        searchPrice(children.item(i),rate);
    }
  }

  protected String getText(Node node)
  {
    StringBuffer buffer = new StringBuffer();
    NodeList children = node.getChildNodes();
    for(int i = 0;i < children.getLength();i++)
    {
      Text text = (Text)children.item(i);
      buffer.append(text.getData());
    }
    return buffer.toString();
  }
}
```

Three Major Differences

The major difference between the Java and the JavaScript versions is that
Java properties have the form getPropertyName().

Therefore, the following JavaScript code from Listing 7.3

```
if(node.localName == "product" &&
   node.namespaceURI== "http://www.psol.com/xbe2/listing7.1")
```

is slightly different in Java:

```
if(element.getLocalName().equals("product") &&
   element.getNamespaceURI().equals(
      "http://www.psol.com/xbe2/listing7.1"))
```

The second difference is that Java is a strongly typed language. Typecasting between `Node` and `Node` descendants is very frequent, such as in the `getText()` method. In JavaScript, the typecasting was implicit:

```
protected String getText(Node node)
{
  StringBuffer buffer = new StringBuffer();
  NodeList children = node.getChildNodes();
  for(int i = 0;i < children.getLength();i++)
  {
    // typecast from Node to Text
    Text text = (Text)children.item(i);
    buffer.append(text.getData());
  }
  return buffer.toString();
}
```

The third difference is in how you start the parser. Although DOM does not define standard methods to load documents, Sun does. The application uses Sun-defined `DocumentBuilderFactory` and `DocumentBuilder` to load a document.

Loading a document is a two-step process. First, create a new `DocumentBuilderFactory` through the `newInstance()` method. Set various properties—in this case, to enable namespace processing and select a non-validating parser.

Next, use the `newDocumentBuilder()` method to acquire a `DocumentBuilder` object. Call its `parse()` method with a `File` object. `parse()` returns a `Document` object and you're back in DOM land:

```
DocumentBuilderFactory factory =
    DocumentBuilderFactory.newInstance();
factory.setNamespaceAware(true);
factory.setValidating(false);
DocumentBuilder builder = factory.newDocumentBuilder();
Document document = builder.parse(new File(args[0]));
```

The Parser

Listing 7.7 was written using the Xerces parser for Java available from xml.apache.org. Xerces is a popular open-source parser. It was originally developed by IBM and is now supported by the Apache Foundation. Xerces is a very useful tool because it supports both DOM and SAX (the event-based interface).

If you download the listings from www.mcp.com or www.marchal.com, it includes a copy of Xerces in the file xerces.jar.

Other Java parsers are available from Oracle (otn.oracle.com/tech/xml), as well as James Clark (www.jclark.com).

DOM in Applications

Every XML application includes a parser. Why? Because every XML application needs to read XML files and reading XML files is what the parser is all about. Let's review a few examples.

Browsers

Obviously, the browser uses the DOM interface everywhere. DOM is not limited to XML islands; any document loaded in a browser is accessible through DOM.

EXAMPLE

Listings 7.8, 7.9, 7.10, and 7.11 show yet another version of the conversion utility. This version loads the XML document in one frame (so, it's not a Microsoft-specific XML island or Netscape's mixture of XHTML and XML; it's a regular document loaded in a frame) and loads the bulk of the utility in another frame.

Listing 7.8 shows the HTML file that creates the frames whereas Listing 7.9 implements the conversion utility. Listing 7.10 is the product list in XML. Notice that, unlike Listing 7.5, it does not use namespaces to work around a bug in Internet Explorer. It also applies a CSS style sheet that is available in Listing 7.11.

Listing 7.8: showparser.html

```
<html>
<head>
   <title>Currency Conversion</title>
</head>
<frameset cols="40%,60%">
   <frame src="controls.html" name="controls">
   <frame src="products3.xml" name="products">
</frameset>
</html>
```

Listing 7.9: controls.html

```
<html>
<head>
   <title>Controls</title>
<script language="JavaScript">
function convert(form,document)
{
   var output = form.output,
       rate = form.rate.value;
   output.value = "";
   var root = document.documentElement;
   walkNode(root,output,rate)
}

function walkNode(node,output,rate)
{
  if(node.nodeType == 1)
  {
    if(node.nodeName == "product")
      walkProduct(node,output,rate);
    else
        {
      var children,
         i;
      children = node.childNodes;
      for(i = 0;i < children.length;i++)
        walkNode(children.item(i),output,rate);
    }
  }
}

function walkProduct(node,output,rate)
{
  var children = node.childNodes,
      i;
  for(i = 0;i < children.length;i++)
  {
    var child = children.item(i);
    if(child.nodeType == 1)
    {
      if(child.nodeName == "price")
        walkPrice(child,output,rate);
      else if(child.nodeName == "name")
        walkName(child,output);
    }
```

Listing 7.9: continued

```
  }
  output.value += "\r";
}

function walkPrice(node,output,rate)
{
  var children = node.childNodes,
      price = "";
  for(i = 0;i < children.length;i++)
  {
    var child = children.item(i);
    if(child.nodeType == 3)
        price += child.data;
  }
  output.value += price * rate;
}

function walkName(node,output,rate)
{
  var children = node.childNodes;
  for(i = 0;i < children.length;i++)
  {
    var child = children.item(i);
    if(child.nodeType == 3)
        output.value += child.data;
  }
  output.value += ": ";
}
</script>
</head>
<body>
<center>
<form id="controls">
Rate: <input type="text" name="rate" value="1.0622" size="5"><br>
<input type="button" value="Convert"
       onclick="convert(controls,parent.products.document)">
<input type="button" value="Clear" onclick="output.value=''"><br>
<!-- make sure there is one character in the text area -->
<textarea name="output" rows="10" cols="30" readonly> </textarea>
</form>
</center>
</body>
</html>
```

Listing 7.10: `products3.xml`

```
<?xml version="1.0"?>
<?xml-stylesheet href="products3.css" type="text/css"?>
<products>
    <product>
        <name>XML Editor</name>
        <price>499.00</price>
    </product>
    <product>
        <name>DTD Editor</name>
        <price>199.00</price>
    </product>
    <product>
        <name>XML Book</name>
        <price>19.99</price>
    </product>
    <product>
        <name>XML Training</name>
        <price>699.00</price>
    </product>
</products>
```

Listing 7.11: `products3.css`

```
product
{
    display: block;
    font-family: Palatino, Garamond, "Times New Roman", serif;
}

name
{
    font-weight: bold;
}
```

Figure 7.10 shows the result in a browser. Note that this code is compatible with both Internet Explorer 5 and Netscape 6.

The code is familiar; for the most part it's copied verbatim from Listing 7.3. The DOM interface gives direct access to the content of the XML frame:

```
<input type="button" value="Convert"
       onclick="convert(controls,parent.products.document)">
```

Figure 7.10: *The result in a browser.*

Editors

XML editors also use DOM. For example, XMetaL from SoftQuad exposes the document being edited through DOM.

For example, macros can access the document to create tables of contents, indexes, and so on. Using macros and DOM, you can customize the editor to suit your needs.

Databases

An XML database stores XML documents in binary format. It is therefore faster to load and manipulate documents.

Such a database exposes its documents to applications using DOM. The application does not even know it is working against a database. Through DOM, it makes no difference whether the document is in a database or in an XML file.

If you would like to experiment with this feature, you can download the GMD-IPSI PDOM engine from `xml.darmstadt.gmd.de/xql`. The engine implements Persistent DOM (PDOM), which is an interface that stores XML documents in binary format. The interface to access the binary document is familiar DOM, which means that any application that works with XML files can be upgraded to binary files with little or no work.

What's Next

This chapter looked at an object-based interface for XML parsers. In the next chapter, you will look at an event-based interface: SAX. It is interesting to compare SAX and DOM.

In Chapter 9, you will learn how to create XML documents. This is the opposite of parsers, but there, again, DOM can be useful.

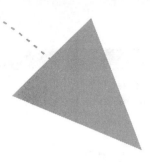

Alternative API: SAX

In the previous chapter you learned how to use DOM, an object-based API for XML parsers. This chapter complements the discussion on XML parsers with an introduction to SAX.

You will see that SAX

- Is an event-based API.

- Operates at a lower level than DOM.

- Gives you more control than DOM.

- Is almost always more efficient than DOM.

- But, unfortunately, requires more work than DOM.

Why Another API?

Don't be fooled by the name. *SAX* may be the *Simple API for XML* but it requires more work than DOM. The reward—tighter code—is well worth the effort.

✔ The "What Is a Parser?" section in Chapter 7, "The Parser and DOM" **(page 211)**, introduced you to XML parsers.

In the previous chapter, you learned how to integrate a parser with an application. Figure 8.1 shows the two components of a typical XML program:

- The *parser*, a software component that decodes XML files on behalf of the application. Parsers effectively shield developers from the intricacies of the XML syntax.

- The *application*, which consumes the file content.

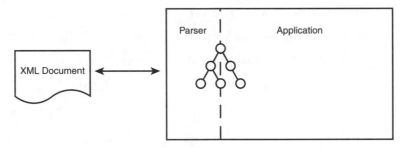

Figure 8.1: *Architecture of an XML program.*

Obviously, the application can be simple (in Chapter 7, we saw an application to convert prices between euros and dollars) or very complex, such as a distributed e-commerce application to order goods over the Internet.

The previous chapter and this chapter concentrate on the dotted line in Figure 8.1—the interface or API (Application Programming Interface) between the parser and the application.

Object-Based and Event-Based Interfaces

In Chapter 7, "The Parser and DOM," you learned that there are two classes of interfaces for parsers: object-based and event-based interfaces.

✔ The section "Getting Started with DOM" in Chapter 7 introduced DOM as the standard API for object-based parsers. DOM was developed and published by the W3C.

DOM is an object-based interface: it communicates with the application by explicitly building a tree of objects in memory. The tree of objects is an exact map of the tree of elements in the XML file.

DOM is simple to learn and use because it closely matches the underlying XML document. It is also ideal for what I call XML-centric applications, such as browsers and editors. XML-centric applications manipulate XML documents for the sake of manipulating XML documents.

However, for most applications, processing XML documents is just one task among many others. For example, an accounting package might import XML invoices, but it is not its primary activity. Balancing accounts, tracking expenditures, and matching payments against invoices are.

Chances are the accounting package already has a data structure, most likely a database. The DOM model is ill fitted, in that case, as the application would have to maintain two copies of the data in memory (one in the DOM tree and one in the application's own structure).

At the very least, it's inefficient. It might not be a major problem for desktop applications but it can bring a server to its knees.

SAX is the sensible choice for non–XML-centric applications. Indeed SAX does not explicitly build the document tree in memory. It enables the application to store the data in the most efficient way.

Figure 8.2 illustrates how an application can map between an XML tree and its own data structure.

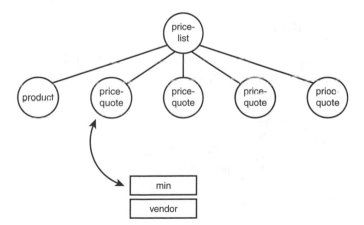

Figure 8.2: *Mapping the XML structure to the application structure.*

Event-Based Interfaces

As the name implies, an event-based parser sends events to the application. The events are similar to user-interface events such as ONCLICK (in a browser) or AWT/Swing events (in Java).

Events alert the application that something happened and the application needs to react. In a browser, events are typically generated in response to user actions: a button fires an ONCLICK event when the user clicks.

With an XML parser, events are not related to user actions, but to elements in the XML document being read. There are events for

- Element opening and closing tags
- Content of elements
- Entities
- Parsing errors

Figure 8.3 shows how the parser generates events as it reads the document.

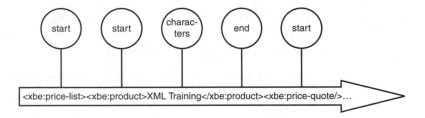

Figure 8.3: *The parser generates events.*

Listing 8.1 is a price list in XML. It lists the prices charged by various companies for XML training. The structure of this document is shown in Figure 8.4.

EXAMPLE

Listing 8.1: pricelist.xml

```
<?xml version="1.0"?>
<xbe:price-list xmlns:xbe="http://www.psol.com/xbe2/listing8.1">
   <xbe:product>XML Training</xbe:product>
   <xbe:price-quote price="999.00"  vendor="Playfield Training"/>
   <xbe:price-quote price="699.00"  vendor="XMLi"/>
   <xbe:price-quote price="799.00"  vendor="WriteIT"/>
   <xbe:price-quote price="1999.00" vendor="Emailaholic"/>
</xbe:price-list>
```

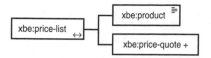

Figure 8.4: *The structure of the price list.*

The XML parser reads this document and interprets it. Whenever it recognizes something in the document, it generates an event.

When reading Listing 8.1, the parser first reads the XML declaration and generates an event for the beginning of the document.

When it encounters the first opening tag, `<xbe:price-list>`, the parser generates its second event to notify the application that it has encountered the starting tag for a `price-list` element.

Next, the parser sees the opening tag for the `product` element (for simplicity, I'll ignore the namespaces and indenting whitespaces in the rest of this discussion) and it generates its third event.

After the opening tag, the parser sees the content of the `product` element: `XML Training`, which results in yet another event.

The next event indicates the closing tag for the `product` element. The parser has completely parsed the `product` element. It has fired five events so far: three events for the `product` element, one event for the beginning of document, and one for `price-list` opening tag.

The parser now moves to the first `price-quote` element. It generates two events for each `price-quote` element: one event for the opening tag and one event for the closing tag.

Yes, even though the closing tag is reduced to the `/` character in the opening tag, the parser still generates a closing event.

There are four `price-quote` elements, so the parser generates eight events as it parses them. Finally, the parser meets `price-list`'s closing tag and it generates its two last events: closing `price-list` and end of document.

As Figure 8.5 illustrates, taken together, the events describe the document tree to the application. An opening tag event means "going one level down in the tree" whereas a closing tag element means "going one level up in the tree."

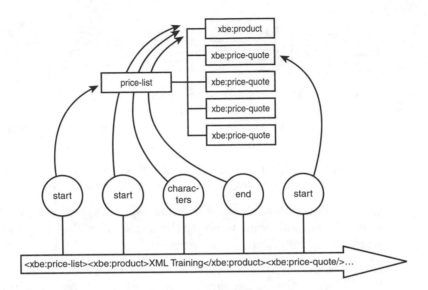

Figure 8.5: *How the parser builds the tree implicitly.*

NOTE

An event-based interface is the most natural interface for a parser: It simply has to report what it sees.

Note that the parser passes enough information to build the document tree of the XML documents but, unlike a DOM parser, it does not explicitly build the tree.

NOTE

If needed, the application can build a DOM tree from the events it receives from the parser. In fact, several DOM parsers are built on top of a SAX parser.

Why Use Event-Based Interfaces?

Now I'm sure you're confused. Which type of API should you use and when should you use it—SAX or DOM? Unfortunately, there is no clear-cut answer to this question. Neither is either of the two APIs intrinsically better; they serve different needs.

The rule of thumb is to use SAX when you need more control and DOM when you want increased convenience. For example, DOM is popular with scripting languages.

The main reason to adopt SAX is efficiency. SAX does fewer things than DOM but it gives you more control over the parsing. Of course, if the parser does less work, it means you (the developer) have more work to do.

Furthermore, as already discussed, SAX consumes fewer resources than DOM, simply because it does not need to build the document tree.

In the early days of XML, DOM benefited from being the official, W3C-approved API. Increasingly, developers trade convenience for power and turn to SAX.

The major limitation of SAX is that it is not possible to navigate backward in the document. Indeed, after firing an event, the parser forgets about it. As you will see, the application must explicitly buffer those events it is interested in.

Of course, whether it implements the SAX or DOM API, the parser does a lot of useful work: It reads the document, enforces the XML syntax, and resolves entities—to name just a few. A validating parser also enforces the document schema.

There are many reasons to use a parser and you should master APIs, SAX, and DOM. It gives you the flexibility to choose the better API depending on the task at hand. Fortunately, modern parsers support both APIs.

SAX: The Power API

SAX was developed by the members of the XML-DEV mailing list as a standard and simple API for event-based parsers. SAX is short for the Simple API for XML.

SAX was originally defined for Java but it is also available for Python, Perl, C++, and COM (Windows objects). More language bindings are sure to follow. Furthermore, through COM, SAX parsers are available to all Windows programming languages, including Visual Basic and Delphi.

Currently SAX is edited by David Megginson (but he has announced that he will retire) and published at www.megginson.com/SAX. Unlike DOM, SAX is not endorsed by an official standardization body, but it is widely used and is considered a de facto standard.

As you have seen, in a browser DOM is preferred API. Therefore, the examples in this chapter are written in Java. If you feel you need a crash course on Java, turn to Appendix A.

Some parsers that support SAX include Xerces, the Apache parser—formerly the IBM parser (available from xml.apache.org); MSXML, the Microsoft parser (available from msdn.microsoft.com); and XDK, the Oracle parser (available from technet.oracle.com/tech/xml). These parsers are the most flexible because they also support DOM.

A few parsers offer only SAX, such as James Clark's XP (available from
www.jclark.com), Ælfred (available from home.pacbell.net/david-b/xml),
and ActiveSAX from Vivid Creations (available from www.vivid-
creations.com).

Getting Started with SAX

EXAMPLE

Listing 8.2 is a Java application that finds the cheapest offering in Listing
8.1. The application prints the best price and the name of the vendor.

Listing 8.2: Cheapest.java

```
/*
 * XML By Example, chapter 8: SAX
 */


package com.psol.xbe2;

import org.xml.sax.*;
import java.io.IOException;
import org.xml.sax.helpers.*;
import java.text.MessageFormat;


/**
 * SAX event handler to find the cheapest offering in a list of
 * prices.
 */

public class Cheapest
   extends DefaultHandler
{
   /**
    * constants
    */
   protected static final String
      NAMESPACE_URI = "http://www.psol.com/xbe2/listing8.1",
      MESSAGE =
         "The cheapest offer is from {0} ({1,number,currency})",
      PARSER_NAME = "org.apache.xerces.parsers.SAXParser";

   /**
    * properties we are collecting: cheapest price & vendor
    */
   protected double min = Double.MAX_VALUE;
   protected String vendor = null;
```

Listing 8.2: continued

```java
/**
 * startElement event: the price list is stored as price
 * elements with price and vendor attributes
 * @param uri namespace URI
 * @param name local name
 * @param qualifiedName qualified name (with prefix)
 * @param attributes attributes list
 */
public void startElement(String uri,
                         String name,
                         String qualifiedName,
                         Attributes attributes)
{
    if(uri.equals(NAMESPACE_URI) && name.equals("price-quote"))
    {
        String attribute =
            attributes.getValue("","price");
        if(null != attribute)
        {
            double price = toDouble(attribute);
            if(min > price)
            {
                min = price;
                vendor = attributes.getValue("","vendor");
            }
        }
    }
}


/**
 * helper method: turn a string in a double
 * @param string number as a string
 * @return the number as a double, or 0.0 if it cannot convert
 * the number
 */
protected static final double toDouble(String string)
{
    Double stringDouble = Double.valueOf(string);
    if(null != stringDouble)
        return stringDouble.doubleValue();
    else
        return 0.0;
}

/**
 * main() method
 * decodes command-line parameters and invoke the parser
 * @param args command-line argument
 * @throw Exception catch-all for underlying exceptions
```

Listing 8.2: continued

```
*/
  public static void main(String[] args)
     throws IOException, SAXException
  {
     // command-line arguments
     if(args.length < 1)
     {
        System.out.println("java com.psol.xbe2.Cheapest file");
        return;
     }

     // creates the event handler
     Cheapest cheapest = new Cheapest();

     // creates the parser
     XMLReader parser =
        XMLReaderFactory.createXMLReader(PARSER_NAME);
     parser.setFeature("http://xml.org/sax/features/namespaces",
                        true);
     parser.setContentHandler(cheapest);

     // invoke the parser against the price list
     parser.parse(args[0]);

     // print the results
     Object[] objects = new Object[]
     {
        cheapest.vendor,
        new Double(cheapest.min)
     };
     System.out.println(MessageFormat.format(MESSAGE,objects));
  }
}
```

Compiling the Example

To compile this application, you need a Java Development Kit (JDK) for your platform. For this example, the Java Runtime is not enough. You can download the JDK from java.sun.com.

You must also download the listings available from www.marchal.com or www.quepublishing.com. The download includes Xerces. As always, I will post updates, if appropriate, on the Web site.

If you have problems with a listing, make sure you visit www.marchal.com or www.quepublishing.com.

Save Listing 8.2 in a file called Cheapest.java. Go to the DOS prompt, change to the directory where you saved Cheapest.java and compile by issuing the following commands at the DOS prompt:

```
mkdir classes
set classpath=classes;lib\xerces.jar
javac -d classes src\Cheapest.java
```

The compilation will install the Java program in the classes directory. These commands assume that you have installed Xerces in the lib directory and Listing 8.2 in the src directory. You might have to adapt the classpath (second command) if you installed the parser in a different directory.

To run the application against the price list, issue the following command:

```
java com.psol.xbe2.Cheapest data\pricelist.xml
```

CAUTION

Be warned that Java has difficulty with paths containing spaces. If Cheapest complains that it cannot find the file, check that the directory does not contain a space somewhere.

The result should be

```
The cheapest offer is from XMLi ($699.00)
```

This command assumes that Listing 8.1 is in a file called data\pricelist.xml. Again, you might need to adapt the path to your system.

CAUTION

The programs in this chapter do essentially no error checking. It simplifies them and helps concentrate on the XML aspects. It also means that if you type incorrect parameters, they crash.

Remember that you cannot compile this example unless you have installed a Java Development Kit.

Finally, an error such as

```
    src\Cheapest.java:7: Package org.xml.sax not found in import.
    import org.xml.sax.*;
```

or

```
    Can't find class com/psol/xbe2/Cheapest or something it requires
```

is most likely one of the following:

- The classpath (second command, classes;lib\xerces.jar) is incorrect.
- You entered an incorrect class name in the last command (com.psol.xbe2.Cheapest).

The Event Handler Step by Step

EXAMPLE

Events in SAX are defined as methods attached to specific Java interfaces. In this section, we will review Listing 8.2 step by step. The following section gives you more information on the main SAX interfaces.

The easiest solution to declare an event handler is to inherit from the SAX-provided DefaultHandler:

```
public class Cheapest
   extends DefaultHandler
```

This application implements only one event handler: startElement() which the parser calls when it encounters a start tag. The parser will call startElement() for every start tag in the document: <xbe:price-list>, <xbe:product> and <xbe:price-quote>.

In Listing 8.2, the event handler is only interested in price-quote, so it tests for it. The handler does nothing with events for other elements:

```
if(uri.equals(NAMESPACE_URI) && name.equals("price-quote"))
{
   // ...
}
```

TIP

Note that this is an event handler. It does not call the parser. In fact, it's just the opposite: the parser calls it.

If you're confused, think of AWT events. An event handler attached to, say, a button does not call the button. It waits for the button to be clicked.

When it finds a price-quote element, the event handler extracts the vendor name and the price from the list of attributes. Armed with this information, finding the cheapest product is a simple comparison:

```
String attribute =
   attributes.getValue("","price");
if(null != attribute)
{
   double price = toDouble(attribute);
   if(min > price)
   {
      min = price;
      vendor = attributes.getValue("","vendor");
   }
}
```

Notice that the event handler receives the element name, namespace and attribute lists as parameters from the parser.

Let's now turn our attention to the `main()` method. It creates an event-handler object and a parser object:

```
Cheapest cheapest = new Cheapest();
XMLReader parser =
    XMLReaderFactory.createXMLReader(PARSER_NAME);
```

`XMLReader` and `XMLReaderFactory` are defined by SAX. An `XMLReader` is a SAX parser. The factory is a helper class to create `XMLReader`s.

`main()` sets a parser feature to request namespace processing and it registers the event handler with the parser. Finally, `main()` calls the `parse()` method with the URI to the XML file:

```
parser.setFeature("http://xml.org/sax/features/namespaces",true);
parser.setContentHandler(cheapest);
parser.parse(args[0]);
```

TIP

It is not required to set `http://xml.org/sax/features/namespaces` to true because the default value is true. However, I find it makes the code more readable.

The innocent-looking `parse()` method triggers parsing of the XML document which, in turn, calls the event handler. It is during the execution of this method that our `startElement()` method will be called. There's a lot happening behind the call to `parse()`!

Last but not least, `main()` prints the result:

```
Object[] objects = new Object[]
{
    cheapest.vendor,
    new Double(cheapest.min)
};
System.out.println(MessageFormat.format(MESSAGE,objects));
```

Wait! When do `Cheapest.vendor` and `Cheapest.min` acquire their values? We don't set them explicitly in `main()`! True; it's the event handler job. And the event handler is ultimately called by `parse()`. That's the beauty of event processing.

Commonly Used SAX Interfaces and Classes

We have looked at only one event (`startElement()`) so far. Before going any further, let's review the main interfaces defined by SAX.

NOTE

There have been two versions of SAX so far: SAX1 and SAX2. This chapter introduces the SAX2 API only.

SAX1 is very similar to SAX2 but it lacks namespace handling.

NOTE

This section is not a comprehensive reference to SAX. Instead it concentrates on the most frequently used classes.

Main SAX Events

SAX groups its events in a few interfaces:

- ContentHandler defines events related to the document itself (such as opening and closing tags). Most applications register for these events.

- DTDHandler defines events related to the DTD. However, it does not define enough events to completely report on the DTD. If you need to parse a DTD, use the optional DeclHandler. DeclHandler is an extension to SAX and it is not supported by all parsers.

- EntityResolver defines events related to loading entities. Few applications register for these events.

- ErrorHandler defines error events. Many applications register for these events to report errors in their own way.

To simplify work, SAX provides a default implementation for these interfaces in the DefaultHandler class. In most cases, it is easier to extend DefaultHandler and override the methods that are relevant for the application rather than to implement an interface directly.

XMLReader

EXAMPLE

To register event handlers and to start parsing, the application uses the XMLReader interface. As we have seen, parse(), a method of XMLReader, starts the parsing:

```
parser.parse(args[0]);
```

XMLReader's main methods are

- parse() parses an XML document. There are two versions of parse(): One accepts a filename or an URL, the other an InputSource object (see the section "InputSource").

- setContentHandler(), setDTDHandler(), setEntityResolver(), and setErrorHandler() let the application register event handlers.

- `setFeature()` and `setProperty()` control how the parser work. They take a property or feature identifier, which is an URI—similar to namespaces—and a value. Features take Boolean values whereas properties take Objects.

The most commonly used features are

- `http://xml.org/sax/features/namespaces` which all SAX parsers recognize. When set to true (the default), the parser recognizes namespaces and resolves prefix when calling `ContentHandler`'s methods.

- `http://xml.org/sax/features/validation` which is optional. If it is set to true, a validating parser validates the document. Nonvalidating parsers ignore this feature.

XMLReaderFactory

EXAMPLE

`XMLReaderFactory` creates the parser object. It defines two versions of `createXMLReader()`: One takes the class name for the parser as a parameter; the second obtains the class name from the `org.xml.sax.driver` system property.

For Xerces, the class is `org.apache.xerces.parsers.SAXParser`. You should use `XMLReaderFactory` because it makes it easy to switch to another SAX parser. Indeed, it requires changing only one line and recompiling:

```
XMLReader parser = XMLReaderFactory.createXMLReader(
                   "org.apache.xerces.parsers.SAXParser");
```

For more flexibility, the application can read the class name from the command line or use the parameterless `createXMLReader()`. It is, therefore, possible to change the parser without even recompiling.

InputSource

`InputSource` controls how the parser reads files, including XML documents and entities.

In most cases, documents are loaded from an URL. However, applications with special needs can override `InputSource`. This is used, for example, to load documents from databases.

ContentHandler

EXAMPLE

`ContentHandler` is the most commonly used SAX interface because it defines events for the XML document.

As we have seen, Listing 8.2 implements `startElement()`, an event defined in `ContentHandler`. It registers the `ContentHandler` with the parser:

```
Cheapest cheapest = new Cheapest();
// ...
parser.setContentHandler(cheapest);
```

ContentHandler declares the following events:

- startDocument()/endDocument() notifies the application of the document's beginning or ending.

- startElement()/endElement() notifies the application of an opening or closing tag. Attributes are passed as an Attributes parameter; see the following section on "Attributes." Empty elements (for example, <img href="logo.gif"/>) generate both startElement() and endElement(),even though there is only one tag.

- startPrefixMapping()/endPrefixMapping() notifies the application of a namespace scope. You seldom need this information because the parser already resolves namespaces when the http://xml.org/sax/features/namespaces is true.

- characters()/ignorableWhitespace() notifies the application when the parser finds text (parsed character data) in an element. Beware, the parser is entitled to spread the text across several events (to better manage its buffer). The ignorableWhitespace event is used for ignorable spaces as defined by the XML standard.

- processingInstruction() notifies the application of processing instructions.

- skippedEntity() notifies the application that an entity has been skipped (that is, when a parser has not seen the entity declaration in the DTD/schema).

- setDocumentLocator()passes a Locator object to the application; see the section Locator that follows. Note that the SAX parser is not required to supply a Locator, but if it does, it must fire this event before any other event.

Attributes

EXAMPLE

In the startElement() event, the application receives the list of attributes in an Attributes parameter:

```
String attribute = attributes.getValue("","price");
```

Attributes defines the following methods:

- getValue(i)/getValue(qName)/getValue(uri,localName) returns the value of the *i*th attribute or the value of an attribute whose name is given.

- getLength() returns the number of attributes.

- getQName(i)/getLocalName(i)/getURI(i) returns the qualified name (with the prefix), local name (without the prefix), and namespace URI of the *i*th attribute.

- getType(i)/getType(qName)/getType(uri,localName) returns the type of the *i*th attribute or the type of the attribute whose name is given. The type is a string, as used in the DTD: "CDATA", "ID", "IDREF", "IDREFS", "NMTOKEN", "NMTOKENS", "ENTITY", "ENTITIES", or "NOTATION".

CAUTION

The Attributes parameter is available only during the startElement() event. If you need it between events, make a copy with AttributesImpl.

Locator

A Locator provides line and column positions to the application. The parser is not required to provide a Locator object.

Locator defines the following methods:

- getColumnNumber() returns the column where the current event ends. In an endElement() event, it would return the last column of the end tag.

- getLineNumber() returns the line in which the current event ends. In an endElement() event, it would return the line of the end tag.

- getPublicId() returns the public identifier for the current document event.

- getSystemId() returns the system identifier for the current document event.

DTDHandler

DTDHandler declares two events related to parsing the DTD:

- notationDecl() notifies the application that a notation has been declared.

- unparsedEntityDecl() notifies the application that an unparsed entity declaration has been found.

EntityResolver

The EntityResolver interface defines only one event, resolveEntity(), which returns an InputSource.

✔ The InputSource is introduced in the section "InputSource" on **page 267**.

Because the SAX parser can resolve most URLs already, few applications implement `EntityResolver`. The exception is catalog files. If you need catalog files in your application, download Norman Walsh's catalog package from
`http://www.arbortext.com/Customer_Support/Updates_and_Technical_Notes/java_form.html`.

✔ Catalog files resolve public identifiers to system identifiers. They were introduced in the section "The DTD Syntax" in Chapter 4 on **page 91**.

ErrorHandler

The `ErrorHandler` interface defines events for errors. Applications that handle these events can provide custom error processing.

After a custom error handler is installed, the parser doesn't throw exceptions anymore. Throwing exceptions is the responsibility of the event handlers.

The interface defines three methods that correspond to three levels or gravity of errors:

- `warning()` signals problems that are not errors as defined by the XML specification. For example, some parsers issue a warning when there is no XML declaration. It is not an error (because the declaration is optional), but it might be worth noting.

- `error()` signals errors as defined by the XML specification.

- `fatalError()` signals fatal errors, as defined by the XML specification.

SAXException

Most methods defined by the SAX standard can throw `SAXException`. A `SAXException` signals an error while parsing the XML document.

EXAMPLE

The error can either be a parsing error or an error in an event handler. To report other exceptions from the event handler, it is possible to wrap exceptions in `SAXException`.

Suppose an event handler catches an `IndexOutOfBoundsException` while processing the `startElement` event. The event handler can wrap the `IndexOutOfBoundsException` in a `SAXException`:

```
public void startElement(String uri,
                         String name,
                         String qualifiedName,
                         Attributes attributes)
```

```
{
   try
   {
      // the code may throw an IndexOutOfBoundsException
   }
   catch(IndexOutOfBounds e)
   {
      throw new SAXException(e);
   }
}
```

The SAXException flows all the way up to the parse() method where it is caught and interpreted:

```
try
{
   parser.parse(uri);
}
catch(SAXException e)
{
   Exception x = e.getException();
   if(null != x)
      if(x instanceof IndexOutOfBoundsException)
         // process the IndexOutOfBoundsException
}
```

Maintaining the State

Listing 8.1 is convenient for a SAX parser because the information is stored as attributes of price elements. The application had to register only for startElement().

EXAMPLE

Listing 8.3 is more complex because the information is scattered across several elements. Specifically, vendors have different prices depending on the delivery delay. If the user is willing to wait, he or she may get a better price. Figure 8.6 illustrates the structure of the document.

Listing 8.3: xtpricelist.xml

```
<?xml version="1.0"?>
<xbe:price-list xmlns:xbe="http://www.psol.com/xbe2/listing8.3">
   <xbe:name>XML Training</xbe:name>
   <xbe:vendor>
      <xbe:name>Playfield Training</xbe:name>
      <xbe:price-quote delivery="5">999.00</xbe:price-quote>
      <xbe:price-quote delivery="15">899.00</xbe:price-quote>
   </xbe:vendor>
   <xbe:vendor>
<xbe:name>XMLi</xbe:name>
```

Listing 8.3: continued

```
    <xbe:price-quote delivery="3">2999.00</xbe:price-quote>
    <xbe:price-quote delivery="30">1499.00</xbe:price-quote>
    <xbe:price-quote delivery="45">699.00</xbe:price-quote>
  </xbe:vendor>
  <xbe:vendor>
    <xbe:name>WriteIT</xbe:name>
    <xbe:price-quote delivery="5">799.00</xbe:price-quote>
    <xbe:price-quote delivery="15">899.00</xbe:price-quote>
  </xbe:vendor>
  <xbe:vendor>
    <xbe:name>Emailaholic</xbe:name>
    <xbe:price-quote delivery="1">1999.00</xbe:price-quote>
  </xbe:vendor>
</xbe:price-list>
```

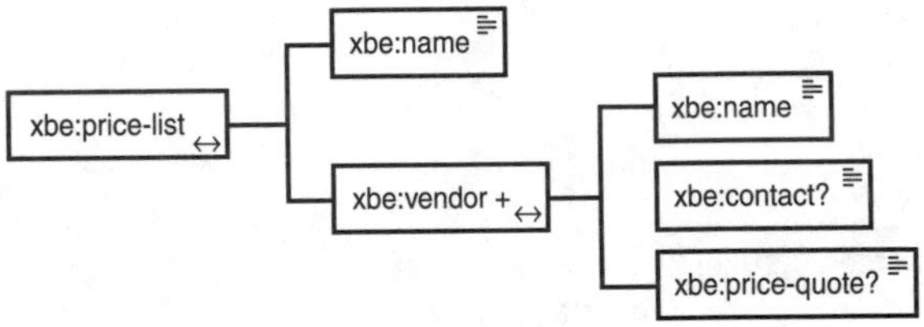

Figure 8.6: *Price list structure.*

To find the best deal, the application must collect information from several elements. However, the parser can generate up to three events for each element (`startElement()`, `characters()`, and `endElement()`). The application must somehow relate events and elements.

> ✔ See the section "Managing the State" in Chapter 7 for a discussion of state (**page 234**). The example in this section achieves the same result but for a SAX parser.

Listing 8.4 is a new Java application that looks for the best deal in the price list. When looking for the best deal, it takes the urgency into consideration. Indeed, from Listing 8.3, the cheapest vendor (XMLi) is also the slowest. On the other hand, Emailaholic is expensive, but it delivers in two days.

Listing 8.4: BestDeal.java

```
/*
 * XML by Example, chapter 8: SAX
 */

package com.psol.xbe2;

import java.util.*;
```

Listing 8.4: continued

```java
import org.xml.sax.*;
import java.io.IOException;
import org.xml.sax.helpers.*;
import java.text.MessageFormat;

/**
 * This class receives events from the SAX2Internal adapter
 * and does the comparison required.
 * This class holds the "business logic."
 * SAX event handling is done in an inner class.
 */

public class BestDeal
{
    /**
     * SAX event handler to adapt from the SAX interface to
     * best deal data structure.
     */

    protected class SAX2BestDeal
        extends DefaultHandler
    {
        /**
         * constants
         */

        /**
         * state constants
         */
        final protected int START = 0,
                            PRICE_LIST = 1,
                            PRICE_LIST_NAME = 2,
                            VENDOR = 3,
                            VENDOR_NAME = 4,
                            VENDOR_PRICE_QUOTE = 5;

        /**
         * the current state
         */
        protected int state = START;

        /**
         * current leaf element and current vendor
         */
        protected String vendorName = null;
        protected StringBuffer buffer = null;
        protected int delivery = Integer.MAX_VALUE;
```

Listing 8.4: continued

```java
/**
 * startElement event
 * @param uri namespace URI
 * @param name local name
 * @param qualifiedName qualified name (with prefix)
 * @param attributes attributes list
 */
public void startElement(String uri,
                         String name,
                         String qualifiedName,
                         Attributes attributes)
    throws SAXException
{
    if(!uri.equals(NAMESPACE_URI))
        return;
    // this accept many combinations of elements
    // it would work if new elements were being added, etc.
    // this ensures maximal flexibility: if the document
    // has to be validated, use a validating parser
    switch(state)
    {
        case START:
            if(name.equals("price-list"))
                state = PRICE_LIST;
            break;
        case PRICE_LIST:
            if(name.equals("name"))
            {
                state = PRICE_LIST_NAME;
                buffer = new StringBuffer();
            }
            if(name.equals("vendor"))
                state = VENDOR;
            break;
        case VENDOR:
            if(name.equals("name"))
            {
                state = VENDOR_NAME;
                buffer = new StringBuffer();
            }
            if(name.equals("price-quote"))
            {
                state = VENDOR_PRICE_QUOTE;
                String st = attributes.getValue("","delivery");
                delivery = Integer.parseInt(st);
                buffer = new StringBuffer();
```

Listing 8.4: continued

```
            }
            break;
        }
    }

    /**
     * content of the element
     * @param chars documents characters
     * @param start first character in the content
     * @param length last character in the content
     */
    public void characters(char[] chars,int start,int length)
    {
        switch(state)
        {
            case PRICE_LIST_NAME:
            case VENDOR_NAME:
            case VENDOR_PRICE_QUOTE:
                buffer.append(chars,start,length);
                break;
        }
    }

    /**
     * endElement event
     * @param uri namespace URI
     * @param name local name
     * @param qualifiedName qualified name (with prefix)
     */
    public void endElement(String uri,
                           String name,
                           String qualifiedName)
    {
        if(!uri.equals(NAMESPACE_URI))
            return;
        switch(state)
        {
            case PRICE_LIST_NAME:
                if(name.equals("name"))
                {
                    state = PRICE_LIST;
                    setProductName(buffer.toString());
                    buffer = null;
                }
                break;
            case VENDOR_NAME:
```

Listing 8.4: continued

```java
                if(name.equals("name"))
                {
                    state = VENDOR;
                    vendorName = buffer.toString();
                    buffer = null;
                }
                break;
            case VENDOR_PRICE_QUOTE:
                if(name.equals("price-quote"))
                {
                    state = VENDOR;
                    double price = 0.0;
                    Double stringDouble =
                        Double.valueOf(buffer.toString());
                    if(null != stringDouble)
                        price = stringDouble.doubleValue();
                    compare(vendorName,price,delivery);
                    delivery = Integer.MAX_VALUE;
                    buffer = null;
                }
                break;
            case VENDOR:
                if(name.equals("vendor"))
                {
                    state = PRICE_LIST;
                    vendorName = null;
                }
                break;
            case PRICE_LIST:
                if(name.equals("price-list"))
                    state = START;
                break;
        }
    }
}

/**
 * constant
 */
protected static final String
    MESSAGE =
        "The best deal is proposed by {0}. " +
        "A(n) {1} delivered in {2,number,integer} days for " +
        "{3,number,currency}",
    NAMESPACE_URI = "http://www.psol.com/xbe2/listing8.3",
    PARSER_NAME = "org.apache.xerces.parsers.SAXParser";
```

Listing 8.4: continued

```java
    /**
     * properties we are collecting: best price, delivery time,
     * product and vendor names
     */
    public double price = Double.MAX_VALUE;
    public int delivery = Integer.MAX_VALUE;
    public String product = null,
                  vendor = null;

    /**
     * target delivery value (refuse elements above this target)
     */
    protected int targetDelivery;

    /**
     * creates a BestDeal
     * @param td the target for delivery
     */
    public BestDeal(int td)
    {
        targetDelivery = td;
    }

    /**
     * called by SAX2Internal when it has found the product name
     * @param name the product name
     */
    public void setProductName(String name)
    {
        product = name;
    }

    /**
     * called by SAX2Internal when it has found a price
     * @param vendor vendor's name
     * @param price price proposal
     * @param delivery delivery time proposal
     */
    public void compare(String vendor,double price,int delivery)
    {
        if(delivery <= targetDelivery)
        {
            if(this.price > price)
            {
                this.price = price;
                this.vendor = vendor;
```

Listing 8.4: continued

```
              this.delivery = delivery;
         }
     }
}

/**
 * return a ContentHandler that populates this object
 * @return the ContentHandler
 */
public ContentHandler getContentHandler()
{
    return new SAX2BestDeal();
}

/**
 * main() method
 * decodes command-line parameters and invoke the parser
 * @param args command-line argument
 * @throw Exception catch-all for underlying exceptions
 */
public static void main(String[] args)
    throws IOException, SAXException
{
    if(args.length < 2)
    {
       System.out.println(
          "java com.psol.xbe2.BestDeal file delivery");
       return;
    }

    BestDeal bestDeal = new BestDeal(Integer.parseInt(args[1]));

    XMLReader parser =
       XMLReaderFactory.createXMLReader(PARSER_NAME);
    parser.setContentHandler(bestDeal.getContentHandler());
    parser.parse(args[0]);

    Object[] objects = new Object[]
    {
        bestDeal.vendor,
        bestDeal.product,
        new Integer(bestDeal.delivery),
        new Double(bestDeal.price)
    };
    System.out.println(MessageFormat.format(MESSAGE,objects));
}
}
```

You compile and run this application like the Cheapest application introduced previously. The results depend on the urgency of the delivery. You will notice that this program takes two parameters: the filename and the longest delay one is willing to wait.

```
java com.psol.xbe2.BestDeal data/xtpricelist.xml 60
```

returns

```
The best deal is proposed by XMLi. A(n) XML Training delivered
➥in 45 days for $699.00
```

whereas

```
java com.psol.xbe2.BestDeal data/xtpricelist.xml 3
```

returns

```
The best deal is proposed by Emailaholic. A(n) XML Training
➥delivered in 1 day for $1,999.00
```

A Layered Architecture

Listing 8.4 is the most complex application you have seen so far. It's not abnormal: The SAX parser is very low level so the application has to take over a lot of the work that a DOM parser would do.

The application is organized around two classes: SAX2BestDeal and BestDeal. SAX2BestDeal manages the interface with the SAX parser. It manages the state and groups events in a coherent way.

BestDeal has the logic to perform price comparison. It also maintains information in a structure that is optimized for the application, not XML. The architecture for this application is illustrated in Figure 8.7. Figure 8.8 shows the class diagram in UML.

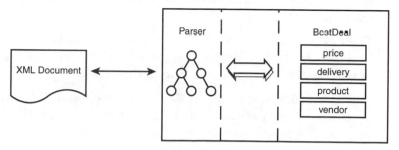

Figure 8.7: The architecture for the application.

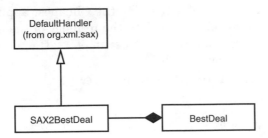

Figure 8.8: *The class diagram for the application.*

SAX2BestDeal handles several events: startElement(), endElement(), and characters(). All along, SAX2BestDeal tracks its position in the document tree.

For example, in a characters() event, SAX2BestDeal needs to know whether the text is a name, the price, or whitespaces that can be ignored. Furthermore, there are two name elements: the price-list's name and the vendor's name.

States

A SAX parser, unlike a DOM parser, does not provide state information. The application is responsible for tracking its own state.

There are several options for this. In Listing 8.4, we identified the meaningful states and the transitions between them. It's not difficult to derive this information from the document structure in Figure 8.6.

It is obvious that the application will first encounter a price-list tag. The first state should, therefore, be "within a price-list." From there, the application will reach a name. The second state is therefore "within a name in the price-list."

The next element has to be a vendor, so the third state is "within a vendor in the price-list." The fourth state is "within a name in a vendor in a price-list," because a name follows the vendor.

The name is followed by a price-quote element and the corresponding state is "in a price in a vendor in a price-list." Afterward, the parser encounters either a price-quote or a vendor for which there are already states.

It's easier to visualize this concept on a graph with states and transitions, such as the one shown in Figure 8.9. Note that there are two different states related to two different name elements, depending on whether you are dealing with the price-list/name or price-list/vendor/name.

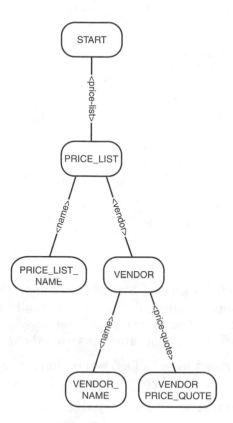

Figure 8.9: State transition diagram.

In Listing 8.4, the state variable stores the current state:

```
final protected int START = 0,
                   PRICE_LIST = 1,
                   PRICE_LIST_NAME = 2,
                   VENDOR = 3,
                   VENDOR_NAME = 4,
                   VENDOR_PRICE_QUOTE = 5;
protected int state = START;
```

Transitions

1. The value of the state variable changes in response to events. In the example, elementStart() updates the state:

```
ifswitch(state)
{
    case START:
        if(name.equals("price-list"))
            state = PRICE_LIST;
```

```
                  break;
          case PRICE_LIST:
            if(name.equals("name"))
                state = PRICE_LIST_NAME;
                // ...
            if(name.equals("vendor"))
                state = VENDOR;
           break;
          case VENDOR:
            if(name.equals("name"))
                state = VENDOR_NAME;
                // ...
            if(name.equals("price-quote"))
                state = VENDOR_PRICE_QUOTE;
                // ...
            break;
        }
```

SAX2BestDeal has a few instance variables to store the content of the current name and price-quote. In effect, it maintains a small subset of the tree.
Note that, unlike DOM, it never has the entire tree because it discards the
name and price-quote when the application has used them.

This is very efficient memorywise. In fact, you could process a file of several
gigabytes because, at any point, there's only a small subset in memory.

EXAMPLE

2. The parser calls characters() for every character data in the document, including indenting. It makes sense to record text only in name
   and price-quote, so the event handler uses the state.

```
switch(state)
{
    case PRICE_LIST_NAME:
    case VENDOR_NAME:
    case VENDOR_PRICE_QUOTE:
        buffer.append(chars,start,length);
        break;
}
```

3. The event handler for endElement() updates the state and calls
   BestDeal to process the current element:

```
switch(state)
{
    case PRICE_LIST_NAME:
        if(name.equals("name"))
        {
            state = PRICE_LIST;
            setProductName(buffer.toString());
```

```
              // ...
           }
           break;
        case VENDOR_NAME:
           if(name.equals("name"))
              state = VENDOR;
              // ...
           break;
        case VENDOR_PRICE_QUOTE:
           if(name.equals("price-quote"))
           {
              state = VENDOR;
              // ...
              compare(vendorName,price,delivery);
              // ...
           }
           break;
        case VENDOR:
           if(name.equals("vendor"))
              state = PRICE_LIST;
              // ...
           break;
        case PRICE_LIST:
           if(name.equals("price-list"))
              state = START;
           break;
     }
   }
```

NOTE

An alternative to using a state variable is to use a Stack. Push the element name (or another identifier) in startElement() and pop it in endElement().

Lessons Learned

Listing 8.4 is typical for a SAX application. There's a SAX event handler (SAX2BestDeal) which packages the events in the format most suitable for the application.

The application logic (in BestDeal) is kept separated from the event handler. In fact, in many cases, the application logic will be written independently of XML.

The layered approach establishes a clean-cut separation between the application logic and the parsing.

The example also clearly illustrates that SAX is more efficient than DOM but that it requires more work from the programmer. In particular, the programmer has to explicitly manage states and transitions between states. In DOM, the state was implicit in the recursive walk of the tree.

Flexibility

XML is a very flexible standard. However, in practice, XML applications are only as flexible as you, the programmer, make them. In this section, we will look at some tips to ensure your applications exploit XML flexibility.

Building for Flexibility

EXAMPLE

The BestDeal application puts very few constraints on the structure of the XML document. Add elements in the XML document and they are simply ignored. For example, BestDeal would accept the following vendor element:

```
<xbe:vendor>
    <xbe:name>Playfield Training</xbe:name>
    <xbe:contact>John Doe</xbe:contact>
    <xbe:price-quote delivery="5">999.00</xbe:price-quote>
    <xbe:price-quote delivery="15">899.00</xbe:price-quote>
</xbe:vendor>
```

but ignores the contact information. In general, it's a good idea to simply ignore unknown elements—as HTML browsers have always done.

Enforce a Structure

EXAMPLE

However it's not difficult to validate their structure from the event handler. The following code snippet (adapted from startElement()) checks the structure and throws a SAXException if a vendor element contains anything but name or price elements.

```
case VENDOR:
    if(name.equals("name"))
    {
        state = VENDOR_NAME;
        buffer = new StringBuffer();
    }
    else if(name.equals("price-quote"))
    {
        state = VENDOR_PRICE_QUOTE;
        String st = attributes.getValue("","delivery");
        delivery = Integer.parseInt(st);
        buffer = new StringBuffer();
    }
    else
        throw new SAXException("Expecting <xbe:name> or <xbe:price-quote>");
    break;
```

Given the listing with a contact element, it reports that

```
org.xml.sax.SAXException: Expecting <xbe:name> or <xbe:price-quote>
```

However, in practice, if your application is really dependent on the structure of the document, it is best to write a schema and use a validating parser.

What's Next

In the previous chapter and in this chapter, you learned how to read XML documents. In the next chapter, you learn how to write documents, thereby closing the loop.

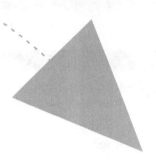

Writing XML

In the last four chapters, you learned how to use XML documents in your applications. You studied style sheets and how to convert XML documents in HTML. You also learned how to read XML documents from JavaScript or Java applications with a parser.

This chapter looks at the mirror problem: how to write XML documents from an application. The mirror component for the parser is called a *generator*. Whereas the parser reads XML documents, the generator writes them.

In this chapter, you learn how to write documents:

- Through DOM, which is ideal for modifying XML documents.

- Through your own generator, which is more efficient.

The Parser Mirror

In practice, most parsers integrate a generator. They can read and write XML documents. Consequently, the term *parser* is often used to symbolize the combination of the parser and the generator.

There are two schools of thought when it comes to generators:

- The first school argues that you need packaged generators for the same reason you need packaged parsers: to shield the programmer from the XML syntax.

- The other school argues that writing XML documents is simple and can be done easily with ad hoc code.

As usual, I'm a pragmatist and I choose one option or the other depending on the needs of the application at hand. If in doubt, remember that it is easier to generate XML documents than to read them. This is because you control what you write, not what you read.

Indeed, when reading a document, you may have to deal not only with tags but also with entities, exotic character sets, and notations[md]not to mention errors and DTD validation.

However, when writing the document, you decide. If your applications don't need entities, don't use them. If you are happy with ASCII, stick to it. Most applications need few of the features of XML besides the tagging mechanism.

Therefore, while a typical XML parser is a thousand lines of code, a simple but effective generator can be written in a dozen lines.

This chapter looks at both approaches. You'll start by using a DOM parser to generate XML documents and then you'll see how to write your own generator. Finally, you will see how to support different DTDs.

Most techniques are illustrated in JavaScript; one example is written in Java. Porting the code to other languages should be easy.

Modifying a Document with DOM

In Chapter 7, you saw how DOM parsers read documents. That is only one half of DOM. The other half is writing XML documents. DOM objects have methods to support creating or modifying XML documents.

✔ The example in the section "A DOM Application" in Chapter 7 **(page 220)** converted the prices in euros and printed the result.

EXAMPLE

With a few small changes to the price converter, it can record the new prices in the original document, that is, modify the XML document. Listing 9.1 illustrates how with Internet Explorer 5. Figure 9.1 shows the result in a browser.

CAUTION

As explained in Chapter 7, by default, Internet Explorer 5 uses an old version of DOM that is not fully compatible with the W3C standard. More specifically, the methods that support namespaces are specific to Microsoft. The code highlights these issues.

You can update Internet Explorer to DOM compliance from msdn.microsoft.com/xml. If you update XML support in your browser, you will need to update the listings as well.

Listing 9.1: conversion-ie5.html

```
<html>
<head>
<title>Currency Conversion</title>
<script language="JavaScript">
var ns = "http://www.psol.com/xbe2/listing9.1"
function convert(form,document)
{
  form.run.disabled = true;
  var output = form.output,
      rate = form.rate.value,
      root = document.documentElement;
  output.value = "";
  walkNode(root,document,rate);
  addHeader(document,rate);
  output.value = document.xml;
}

function walkNode(node,document,rate)
{
  if(node.nodeType == 1)
  {
    // with true DOM, it would be localName
    if(node.baseName == "product" && node.namespaceURI == ns)
      walkProduct(node,document,rate);
    else
    {
      var children,
          i;
      children = node.childNodes;
      for(i = 0;i < children.length;i++)
        walkNode(children.item(i),document,rate);
```

Listing 9.1: continued

```
      }
    }
  }

  function walkProduct(node,document,rate)
  {
    var price,
        children,
        i;
    children = node.childNodes;
    for(i = 0;i < children.length;i++)
    {
      var child = children.item(i);
      if(child.nodeType == 1)
        // with true DOM, it would be localName
        if(child.baseName == "price" && child.namespaceURI == ns)
          price = child;
    }
    // append the new child after looping to avoid infinite loop
    // with true DOM, it would be createElementNS()
    var element = document.createNode(1,"price",ns),
        text = document.createTextNode(getText(price) * rate);
    element.setAttribute("currency","eur");
    element.appendChild(text);
    node.appendChild(element);
    price.setAttribute("currency","usd");
  }

  function addHeader(document,rate)
  {
    var comment = document.createComment(
                      "Rate used for this conversion: " + rate),
        stylesheet = document.createProcessingInstruction(
                        "xml-stylesheet",
                        "href=\"common.css\" type=\"text/css\""),
        root = document.documentElement;
    document.insertBefore(comment,root);
    document.insertBefore(stylesheet,comment);
  }

  function getText(node)
  {
    var children = node.childNodes,
        text = "";
    for(i = 0;i < children.length;i++)
```

Listing 9.1: continued

```
  {
    var n = children.item(i);
    if(n.nodeType == 3)
      text += n.data;
  }
  return text;
}
</script>
</head>
<body onload="controls.output.value=''">
<center>
<form id="controls">
Rate: <input type="text" name="rate" value="1.0622" size="5">
<input type="button" value="Convert" name="run"
       onclick="convert(controls,products)"><br>
<!-- need one character in the text area -->
<textarea name="output" rows="22" cols="70" readonly> </textarea>
</form>
<xml id="products">
<?xml version="1.0"?>
<xbe:products xmlns:xbe="http://www.psol.com/xbe2/listing9.1">
  <xbe:product>
    <xbe:name>XML Editor</xbe:name>
    <xbe:price>499.00</xbe:price>
  </xbe:product>
  <xbe:product>
    <xbe:name>DTD Editor</xbe:name>
    <xbe:price>199.00</xbe:price>
  </xbe:product>
  <xbe:product>
    <xbe:name>XML Book</xbe:name>
    <xbe:price>19.99</xbe:price>
  </xbe:product>
  <xbe:product>
    <xbe:name>XML Training</xbe:name>
    <xbe:price>699.00</xbe:price>
  </xbe:product>
</xbe:products>
</xml>
</center>
</body>
</html>
```

OUTPUT

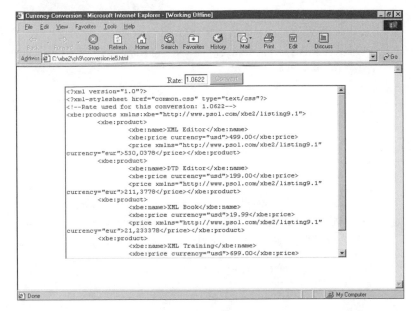

Figure 9.1: *Result in a browser.*

This example displays the XML document in a form. The section "Doing Something with the XML Documents" explains how to save it or send it to the server.

Inserting Nodes

EXAMPLE

Most of Listing 9.3 is familiar. It walks through the price list and converts prices from dollars to euros. The novelty is that it inserts new price elements in the list for the prices in euros. It also adds a currency attribute to every price element.

```
function walkProduct(node,document,rate)
{
  var price,
      children,
      i;
  children = node.childNodes;
  for(i = 0;i < children.length;i++)
  {
    var child = children.item(i);
    if(child.nodeType == 1)
      // with true DOM, it would be localName
```

```
        if(child.baseName == "price" && child.namespaceURI == ns)
          price = child;
      }
      // append the new child after looping to avoid infinite loop
      // with true DOM, it would be createElementNS()
      var element = document.createNode(1,"price",ns),
          text = document.createTextNode(getText(price) * rate);
      element.setAttribute("currency","eur");
      element.appendChild(text);
      node.appendChild(element);
      price.setAttribute("currency","usd");
    }
```

Modifying the DOM tree created by the parser is easy because the DOM
Document object has methods to create elements, comments, text nodes, processing instructions, and so on. The walkProduct() function uses both
createNode() (a Microsoft-specific method, the DOM equivalent would be
createElementNS()) and createTextNode().

Furthermore, the DOM Node object has methods for adding and removing
objects from the document tree. Because most DOM objects are derived
from Node, they inherit these methods. The walkProduct() function uses
appendChild() to insert the new nodes.

Finally, Element has a setAttribute() method that creates new attributes.

CAUTION

Don't add children to a node while looping through them, or you will create an infinite
loop.

EXAMPLE

While modifying the document, we also attach a CSS style sheet to it. The
addHeader() function appends a small header at the beginning of the document with a style sheet (using DOM's createProcessingInstruction()) and
a comment (through DOM's createComment()).

```
function addHeader(document,rate)
{
  var comment = document.createComment(
                  "Rate used for this conversion: " + rate),
      stylesheet = document.createProcessingInstruction(
                  "xml-stylesheet",
                  "href=\"common.css\" type=\"text/css\""),
      root = document.documentElement;
  document.insertBefore(comment,root);
  document.insertBefore(stylesheet,comment);
}
```

To attach a style sheet, you can simply create a processing instruction. `addHeader()` uses `insertBefore()` to control where the new nodes are being added.

Saving As XML

EXAMPLE

As you can see, it's not difficult to modify an XML document after Internet Explorer has loaded it in an XML island, but how do you retrieve the DOM tree as an XML document?

Unfortunately, as discussed in Chapter 7, the DOM recommendation available at the time of this writing does not specify how to retrieve the actual XML markup from the parser. Each vendor has come up with a different solution. In the Microsoft implementation, the `Document` object has an `xml` property, which returns the document in text. The script uses it to load the document in a text area onscreen:

```
walkNode(root,document,rate);
addHeader(document,rate);
output.value = document.xml;
```

Exploring Netscape Support for DOM

Theoretically, it should be possible to modify an XML document that is being displayed by the browser (for example, with a CSS). However, in practice, the support for DOM in Internet Explorer is not strong enough.

With Internet Explorer, true support for DOM is limited to the proprietary XML islands. As you saw in Chapter 7, documents being displayed are also available as DOM objects but there are many limitations to what you can do to them. In particular, it is not possible to manipulate them. This limitation will probably be fixed in future versions of the browser.

EXAMPLE

In the meantime, you can turn to Netscape 6. The mixed XHTML/XML mode for Netscape 6 has its own faults (for example, its support for forms has problems, to say the least) but it boasts strong support for DOM.

Listings 9.2 and 9.3 build a similar application written for Netscape 6. This time when you hit the convert button, the browser modifies the document and the update is immediately reflected onscreen. Figures 9.2 and 9.3 illustrate the result.

Listing 9.2: conversion-ns6.xml

```
<?xml version="1.0"?>
<?xml-stylesheet href="common.css" type="text/css"?>
<html:html xmlns:html="http://www.w3.org/1999/xhtml">
<html:head>
<html:title>Currency Conversion</html:title>
```

Listing 9.2: continued

```
<html:script language="JavaScript"><![CDATA[
var ns = "http://www.psol.com/xbe2/listing9.2"
function convert()
{
  var rate = "1.0622",
      root = document.documentElement,
      products = root.getElementsByTagNameNS(ns,"products");
  walkNode(products.item(0),document,rate);
}

function walkNode(node,document,rate)
{
  if(node.nodeType == 1)
  {
    if(node.localName == "product" && node.namespaceURI == ns)
      walkProduct(node,document,rate);
    else
    {
      var children,
          i;
      children = node.childNodes;
      for(i = 0;i < children.length;i++)
        walkNode(children.item(i),document,rate);
    }
  }
}

function walkProduct(node,document,rate)
{
  var price,
      children,
      i;
  children = node.childNodes;
  for(i = 0;i < children.length;i++)
  {
    var child = children.item(i);
    if(child.nodeType == 1)
      if(child.localName == "price" && child.namespaceURI == ns)
        price = child;
  }
  // append the new child after looping to avoid infinite loop
  var element = document.createElementNS(ns,"xbe:price"),
      text = document.createTextNode(getText(price) * rate);
  element.setAttribute("currency","eur");
  element.appendChild(text);
```

Listing 9.2: continued

```
    node.appendChild(element);
    price.setAttribute("currency","usd");
}

function getText(node)
{
  var children = node.childNodes,
      text = "";
  for(i = 0;i < children.length;i++)
  {
    var n = children.item(i);
    if(n.nodeType == 3)
      text += n.data;
  }
  return text;
}
]]></html:script>
</html:head>
<html:body>
<html:center>
<html:form>
<html:input type="button" value="Convert" name="run"
            onclick="convert()"/><br/>
</html:form>
</html:center>
<xbe:products xmlns:xbe="http://www.psol.com/xbe2/listing9.2">
  <xbe:product>
    <xbe:name>XML Editor</xbe:name>
    <xbe:price>499.00</xbe:price>
  </xbe:product>
  <xbe:product>
    <xbe:name>DTD Editor</xbe:name>
    <xbe:price>199.00</xbe:price>
  </xbe:product>
  <xbe:product>
    <xbe:name>XML Book</xbe:name>
    <xbe:price>19.99</xbe:price>
  </xbe:product>
  <xbe:product>
    <xbe:name>XML Training</xbe:name>
    <xbe:price>699.00</xbe:price>
  </xbe:product>
</xbe:products>
</html:body>
</html:html>
```

Listing 9.3: `common.css`

```css
product
{
    display: block;
    text-align: center;
    margin-top: 0.5em;
}

price
{
    display: block;
    font-style: italic;
}

price:after
{
    content: " dollars";
}

price[currency='eur']:after
{
    content: " euros";
}
```

Most of the Netscape code is similar to the Internet Explorer code, but it uses the standard DOM properties and methods, such as `localName` and `createElementNS()`. Incidentally, note that `createElementNS()` expects an element name that includes the prefix

```
function walkNode(node,document,rate)
{
  if(node.nodeType == 1)
  {
    if(node.localName == "product" && node.namespaceURI == ns)
      walkProduct(node,document,rate);
    else
    {
      var children,
          i;
      children = node.childNodes;
      for(i = 0;i < children.length;i++)
        walkNode(children.item(i),document,rate);
    }
  }
}
```

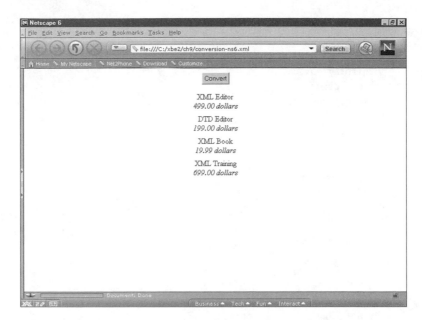

Figure 9.2: *Before hitting the Transform button.*

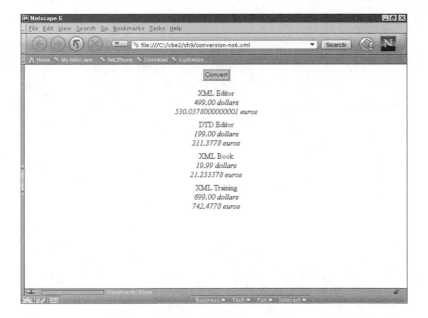

Figure 9.3: *After hitting the Transform button.*

DOM Methods to Create and Modify Documents

This section defines properties and methods of DOM Level 2 that are related to document manipulation. These methods and properties are in addition to the properties introduced in Chapter 7.

> ✔ You will find the list of methods and properties to read XML documents in the section "Getting Started with DOM" in Chapter 7 **(page 219)**.

Document

In addition to the properties introduced in Chapter 7, Document defines the following methods:

- createAttributeNS(uri,name)/createAttribute(name) creates an Attr object called name, respectively with and without the uri namespace. If using the namespace-enabled version, the name must be a qualified name—in other words, it must include a prefix (as in xbe:product).

- createCDATASection(data) creates a CDATASection object with the data.

- createComment(data) creates a Comment object.

- createDocumentFragment() creates an empty DocumentFragment object.

- createElementNS(uri,name)/createElement(name) creates an Element object with name and namespace URI. Like createAttribute(), there are two versions of the method with and without a namespace.

- createEntityReference(name) creates an EntityReference object called name.

- createProcessingInstruction(target,data) creates a ProcessingInstruction object for the target.

- createTextNode(data) creates a TextNode object.

Internet Explorer 5 does not support the namespace-aware methods. Instead, it uses createNode(type,name,uri) where type is the node being created (1 for element, 2 for attribute), name is the element or attribute's name, and uri is the namespace URI.

Node

Node defines the following methods for adding and removing objects to/from the document tree. Because many DOM objects are derived from Node, they inherit these methods:

- `appendChild(child)` appends `child` to the end of the list of the children.

- `insertBefore(child,before)` appends `child` before the node `before`. `before` must be a child of the node.

- `replaceChild(child,toReplace)` replaces `toReplace` with `child`; `toReplace` must be a child of the node.

- `removeChild(child)` removes `child` from the node's children.

- `cloneNode(deep)` creates a copy of the node. If `deep` is `true`, it also clones all the children of the node recursively.

- `hasChildNodes()` returns `true` if the node has children; `false` otherwise.

CharacterData

`CharacterData` defines the following methods. These methods are inherited by `Text`, `Comment`, and `CDATASection`:

- `appendData(data)` appends `data` at the end of the text.

- `insertData(offset,data)` inserts `data` in the current text starting at `offset`.

- `deleteData(offset,length)` deletes `length` characters starting at `offset`.

- `replaceData(offset,length,data)` inserts `data` in place of the characters at `offset` for a `length`.

- `substringData(offset,length)` returns the characters starting at `offset` for a `length`.

Element

`Element` has the following methods for manipulating the XML document:

- `setAttributeNS(uri,name,value)`/`setAttribute(name,value)` creates an attribute called `name` with the `value`, possibly in the `uri` namespace.

- `getAttributeNS(uri,name)`/`getAttribute(name)` returns the value of the attribute called `name`, possibly in the `uri` namespace.

- `removeAttributeNS(uri,name)`/`removeAttribute(name)` remove the attribute called `name` from the element, possibly in the `uri` namespace.

- `setAttributeNode(attr)`/`getAttributeNode(name)`/`remove AttributeNote(attr)` are similar to `setAttribute()`, `getAttribute()` and `removeAttribute()` except that they accept or return `Attr` objects.

NOTE

There are two solutions for creating attributes:

- Create the attribute with `Document.createAttributeNS()` and attach it to the element with `setAttribute()`.

- Create the element and attach it to the element in one step with `Element.setAttributeNS()`.

Text

Text inherits its properties and methods from `CharacterData`. It defines one new method for manipulating the XML document:

> `splitText(offset)` splits the `Text` object into two `Text` objects. The new objects replace the existing one in the tree.

Creating a New Document with DOM

In most cases, in a browser you will use DOM to modify existing documents. However, DOM can also create documents from scratch as illustrated by Listing 9.4.

EXAMPLE

Listing 9.4: `ProductsCreator.java`

```java
package com.psol.xbe2;

import java.io.*;
import java.awt.*;
import org.w3c.dom.*;
import java.awt.event.*;
import javax.xml.parsers.*;
import org.apache.xml.serialize.*;

public class ProductsCreator
    extends Frame
{
    protected TextComponent xmlText,
                            name,
                            price;
    protected Choice currencies;
    protected Document document;
    protected static final String[] currencyCode =
    {
        "usd", "eur"
    };
    protected static final String NS =
        "http://www.psol.com/xbe2/listing9.4";
```

Listing 9.4: continued

```java
public ProductsCreator()
   throws ParserConfigurationException
{
   super("Price List Creator");
   setResizable(false);
   setBackground(Color.lightGray);
   addWindowListener(new WindowAdapter()
   {
      public void windowClosing(WindowEvent event)
         { System.exit(0); }
   });
   GridBagLayout gridbag = new GridBagLayout();
   GridBagConstraints constraints = new GridBagConstraints();
   setLayout(gridbag);
   xmlText = new TextArea(10,40);
   xmlText.setEditable(false);
   constraints.gridwidth = GridBagConstraints.REMAINDER;
   constraints.fill = GridBagConstraints.BOTH;
   constraints.insets = new Insets(3,3,3,3);
   gridbag.setConstraints(xmlText,constraints);
   add(xmlText);
   Component component = new Label("Name:");
   constraints.gridwidth = 1;
   gridbag.setConstraints(component,constraints);
   add(component);
   name = new TextField(25);
   constraints.gridwidth = GridBagConstraints.REMAINDER;
   gridbag.setConstraints(name,constraints);
   add(name);
   component = new Label("Price:");
   constraints.gridwidth = 1;
   gridbag.setConstraints(component,constraints);
   add(component);
   price = new TextField(15);
   constraints.gridwidth = GridBagConstraints.RELATIVE;
   gridbag.setConstraints(price,constraints);
   add(price);
   currencies = new Choice();
   currencies.add("Dollars");
   currencies.add("Euros");
   constraints.gridwidth = GridBagConstraints.REMAINDER;
   gridbag.setConstraints(currencies,constraints);
   add(currencies);
   Button creator = new Button("Create new product");
   constraints.fill = GridBagConstraints.NONE;
```

Listing 9.4: continued

```java
        constraints.gridwidth = GridBagConstraints.REMAINDER;
        gridbag.setConstraints(creator,constraints);
        creator.addActionListener(new ActionListener()
        {
            public void actionPerformed(ActionEvent event)
                { doCreate(); }
        });
        add(creator);
        DocumentBuilderFactory factory =
            DocumentBuilderFactory.newInstance();
        factory.setNamespaceAware(true);
        DocumentBuilder builder = factory.newDocumentBuilder();
        document = builder.newDocument();
        DOMImplementation implementation =
            document.getImplementation();
        document =
            implementation.createDocument(NS,"xbe:products",null);
        document.getDocumentElement().setAttribute("xmlns:xbe",NS);
    }

    protected void doCreate()
    {
        Element root = document.getDocumentElement(),
                elProduct = document.createElementNS(NS,
                                                "xbe:product"),
                elName = document.createElementNS(NS,"xbe:name"),
                elPrice = document.createElementNS(NS,"xbe:price");
        String currency =
            currencyCode[currencies.getSelectedIndex()];
        elPrice.setAttribute("currency",currency);
        Text text = document.createTextNode(name.getText());
        elName.appendChild(text);
        text = document.createTextNode(price.getText());
        elPrice.appendChild(text);
        elProduct.appendChild(elName);
        elProduct.appendChild(elPrice);
        root.appendChild(elProduct);
        updateDisplay();
    }

    protected void updateDisplay()
    {
        StringWriter writer = new StringWriter();
        try
        {
```

Listing 9.4: continued

```
            OutputFormat format = new OutputFormat(document);
            format.setIndenting(true);
            XMLSerializer serializer =
                new XMLSerializer(writer,format);
            serializer.asDOMSerializer();
            serializer.serialize(document.getDocumentElement());
        }
        catch(IOException e)
        {
            e.printStackTrace(new PrintWriter(writer));
        }
        xmlText.setText(writer.toString());
    }


    public static void main(String[] params)
        throws ParserConfigurationException
    {
        Frame frame = new ProductsCreator();
        frame.pack();
        frame.show();
    }
}
```

This listing is in Java because you seldom create new documents from scratch in a browser. In most cases, you will use DOM as a generator from regular programs, not from within a browser.

This listing highlights the usual differences between Java and JavaScript, as explained in Chapter 7. More specifically in Java, you access properties through getter and setter methods (getXXX() and setXXX() methods). Java also enforces a stricter type system.

However, note that nothing prevents you from creating a document in a browser. The next section includes such examples.

To create a new element in the XML document, the user enters the product name and price in dollars or in euros and presses the Create new product button. This updates the XML document in the text area. Figure 9.4 shows the result.

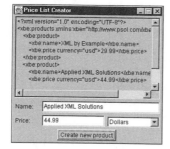

Figure 9.4: *Creating an XML document from scratch.*

Creating Nodes

The following application simply creates new DOM objects and inserts them in the document tree. It takes care to insert the new elements in the appropriate order. Except that there are more elements to create, this process is very similar to modifying an existing document.

```
protected void doCreate()
{
    Element root = document.getDocumentElement(),
            elProduct = document.createElementNS(NS,
                                                "xbe:product"),
            elName = document.createElementNS(NS,"xbe:name"),
            elPrice = document.createElementNS(NS,"xbe:price");
    String currency =
        currencyCode[currencies.getSelectedIndex()];
    elPrice.setAttribute("currency",currency);
    Text text = document.createTextNode(name.getText());
    elName.appendChild(text);
    text = document.createTextNode(price.getText());
    elPrice.appendChild(text);
    elProduct.appendChild(elName);
    elProduct.appendChild(elPrice);
    root.appendChild(elProduct);
    updateDisplay();
}
```

Creating the Root Element and Document Object

Of course, when creating a document from scratch, you need to create the original Document object. DOM offers the createDocument() method on the DOMImplementation class. Unfortunately, to obtain a DOMImplementation, you need a Document object already!

Although this appears silly, bear in mind that DOM was originally developed for browsers. In that context, the browser provides you with the initial Document object.

Fortunately, we can use the DocumentBuilder, specified by Sun, to create an initially empty Document object.

Note that createDocument() also creates the root element:

```
DocumentBuilderFactory factory =
    DocumentBuilderFactory.newInstance();
factory.setNamespaceAware(true);
DocumentBuilder builder = factory.newDocumentBuilder();
document = builder.newDocument();
DOMImplementation implementation =
    document.getImplementation();
document =
    implementation.createDocument(NS,"xbe:products",null);
document.getDocumentElement().setAttribute("xmlns:xbe",NS);
```

CAUTION

Note that the code explicitly creates the xmlns:xbe attribute to declare the http://www.psol.com/xbe2/listing9.4 namespace. This is a limitation of Xerces 1.3.

NOTE

The code above follows the DOM logic to the absurd. It is also possible to use the Document object returned by DocumentBuilder directly, but I like the previous construct better.

Displaying the Result

EXAMPLE

If Sun has defined objects to create DOM parsers, it provides nothing to write documents. Because neither the W3C nor Sun has defined a standard, you'll have to resort to parser-specific code.

Listing 9.4 uses the XMLSerializer class from Xerces 1.3. Using a Xerces serializer is easy. Just creates a serializer object, passing it a Writer and OutputFormat. Next set the serializer in DOM mode with asDOMSerializer() and use the serialize() method passing it the root element.

```
protected void updateDisplay()
{
    StringWriter writer = new StringWriter();
    try
    {
        OutputFormat format = new OutputFormat(document);
        format.setIndenting(true);
        XMLSerializer serializer =
            new XMLSerializer(writer,format);
        serializer.asDOMSerializer();
        serializer.serialize(document.getDocumentElement());
```

```
   }
   catch(IOException e)
   {
      e.printStackTrace(new PrintWriter(writer));
   }
   xmlText.setText(writer.toString());
}
```

Using DOM to Create Documents

As you have seen, it is very easy to create or modify XML documents with DOM. The parser creates a Document object and you can use it to add (or modify) objects to the document tree.

The main advantage to using DOM is the same reason you use a parser in the first place: It shields the application from the XML syntax.

The parser also enforces syntactical rules: It accepts only one element at the top level. Unfortunately, at the time of writing, DOM does not fully support DTDs; therefore, it is not possible to force the parser to validate a document as it is being created.

On the downside, the application has to explicitly create the DOM tree for the document. As always, it is inefficient if the application already has its own data structure. In this case, it might be more efficient to skip DOM and write the XML document directly from the application's own data structure. The next section discusses this approach.

Creating Documents Without DOM

It is not difficult, either, to write XML documents without the help of a parser/generator. Indeed, the core of the XML syntax (what most applications use) is not complex.

EXAMPLE

Listing 9.5 is a JavaScript application to create, edit, and manage a list of products in an HTML form. Users can add or remove products from the list. The application has its own data structure (not DOM), but it can still export the list in XML.

Listing 9.5: editor.html

```
<html>
<head>
<title>Price List Editor</title>
<script language="JavaScript">
var products = new Array(),
    ns = "http://www.psol.com/xbe2/listing9.5";
```

Listing 9.5: continued

```
function addProduct(form)
{
   // collects data from the form
   var name = form.name.value,
       dollars = form.dollarsamount.value,
       euros = form.eurosamount.value,
       productList = form.productlist;
   // creates the various objects
   var dollarsPrice = new Price(dollars,"usd"),
       eurosPrice = new Price(euros,"eur"),
       prices = new Array(dollarsPrice,eurosPrice),
       product = new Product(name,prices);
   // arrays are zero-based so products.length points
   // to one past the latest product
   // JavaScript automatically allocates memory
   var pos = products.length;
   products[pos] = product;
   var option = new Option(name,pos);
   productList.options[productList.length] = option;
}

function deleteProduct(form)
{
   var productList = form.productlist,
       pos = productList.selectedIndex;
   if(pos != -1)
   {
      var product = productList.options[pos].value;
      productList.options[pos] = null;
      products[product] = null;
   }
}

function exportProduct(form)
{
   form.output.value = makeXML();
}

function makeXML()
{
   var xmlCode = "";
   var i;
   for(i = 0;i < products.length;i++)
      if(products[i] != null)
         xmlCode += products[i].toXML();
```

Listing 9.5: continued

```
    return element("xbe:products","xmlns:xbe=\"" + ns + "\"",
                   xmlCode);
}

function resetAll(form,document)
{
    priceList = null;
    form.output.value = "";
}

function element(name,attributes,content)
{
    var result = "<" + name;
    if(attributes != "")
        result += " " + attributes;
    result += ">";
    result += content;
    result += "</" + name + ">\r";
    return result;
}

function escapeXML(string)
{
    var result = "",
        i,
        c;
    for(i = 0;i < string.length;i++)
    {
        c = string.charAt(i);
        if(c == '<')
            result += "&lt;";
        else if(c == '&')
            result += "&amp;";
        else
            result += c;
    }
    return result;
}

// declares two JavaScript objects

// product object

function Product(name,prices)
{
    this.name = name;
```

Listing 9.5: continued

```
      this.prices = prices;
      this.toXML = product_toXML;
}

function product_toXML()
{
   var result = element("xbe:name","",escapeXML(this.name)),
       i;
   for(i = 0;i < this.prices.length;i++)
      result += this.prices[i].toXML();
   return element("xbe:product","",result);
}

// price object

function Price(amount,currency)
{
   this.amount = amount;
   this.currency = currency;
   this.toXML = price_toXML;
}

function price_toXML()
{
   return element("xbe:price",
                  "currency=\"" + this.currency + "\"",
                  escapeXML(this.amount));
}
</script>
</head>
<body>
<center>
<!-- name works with Netscape & IE -->
<form name="controls" action="http://localhost:5301/dump"
      method="post">
Product name: <input type="text" name="name">
Price (USD): <input type="text" name="dollarsamount" size="7">
Price (EUR): <input type="text" name="eurosamount" size="7"><br>
<select name="productlist" size="5" width="250">
</select><br>
<input type="button" value="Add"
                onclick="addProduct(controls)">
<input type="button" value="Delete"
                onclick="deleteProduct(controls)">
<input type="button" value="Export to XML"
                onclick="exportProduct(controls)">
```

Listing 9.5: continued

```
<input type="button" value="Clear"
            onclick="resetAll(controls)">
<input type="submit" value="Send to server"
            onclick="exportProduct(controls)"><br>
<!-- there must be one character in the text area -->
<textarea name="output" rows="12" cols="50" readonly> </textarea>
</form>
</center>
</body>
</html>
```

OUTPUT

Because this application does not use DOM, it works with browsers that have no XML support (obviously, they need to support JavaScript), such as older browsers. Figure 9.5 shows the result in a browser.

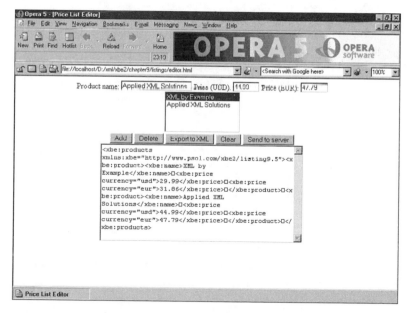

Figure 9.5: The result in the Opera browser.

A Non-DOM Data Structure

This application is radically different from the other applications introduced in this chapter. Internally, the application does not use XML, but uses its own data structure instead. In other words, it does not create Element objects; it creates Product and Price JavaScript objects.

In JavaScript, an object constructor is simply a function that sets the object properties. A method is a property that is assigned a function.

EXAMPLE

In this example, the constructor for Product declares two properties (name and prices) and one method (toXML).

```
function Product(name,prices)
{
   this.name = name;
   this.prices = prices;
   this.toXML = product_toXML;
}
```

These objects are created with the new operator like built-in JavaScript objects:

```
var product = new Product(name,prices);
```

JavaScript objects are used like built-in objects:

```
xmlCode += products[i].toXML();
```

Writing XML

EXAMPLE

The Product and Price objects are XML-aware because they know how to save (serialize) themselves as XML objects through the toXML() function. The makeXML() function is trivial: It iterates over the list of products calling the toXML() function. It wraps the result in a products element:

```
function makeXML()
{
   var xmlCode = "";
   var i;
   for(i = 0;i < products.length;i++)
      if(products[i] != null)
          xmlCode += products[i].toXML();
   return element("xbe:products","xmlns:xbe=\"" + ns + "\"",
               xmlCode);
}
```

Notice that this approach is recursive. Product implements its toXML() method partly by serializing the list of Price and wrapping it in a product element.

```
function product_toXML()
{
   var result = element("xbe:name","",escapeXML(this.name)),
       i;
   for(i = 0;i < this.prices.length;i++)
      result += this.prices[i].toXML();
   return element("xbe:product","",result);
}
function price_toXML()
{
   return element("xbe:price",
```

```
                              "currency=\"" + this.currency + "\"",
                              escapeXML(this.amount));
    }
```

XML is a convenient format because elements can nest in a way that is very similar to how objects are referenced by other objects.

Hiding the Syntax

This application needs to know very little about the XML syntax. Its knowledge is completely encapsulated in two functions[md]element() and escapeXML().

EXAMPLE

element() is in charge of the tagging. Again, the core XML syntax function is simple and it shows in this function.

```
function element(name,attributes,content)
{
    var result = "<" + name;
    if(attributes != "")
        result += " " + attributes;
    result += ">";
    result += content;
    result += "</" + name + ">\r";
    return result;
}
```

EXAMPLE

escapeXML() ensures that the angle bracket and ampersand characters are escaped. These characters are not allowed in the text of an element.

```
function escapeXML(string)
{
    var result = "",
        i,
        c;
    for(i = 0;i < string.length;i++)
    {
        c = string.charAt(i);
        if(c == '<')
            result += "&lt;";
        else if(c == '&')
            result += "&amp;";
        else
            result += c;
    }
    return result;
}
```

Creating Documents from Non-XML Data Structures

For most applications, it is easy to write an XML generator. Indeed, the core XML syntax (essentially composed of tags) is not complex. Furthermore, XML elements nest in a way that is very convenient for object-oriented applications.

Typically, creating documents from non-XML data structures is more efficient than the DOM-based approach because the application doesn't have to duplicate its data structure. Figure 9.6 compares the two approaches.

TIP

So, when do you use DOM and when do you write your own generator? I find that DOM is ideal for modifying existing documents. In most other cases, I prefer my own generator.

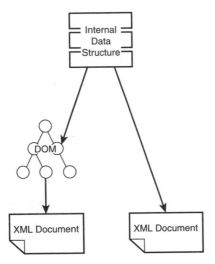

Figure 9.6: *Comparing DOM with an ad hoc generator.*

Doing Something with the XML Documents

Now that you can create XML documents, you probably want to do something more involved than displaying the XML code in an HTML form. In most cases, the application can either save the document to a file or send it to a server.

Sending the Document to the Server

There are two options to send the document to the server. You can place the XML document in an HTML form and have it sent along with the form, or you can use a JavaBean or an ActiveX control to post the XML document to the Web server.

EXAMPLE

Sending the XML document in a form is the more portable approach. Listing 9.3 demonstrates it. It suffices to have a submit button on the form; the browser will send the form content (including the text area with the XML document) to the server:

```
<input type="submit" value="Send to server"
          onclick="exportProduct(controls)"><br>
```

In most cases, you would want to change the text area in a hidden input field so the XML document does not appear onscreen.

The Web server will receive the XML document in a parameter called *output*. You would need to write a servlet, a CGI script, or an ASP page to process this form, as you would for any other form.

✔ The section "Viewer and Editor" in Chapter 12 **(page 391)** shows such a servlet.

CAUTION

Listing 9.3 uses the Dump service that ships with Jetty, the Web server used in this book. Dump returns a document that contains whatever it originally received. It is convenient for testing.

If you download the listings from www.marchal.com or www.quepublishing.com, it includes a copy of Jetty with a properly configured Dump service.

TIP

Jetty's Dump returns an HTML document which contains the POST parameters. Choose "View Source" in your browser options to see the XML document.

✔ Section "Servlet Engine" in Appendix A explains how to install Jetty.

Alternatively, you can post the data directly to the Web server, without going through a form. This method has the added benefit of not changing the current page. However, you have to go through an ActiveX object (Internet Explorer), a plug-in (all browsers), or a JavaBean (all browsers, all platforms).

EXAMPLE

Internet Explorer 5.0 ships with XMLHTTP, an ActiveX control that can send XML documents from JavaScript. Listing 9.6 shows how to use XML-HTTP.

Listing 9.6: Script to Post an XML Document Through XMLHTTP

```
function send()
{
    var http = new ActiveXObject("Microsoft.XMLHTTP");
    http.open("POST","http://localhost:5301/dump",false);
```

```
http.setRequestHeader("Content-type","application/xml");
http.send(makeXML());
document.open();
document.write(http.responseText);
}
```

The ActiveX object has the following methods:

- `open(protocol,url,asynchronous)` connects to a url. Set the `protocol` to `POST`. Set `asynchronous` to `false` to send synchronously.

- `setRequestHeader(keyword,value)` adds a new `keyword` in the header of the document; you must use this function to set the content-type.

- `send(data)` posts the `data` to the server.

Again, you need a servlet or CGI script on the server to receive the XML document.

Saving the Document

EXAMPLE

From Java, it's easy to save a document to a file. As Listing 9.4 illustrated, Xerces expects a `java.io.Writer` to serialize a document. Although, in Listing 9.4, you choose to serialize to a string, you could have used a FileWriter and serialized to a regular file:

```
try
{
    Writer writer = new FileWriter("mydocument.xml");
    OutputFormat format = new OutputFormat(document);
    format.setIndenting(true);
    XMLSerializer serializer =
        new XMLSerializer(writer,format);
    serializer.asDOMSerializer();
    serializer.serialize(document.getDocumentElement());
    writer.close();
}
catch(IOException e)
{
    e.printStackTrace();
}
```

EXAMPLE

JavaScript running in a browser cannot access the local hard disk unless it has been signed. Therefore, it is not common to save the XML on file from a browser.

However, when using JavaScript on servers (for example, from an ASP page), you want to save XML documents often. The Microsoft DOM parser offers the `save()` function for that purpose.

However, as I have just explained, this extension does not work on the browser. It is therefore useful only when writing CGI scripts or ASP pages. The example in Listing 9.7 shows how to save a file from JavaScript in an ASP server.

Listing 9.7: Saving XML Documents with Microsoft Parser

```
<%
   var xmldoc = new ActiveXObject("Microsoft.XMLDOM");
   // creates the XML document here
   // ...
   xmldoc.save(Server.MapPath("mydocument.xml"));
%>
```

NOTE

To create an XML parser from ASP, you cannot use XML islands. Instead, create the XML parser directly as an ActiveX Object as in

```
var xmldoc = new ActiveXObject("Microsoft.XMLDOM");
```

Writing with Flexibility in Mind

One of the major advantages of XML is that it is extensible. Anybody can create a markup language with tags specific to his or her application.

On the other hand, it means applications must be able to support different models. For example, your company can have its own model for internal exchange. However, when exchanging documents with other companies, you may have to use another model.

There are also so-called "standard DTDs" or "standard Schemas" developed by various standardization committees. In fact, developing DTDs has become a favorite activity in standard bodies lately so expect more choice in the future. Unfortunately, so many committees are actively developing standards that they result in numerous incompatible standards that you then need to support in your applications.

There are essentially two solutions to this problem. Either you define several functions, one for each model that you want to support, and have each function generate the XML code for a given model, or you turn to XSLT.

In most cases, I would advocate using XSLT. It is a waste of time to write as many functions as there are models. XSLT is also more flexible because you don't have to write code to add new models or when a model changes (and it happens more often than you might think).

Supporting Several XML Models with XSLT

EXAMPLE

Listing 9.8 shows how to use XSLT to support several models. The user can choose the model from a listbox. Unlike the previous listing, this uses DOM and the XSLT processor of Internet Explorer 5. It would not run on another browser.

TIP

If you need to support both browsers, you can replace the Internet Explorer XSLT processor with Xalan and create the XML document without DOM.

Xalan comes with several examples that show how to use it in a browser. However, it is not as stable as using the built-in XSLT processor, which explains why I decided to stick to Internet Explorer.

Listing 9.8: `multi.html`

```
<html>
<head>
<title>Price List Editor</title>
<script language="JavaScript">
var ns = "http://www.psol.com/xbe2/listing9.8";

function create(form,xmlIsland,xslt)
{
   var name = form.name.value,
       price = form.price.value,
       currency = form.currency.value,
       root = xmlIsland.documentElement;
   if(root == null)
   {
      root = xmlIsland.createNode(1,"products",ns);
      xmlIsland.appendChild(root);
   }
   var elProduct = xmlIsland.createNode(1,"product",ns),
       elName = xmlIsland.createNode(1,"name",ns),
       elPrice = xmlIsland.createNode(1,"price",ns);
   elPrice.setAttribute("currency",currency);
   var text = xmlIsland.createTextNode(name);
   elName.appendChild(text);
   text = xmlIsland.createTextNode(price);
   elPrice.appendChild(text);
   elProduct.appendChild(elName);
   elProduct.appendChild(elPrice);
   root.appendChild(elProduct);
   updateDisplay(form,xmlIsland,xslt);
}
```

Listing 9.8: continued

```
function updateDisplay(form,xmlIsland,xslt)
{
   var selected = form.format.selectedIndex,
       format = form.format.options[selected].value,
       output = form.output;
   if(format == "default")
      output.value = xmlIsland.xml;
   else
      output.value = xmlIsland.transformNode(xslt.XMLDocument);
}

function resetAll(form,xmlIsland)
{
   var root = xmlIsland.documentElement,
       output = form.output;
   document.removeChild(root);
   output.value = "";
}
</script>
</head>
<body>
<center>
<form name="controls">
Product name: <input type="text" name="name">
Price: <input type="text" name="price" size="7">
<select name="currency">
   <option value="eur">Euros</option>
   <option value="usd" selected>Dollars</option>
</select><br>
<input type="button" value="Create"
       onclick="create(controls,xmlIsland,xslt)">
<input type="button" value="Update"
       onclick="updateDisplay(controls,xmlIsland,xslt)">
<select name="format">
   <option value="default" selected>products</option>
   <option value="external">price-list</option>
</select>
<input type="button" value="Clear"
       onclick="resetAll(controls,xmlIsland)"><br>
<!-- there must be one character in the text area -->
<textarea name="output" rows="12" cols="50" readonly> </textarea>
</form>
</center>
<xml id="xmlIsland"></xml>
<xml id="xslt">
<?xml version="1.0"?>
```

Listing 9.8: continued

```
<xsl:stylesheet xmlns:xsl="http://www.w3.org/TR/WD-xsl">
<!-- I.E. 5.0 style sheet: no built-in rule and old URI-->

<xsl:template match="/">
   <xsl:apply-templates/>
</xsl:template>

<xsl:template match="products">
   <price-list>
      <xsl:apply-templates/>
   </price-list>
</xsl:template>

<xsl:template match="product">
   <xsl:apply-templates/>
</xsl:template>

<xsl:template match="price">
   <line>
      <xsl:attribute name="name"><xsl:value-of
         select="../name"/></xsl:attribute>
      <xsl:attribute name="price"><xsl:value-of
         select="."/></xsl:attribute>
      <xsl:attribute name="currency"><xsl:value-of
         select="@currency"/></xsl:attribute>
   </line>
</xsl:template>

</xsl:stylesheet>
</xml>
</body>
</html>
```

The application creates a document following a default model. A style sheet converts it to another model, if required. Obviously, it is an Internet Explorer style sheet. As explained in Chapter 5, Internet Explorer uses an old draft of XSLT and the style sheet is not strictly compliant with the standard. Furthermore, it does not support namespaces.

Figures 9.7 and 9.8 illustrate the difference between the two models. Figure 9.7 relies on elements extensively. It needs more levels of nesting. Figure 9.8, on the other hand, has a flat structure with few elements and many attributes.

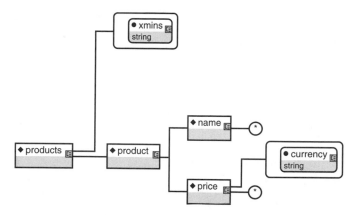

Figure 9.7: *The nested structure.*

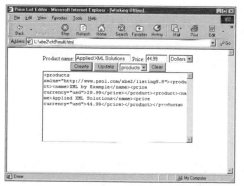

Figure 9.8: *The flat structure.*

Figures 9.9 and 9.10 show the difference when selecting one or the other output format in the browser.

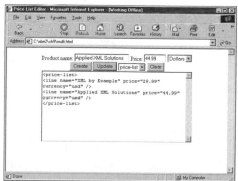

Figure 9.9: *Generating according to one model.*   ***Figure 9.10:*** *And the other.*

Calling XSLT

EXAMPLE

Most of the code in Listing 9.8 is familiar. The novelty is the `updateDisplay()` method which may apply a style sheet to the document.

```
function updateDisplay(form,xmlIsland,xslt)
```

```
{
  var selected = form.format.selectedIndex,
      format = form.format.options[selected].value,
      output = form.output;
  if(format == "default")
    output.value = xmlIsland.xml;
  else
    output.value = xmlIsland.transformNode(xslt.XMLDocument);
}
```

Unfortunately, the DOM standard does not specify how to apply an XSLT style sheet to a document. Again, you can use a browser-specific extension. For Internet Explorer, the XSL processor is called by the transformNode() method.

Note that the XSLT style sheet was loaded in its own XML island.

Which Structure for the Document?

If your application supports several models, you may wonder which one to use as the "default" model. Experience shows that it pays to be dumb when designing this "default" model.

I like to define a model that is very similar to my object structure. So, if the application has Product and Price objects, I create two elements: product and price.

There are two main advantages to designing a model that is close to the internal data structure:

- It is easy to generate the XML document.

- The resulting document is as expressive as the internal data structure.

XSLT Versus Custom Functions

XSLT has been designed specifically to convert XML documents. It offers a simple solution to cleanly separate the model from the application code. This separation of roles offers many advantages:

- If the format changes, you don't have to change your application, only the style sheet.

- Somebody else can write and maintain the style sheet while you concentrate on the application; this is a simple solution for separating work in a team.

- After the system is in place, it's easy to provide 5, 10, or 100 style sheets.

- Conversely, you can deploy the application with only those few style sheets the users really need. Therefore, the application loads faster.

CAUTION

Using XSLT is less efficient than custom export functions. If you decide not to use XSLT (or cannot, for performance reasons), I advise you to investigate the visitor pattern, described in "Design Patterns" by Gamma et al. The visitor pattern is a clean solution for separating the various XML structures from the objects.

What's Next

The next chapter returns to modeling. Armed with a better understanding of how to manipulate XML documents, you will learn several useful standard models. These provide a good starting point for many XML applications.

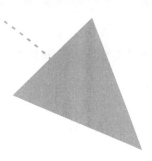

Important XML Models

You are reaching the end of your tour of XML. In the previous chapters, you learned not only XML syntax but also how to manipulate XML. The next two chapters are devoted to a real-life e-commerce application based on XML.

In this chapter, you review some aspects of XML flexibility. In particular, you revisit some concepts related to modeling documents. I hope the previous chapters have convinced you that XML is a flexible solution for many applications.

You have already learned about some of the topics we'll cover now in other chapters. This discussion consolidates previous discussions. More specifically, you learn about the following:

- How to take advantage of XML extensibility through namespaces

- Some standards under development by the W3C

- "Warning signs" that may point to problems in an XML document

- The raging debate in the XML community: attributes versus elements

Structured and Extensible

When I wrote the first edition of *XML by Example*, few XML models were available. I had to make up most of the tags in the example.

In a year and half, much has changed in this respect. The XML developer can choose from a large variety of existing models. These models were developed by various standard bodies, including the W3C (www.w3.org), OASIS (www.oasis-open.org), ebXML (www.ebxml.org), the OMG (www.omg.org), the WAP Forum (www.wapforum.org), or software vendors, such as CommerceOne (www.commerceone.com). You can find a good selection of models in the online repository at www.xml.org.

It is not possible, in this book, to review all these XML-based markup languages. One would need more than one book. In this chapter, you'll learn what you should look for as you select and adapt the models suitable to your needs.

As you learned in Chapter 1, "The XML Galaxy," and as you saw demonstrated in Chapters 2 through 9, unlike HTML, XML encourages you to focus on the structure of the information. How you eventually use the document is derived from its structure. Style sheets are typical of this approach because they let you render a document onscreen or on paper based on its structure.

To this end, XML is extensible. In practice, it means that you can define your own elements, tags, and attributes and decide how to combine them.

The challenge in making a successful XML application is to channel XML extensibility in a sensible way. The first generation of models, directly inspired from SGML, would tend to limit the flexibility; they attempt to build a superset model.

However, a second generation is appearing that builds on the extensibility as an essential part of the application. These models are broken down in modules.

The Superset Model Approach

DocBook is a typical example of this approach. You will remember DocBook from Chapter 5, "XSL Transformations," and Chapter 6, "XSL Formatting Objects and Cascading Style Sheets." DocBook was originally developed as an SGML DTD for technical documentation.

At the time of this writing, DocBook is in its fourth revision, and it has been ported from SGML to XML. DocBook defines tags for every concept you might need when working with technical documentation, including the following:

- Book, chapter, article

- Sections, appendixes, index, table of contents, glossary

- Paragraphs, lists, figures, listings, tables, notes

- Footnotes, hyperlinks, emphasis

In short, DocBook is a comprehensive solution that offers every tag you would need when producing books or articles. Although DocBook is best tailored for technical documentation, it should work for any book.

EXAMPLE

Listing 10.1 is an example of a DocBook document. You may remember it from Chapters 5 and 6. For examples of style sheets, turn to Chapter 5.

Listing 10.1: docbook.xml

```
<?xml version="1.0"?>
<article>
<articleinfo>
 <title>XSL -- First Step in Learning XML</title>
 <author><firstname>Beno&#238;t</firstname>
  <surname>Marchal</surname></author>
</articleinfo>
<sect1><title>The Value of XSL</title>
 <para>This is an excerpt from the September 2000 issue of
  Pineapplesoft Link. To subscribe free visit
  <ulink url="http://www.marchal.com">marchal.com</ulink>.</para>
 <para>Where do you start learning XML? Increasingly my answer
  is with XSL. XSL is a very powerful tool with many
  applications. Many XML applications depend on it. Let's take
  two examples.</para>
</sect1>
<sect1>
 <title>XSL and Web Publishing</title>
 <para>As a webmaster you would benefit from using XSL.</para>
 <para>Let's suppose that you decide to support smartphones.
  You will need to redo your web site using WML, the
  <emphasis>wireless markup language</emphasis>, instead of
  HTML. While learning WML is easy, it can take days if not
  months to redo a large web site. Imagine having to edit every
  single page by hand!</para>
 <para>In contrast with XSL, it suffices to update one style
  sheet the changes flow across the entire web site.</para>
</sect1>
<sect1>
 <title>XSL and Programming</title>
 <para>The second facet of XSL is the scripting language. XSL
```

Listing 10.1: continued

```
has many features of scripting languages including loops,
function calls, variables and more.</para>
<para>In that respect, XSL is a valuable addition to any
programmer toolbox. Indeed, as XML popularity keeps growing,
you will find that you need to manipulate XML documents
frequently and XSL is the language for so doing.</para>
</sect1>
<sect1>
<title>Conclusion</title>
<para>If you're serious about learning XML, learn XSL. XSL is
a tool to manipulate XML documents for web publishing or
programming.</para>
</sect1>
</article>
```

This simple example shows some of the benefits of maintaining documents in XML:

- As you saw in Chapter 5 and 6, the same document can be reused in different contexts; in this case, HTML, WML, and PDF versions of the document were produced automatically.

- It is easy to change the presentation, just update the style sheet.

- As you saw in Chapter 1, several excellent XML editors make it easy to write and maintain the document.

- If the document grows and special needs arise, it is possible to write specialized software (using SAX or DOM) to further manipulate the article.

- If you have many such articles, it is possible to move to an XML database for better performance.

In other words, XML and DocBook offer you a good file format to author, maintain, and publish documents. Furthermore, XML is supported by many high-quality off-the-shelf software applications that you can use to manipulate the document quickly and inexpensively.

DocBook has tags for every situation a book author might face and more. It is one of the most comprehensive models of technical documentation; it covers all the bases. Indeed, if yours is a document publishing application, I strongly recommend you check DocBook (the official Web site is www.oasis-open.org/docbook).

If your application relates to technical documentation, there is no room for doubt: you need DocBook.

However, this richness is a strength and a weakness. First, DocBook is a large and complex standard—so large and so complex that you cannot use it as is. In practice, you need to simplify the standard and retain only those pieces that are sensible to you.

For example, there are no book or chapter tags in Listing 10.1. Also, although DocBook defines up to five levels of sections (from sect1 to sect5), Listing 10.1 uses only the first level.

Furthermore, such a large standard is difficult to learn and to maintain. The DocBook committee is doing a fabulous job, but it's a lot of work.

The Modular Approach

Because large models are expensive to build and difficult to use, a new approach, defined as modular, has emerged. This new approach takes advantage of two XML features: namespaces and well-formed documents.

The idea is to break large models into a set of smaller modules and to design these modules so that they can be combined at will.

EXAMPLE

Listing 10.2 illustrates this with XML digital signature. The heart of this document is Listing 10.1, but it has wrapped around a digital signature.

> **CAUTION**
>
> At the time of writing, the XML digital signature standard is still under development. This document is based on the 31-October-2000 working draft. It was created with IBM's XML Security Suite, which currently is available from www.alphaworks.ibm.com.
>
> IBM tends to move software from Alphaworks into products on a regular basis. By the time you read this, the XML Security Suite may have moved.

> **CAUTION**
>
> I had to reformat the document so that it would print on one page. The actual document is slightly different. You can download the actual document from www.quepublishing.com or www.marchal.com.

Listing 10.2: signed.xml

```
<?xml version='1.0' encoding='UTF-8'?>
<Signature xmlns="http://www.w3.org/2000/09/xmldsig#">
  <SignedInfo>
    <CanonicalizationMethod
     Algorithm="http://www.w3.org/TR/2000/WD-xml-c14n-20000119"/>
    <SignatureMethod
     Algorithm="http://www.w3.org/2000/09/xmldsig#dsa-sha1"/>
    <Reference URI="#Res0">
      <Transforms>
```

Listing 10.2: continued

```xml
      <Transform
    Algorithm="http://www.w3.org/TR/2000/WD-xml-c14n-20000119"/>
      </Transforms>
      <DigestMethod
       Algorithm="http://www.w3.org/2000/09/xmldsig#sha1"/>
      <DigestValue>EnjbDLqPu+IJvjobZ0KnvL30k0M=</DigestValue>
    </Reference>
  </SignedInfo>
  <SignatureValue>
      lzJVXLLvTPEOWm89JxJfDr2UBDh8eD6cy+LbeiRj1m9vRlwxAT3erg==
  </SignatureValue>
  <KeyInfo>
    <KeyValue>
      <DSAKeyValue>
<P>
/X9TgR11EilS30qcLuzk5/YRt1I870QAwx4/gLZRJmlFXUAiUftZPY1Y+r/F9bow9s
ubVWzXgTuAHTRv8mZgt2uZUKWkn5/oBHsQIsJPu6nX/rfGG/g7V+fGqKYVDwT7g/bT
xR7DAjVUE1oWkTL2dfOuK2HXKu/yIgMZndFIAcc=
</P>
<Q>l2BQjxUjC8yykrmCouuEC/BYHPU=</Q>
<G>
9+GghdabPd7LvKtcNrhXuXmUr7v6OuqC+VdMCz0HgmdRWVeOutRZT+ZxBxCBgLRJFn
Ej6EwoFhO3zwkyjMim4TwWeotUfI0o4KOuHiuzpnWRbqN/C/ohNWLx+2J6ASQ7zKTx
vqhRkImog9/hWuWfBpKLZl6Ae1UlZAFMO/7PSSo=
</G>
<Y>
ExRJP2t4T0h07oLAqlgv9mXNFKX8X+tIgjA6860srebYoWLaxFTdEV6dq0DM5ffejf
1tkmPYS5wIsUXMrILPJpTpp/4c/AROv2dqnqAch4KqE7sJ16hKUxJyB8r2Rw6LIZmZ
m80S5nWt2UxC3rLy/lBmSTLCHBbx3/lGR+gfiOs=
</Y>
      </DSAKeyValue>
    </KeyValue>
    <X509Data>
      <X509IssuerSerial>
        <X509IssuerName>
          CN=Benoît Marchal, O=Pineapplesoft, L=Namur, C=BE
        </X509IssuerName>
        <X509SerialNumber>982695798</X509SerialNumber>
      </X509IssuerSerial>
      <X509SubjectName>
        CN=Benoît Marchal, O=Pineapplesoft, L=Namur, C=BE
      </X509SubjectName>
      <X509Certificate>
MIIC0DCCAo4CBDqSv3YwCwYHKoZIzjgEAwUAME4xCzAJBgNVBAYTAkJFMQ4wDAYDVQQHEwVOYW11
cjEWMBQGA1UEChMNUGluZWFwcGxlc29mdDEXMBUGA1UEAxMOQmVub690IE1hcmNoYWwwHhcNMDEw
MjIwMTkwMzE4WhcNMDEwNTIxMTkwMzE4WjBOMQswCQYDVQQGEwJCRTEOMAwGA1UEBxMFTmFtdXIx
```

Listing 10.2: continued

```
FjAUBgNVBAoTDVBpbmVhcHBsZXNvZnQxFzAVBgNVBAMTDkJlbm+vdCBNYXJjaGFsMIIBtzCCASwG
ByqGSM44BAEwggEfAoGBAP1/U4EddRIpUt9KnC7s5Of2EbdSP09EAMMeP4C2USZpRV1AIlH7WT2N
WPq/xfW6MPbLm1Vs14E7gB00b/JmYLdrmVClpJ+f6AR7ECLCT7up1/63xhv4O1fnxqimFQ8E+4P2
08UewwI1VBNaFpEy9nXzrith1yrv8iIDGZ3RSAHHAhUAl2BQjxUjC8yykrmCouuEC/BYHPUCgYEA
9+GghdabPd7LvKtcNrhXuXmUr7v6OuqC+VdMCz0HgmdRWVeOutRZT+ZxBxCBgLRJFnEj6EwoFhO3
zwkyjMim4TwWeotUfI0o4KOuHiuzpnWRbqN/C/ohNWLx+2J6ASQ7zKTxvqhRkImog9/hWuWfBpKL
Z16Ae1UlZAFMO/7PSSoDgYQAAoGAExRJP2t4T0h07oLAqlgv9mXNFKX8X+tIgjA6860srebYoWLa
xFTdEV6dq0DM5ffejf1tkmPYS5wIsUXMrILPJpTpp/4c/AROv2dqnqAch4KqE7sJ16hKUxJyB8r2
Rw6LIZmZm80S5nWt2UxC3rLy/lBmSTLCHBbx3/lGR+gfiOswCwYHKoZIzjgEAwUAAy8AMCwCFG/V
auq62IHCx0o2wCqWb6x0hXRNAhQ8wEQ0yznxVqcVZ60bxOuCr5V30Q==
```

```
      </X509Certificate>
     </X509Data>
   </KeyInfo>
   <dsig:Object Id="Res0" xmlns=""
    xmlns:dsig="http://www.w3.org/2000/09/xmldsig#"><article>
<articleinfo>
 <title>XSL -- First Step in Learning XML</title>
 <author><firstname>Benoît</firstname>
  <surname>Marchal</surname></author>
</articleinfo>
<sect1><title>The Value of XSL</title>
 <para>This is an excerpt from the September 2000 issue of
  Pineapplesoft Link. To subscribe free visit
   <ulink url="http://www.marchal.com">marchal.com</ulink>.</para>
 <para>Where do you start learning XML? Increasingly my answer
  is with XSL. XSL is a very powerful tool with many
  applications. Many XML applications depend on it. Let's take
  two examples.</para>
</sect1>
<sect1>
 <title>XSL and Web Publishing</title>
 <para>As a webmaster you would benefit from using XSL.</para>
 <para>Let's suppose that you decide to support smartphones.
  You will need to redo your web site using WML, the
   <emphasis>wireless markup language</emphasis>, instead of
  HTML. While learning WML is easy, it can take days if not
  months to redo a large web site. Imagine having to edit every
  single page by hand!</para>
 <para>In contrast with XSL, it suffices to update one style
  sheet the changes flow across the entire web site.</para>
</sect1>
<sect1>
 <title>XSL and Programming</title>
 <para>The second facet of XSL is the scripting language. XSL
  has many features of scripting languages including loops,
  function calls, variables and more.</para>
```

Listing 10.2: continued

```
<para>In that respect, XSL is a valuable addition to any
 programmer toolbox. Indeed, as XML popularity keeps growing,
 you will find that you need to manipulate XML documents
 frequently and XSL is the language for so doing.</para>
</sect1>
<sect1>
 <title>Conclusion</title>
 <para>If you're serious about learning XML, learn XSL. XSL is
 a tool to manipulate XML documents for web publishing or
 programming.</para>
</sect1>
</article></dsig:Object>
</Signature>
```

NOTE

Increasingly, you will need digitally signed documents. A digital signature guarantees that an electronic document was written (or approved) by the signer, just like a regular signature guarantees that a paper document was approved by the signer.

For example, electronic prescriptions would have to be signed. If you receive a prescription from your doctor via e-mail (don't laugh, some people are seriously considering this), you want to be sure that it really originated from your doctor: you don't want anybody else to prescribe you medicine!

The same holds true for commercial and administrative documents, such as orders, payments, passports, or even concert tickets. You want to make sure that your tickets are valid—so does the show manager.

The idea with this document is to build on a toolkit of standard elements and attributes defined by the W3C or another standard body. Those elements and attributes are placed in a special namespace, and they support commonly used features. Over time, the W3C and other groups will build a large toolbox of elements that you can use in your documents.

Listing 10.2 is based on the signature standard currently being developed by the W3C and the IETF (Internet Engineering Task Force). Although it has nothing to do with links or product prices, it is based on the idea of standardizing a few elements required for a specific application. The application is cryptographic software in this case.

The `xmldsig` working group aims at developing a set of elements and attributes to represent digital signatures in XML documents.

In Listing 10.2, the elements for digital signature are in the `http://www.w3.org/2000/09/xmldsig#` namespace and a few other namespaces derived from it (such as `http://www.w3.org/2000/09/xmldsig#dsa-sha1`).

By virtue of being in their own namespace, it is easy for software to pick up the relevant elements and process them. The beauty of this approach is that the digital signature elements can be combined with other elements—in this case, DocBook element—to create a new markup language that is the sum of two original markup languages.

Indeed, by adding the digital signature elements to Listing 10.1, we have created a digitally signed version of the article.

Furthermore, because the elements are in different namespaces, software can still pick them apart. In most cases, when you receive a digitally signed electronic document you want to do two things:

1. Validate that the signature is indeed correct; this is done with a cryptographic toolkit.

2. Display the document so that you can read it. This is done, for example, with XSLT.

Figure 10.1 illustrates how to validate the signature. It uses the IBM cryptographic toolkit mentioned previously. Bear in mind that this toolkit does not know and does not need to know about DocBook. It is concerned only about cryptographic elements that it can recognize by their namespace.

In other words, I could use the same toolkit to verify the signature of a completely different class of documents, such as the price lists introduced in Chapters 7, 8, and 9.

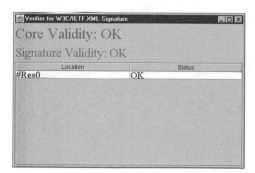

Figure 10.1: *Verifying the signature.*

Conversely, to display the document, I could use the style sheet in Listing 10.3. This style sheet need not know anything about cryptographic elements.

Listing 10.3: `view.xsl`

```
<?xml version="1.0"?>
```

Listing 10.3: continued

```
<xsl:stylesheet
   xmlns:xsl="http://www.w3.org/1999/XSL/Transform"
   version="1.0">

<xsl:output method="html"/>

<xsl:template match="/">
   <xsl:apply-templates select="//article"/>
</xsl:template>

<xsl:template match="article">
<html>
   <head>
      <title><xsl:value-of
         select="articleinfo/title"/></title>
   </head>
   <body>
      <xsl:apply-templates/>
   </body>
</html>
</xsl:template>

<xsl:template match="articleinfo/title">
   <h1><xsl:apply-templates/></h1>
</xsl:template>

<xsl:template match="sect1/title">
   <h2><xsl:apply-templates/></h2>
</xsl:template>

<xsl:template match="ulink">
   <a href="{@url}"><xsl:apply-templates/></a>
</xsl:template>

<xsl:template match="emphasis">
   <b><xsl:apply-templates/></b>
</xsl:template>

<xsl:template match="para">
   <p><xsl:apply-templates/></p>
</xsl:template>

<xsl:template match="author">
   <p>by <xsl:value-of select="firstname"/>
   <xsl:text> </xsl:text>
   <xsl:value-of select="surname"/></p>
```

Listing 10.3: continued

```
</xsl:template>

</xsl:stylesheet>
```

Because the template for the root is written to look for `articles` wherever they are, it will work with both Listing 10.1 (nonsigned version) and Listing 10.2 (signed version)! Figure 10.2 shows the result in a browser.

```
<xsl:template match="/">
   <xsl:apply-templates select="//article"/>
</xsl:template>
```

OUTPUT

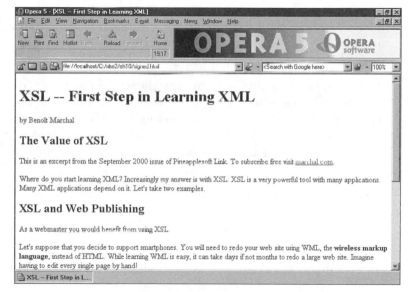

Figure 10.2: *The result in a browser.*

Again, this style sheet demonstrates the flexibility of the modular approach: The style sheet processes only the elements it knows about and ignores cryptographic elements. This is similar (although opposite) to the cryptographic toolkit that ignores DocBook elements and processes only cryptographic elements.

Figure 10.3 illustrates how this application takes advantage of XML extensibility. The document consists of two sets of tags: DocBook, which is required by the style sheet, and XML signature, which is required by the cryptographic toolkit. The style sheet and the application recognize their elements from their namespaces.

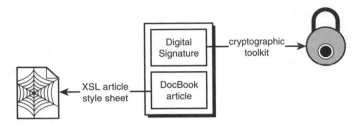

Figure 10.3: *The document consists of an article and cryptographic elements. Both are intended for different applications.*

Lessons Learned

Most current XML applications are similar to DocBook: They are defined independently from other works, and they aim to provide a complete set of tags for one particular application.

However, building and maintaining these models are expensive, and there is much overlap. For example, the digital signature can be used with electronic copy articles (to claim ownership), with electronic purchase orders (to guarantee the validity of the order), with electronic prescriptions (to make sure that it was written by your doctor), and much more.

It would just be too expensive to keep on redeveloping digital signature facilities in all these cases. Indeed, bear in mind that developing a new set of tags for digital signature means that you need to develop new cryptographic software (or at least adapt existing ones). So, the challenge is not limited to the markup; it impacts software development as well.

Increasingly, it makes more sense to develop specific markup modules for certain applications and combine them as needed.

XLink

Besides electronic signature, the W3C is working on several other markup modules for specific applications. Some of the most important such modules are as follows:

- XLink and XPointer define markup for hyperlinks (similar to the <a> tag in HTML).

- XHTML, an XML rewriting of HTML, serves as a basis for markup languages.

- XForms defines support for advanced forms.

- RDF, the Resource Description Framework, is a standard syntax to organize resources in directed graphs.

- SMIL, the Synchronized Multimedia Integration Language, defines how to create multimedia streaming documents (similar to RealAudio/Video). SMIL 1.0 is a monolithic markup language, but SMIL 2.0 is being rewritten as a set of modules.

- SVG, the Scalable Vector Graphics, is a module to represent images in XML.

You can find more information on these standards at the W3C Web site: www.w3.org. This chapter introduces XLink and XHTML. It does not pretend to be a complete reference on both standards and introduces them mainly as illustration of this modular attitude to markup language development.

CAUTION

At the time of writing, the XLink standard is not final. Although the concepts seem stable, it is possible that the published standard will differ significantly from the material presented in this section.

Furthermore, it appears that a Sun patent may conflict with some parts of XLink/XPointer. Consequently, the W3C has delayed releasing XLink until a solution has been found.

The latest version of XLink is available from www.w3.org/TR/xlink.

XLink allows you specify links between documents. It recognizes two types of links:

- *Simple links* are similar to HTML links, such as the anchor tag (<a>) or the image tag (<img>).

- *Extended links* make it possible to link several documents.

Simple Links

EXAMPLE

The simple link is familiar because it closely mimics the features of HTML links. At its simplest, an XLink looks like

```
<bookmark xmlns:xlink="http://www.w3.org/1999/xlink"
          xlink:href="http://www.marchal.com"
          xlink:type="simple">Listings are here</bookmark>
```

As the example illustrates, XLink defines a number of attributes in the http://www.w3.org/1999/xlink namespace. The attributes control how the link behaves.

Following this model, any XML element can become an XLink; it suffices to add the appropriate attributes. Browsers recognize the XLink attributes when they read the document and display the elements accordingly.

At the time of writing, Netscape 6 is the only browser to support XLink. Figure 10.4 shows the document in Netscape. Notice that it has turned into a hyperlink.

OUTPUT

Figure 10.4: *Netscape 6 renders a simple XLink.*

XLink needs many attributes to offer the same richness as HTML links. Some of these attributes are self-explanatory, such as `xlink:type` or `xlink:href`. Indeed, the only difference between `xlink:href` and its HTML counterpart is the namespace!

The other attributes are

- `type`: Select a simple or extended link. The only acceptable values are `simple` and `extended`.

- `href`: The URI the link is pointing to.

- `role`: It defines a property of the resource. It must be a URI. Tools use this to recognize special links, similar to how they recognize certain elements by their namespace.

- `arcrole`: It defines a property of the link. Again, it must be a URI.

- `title`: This is a human-readable name for the link. Tools may use this for display.

- `show`: Indicates what happens when the link is activated. Acceptable values are `new`, `replace`, `embed`, `other`, and `none`.

- `actuate`: Determines when the link is activated. Acceptable values are `onLoad`, `onRequest`, `other`, and `none`.

show and actuate are probably the least intuitive attributes. In HTML, there are several types of links. Compare the following:

```
<a href="http://www.marchal.com">Listings are here</a>
<img src="http://www.pineapplesoft.com/images/logo.gif">
```

To active the first link, the user must click it. When clicked, the link replaces the current document with the link content.

Conversely, the link in the image tag is immediately activated: The browser downloads the image when it loads the page. Furthermore, the image is integrated in the current document—it does not replace it.

The combination of show and actuate controls this behavior for XLink. With show, new means that the browser should open a new window to display the link's content. embed means that the link's content should be parsed and integrated in the current document. replace means that the browser should replace the current document with the content of the link. replace is the default behavior for an HTML anchor.

The behavior of other and none is not specified by XLink. The browser needs to decide what to do based on other markup (for example, the value of role).

With actuate, onRequest means that the user must click on the link (or otherwise select it), whereas onLoad means that the browser should automatically traverse the link when the document is being loaded.

The following example illustrates the use of actuate and show. It is equivalent to `<img src="logo.gif">` in HTML:

```
<image xmlns:xlink="http://www.w3.org/1999/xlink"
       xlink:href="logo.gif" actuate="onLoad" show="embed"
       xlink:type="simple"/>
```

Extended Links

Extended links are more powerful. Some of the most exciting features of extended links include the capability to establish links between more than two resources or even links that do not reside in the document.

The latter means that it is possible to maintain links independently of the documents. This is useful in at least two cases:

- It is possible to store all the links in a single, central document. This should simplify maintenance of the links (because there is only one document to search when a link must be updated) and may help reduce broken links.

- It is possible to add links to documents that cannot be modified, such as documents residing on another server or a document in non-XML format.

EXAMPLE

Listing 10.4 is an example of an extended link.

Listing 10.4: `extended-xlink.xml`

```
<bookmark xmlns:xlink="http://www.w3.org/1999/xlink"
          xlink:type="extended">
   <display xlink:type="resource"
            xlink:label="local">Listings are here</display>
   <address xlink:href="http://www.quepublishing.com"
            xlink:type="locator"
            xlink:title="Que"
            xlink:label="remote1"/>
   <address xlink:href="http://www.marchal.com"
            xlink:type="locator"
            xlink:title="marchal.com"
            xlink:label="remote2"/>
   <go      xlink:type="arc"
            xlink:from="local"
            xlink:to="remote1"/>
   <go      xlink:type="arc"
            xlink:from="local"
            xlink:to="remote2"/>
   <go      xlink:type="arc"
            xlink:from="remote1"
            xlink:to="remote2"/>
   <go      xlink:type="arc"
            xlink:from="remote2"
            xlink:to="remote1"/>
</bookmark>
```

Links are established between resources, and, as you can see, the `type` attribute takes on new values to let you represent both local and remote resources as well as any links between those resources:

- `extended` for the element representing the link itself.

- `resource` for the element that contains resource local to the document; that is, a resource that appears within the document—typically a text or the image the user clicks on. In some cases, there are no local resources. `resource-type` elements have a `label` attribute that acts as identifier for the resource.

- `locator` for elements referencing external resources. Typically, this element will repeat. Like `resource-type` elements, `locator`-type elements have a `label` attribute.

- arc describes a traversal between two resources (which can be local or remote). An arc has a starting point (in the `from` attribute) and an end point (the `to` attribute). As the names imply, the link goes from the first resource to the other resource.

Extended links are powerful because it is possible to establish any relationships between resources. The first two arcs in the example are between the document and other documents.

OUTPUT

Unfortunately, current browsers do not support extended links. However you can imagine that, to render an extended link, the browser will need to offer a menu when the user clicks on the link.

Figures 10.5 and 10.6 simulate this behavior through JavaScript. When the user clicks the link, it opens a new window.

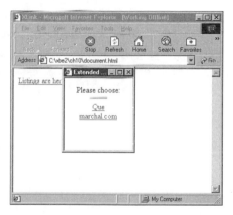

Figure 10.5: *The extended link before the user clicks.*

Figure 10.6: *The extended link after the user has clicked.*

The last two links illustrate how rich XLink is because they link two remote Web sites. This is powerful because it means that you can establish links between documents without modifying the document.

Indeed in this link, there is no need to edit either `http://www.marchal.com` or `http://www.mcp.com`. The link exists independently from the Web site (at least, it will be when browsers step up support for XLink).

Figure 10.7 illustrates the various resources and the links between these resources that the document establishes.

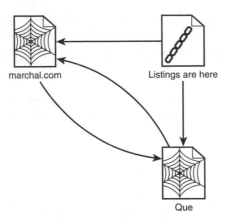

Figure 10.7: *The links between various resources in this document.*

EXAMPLE

The following is a rewriting of the simple link from the beginning of this section as an extended link. As you can see, the simple link is easier to use:

```
<entry      xmlns:xlink="http://www.w3.org/1999/xlink"
            xlink:type="extended">
   <local   xlink:type="resource"
            xlink:label="text">Listings are here</local>
   <remote  xlink:href="http://www.marchal.com"
            xlink:type="locator"
            xlink:label="site"/>
   <traverse xlink:type="arc"
            xlink:from="text"
            xlink:to="site"/>
</entry>
```

This link, of course, needs only to define one local resource, one remote one and one arc between the two.

XLink and Browsers

At the time of this writing, Netscape 6 is the only browser with limited support for XLink (it supports only simple links). This might change when the W3C officially approves XLink.

Notice how similar the implementation of XLink is to digital signatures: the W3C has defined a limited set of attributes in a specific namespace. When browsers read the document, they use a style sheet to control the display.

However, they also pick XLink attributes from their namespace and render them as link. Again we see two components (style sheet and XLink) working hand-in-hand to achieve the final result. Each component recognizes "its" elements from its namespace.

XHTML

The W3C didn't stop with digital signatures and XLink. It realized that, with HTML, it has a fabulous legacy that can serve as the basis for future markup language developments.

What Is XHTML?

Indeed, although XML is not limited to Web publishing, it is clear that many applications are being and will be built around some form of Web publishing. Some of these applications will use HTML; many more won't.

For example, as mentioned in Chapter 1, HTML is too complex and ill-suited for the current generation of mobile phones. There have been several attempts at simplifying HTML specifically targeted at mobile phones. The two most popular being WAP (www.wapforum.org, in Europe) and i-mode (in Japan).

The W3C is working to unify the two standards around a simplified version of HTML with some success. The effort falls under the XHTML banner.

It is expected that other markup languages, such as those developed for eBooks (www.openebook.org) or Palm PDAs (WebClip at www.palmos.com), will eventually follow suit.

What do these markup languages have in common? They all offer tags for text (paragraphs, boldness, italic, and so on), images, forms, and so on. So does HTML, and, furthermore, everybody is already familiar with HTML, so it makes sense to base new developments on HTML.

EXAMPLE

This leads to XHTML 1.0. With XHTML 1.0, the W3C has rewritten HTML using the XML syntax. In practice, it means that in an XHTML document, every element must have an opening and closing tag, as in

```
<p>In XHTML, every element has an opening and closing tag.</p>
```

Furthermore, empty elements now follow the XML syntax (and, of course, don't forget the quotation marks around attributes):

```
<img src="logo.gif"/>
```

Otherwise, the XHTML tags are identical to the HTML ones. In other words, every tag defined in HTML 4.0 has an XHTML equivalent and vice versa. Because HTML is one of the prerequisites for this book, I won't bother you with a long discussion of the XHTML tags—you already know them!

TIP

Make sure that older browsers can read XHTML documents. In practice, the only serious problem is XML special syntax for empty elements. Old browsers choke over the following:

```
<img src="logo.gif"/>
```

Fortunately, there's a trick. Just insert a blank before the slash, and both HTML and XML browsers will recognize your document. The img tag would be written as follows:

```
<img src="logo.gif" />
```

Likewise, you should write line breaks as <br />.

What Is XHTML Good At?

At this stage, you might wonder: "why bother?" If XHTML 1.0 has the same tags as HTML, why not stick to HTML?

XHTML 1.0 is but only the first step in the development of XHTML. The next step will be to break XHTML in modules. The ultimate goal, of course, is to combine these modules with other XML markup languages or to create a subset of XHTML by selecting only those modules. To that purpose, XHTML has been assigned its own namespace (http://www.w3.org/1999/xhtml).

CAUTION

At the time of writing, the modularization effort is still very much a work in progress. This discussion is based on the Candidate Recommendation from 20 October 2000.

The latest recommendation can be found at www.w3.org/TR/xhtml-modularization.

For example, a simplified version of XHTML designed for smartphones may consist of only the core modules, leaving out, for example, tags for Java applets or legacy tags.

TIP

For compatibility with HTML browsers, you will want to use the default prefix for XHTML documents. For example, if you want your document to be compatible with HTML and XHTML browsers, don't write

```
<html:html xmlns:html=" http://www.w3.org/1999/xhtml">
<!-- some parts deleted -->
</html:html>
```

but use the following instead:

```
<html xmlns=" http://www.w3.org/1999/xhtml">
<!-- some parts deleted -->
 </html>
```

Don't overlook this modularization effort. Indeed, recall that the W3C developed XML in answer to conflicting user requests (where some users wanted more markup options, and other users wanted fewer options). The modularization of XHTML is the ultimate answer to those conflicting requests.

Users who want more will adopt all the modules and then some; users who need simplified markup will ignore some modules.

e-Commerce, XML/EDI, and ebXML

Just as the W3C is working on a modular markup language for Web publishing (based on XHTML modules), other groups are working on modular markup languages for e-commerce.

Which e-Commerce?

You might think of e-commerce as buying and selling books on the Internet. Obviously, that is part of e-commerce, but that is only one facet of it.

Selling books or other goods to consumers (toys, electronics, cars, insurance, or banking) over the Internet is known as Business-to-Consumer e-commerce (B2C).

It's easy to get started with B2C. Register a domain, select an ISP (Internet service provider), and ask for a shopping cart option. Hire a designer, and you can start building a great electronic shop. Within days, you can have a shop online.

What happens when the customers find your shop, and orders start flying? As long as there are few of them, you can probably process the orders manually. Indeed that's how most small- to medium-size shops operate.

However, larger shops need to automate the process. It is well known that Amazon.com has invested heavily in its infrastructure and the logistics to support a large volume of sales.

Indeed bookstores (be they online or offline), don't manufacture books; they buy them from publishers. But if you buy books one at a time, large bookstores buy them by the thousand.

When a company orders from its providers, it's called business-to-business (B2B) commerce, as opposed to B2C. The major difference between B2C and B2B is the volume. Consumers order goods in small quantities; businesses order in large batches.

Furthermore, to manufacture the goods, the business needs to buy raw materials or use the services of other businesses. Publishers, for example, have the books manufactured by printers. Printers in turn buy paper and ink. To make paper, you need wood pulp.

Consequently, because the goods are bought and sold several times before reaching the customer, the value of B2B transactions will dwarf B2C, which makes it all the more attractive to automate things.

XML and e-Commerce

Theoretically, it would be possible to devise a common XML model to accommodate the needs of all the merchants involved in B2B transactions. In practice, however, this is a difficult exercise because the common models must take into account differences in culture between the organizations.

Furthermore, merchants are competitors. In practice, trying to reach agreement on anything but the most basic elements quickly degenerates into a political fight.

Electronic Data Interchange (EDI) shows the limits of trying to build a universal data structure. The idea behind EDI is a promising one: a large number of paper documents printed by computers are rekeyed at the receiving site. Why not skip the paper?

In other words, your organization's accounting package prints invoices. The invoices are mailed to your customer, who reenters the information in his or her accounting package—likewise for orders, delivery instructions, tax declarations, and checks. It would be more efficient to exchange the information electronically.

EDI tried to remove the paper from the equation. To that effect, a number of standards (X.12, UN/EDIFACT, Odette) were developed. These standards specified almost universal electronic formats for administrative and business documents.

The only problem is the universality. Accommodating the business practices of all the companies in various countries is an immense task. Remember that we are talking about different countries with radically different cultures and legislation.

In practice, the electronic documents become so complex that people have to first simplify them before they can use them. Worse, they often find that, despite all the options, some elements still are missing. It is an endless fight for the standard to keep up with evolution. It results in too much complexity.

This discussion of EDI should remind you of the problem the W3C was facing for the evolution of HTML (some people asking for more tags; others complaining there are too many tags) discussed in Chapter 1.

As you can imagine, XML has raised interest in relation to EDI and, more generally speaking, B2B e-commerce. One approach is to use modular components that would be combined as needed to accommodate the needs of the vendors.

XML combines the best of both worlds: commonality where it is practical and extension or customization where it is required.

This raises many interesting questions. If each party can create its own elements, how do you read them? One solution is to use a style sheet, as we have just done, to describe how to render the new elements.

Another solution is to use the DTD or the schema to describe the new elements and their structure. Several companies, such as Influe (www.influe.com), Mercator (www.mercator.com), and Microsoft (www.microsoft.com), offer so-called integration servers. The integration server helps you import the XML documents you received from a commercial partner in your ERP package or other business applications.

e-Commerce Initiative

There have been a number of initiatives to combine the power of EDI, XML, and the Internet. One of the most promising such initiatives is ebXML run by the UN/CEFACT (a well-established EDI standard body) and OASIS (the association of XML/SGML users). At the time of this writing, they have not published much information, but you can find more at www.ebxml.org.

Microsoft has launched a competing initiative at www.biztalk.org.

Another important initiative in this space is RosettaNet. RosettaNet specifies how to automate commercial relationships in the computer industry. For more information, see its Web site at www.rosettanet.org.

Last but not least, in 1997, I helped cofound the XML/EDI Group. If you are interested in this topic and if you want a nonpartisan view on the progress of the various groups, I encourage you to visit our Web site at www.xmledi.com.

Lessons Learned

This concludes our discussion of modular markup language. However, keep these concepts in mind as you build your XML applications. You might find that

- You can reuse existing modules, such as digital signatures or XHTML, saving you development time both when preparing the XML markup and when writing the software to support it.

- You can also develop your own markup in a modular way so that others can benefit from it in their applications.

In the rest of this chapter, you'll learn about other problems to watch for when developing XML applications.

The Right Level of Abstraction

When designing XML applications and, more specifically, XML models, it is not always easy to decide what to include in the markup and what to leave out. This section provides some guidance.

Note that this section applies equally to DTDs and schemas. Indeed, in this section, we are concerned with the document model, not its expression in a specific language (DTD or schema).

Destructive and Nondestructive Transformations

I know from firsthand experience that it takes very little effort to turn an office into a mess: Just start piling old files and let documents accumulate in the inbox. In no time, the mess gets out of control. It requires continuous effort to keep the office tidy.

Unfortunately, the same is true for XML documents. It is easy to turn XML documents into a mess, but it is difficult to keep them tidy. Also it takes a lot of effort to clean up documents that have been degraded.

EXAMPLE

In particular, it is easy to lose information when transforming an XML document. Listing 10.5 is yet another product list, and it helps illustrate the point.

Listing 10.5: `products-el.xml`

```
<?xml version="1.0"?>
<xbe:products xmlns:xbe="http://www.psol.com/xbe2/listing10.5">
    <xbe:product>
        <xbe:name>XML Editor</xbe:name>
        <xbe:price>499.00</xbe:price>
    </xbe:product>
```

Listing 10.5: continued

```
    <xbe:product>
        <xbe:name>DTD Editor</xbe:name>
        <xbe:price>199.00</xbe:price>
    </xbe:product>
    <xbe:product>
        <xbe:name>XML Book</xbe:name>
        <xbe:price>19.99</xbe:price>
    </xbe:product>
    <xbe:product>
        <xbe:name>XML Training</xbe:name>
        <xbe:price>699.00</xbe:price>
    </xbe:product>
</xbe:products>
```

Listing 10.6 is an XSLT style sheet that transforms this document into another XML document.

Listing 10.6: el2at.xsl

```
<?xml version="1.0"?>
<xsl:stylesheet xmlns:xsl="http://www.w3.org/1999/XSL/Transform"
                xmlns:xbe5="http://www.psol.com/xbe2/listing10.5"
                xmlns:xbe="http://www.psol.com/xbe2/listing10.7"
                version="1.0">


<xsl:output method="xml"/>

<xsl:template match="xbe5:products">
    <xbe:products>
        <xsl:apply-templates/>
    </xbe:products>
</xsl:template>

<xsl:template match="xbe5:product">
    <xbe:product name="{xbe5:name}" price="{xbe5:price}"/>
</xsl:template>


</xsl:stylesheet>
```

Listing 10.7 shows the result of applying the style sheet to the product list.

Listing 10.7: products-at.xml

```
<?xml version="1.0" encoding="UTF-8"?>
<xbe:products xmlns:xbe="http://www.psol.com/xbe2/listing10.7">
    <xbe:product price="499.00" name="XML Editor"/>
    <xbe:product price="199.00" name="DTD Editor"/>
    <xbe:product price="19.99" name="XML Book"/>
    <xbe:product price="699.00" name="XML Training"/>
</xbe:products>
```

This transformation has not degraded the original document because Listing 10.7 carries as much information as Listing 10.5. Furthermore, the information has the same structure as the information in Listing 10.5. This transformation is therefore labeled nondestructive—it does not lose any information.

EXAMPLE

To prove that the transformation is nondestructive, Listing 10.8 shows another style sheet that does the reverse operation. Applying Listing 10.8 to Listing 10.7 results in Listing 10.5.

Listing 10.8: at2el.xsl

```
<?xml version="1.0"?>
<xsl:stylesheet
    xmlns:xsl="http://www.w3.org/1999/XSL/Transform"
    xmlns:xbe="http://www.psol.com/xbe2/listing10.5"
    xmlns:xbe7="http://www.psol.com/xbe2/listing10.7"
    exclude-result-prefixes="xbe7"
    version="1.0">

<xsl:output method="xml"/>

<xsl:template match="xbe7:products">
    <xbe:products>
        <xsl:apply-templates/>
    </xbe:products>
</xsl:template>

<xsl:template match="xbe7:product">
    <xbe:product>
        <xbe:name><xsl:value-of select="@name"/></xbe:name>
        <xbe:price><xsl:value-of select="@price"/></xbe:price>
    </xbe:product>
</xsl:template>

</xsl:stylesheet>
```

From a data-management point of view, nondestructive transformations are ideal because they preserve the quality of the information.

EXAMPLE

On the other hand, destructive transformations (those that destroy the structure of the information) are useful in practice, if only because publishing is often a destructive transformation. Listing 10.9 illustrates this with a style sheet to convert the price list in Listing 10.5 to HTML.

Listing 10.9: el2html.xsl

```
<?xml version="1.0"?>
<xsl:stylesheet xmlns:xsl="http://www.w3.org/1999/XSL/Transform"
```

Listing 10.9: continued

```
                    xmlns:xbe="http://www.psol.com/xbe2/listing10.5"
                    exclude-result-prefixes="xbe"
                    version="1.0">

<xsl:output method="html"/>

<xsl:template match="/">
   <html>
      <head><title>Product List</title></head>
      <body>
         <p>Product List</p>
         <xsl:for-each select="xbe:products/xbe:product">
            <p>
               <xsl:value-of select="xbe:name"/>
               <xsl:text>, $</xsl:text>
               <xsl:value-of select="xbe:price"/>
            </p>
         </xsl:for-each>
      </body>
   </html>
</xsl:template>

</xsl:stylesheet>
```

Unfortunately, this transformation is a destructive conversion. The result of applying Listing 10.9 to Listing 10.5 is shown in Listing 10.10.

Listing 10.10: products.html

OUTPUT

```
<html>
   <head>
      <title>Product List</title>
   </head>
   <body>
      <p>Product List</p>
      <p>XML Editor, $499.00</p>
      <p>DTD Editor, $199.00</p>
      <p>XML Book, $19.99</p>
      <p>XML Training, $699.00</p>
   </body>
</html>
```

The tags in the HMTL version are meaningless. They do not reflect the structure, and it is not possible to perform further conversions from the HTML tags alone. For example, the <p> tag is ambiguous because it is used both for the list label and the product information. Also there are no tags for product price and name. No XSLT style sheet could transform this document back into XML, which is the sign of a destructive transformation.

Why is that so? Because with XML, transformations are driven by the structure. If the structure is ambiguous with one tag used for different purposes (as is the case for the <p>), it is impossible (or, at the very least, extremely difficult) to further manipulate the document.

This is similar to turning the office into a mess. It takes a significant effort to return to a tidy desk. Likewise, it takes a significant effort to re-create the original XML file—and, in some cases, it might be impossible. (For example, if you had a product code element whose content would be ignored in the conversion to HTML, it would be impossible to re-create the original XML document because the product code would be missing.)

Mark It Up!

The previous section introduces the distinction between destructive and nondestructive transformations. It reinforces the importance of structure and proper markup. In XML, everything is derived from the structure, and it is therefore important that the structure be sound.

Figure 10.8 illustrates the optimal situation. The information is maintained in a highly structured format. To create new documents, transformations are applied to the highly structured document. Some transformations will be nondestructive, but most useful transformations are destructive.

Indeed, to publish a document (in HTML, WML, FO/PDF, or another format) requires a destructive transformation—one that cannot be undone without a great deal of effort.

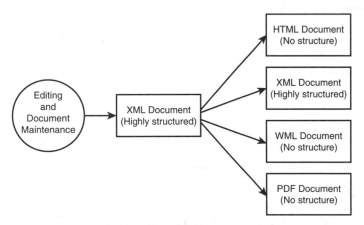

Figure 10.8: How to best use XML.

The logical conclusion is to introduce as much structure as possible in your document. You should mark up all the major components of the document with either tags or attributes. Why? Because you know you'll need to transform these documents, and you know the tags or the structure drive the transformations.

EXAMPLE

In your markup, concentrate on high-level structures. In the following document, it is easy to recognize that there is a name, address, and phone number:

```
John Doe
34 Fountain Square Plaza
Cincinnati, OH 45202
US
513-744-8889
```

This structure results in the following markup (for simplicity, it does not use namespaces):

```
<entry>
   <name>John Doe</name>
   <address>34 Fountain Square Plaza
Cincinnati, OH 45202
US</address>
   <tel>513-744-8889</tel>
</entry>
```

The difficulty is finding the appropriate granularity. Is the previous example enough? Unlikely. It is probably best to mark up some more. For example:

```
<entry>
   <name>John Doe</name>
   <address>
      <street>34 Fountain Square Plaza</street>
      <region>OH</region>
      <postal-code>45202</postal-code>
      <locality>Cincinnati</locality>
      <country>US</country>
   </address>
   <tel>513-744-8889</tel>
</entry>
```

Is this enough or do you need to further break some of the elements, such as

```
<name>
   <fname>John</fname>
   <lname>Doe</lname>
</name>
```

The question is where do you stop. What is the correct granularity for an XML document? Unfortunately, there are no strict criteria. Your experience will guide you. It is, however, a good idea to mark up as much as is convenient.

The end user's convenience is the best guideline when deciding where to stop breaking a document into smaller pieces.

Indeed, if the DTD is too detailed and requires the user to identify details, it won't work. The document may be highly structured, but, on closer analysis, most of the markup will prove to be incorrect. This problem is often experienced by database administrators who have good data schemas but poor information in the database.

For example, if you were to ask users to break the street into further components such as these:

```
<street>
    <nr>34</nr>
    <name>Fountain Square</name>
    <type>Plaza</type>
</street>
```

It probably wouldn't work. Realistically, few people would know where to insert the markup. Is it `<type>Plaza</type>` or

```
<street>
    <nr>34</nr>
    <name>Fountain</name>
    <type>Square Plaza</type>
</street>
```

Likewise, you wouldn't want to mark up every letter of every word:

```
<l>J</l><l>o</l><l>h</l><l>n</l>
```

The only way to know when to stop breaking a document into smaller pieces is to write sample documents or even small prototypes as you design the DTD. As you gain experience with XML, this becomes easier.

Use the sample documents or the prototype to test the usability of the DTD. Does it accurately capture all the information? Does it capture enough details? Is it nonobtrusive? You don't want to capture too many details and alienate the users.

I stress the importance of not alienating the users because they are the ones marking up the documents. If you ask them to introduce too much markup, they may be confused, or they may start cheating—inserting incorrect markup or even incorrect information just to get the task done.

The result is beautifully marked-up documents with lots of structural information, but, unfortunately, in practice they are not usable. Why? Because, although there is a lot of markup, most of it is incorrect.

CAUTION

Be sensitive to cultural differences when designing your markup. Let me offer an example. I live in Belgium, and, although Belgium is a federal country, we do not include the state in our addresses.

Yet many models designed in North America require states in addresses. This is unfortunate because I never know what to put there.

Should I follow the markup and insert the state, which is guaranteed to confuse the post office and might result in the mail not being delivered?

Should I use the province, which is uncommon in Belgian addresses but at least does not confuse the postman? Or should I insert what is known here as a "commune" which, again, is unused by the postal office but is guaranteed harmless?

Avoiding Too Many Options

As you finalize your DTD, proofread it to check for excessive use of options.

A warning bell should ring in your head if the DTD leaves too many options open. This is usually a sign that you need to be stricter in the markup.

The DTD in Listing 10.11 leaves too many options open. Figure 10.9 is a graphical view of the DTD.

EXAMPLE

Listing 10.11: order.dtd

```
<!ENTITY % company        "(name,address)">
<!ELEMENT order           (date,sender,receiver,lines)>
<!ELEMENT date            (#PCDATA)>
<!ELEMENT sender          %company;>
<!ELEMENT receiver        %company;>
<!ELEMENT lines           (reference*,description*,quantity?,
                           time-material*,price?)+>
<!ELEMENT reference       EMPTY>
<!ATTLIST reference       href CDATA #IMPLIED>
<!ELEMENT description     (#PCDATA)>
<!ELEMENT quantity        (#PCDATA)>
<!ELEMENT time-material   (#PCDATA)>
<!ELEMENT price           (#PCDATA)>
<!ATTLIST price           currency (usd | eur) #IMPLIED>
<!ELEMENT name            (#PCDATA)>
<!ELEMENT address         (street,region?,postal-code,
                           locality,country)>
<!ELEMENT street          (#PCDATA)>
<!ELEMENT region          (#PCDATA)>
```

Listing 10.11: continued

```
<!ELEMENT postal-code    (#PCDATA)>
<!ELEMENT locality       (#PCDATA)>
<!ELEMENT country        (#PCDATA)>
```

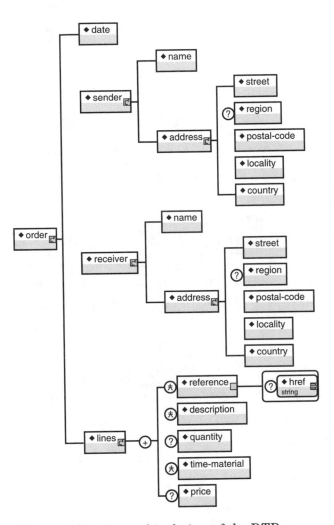

Figure 10.9: *A graphical view of the DTD.*

The problem with this DTD is the content model for `lines`:

```
<!ELEMENT lines (reference*,description*,quantity?,
                 time-material*,price?)+>
```

This model has so many options that the document in Listing 10.12 is valid, even though the `lines` element has no content! This is probably not what the model designer intended because it makes no sense to issue an order that contains only names and addresses.

Listing 10.12: `order.xml`

```
<?xml version="1.0"?>
<!DOCTYPE order SYSTEM "order.dtd">
<order>
    <date>19990727</date>
    <sender>
        <name>Playfield Software</name>
        <address>
            <street>38 Fountain Square Plaza</street>
            <region>OH</region>
            <postal-code>45263</postal-code>
            <locality>Cincinnati</locality>
            <country>US</country>
        </address>
    </sender>
    <receiver>
        <name>Que Publishing</name>
        <address>
            <street>201 West 103rd Street</street>
            <region>IN</region>
            <postal-code>46290</postal-code>
            <locality>Indianapolis</locality>
            <country>US</country>
        </address>
    </receiver>
    <lines/>
</order>
```

This creates a hole in the document. The solution is to use the or connector more often. A more realistic content model might be

```
<!ELEMENT lines ((reference | description)+,
                 (quantity | time-material+),price?)+>
```

This model states there is at least one reference or one description for each product (there may be several references or several descriptions). Also, the order is either for a certain quantity or on a time and material basis; one of the two elements must be present. Figure 10.10 illustrates this structure.

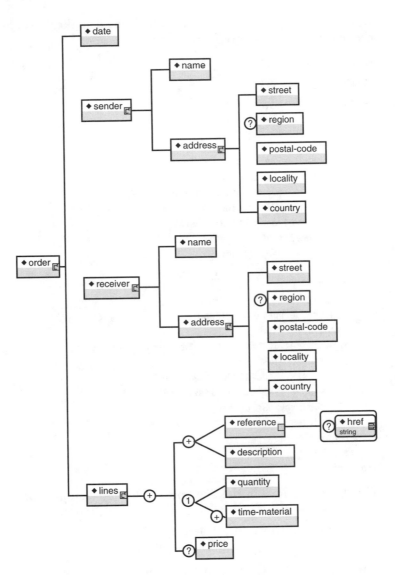

Figure 10.10: *The structure of the new DTD.*

When resolving these problems, it is important to avoid introducing ambiguities in the DTD. The following model would have been ambiguous:

```
<!ELEMENT lines ((reference+ | (reference+, description+) |
                 description+),
                (quantity | time-material+),price?)+>
```

It says that a line has either references or descriptions or both. Unfortunately, it is ambiguous (which, you might remember from

Chapter 4, "XML Models," is not authorized). To remove the ambiguity, you can introduce a new element such as

```
<!ELEMENT line      ((ref-desc | reference+ | description+),
                     (quantity | time-material+ | price?))+>
<!ELEMENT ref-desc (reference+,description+)>
```

Attributes Versus Elements

As you have seen in the section "The Right Level of Abstraction," you can use elements or attributes interchangeably to record the information in a DTD.

This has led to heated debates in the XML community between the proponents of attributes and the proponents of elements. Specifically, the debate is whether it is better to store content in attributes or in elements.

Both sides have convincing arguments and support their claims with good examples that clearly demonstrate the superiority of attributes over elements, or elements over attributes. The only problem is that both sides are right.

This debate is similar to the debate between inheritance and aggregation in object-oriented modeling. There are some clear arguments for and against each approach. And yet, when you have a blank sheet of paper in front of you, the solution is sometimes obvious, sometimes not.

I don't believe one approach is intrinsically better than the other. I try to keep an open mind and adapt to the needs of the application at hand. For some applications, attributes just seem to work better; for others, elements are the clear winner. I always keep in mind that conversion is an option provided the structure is good enough.

Your experience will guide you as well. The next two sections present some of the reasons you might use attributes or elements.

Using Attributes

EXAMPLE

A major advantage of attributes is that they establish a strong relationship with their parent element. This makes it easy to process all the attributes attached to an element. This is particularly true for SAX parsers, as illustrated by the following code excerpt:

```
public void startElement(String uri,
                         String name,
                         String qualifiedName,
                         Attributes attributes)
{
```

```
if(uri.equals(NAMESPACE_URI) && name.equals("price-quote"))
{
   String attribute =
      attributes.getValue("","price");
   if(null != attribute)
   {
      double price = toDouble(attribute);
      if(min > price)
      {
         min = price;
         vendor = attributes.getValue("","vendor");
      }
   }
}
}
```

In contrast, it is more difficult to walk down the element tree and collect information from the children of an element with SAX. Because DOM gives you the entire document tree, it is not much more difficult to walk down to a child element than to use attributes.

Elements are naturally organized in a hierarchy, whereas attributes cannot nest.

EXAMPLE

This provides a clean-cut separation between elements and attributes that has led some to argue that elements should be used to express the structure (the relationship between elements) and attributes to hold the content.

This approach suggests that leaf elements should be turned into attributes:

```
<entry>
   <name name="John Doe"/>
   <address street="34 Fountain Square Plaza"
            region="OH"
            postal-code="45202"
            locality="Cincinnati"
            country="US"/>
   <tel tel="513-744-8889"/>
</entry>
```

Finally, attributes are also popular because the DTD gives you more control over the type and value of attributes than over the type and value of elements.

EXAMPLE

You can restrict an attribute to a list of values, whereas the type of an element is essentially text:

```
<!ATTLIST price currency (usd | eur) #IMPLIED>
```

This argument, however, will soon disappear. The new XML schema offers better data-typing for elements.

Using Elements

EXAMPLE

If attributes are easier to manipulate for the programmer, elements are typically easier to work with in XML editors or browsers. For one thing, it is impossible to display attributes with CSS. This would suggest that attributes are great for abstract data, and elements are ideal for human data.

```
url[protocol='mailto'] {
  text-decoration: none;
}
```

Incidentally, this was the original justification for attributes. In publishing models such as DocBook, elements typically contain the document text, whereas attributes contain other information (such as URLs for hyperlinks).

EXAMPLE

Elements can be repeated through the + and * occurrence indicators; attributes cannot.

```
<?xml version="1.0"?>
<entry>
   <name>John Doe</name>
   <tel preferred="true">513-744-8889</tel>
   <tel>513-744 7090</tel>
</entry>
```

EXAMPLE

Generally, elements offer more room for extension and reuse than attributes because elements are highly structured.

For example, in Listing 10.12, the address element is reused in the sender and receiver elements. It is reused with its complete structure.

Lessons Learned

It is clear that elements and attributes have different characteristics. Unfortunately, nobody seems to agree on how to exploit them best.

Over time, you will develop your own set of rules for when to use an attribute and when to use an element. My set of rules is not to lose any sleep on this debate because I can convert back and forth with simple style sheets! However, I try to be consistent, so in one model I would use attributes and elements consistently.

TIP

Gray areas like this, where there are no clear rules, are unavoidable in XML. XML wouldn't be so powerful and flexible if it didn't offer several solutions for each problem.

Don't waste too much time trying to find the best rule because there probably isn't one. Pick one approach, document it in as nonambiguous terms as possible, and try to be consistent.

What's Next

The next two chapters put all the knowledge of XML you have acquired to the test because they help you build a realistic e-commerce application based on XML.

The application demonstrates many of the techniques you have studied in a real-life context. It also shows how to use XML for distributed applications.

N-Tiered Architecture and XML

You are now familiar with every major aspect of XML:

- How to read and write XML documents as well as XML models

- How to publish XML documents through style sheets

- How to manipulate XML documents with a parser

This chapter and Chapter 12, "Putting It All Together: An e-Commerce Example," demonstrate how to put these techniques to use in a medium-size example. Not many new techniques are introduced in these chapters, but they illustrate how to apply what you have learned to a real-world application. In particular, you learn

- How to use XML for interapplication communication. You also learn about a new communication standard based on XML, SOAP (Simple Object Access Protocol).

- How XML benefits Web applications and, in particular, electronic commerce.

- How to integrate XML tools in an application. We will pay special attention to XSLT processors.

Throughout these two chapters, you'll develop a multi-tiered Web shop, dubbed XCommerce (XML Commerce). Bear in mind that XCommerce does not compete with commercial products because it lacks some important shop features such as the capability to process credit card payments. Still, as it stands, XCommerce is a good demonstration of a multi-tiered XML application.

You must read this chapter in conjunction with Chapter 12. This chapter introduces many of the ideas underlying the XCommerce application and includes some code snippets and partial listings used to illustrate a point. The complete source code is in Chapter 12.

What Is an N-Tiered Application?

Most medium and large-scale XML applications are *distributed applications*, meaning that they involve several servers linked over a network (typically the Internet or a LAN).

Because they are distributed over several computers, these applications are referred to as n-tiered. In this context, a *tier* simply means a component in a distributed application. XCommerce is an n-tiered application. Essentially, n-tiered applications are a specialized form of client/server applications.

CAUTION

In this context, a *server* refers to a software server, which might not equate with a computer.

Indeed, it is common to run several software servers on one computer. For example, the same machine (the hardware notion of server) may run a Web server, database server, mail server, and much more. In fact, with ISPs, it's not uncommon to run several Web servers on one machine.

EXAMPLE

Client/Server Applications

As Figure 11.1 illustrates, the Web is a good example of a client/server application, so you are already familiar with the basic ideas. On the left side is the Web client also known as the *browser*. On the right side is the Web server.

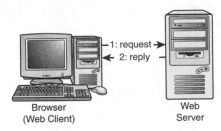

1: request →
← 2: reply

Browser
(Web Client)

Web
Server

Figure 11.1: *The Web is a client/server application.*

At the user initiative, the browser requests Web pages from the server. The server delivers the pages, and the client displays them. In effect, the client is a tool for the user to interact with the server.

Client/server applications have two essential characteristics:

- They are distributed applications, meaning that pieces of software are connected over a network (and they typically run on different computers, although it need not be the case).

- The two pieces of software have specific roles.

The second point differentiates client/server applications from other forms of distributed applications (such as the much-hyped peer-to-peer mode). It means that there is a client and server and that their roles differ.

The server provides *services* to the client. The server is the producer, and the client is the consumer. However, the server provides services only at the client's request. This is a sort of master/slave relationship where the master (the client) requests services from the slave (the server).

EXAMPLE

The Web is but one example of client/server. Other examples include

- Internet mail, where the mail client (such as Eudora or Outlook) interacts with the mail server to deliver and receive e-mail.

- Windows file sharing, where the dedicated stations on a LAN can store files or print documents on a server.

- Departmental client/server development environments such as Delphi, PowerBuilder, and other 4GL applications. In this mode, a local client interacts with a database server for administrative applications.

Generally, the server has access to resources that the client does not have access to or that are too difficult for the client to manage. With the Web, the resources are HTML files and servlets. You realize that the page must be on servers if you remember that there are millions of pages, and they are updated all the time. It would not be realistic to keep a local copy of every Web page on every computer connected to the Web! It makes more sense for a client to request pages from the server.

For e-mail, the resource is a 24/7 Internet connection. A client on a dial-up connection could send e-mails directly, but it makes more sense to pass the burden to a dedicated server that handles errors and retries.

Windows servers may have printers and plenty of hard disks. In most setups, it is not cost-effective to give every user a fast printer, and it is safer and more efficient to store files on a central location. Among other things, it simplifies backups.

Database servers provide a central storage for the data in the organization. Therefore, a database server has more information than what is available to a given PC.

EXAMPLE

3-Tiered Applications

As we enter an increasingly wired world, the server itself needs to rely on other servers. Webmail is a good example of an n-tiered application. Webmail are those Web services that let you read and compose e-mails through a Web site. Popular Webmails include Hotmail (www.hotmail.com) and Mailstart (www.mailstart.com).

As Figure 11.2 illustrates, in this setup, a server can also act as a client to another server. Indeed, the browser is the original client. The e-mail server is, of course, a server. But the Web server is both a client and a server: It is a server when talking to the browser and a client when talking to the e-mail server.

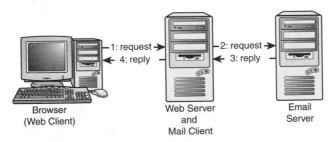

| 1: request → | 2: request → |
| ← 4: reply | ← 3: reply |

Browser (Web Client)   Web Server and Mail Client   Email Server

Figure 11.2: *The Web server plays both roles.*

Another way to look at this application is to decompose it in two client/server applications chained together. The architecture depicted in Figure 11.2 is known as a three-tiered application because three tiers (or parties) are involved.

To differentiate between the various clients and servers, the leftmost client is often called the *presentation tier* because it is the interface for the end-user. The machine in the middle, the one that plays both client and server, is often referred to as a *middle tier*. This tier encapsulates the business rules of the system.

In most cases, but not in this example, the rightmost server is a database server and is therefore often called the *data tier*.

EXAMPLE

N-Tiers

It is possible to add more parties by chaining together more client/server applications. For example, some e-mail servers depend on a database. The Webmail application would look like Figure 11.3 where there are four parties or tiers; this is a four-tiered application.

You can build five-tiered or six-tiered applications, or even more (although having more than four tiers is uncommon and may be counterproductive). The term *n-tiers* is generic for client/servers with three or more tiers.

NOTE

Just to confuse things further, there's a growing tendency not to count the Web browser as a tier in its own right. The reasoning is that the Web browser is so common, it's not worth mentioning anymore.

Figure 11.3: *Adding one more tier.*

The XCommerce Application

Chapter 12 contains the source code with comments for XCommerce. As explained earlier, this is a simple online shop built as an n-tiered application.

Figure 11.4 is a breakdown of XCommerce. The main components are the shop, which manages the interaction with shoppers, the middle-tier server, which implements the logic for product selection and order taking, and the data-tier, which is a SQL database.

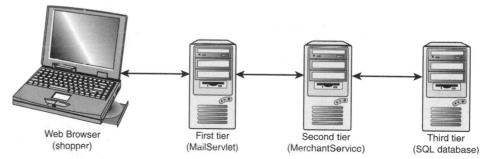

Figure 11.4: *The main components of XCommerce.*

Simplifications

XCommerce is representative of a real shop. However, because this is a book on XML, not on building online shops, I have made a few simplifications. These simplifications are not related to the use of XML in any way:

- There is no provision for payments. Processing payments typically requires credit card processing and a merchant account and is clearly outside the scope of this book.

- The database is the open-source Hypersonic SQL. Hypersonic SQL is a fine database for prototyping and demonstrations, but it lacks many characteristics of more advanced products.

- Presentation is minimalist. You would want to include more graphics and better layout in a real shop.

Additionally, security is nonexistent. It is possible to add encryption, but it is clearly outside the scope of this book.

Why Bother?

By now you're probably asking yourself why bother? What is the point of this separation across several servers? There are many advantages to n-tiered architectures that make them popular. The main ones are

- An n-tiered application scales better than a monolithic application. Indeed, if more processing is required, it suffices to move one of the servers to a different machine or a more powerful one. Load balancing across several servers is another option for high-end applications.

- Because the servers and clients are independent, it is possible to upgrade or maintain them separately.

- It is possible to connect more users with fewer database licenses (which tend to be expensive). Indeed, the server in front of the database may be able to serve several clients with only one database connection.

  Depending on the load, it's not uncommon to serve from twenty to hundreds of clients with only one database connection (compared to one database connection per client otherwise).

- It is possible to write the various tiers in different languages or run them on different platforms. This is particularly valuable if one of the servers is a legacy application that has special needs.

- It is possible to have more than one implementation of a tier, each optimized for different needs.

- It is possible to run the different tiers across several sites. This is particularly useful for e-commerce when the middle-tier server may be at a supplier site.

How XML Helps

Any form of client/server application needs a communication mechanism between the tiers. This is even more true for n-tiered applications where there are more parties.

Currently, two approaches are particularly popular for client/server applications:

- Middleware such as CORBA (Common Object Request Broker Architecture), DCOM (Distributed Component Object Model), or RPC (Remote Procedure Call).

- Exchange files, such as comma-delimited files, EDI HTML, or others, typically over a file exchange protocol such as HTTP or FTP.

We'll look at a third approach that builds on XML to combine benefits from middleware and more file-oriented solutions: SOAP, the Simple Object Access Protocol.

Middleware

I won't cover middleware in great detail (again, this is an XML book, not a middleware book), but I want to provide enough information for a comparison.

The basic idea behind middleware is to reduce the effort required to write distributed applications. Networks are not always safe, reliable, and dependable. In fact, you could argue that they are exactly the opposite. To work around these limitations, programmers have to implement specific protocols.

It is not uncommon for network-specific code to amount to more than ten times the business code. This enormous amount of time spent on plumbing explains why writing distributed applications takes time. Clearly, if 90 percent of the code deals with technical plumbing instead of business problems, it is not very productive. Indeed, the time spent wrestling with the network and its security is not spent solving actual business problems.

Middleware includes tools that deal with the network. For example, a network might fail, so a middleware has logic to gracefully recover from these failures. Also, on a network, several computers need to collaborate; middleware offers tools to manage the interaction between these computers.

Middleware is based on specific protocols, but those protocols are generally not accessible directly to programmers. Indeed, the goal of middleware is not to overwhelm programmers with details but to hide those details. It stands to reason that the protocols are not directly accessible. This encourages programmers to concentrate on business issues and, hopefully, be more productive.

EXAMPLE

Listing 11.1 illustrates this. This is a simple CORBA client that appends one line to an order and confirms it. A server maintains the order.

Listing 11.1: Small CORBA Example

```java
import org.omg.CORBA.*;

public class StockExchangeClient
{
    static public void main(String[] args)
    {
        String order = args[0],
               product = args[1];
        int quantity = Integer.parseInt(args[2]);
        ORB orb = ORB.init(args,null);
        Order remoteOrder = OrderHelper.bind(orb,order);
        remoteOrder.appendLine(product,quantity);
        remoteOrder.confirm();
    }
}
```

Listing 11.1 is interesting because you can hardly tell it is a distributed application. The only lines that deal with networks explicitly are these two:

```java
ORB orb = ORB.init(args,null);
Order remoteOrder = OrderHelper.bind(orb,order);
```

and they are not very difficult. Without going into any details, they let the client connect to a remote order object. This object exists only on the server.

More interestingly, in the remainder of the client, it manipulates the order object, which resides on the server, as if it were a local object:

```java
remoteOrder.appendLine(product,quantity);
remoteOrder.confirm();
```

That's the power of middleware; it completely hides the distributed nature of this application. In Listing 11.1, the client calls methods on a remote object as if they were local objects. The middleware takes care of network communication.

Experience shows that middleware works better on LANs or intranets than on cross-enterprise applications. This is because, with middleware, the client directly manipulates objects on the server. This leads to a tight coupling between the client and the server. It is therefore difficult to set up unless both parties are controlled by the same organization.

NOTE

Middleware gurus are quick to point out that it doesn't have to be that way. Indeed, several mechanisms, including dynamic invocation, support flexible coupling through middleware.

Although it is correct technically, in practice, experience shows that most solutions based on middleware are relatively inflexible and are therefore best suited for internal use.

Exchange Files

For applications that work across several enterprises, it is common to prepare files with the appropriate data and exchange those files.

EXAMPLE

You're familiar with this process because this is how the Web works: to publish a Web site, the Webmaster prepares HTML documents, say with a product description. The documents are made available through a server. When the browser needs information (in this example, the product description), it requests the document from the server (see Listing 11.2).

Unlike middleware, this crude mechanism based on files has proved to scale well to millions of users. See the Web if you need more convincing.

Listing 11.2: Product Description in HTML

```
<html>
<head><title>Safest Safe</title></head>
<body>
<form method="post" action="/shop/shoppingcart">
<b>Safest Safe</b><br>
<small>by </small>Top-notch Security, Inc.<br>$ 1999.0<br>
<i>Choose the authentic Safest Safe</i><br>
<small>Warranty: </small>Lifetime<br>
<small>Quantity: </small>
<input name="quantity" value="1" size="3" type="text">
<input value="Buy" type="submit">
</form>
</body>
</html>
```

EXAMPLE

HTML is just one example, albeit the most popular. Many other distributed applications use specialized formats, such as CSV (comma-separated value), EDI (Electronic Data Interchange), or other formats—such as XML itself.

Listing 11.3 illustrates this with a list of products in comma-separated format. Such a file would be made available on a server (typically an FTP server) for the client to retrieve.

Listing 11.3: A List of Products in CSV

```
id,name,manufacturer,price,warranty,description
0,"Ultra Word Processor","Word Processing, Inc.",799.99,"1 year",
➥"More words per minute than the competition"
1,"Super Calculator","WhizBang Corp.",5.99,"5 days",
➥"Cheap and reliable with power saving"
2,"Safest Safe","Top-notch Security, Inc.",1999.0,"Lifetime",
➥"Choose the authentic Safest Safe"
```

The main benefits of using files are

- It promotes a cleaner separation between client and server. Middleware offers a programming interface. In practice, it forces the server to offer an API to the client. This promotes tighter coupling between the two.

- It is often easier to add new parties. Again the coupling between client and server is not so strong, making it easier to add new parties.

- The system may scale better. Files are well-suited for advanced caching. Programmatic APIs make caching more difficult.

- It makes it easier to retrofit legacy applications as servers. Indeed, just about any application can save its data in files (thereby becoming a server), but few applications are designed to integrate with middleware from the onset.

Simple Object Access Protocol (SOAP)

Microsoft, IBM, Userland, and DevelopMentor teamed to develop a standard, based on XML, that would combine the benefits of middleware and file-based architecture. The result is SOAP, the Simple Object Access Protocol.

SOAP recognizes that the Web provides a good basis for client/server architecture. However, HTML is intended for human consumption only. XML, as you have seen, is similar but can be manipulated by applications. So, SOAP attempts to merge the two.

SOAP clients and servers use HTTP, the Web protocol, to communicate. In practice, it means that a SOAP server is a Web server, whereas a SOAP client borrows code from a Web browser. A SOAP server is known as a *SOAP endpoint.*

The SOAP client encodes its request as an XML document. The response from the server also comes in XML. Listing 11.4 is an example of such a SOAP response: This is the XML document that the server returns to the client. Notice that it includes the same data as Listing 11.2, but the markup is XML.

Having XML markup instead of HTML markup means that the client can retrieve the structure of the information and do more processing than would be possible with HTML.

Listing 11.4: Product Description with SOAP

```
<?xml version='1.0' encoding='UTF-8'?>
<SOAP-ENV:Envelope
    xmlns:SOAP-ENV="http://schemas.xmlsoap.org/soap/envelope/"
    xmlns:xsi="http://www.w3.org/1999/XMLSchema-instance"
    xmlns:xsd="http://www.w3.org/1999/XMLSchema">
<SOAP-ENV:Body>
<ns1:getProductDetailsResponse
    xmlns:ns1="http://www.psol.com/xbe2/chapter12"
    SOAP-ENV:encodingStyle="http://schemas.xmlsoap.org/soap/encoding/">
<return xsi:type="ns1:ProductDetails">
<name xsi:type="xsd:string">Safest Safe</name>
<warranty xsi:type="xsd:string">Lifetime</warranty>
<manufacturer xsi:type="xsd:string">Top-notch Security,
➥Inc.</manufacturer>
<description xsi:type="xsd:string">Choose the authentic
➥Safest Safe</description>
<price xsi:type="xsd:double">1999.0</price>
<id xsi:type="xsd:int">2</id>
</return>
</ns1:getProductDetailsResponse>
</SOAP-ENV:Body>
</SOAP-ENV:Envelope>
```

In Listing 11.4, you'll notice that same elements are in a SOAP-defined namespace:

```
xmlns:SOAP-ENV="http://schemas.xmlsoap.org/soap/envelope/"
```

These elements are specified by the SOAP standard. Other elements are in a namespace defined by our application:

```
xmlns:ns1="http://www.psol.com/xbe2/chapter12"
```

The namespace refers to chapter 12 because this is excerpted from the e-commerce application you'll develop in the next chapter. It's not a problem because, as you'll remember, there are no other constraints on namespaces than making sure they are unique!

SOAP appears more attractive than regular middleware because it is based on XML:

- XML is structure-rich, which allows the middle server to process product information (such as extracting prices).

- XML is versatile; therefore, most data in the application are stored in XML. In particular, XML is used for configuration information (the list of merchants), for product information, and to store the orders themselves.

- The combination of XML and HTTP scales well. Indeed Web servers have proved extremely scalable, and most organizations have learned how to scale their Web presence as traffic grows. Few organizations have that sort of experience with middleware.

- As a secondary benefit of scalability, XML and SOAP give the company flexibility in deploying its solutions. The business can start with a simple Web server and upgrade as the business expands.

- XML is based on the Web; therefore, it is often possible to reuse HTML investments.

- XML is textual, which simplifies testing and debugging (this should not be neglected; few applications work flawlessly the first time).

- It's easy to convert XML into any presentation format, including HTML, WML, and PDF, using style sheets.

- Yet SOAP, not unlike a regular middleware, allows access to Java objects. In practice, it means that the developers benefit from maximum flexibility: they can treat SOAP as a file exchange mechanism (essentially raw XML) when it suits them and as a middleware where it's more appropriate.

- XML is cost-effective to deploy because many vendors support it; companion standards are also available.

Programming SOAP

Because SOAP is a standard, there are toolkits that implement it. These toolkits play a role similar to parsers, XSL processors, and other XML tools: They cut down on your work.

For XCommerce, I choose the Apache SOAP toolkit, which is available from `xml.apache.org`. The Apache toolkit is implemented in Java as a servlet. It is compatible with many servlet-based Web servers.

CAUTION

At the time of this writing, the Apache toolkit is still in its first revisions, so it is subject to unexpected changes.

The code published here was tested against Apache SOAP toolkit revision 2.1. Beware that future evolutions may be slightly incompatible with the code published here.

If in doubt, consult `www.marchal.com` or `www.quepublishing.com` for updates.

Writing a SOAP Endpoint

It's easy to write a SOAP endpoint with the Apache toolkit. In fact, it suffices to write a regular Java class and export some methods to the toolkit.

Listing 11.5 is an excerpt from XCommerce endpoint (see Chapter 12 for the complete code). As you can see, it's a regular Java class, and it defines three methods.

Where's the XML? That's precisely what makes SOAP attractive: you only bother with XML where and when it makes sense. In this case, it is simpler and faster to write a regular Java class and let the SOAP toolkit convert it to XML. At this level, SOAP buys you the same benefits as a regular middleware.

Listing 11.5: Excerpt from `MerchantService.java`

```java
package com.psol.xbe2;

import java.sql.*;
import java.util.*;

public class MerchantService
{
   // ...
   public Product[] getProductList()
      throws SQLException
   {
      // ...
   }

   public ProductDetails getProductDetails(int id)
      throws SQLException
   {
      // ...
   }

   public boolean addOrder(String name,
                           String company,
                           String street,
                           String region,
                           String postalCode,
                           String locality,
                           String country,
                           String email,
                           OrderLine[] lines)
   {
      // ...
   }
}
```

You still need to declare the Java class with the SOAP toolkit. This is done through a so-called deployment descriptor similar to Listing 11.6.

Listing 11.6: `DeploymentDescriptor.xml`

```
<isd:service
    xmlns:isd="http://xml.apache.org/xml-soap/deployment"
    id="http://www.psol.com/xbe2/chapter12">
    <isd:provider scope="Application"
        type="java"
        methods="getProductList getProductDetails addOrder">
      <isd:java class="com.psol.xbe2.MerchantService"
          static="false"/>
    </isd:provider>
    <isd:mappings>
      <isd:map
          encodingStyle="http://schemas.xmlsoap.org/soap/encoding/"
          xmlns:xbe2="http://www.psol.com/xbe2/chapter12"
          qname="xbe2:Product"
          javaType="com.psol.xbe2.Product"
          java2XMLClassName=
              "org.apache.soap.encoding.soapenc.BeanSerializer"
          xml2JavaClassName=
              "org.apache.soap.encoding.soapenc.BeanSerializer"/>
      <isd:map
          encodingStyle="http://schemas.xmlsoap.org/soap/encoding/"
          xmlns:xbe2="http://www.psol.com/xbe2/chapter12"
          qname="xbe2:ProductDetails"
          javaType="com.psol.xbe2.ProductDetails"
          java2XMLClassName=
              "org.apache.soap.encoding.soapenc.BeanSerializer"
          xml2JavaClassName=
              "org.apache.soap.encoding.soapenc.BeanSerializer"/>
      <isd:map
          encodingStyle="http://schemas.xmlsoap.org/soap/encoding/"
          xmlns:xbe2="http://www.psol.com/xbe2/chapter12"
          qname="xbe2:OrderLine"
          javaType="com.psol.xbe2.OrderLine"
          java2XMLClassName=
              "org.apache.soap.encoding.soapenc.BeanSerializer"
          xml2JavaClassName=
              "org.apache.soap.encoding.soapenc.BeanSerializer"/>
    </isd:mappings>
  </isd:service>
```

The deployment descriptor has three important elements:

- service, which is the root element and declares an id for the SOAP endpoint.

- provider, which declares a Java class that implements the endpoint.

- map, which specifies how to convert parameters in XML. map elements are grouped in a mapping element.

The only important attribute of service is id. This attribute is mandatory, and it contains a namespace for the SOAP endpoint. You'll see in the next section that the client must match this URI:

```
id="http://www.psol.com/xbe2/chapter12"
```

As a reminder, although namespaces are URIs, they do not point to Web sites. Namespaces are used only as identifiers; they do not have to point to an actual resource.

In Listing 11.6, the provider declares three methods (getProductList, getProductDetails, and addOrder) through the methods attribute. These three methods match the three methods in the MerchantService class introduced in Listing 11.5:

```
<isd:provider scope="Application"
    type="java"
    methods="getProductList getProductDetails addOrder">
  <isd:java class="com.psol.xbe2.MerchantService"
      static="false"/>
</isd:provider>
```

The java element nested in provider associates one or more Java classes through the class attribute (including their complete package names), with the endpoint.

The map elements specify how to encode parameters in XML. Indeed the SOAP toolkit knows how to encode built-in Java types such as String or int, but it does not know about the classes you declare, unless you associate a map to them.

In Listing 11.6, the map mostly uses default values. If in doubt, you can often enter the same values when writing your own maps:

```
<isd:map
    encodingStyle="http://schemas.xmlsoap.org/soap/encoding/"
    xmlns:xbe2="http://www.psol.com/xbe2/chapter12"
    qname="xbe2:Product"
    javaType="com.psol.xbe2.Product"
```

```
java2XMLClassName=
    "org.apache.soap.encoding.soapenc.BeanSerializer"
xml2JavaClassName=
    "org.apache.soap.encoding.soapenc.BeanSerializer"/>
```

The attributes are

- encodingStyle, which selects how the SOAP toolkit should produce the XML document. The default value is http://schemas.xmlsoap.org/soap/encoding/.

- javaType, which declares the Java type the map controls. In most cases, it's a Java class. The example declares a map for the class com.psol. xbe2.Product.

- qname, which specifies an XML element to map the object to. This may be confusing; why declare XML elements in a mapping?

  Keep in mind that, for the communication between client and server, SOAP creates an XML document with data from these Java classes. The qname controls the name of the elements in this XML document. In practice, whenever SOAP creates an XML document containing instances com.psol.xbe2.Product, it calls them xbe2:Product.

  Notice that I declared a namespace to use in this qname.

- java2XMLClassName and xml2JavaClassName select the Java class responsible to create the XML document. You could write your own, but it's easier to use the one provided by the toolkit.

TIP

In most cases, you will want to use a SOAP toolkit such as the Apache toolkit introduced here. However, there are cases where you would rather roll up your sleeves and write your own implementation.

Fortunately, because it is based on XML and HTTP, writing your own SOAP server or client is not that difficult. If you want an example with complete source code, check my other book, *Applied XML Solutions*.

Writing a SOAP Client

What about the client? Writing a SOAP client is, unfortunately, more involved than writing an endpoint, but most of the code is repetitive, so you can often hide it away in a special method.

Here's how to call the getProductDetails method defined in the previous section:

```
BeanSerializer serializer = new BeanSerializer();
SOAPMappingRegistry registry = new SOAPMappingRegistry();
```

```
registry.mapTypes(Constants.NS_URI_SOAP_ENC,
                new QName(
                    "http://www.psol.com/xbe2/chapter12",
                    "Product"),
                Product.class,serializer,serializer);
registry.mapTypes(Constants.NS_URI_SOAP_ENC,
                new QName(
                    "http://www.psol.com/xbe2/chapter12",
                    "ProductDetails"),
                ProductDetails.class,serializer,serializer);
Vector params = new Vector();
params.addElement(new Parameter("id",Integer.class,
                            new Integer(productId),
                            null));
Call call = new Call();
call.setSOAPMappingRegistry(registry);
call.setTargetObjectURI("http://www.psol.com/xbe2/chapter12");
call.setMethodName("getProductDetails");
call.setEncodingStyleURI(Constants.NS_URI_SOAP_ENC);
call.setParams(params);
Response resp =
    call.invoke(new URL("http://localhost:5401/soap/servlet/rpcrouter"),
                "http://www.psol.com/xbe2/soapaction");
if(!resp.generatedFault())
    return (ProductDetails)resp.getReturnValue().getValue();
else
    System.out.println(resp.getFault().getFaultString());
}
```

That's a lot of code, so let's review it line by line. First, we create a
SOAPMappingRegistry. This object plays a role similar to the deployment
descriptor on the server. You'll notice that it introduces the same mappings:

```
BeanSerializer serializer = new BeanSerializer();
SOAPMappingRegistry registry = new SOAPMappingRegistry();
registry.mapTypes(Constants.NS_URI_SOAP_ENC,
                new QName(
                    "http://www.psol.com/xbe2/chapter12",
                    "Product"),
                Product.class,serializer,serializer);
registry.mapTypes(Constants.NS_URI_SOAP_ENC,
                new QName(
                    "http://www.psol.com/xbe2/chapter12",
                    "ProductDetails"),
                ProductDetails.class,serializer,serializer);
```

Next, prepare a `Vector` with parameter objects. There's one `Parameter` object for every parameter in the call. In this case, `getProductDetails` takes only one parameter:

```
Vector params = new Vector();
params.addElement(new Parameter("id",Integer.class,
                                new Integer(productId),
                                null));
```

We're now ready to create and initialize a `Call` object. Most of the initialization is setting default values so that you can copy it verbatim. The last line invokes the remote method—that is, it executes the call:

```
Call call = new Call();
call.setSOAPMappingRegistry(registry);
call.setTargetObjectURI("http://www.psol.com/xbe2/chapter12");
call.setMethodName("getProductDetails");
call.setEncodingStyleURI(Constants.NS_URI_SOAP_ENC);
call.setParams(params);
Response resp =
    call.invoke(new URL("http://localhost:5401/soap/servlet/rpcrouter"),
              "http://www.psol.com/xbe2/soapaction");
```

The only difficulty with the `Call` object is that it uses three URLs. There's much confusion around these URLs, especially because two of them are not real URLs but namespaces:

- The target object URI (in `setTargetObjectURI()`) is a namespace that must match the `id` parameter in the deployment descriptor.

  Remember that the `id` is a namespace, so it's not pointing to an actual Web site.

- `invoke` takes two URLs. The first one is a real URL. It points to the HTTP server that hosts the SOAP endpoint.

  The second URL, however, is again a namespace. SOAP proxies use this namespace to recognize SOAP requests. You could put any value here; it does not have to match anything in the deployment descriptor.

The call has been executed. The last step is to test whether it ran smoothly or whether there's been an error. This is done with the `getGeneratedFault()` method.

If it reports no error, you can access the returned value and typecast it into whatever is appropriate. Otherwise, process the error:

```
if(!resp.generatedFault())
    return (ProductDetails)resp.getReturnValue().getValue();
else
    System.out.prinltn(resp.getFault().getFaultString());
```

If writing a SOAP endpoint is easy, it appears that writing the client is more work. On the client, SOAP is much more involved than regular middleware, at least with the version of the Apache SOAP Toolkit available at the time of writing. Is it really worth it? Yes, because SOAP brings you enormous flexibility.

Flexibility Illustrated

In the previous section, you learned how to issue a SOAP request and retrieve the result as a Java object. This is particularly valuable when you want to further process the result in Java.

However, there are cases where you just want to take the result from the SOAP request and present it onscreen. In such cases, your best bet is to access the raw XML document and apply a style sheet.

Because SOAP builds on XML, you can do both. The following code illustrates how to retrieve the result as an XML document instead of a Java object:

```
// call initialization: see previous section
Response resp =
   call.invoke(new URL("http://localhost:5401/soap/servlet/rpcrouter"),
               "http://www.psol.com/xbe2/soapaction");
if(!resp.generatedFault())
{
   BodyPart bp = resp.getBodyPart(0);
   InputStream in = bp.getInputStream();
   for(int c = in.read();c != -1;c = in.read())
      System.out.print((char)c);
}
else
   System.out.prinltn(resp.getFault().getFaultString());
```

The call initialization is identical to the previous section. The only difference is that instead of typecasting the returned value into a Java object, this code retrieves it into a BodyPart object.

Through the BodyPart.getInputStream() method, it is now easy to read the raw XML document. This is the XML document generated by the SOAP toolkit on the server, so it would be similar to Listing 11.4. Of course, it's easy to feed this raw XML document into an XSL processor.

TIP

With SOAP, it's not one or the other, but both. SOAP requests are encoded as XML documents, but the SOAP toolkit takes care to decode them into Java objects.

You can always mix and match between XML and Java objects as needed.

XCommerce Architecture

Figure 11.4, shown earlier in the chapter, illustrates the architecture of XCommerce. It's a distributed application that consists of four tiers:

- A standard Web browser for interaction with the shopper.

- A presentation server written as a servlet.

- A middle-tier server that mediates between the presentation and the database. This is a SOAP endpoint.

- A SQL database to store product information and orders.

Web Browser

Why bother with a presentation server? Aren't we using XML? Ultimately, it will be possible to send XML to the client and apply style sheets on the client. Currently, I would advise against so doing. It makes more sense to convert to HTML on a server, which is the primary role of the presentation server.

There are several problems with XML on the client:

- Currently, XML is supported only by the latest generation of browsers. Studies show that surfers are less likely to update their browsers than they were in the past, so implementation may take a while.

- Even if your target audience has XML-capable browsers, not all browsers are born equal. There are important differences between version 4.0 and version 5.0 of Internet Explorer and Netscape 6.0, for example.

- XSL implementations are particularly unstable. Internet Explorer 4.0 supported an early version of XSL. Internet Explorer 5.0 is closer to the standard, but needs updates. Full support of XSL is available as a separate download, but how many users download patches?

  Things will get even more confusing when Internet Explorer 6.0 is released because it should support standard XSLT.

In conclusion, it probably will take more than two years before XML will be common in browsers. Currently, converting XML to HTML on the server is the safe solution. It buys you the best of both worlds: It works with older browsers but still allows you to take advantage of XML in your applications.

In the previous chapters, you saw many examples that performed a lot of processing on the client side. However, in each case, I warned that it would work only with specific browsers. XCommerce relies heavily on server-side conversion because it is a more realistic example.

NOTE

I advise against sending XML to the client because there are not enough XML-capable browsers.

This might not be true on an intranet. An intranet is a controlled environment; thus, you might be able to control which browser (including the patch level!) is being used. Therefore, you can tailor your documents to the appropriate browsers.

If, however, the intranet is large, stick to server-side conversion of XML. In a large intranet, it is difficult to upgrade all the users simultaneously. If your application depends on Internet Explorer 5.0 and a third of the intranet users have applied a patch, it may not be possible for them to access your application. What makes it worse is that it breaks when they apply the patch!

Presentation Server

The presentation layer is not very complex because most of the operations are performed on the middle-tier server.

The servlet essentially issues SOAP requests as appropriate and applies style sheets to the result. The most involving aspect of this servlet is that it manages a shopping cart, giving shoppers the capability to order several items at once.

Middle-Tier

The middle tier is a SOAP endpoint. It translates requests from the presentation layer into SQL statements. This middle-tier layer manages the connection with the databases.

The Database

Because this book concentrates on XML, not on database programming, XCommerce uses a simple open-source database called Hypersonic SQL.

Hypersonic SQL imposes some simplifications when compared to a full-blown database, but it is ideal for demonstrations for two reasons:

- It is entirely written in Java, so it runs on any Java platform.

- It supports SQL and JDBC (Java Database Connectivity), so it is possible to share a lot of code with other, more powerful databases.

Server-Side Programming Language

XCommerce relies extensively on XSL. From a certain point of view, XSL is used as a scripting language for XML documents.

However, certain features cannot be implemented in XSL. For example, there is no mechanism to access databases from XSL.

Therefore, XSL is not enough. A medium-size XML application often needs a combination of XSL and a more traditional programming language to compile new documents, handle user authentication, access databases, and more—all features that are not being covered, or not properly covered, by XSL.

The main options for server-side programming languages that work well with XML are Perl, JavaScript, Python, Omnimark, and Java.

Perl

Perl is a scripting language. It is popular for CGI scripting because it offers superior text manipulation. However, with XML, you might prefer to use XSL to manipulate documents. Therefore, Perl is less attractive.

JavaScript

JavaScript is also a scripting language. It is particularly popular for browsers. Many examples in this book rely on JavaScript. There are server-side versions of JavaScript from Microsoft and iPlanet (formerly Netscape). Microsoft offers Active Server Page (ASP). iPlanet supports Server-Side JavaScript (SSJS).

EXAMPLE

Although ASP and SSJS are similar, they are incompatible. ASP and SSJS encourage you to mix JavaScript statements in an HTML or an XML page. The server, not the browser, executes the script to generate the final page. Listing 11.7 shows how to use SSJS to create an XML document with product information.

Listing 11.7: Creating XML with SSJS

```
<SERVER>
deleteResponseHeader("content-type")
addResponseHeader("content-type","application/xml")
database.connect("ODBC","products","SYSDBA","masterkey","")
product = database.cursor("select * from products where id = '" +
➥request.id + "'")
product.next()
</SERVER><product>
<name><SERVER>write(product.name)</SERVER></name>
<description><SERVER>write(product.description)</SERVER></description>
<price><SERVER>write(product.price);product.close()</SERVER></price>
</product>
```

The first few lines change the type of the document to XML. Next it connects to the database. Finally, it reads various information from the database and inserts it in an XML document.

The major problem with JavaScript is that it is not portable. An application developed with Microsoft's ASP does not work on iPlanet servers and vice versa. Although ChiliSoft offers a version of ASP for Unix systems, it remains primarily a Windows technology.

Python

Python is an object-oriented scripting language with a pleasant syntax. Python supports XML and XSL. Although Python is rapidly gaining in popularity, it is yet not as popular as Perl and JavaScript.

There is a Java implementation of Python that gives you access to all the Java tools.

Omnimark

Omnimark is another scripting language. Unlike the other languages introduced so far, it was developed specifically to process SGML documents. Obviously, it was later extended to support XML. If you need a scripting language to manipulate XML documents, Omnimark is a good choice.

However, Omnimark is not well known outside SGML circles, and it is a proprietary language.

Java

The last option is Java. This is the language I have used for XCommerce. Keep in mind that this use of Java is not for client-side applets, but Java servlets or code running on a server.

Java has many strong points for XML development:

- Many XML tools are available in Java. Indeed, most of the XML tools (parser, XSL processor, FO processor, and so on) were first made available for Java.

- Java is highly portable. There are versions of Java for the major Web servers and then some.

- Java is a typed language, and it is compiled. The compiler catches many errors. This is important for server-side programming because a faulty script can crash your server.

- Several high-quality development environments are available, so you can choose the one that works best for you.

- Many vendors support Java. You have an ample supply of books, components, and services.

If you are familiar with JavaScript but you think Java is too complex, think twice. With XML, you will write more XSL code than Java or JavaScript code anyway. You really need not worry about complex concepts in Java.

✔ If you are not familiar with Java but you want to learn enough Java to run the examples, turn to Appendix A, "Crash Course on Java."

What's Next

Chapter 12 contains the entire source code for XCommerce. It provides a good illustration of what is possible with XML.

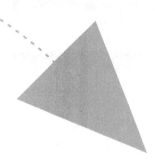

12

Putting It All Together: An e-Commerce Example

We're almost at the end of our journey. You have learned many useful XML concepts, and you have seen many practical examples. You know how to create XML documents, model them and validate them against the models, view or print them in HTML and PDF, and manipulate XML documents from your own applications.

You have learned enough to go and deploy XML in your organization. Before so doing, this chapter shows you how to use all the skills you've acquired in a midsize project. It contains the source code for XCommerce, an electronic mall that relies extensively on XML and, more specifically, SOAP and XSLT.

In this chapter, you learn

- How to use XML in a medium-size application

- How to organize a three-tiered application using SOAP

- How XSLT and XML make it easy to build sophisticated applications

- How to build and install a complete application

If you are not reading this book from cover to cover, make sure that you read Chapter 11, "N-Tiered Architecture and XML," first. Chapter 11 introduces the three-tiered concept used in XCommerce.

Building XCommerce

Although I've included the listings and a comprehensive installation procedure in this chapter, I urge you to download a working copy of XCommerce from www.marchal.com or www.quepublishing.com.

As you will see in the next few sections, XCommerce is larger than the examples in previous chapters. Installing it requires several steps, and it's easy to make a mistake. The download is both easier and safer.

CAUTION

Some of the components I used to prepare this chapter, such as the SOAP toolkit, are still at an early stage, so regardless of whether you want to download the XCommerce package, be sure to visit the Web sites for updates.

JDK

XCommerce depends on the SOAP library from Apache (xml.apache.org). At the time of this writing, the SOAP library uses JSP (Java Server Page). JSP, in turn, needs a Java compiler. The conclusion from all this is that, unlike many other Java applications, XCommerce requires a JDK (Java Development Kit). A JRE (Java Runtime Environment), lacking a compiler, is not appropriate.

Make sure that you download and install JDK 1.3 or above from java.sun.com before you attempt to run XCommerce.

CAUTION

XCommerce won't work unless JDK 1.3 or above is installed on your computer. Installing a JRE is not enough.

Classpath and Properties

XCommerce uses several libraries in addition to its own classes. Make sure that they are all properly installed, or it won't run. Specifically, you will need the following libraries:

- As you can imagine, an XML parser is required. I used Xerces, the XML parser from Apache (xml.apache.org). Most components in XCommerce manipulate XML documents and therefore need Xerces.

- Xalan, the XSLT processor. You can download Xalan from xml.apache.org. XCommerce uses XSLT to create HTML pages.

- The Apache SOAP toolkit, which you can download from xml.apache.org. SOAP provides the communication between the three tiers in XCommerce.

- The SOAP toolkit needs JavaMail and the JavaBeans Activation Framework. Both can be downloaded from java.sun.com.

- Because XCommerce is Web-based, it needs a servlet engine. I chose Jetty, which is available at jetty.mortbay.com. Switching to another servlet engine, such as Tomcat, is possible, but you need to adapt the configuration files.

- A JDBC database. I have tested this package with Hypersonic SQL, an open-source database available from (sourceforge.net/ projects/hsqldb). It should be easy to switch to another JDBC database, but you might need to adapt some of database code slightly.

As you can see, this project uses many open-source libraries. In fact, XCommerce illustrates the value of open-source libraries: So much code is already provided for us.

You need to tell the Java environment where to find these files, and the easiest solution is to add them to the classpath, as explained in Appendix A, "Crash Course on Java." Your classpath should look like

```
-classpath lib/hsql.jar;lib/xalan.jar;lib/xcommerce.jar;
➥%JAVA_HOME%/lib/tools.jar;lib/javax.servlet.jar;
➥lib/com.mortbay.jetty.jar;lib/activation.jar;lib/mail.jar;
➥lib/org.apache.jasper.jar;lib/xerces.jar;lib/soap.jar
```

Obviously, you may have to adapt these paths to your machine.

Furthermore, you need to tell Jetty to use Xerces as its XML parser. This is done by setting the org.xml.sax.parser environment variable to org.apache.xerces.parsers.SAXParser. You can use the -D parameter to the Java command, as in the following:

```
-Dorg.xml.sax.parser=org.apache.xerces.parsers.SAXParser
```

Configuration Files

EXAMPLE

You will need four configuration files: three for Jetty, the servlet engine, and one for the SOAP toolkit.

First Jetty, like any other servlet engine, needs web.xml files for each servlet package. In this case, two web.xml files are required: one for XCommerce itself and another one for the SOAP toolkit.

This file, which is defined by the servlet API, controls the configuration of servlets. Listing 12.1 is the web.xml file I use for XCommerce. It declares two servlets: mall and console.

As you will see, `mall` implements the shopping mall (the third tier) whereas console is just a tool to configure the database (the first tier).

✔The three tiers (the `mall` servlet, the merchant SOAP service, and the database) were introduced in Chapter 11.

CAUTION

Pay attention to the `rpc.router` property in Listing 12.1. It points to the SOAP end-point. If you change the SOAP configuration, you may need to adapt this property.

Listing 12.1: `web.xml`

```
<?xml version="1.0" encoding="ISO-8859-1"?>

<!DOCTYPE web-app
    PUBLIC "-//Sun Microsystems, Inc.//DTD Web Application 2.2//EN"
    "http://java.sun.com/j2ee/dtds/web-app_2_2.dtd">

<web-app>
  <display-name>XCommerce</display-name>
  <description>XML by Example, 2nd Edition -- Chapter 12</description>
  <servlet>
    <servlet-name>mall</servlet-name>
    <display-name>XCommerce Mall</display-name>
    <description>XML by Example, 2nd Edition -- Chapter 12</description>
    <servlet-class>com.psol.xbe2.MallServlet</servlet-class>
    <init-param>
      <param-name>rpc.router</param-name>
      <param-value>http://localhost:5401/soap/servlet/rpcrouter
➥</param-value>
    </init-param>
  </servlet>
  <servlet>
    <servlet-name>console</servlet-name>
    <display-name>Merchant Console</display-name>
    <description>XML by Example, 2nd Edition -- Chapter 12</description>
    <servlet-class>com.psol.xbe2.MerchantConsole</servlet-class>
  </servlet>

  <servlet-mapping>
    <servlet-name>mall</servlet-name>
    <url-pattern>/*</url-pattern>
  </servlet-mapping>
  <servlet-mapping>
    <servlet-name>console</servlet-name>
    <url-pattern>/console/*</url-pattern>
```

Listing 12.1: continued

```
  </servlet-mapping>

</web-app>
```

In addition to Listing 12.1, you'll need another web.xml file for the SOAP toolkit. However, this one should have been included in the toolkit download.

EXAMPLE

Next you need to configure Jetty to instantiate both the XCommerce servlet (essentially Listing 12.1) and the SOAP toolkit (see instructions in the SOAP toolkit download). Listing 12.2 is the configuration file for Jetty 3.0.

NOTE

If port 5401 is already in use on your computer, you will need to change this file and, more specifically, the following line:

```
<Set name="Port">5401</Set>
```

Be sure to update all the URLs, such as the rpc.route property in Listing 12.1.

Listing 12.2: jetty.xml

```
<?xml version="1.0" encoding="ISO-8859-1"?>

<!DOCTYPE Configure PUBLIC
    "-//Mort Bay Consulting//DTD Configure 1.0//EN"
    "http://jetty.morthay.com/configure_1_0.dtd">

<Configure class="com.mortbay.HTTP.HttpServer">

    <Call name="addListener">
      <Arg>
        <New class="com.mortbay.HTTP.SocketListener">
            <Set name="Port">5401</Set>
            <Set name="MinThreads">5</Set>
            <Set name="MaxThreads">255</Set>
            <Set name="MaxIdleTimeMs">60000</Set>
            <Set name="MaxReadTimeMs">60000</Set>
        </New>
      </Arg>
    </Call>

    <Set name="LogSink">
      <New class="com.mortbay.Util.WriterLogSink">
        <Arg><SystemProperty name="jetty.log" default="etc/logs"/>
➥/yyyy_mm_dd.request.log</Arg>
        <Set name="RetainDays">90</Set>
```

Listing 12.2: continued

```
        <Set name="Append">true</Set>
      </New>
    </Set>

    <Call name="addWebApplication">
      <Arg>/mall/*</Arg>
      <Arg><SystemProperty name="jetty.home" default="."/>
➡/webapps/xcommerce</Arg>
      <Arg><SystemProperty name="jetty.home" default="."/>
➡/webapps/xcommerce/WEB-INF/web.xml</Arg>
    </Call>

    <Call name="addContext">
      <Arg>/mall/*</Arg>
      <Set name="ResourceBase"><SystemProperty name="jetty.home"
          default="."/>/webapps/xcommerce</Set>
      <Set name="ServingResources">false</Set>
    </Call>

    <Call name="addWebApplication">
      <Arg>/soap/*</Arg>
      <Arg><SystemProperty name="jetty.home" default="."/>
➡/webapps/soap</Arg>
      <Arg><SystemProperty name="jetty.home" default="."/>
➡/webapps/soap/WEB-INF/web.xml</Arg>
      <Arg type="boolean">false</Arg>
    </Call>

    <Call name="addContext">
      <Arg>/soap/*</Arg>
      <Set name="ResourceBase"><SystemProperty name="jetty.home"
          default="."/>/soap/</Set>
      <Set name="ServingResources">true</Set>
      <Set name="HttpServerAccess">true</Set>
    </Call>

    <Call name="addContext">
      <Arg>/soap/admin/*</Arg>
      <Set name="ResourceBase"><SystemProperty name="jetty.home"
          default="."/>/soap/admin/</Set>
      <Set name="ClassPath"><SystemProperty name="jetty.home"
          default="."/>/soap/admin/</Set>
      <Set name="ServingResources">true</Set>
      <Call name="addServlet">
        <Arg>JSP</Arg>
```

Listing 12.2: continued

```
            <Arg>/soap/admin/*.jsp</Arg>
            <Arg>org.apache.jasper.servlet.JspServlet</Arg>
        </Call>
        <Set name="HttpServerAccess">true</Set>
    </Call>

</Configure>
```

EXAMPLE

Finally, you need a configuration file for SOAP itself. This file declares the SOAP services as well as specifies encoding routines for Java objects. You can use the deployment descriptor in Listing 12.3.

Listing 12.3: DeploymentDescriptor.xml

```
<isd:service
    xmlns:isd="http://xml.apache.org/xml-soap/deployment"
    id="http://www.psol.com/xbe2/chapter12">
    <isd:provider scope="Application"
        type="java"
        methods="getProductList getProductDetails addOrder">
        <isd:java class="com.psol.xbe2.MerchantService"
            static="false"/>
    </isd:provider>
    <isd:mappings>
      <isd:map
            encodingStyle="http://schemas.xmlsoap.org/soap/encoding/"
            xmlns:xbe2="http://www.psol.com/xbe2/chapter12"
            qname="xbe2:Product"
            javaType="com.psol.xbe2.Product"
            java2XMLClassName=
                "org.apache.soap.encoding.soapenc.BeanSerializer"
            xml2JavaClassName=
                "org.apache.soap.encoding.soapenc.BeanSerializer"/>
      <isd:map
            encodingStyle="http://schemas.xmlsoap.org/soap/encoding/"
            xmlns:xbe2="http://www.psol.com/xbe2/chapter12"
            qname="xbe2:ProductDetails"
            javaType="com.psol.xbe2.ProductDetails"
            java2XMLClassName=
                "org.apache.soap.encoding.soapenc.BeanSerializer"
            xml2JavaClassName=
                "org.apache.soap.encoding.soapenc.BeanSerializer"/>
      <isd:map
            encodingStyle="http://schemas.xmlsoap.org/soap/encoding/"
            xmlns:xbe2="http://www.psol.com/xbe2/chapter12"
            qname="xbe2:OrderLine"
            javaType="com.psol.xbe2.OrderLine"
```

Listing 12.3: continued

```
        java2XMLClassName=
            "org.apache.soap.encoding.soapenc.BeanSerializer"
        xml2JavaClassName=
            "org.apache.soap.encoding.soapenc.BeanSerializer"/>
    </isd:mappings>
</isd:service>
```

Compiling and Running the Application

EXAMPLE

This section contains complete instructions to rebuild the project. Again, I urge you to download the listings from www.marchal.com or www.quepublishing.com instead. You can then proceed directly to the next section "A Simpler Alternative."

Before running this application, you must compile all the Java files. I have found that for midsize projects, it is easier to use Ant (introduced in Appendix A). Listing 12.4 is the Ant build.xml file. This file is suitable for Ant 1.2 available from jakarta.apache.org.

Listing 12.4: build.xml

```
<?xml version="1.0"?>

<!-- Ant 1.2 build file: jakarta.apache.org -->

<project name="XBE2, Chapter 12" default="jar" basedir=".">
    <property name="src"        value="src"/>
    <property name="target"     value="classes"/>
    <property name="doc"        value="javadoc"/>
    <property name="etc"        value="etc"/>
    <property name="lib"        value="lib"/>
    <property name="db"         value="db"/>
    <property name="classpath" value="lib/soap.jar;lib/mail.jar;
➥lib/activation.jar;lib/xerces.jar;lib/xalan.jar;
➥lib/javax.servlet.jar"/>

    <target name="jar" depends="compile">
        <jar jarfile="${lib}/xcommerce.jar"
            basedir="${target}"/>
    </target>
    <target name="compile" depends="prepare">
        <javac srcdir="${src}"
                destdir="${target}"
                classpath="${classpath}"/>
```

Listing 12.4: continued

```
        <copy todir="${target}">
           <fileset dir="${src}" includes="**/*.xsl"/>
        </copy>
    </target>
    <target name="prepare">
        <mkdir dir="${target}"/>
        <mkdir dir="${etc}"/>
        <mkdir dir="${db}"/>
    </target>
</project>
```

Now you are ready to launch Jetty. Here's the command line, as explained before it sets the classpath and the org.xml.sax.parser property:

```
java -classpath lib/hsql.jar;lib/xalan.jar;lib/xcommerce.jar;
➥c:/jdk1.3/lib/tools.jar;lib/javax.servlet.jar;
➥lib/com.mortbay.jetty.jar;lib/activation.jar;lib/mail.jar;
➥lib/org.apache.jasper.jar;lib/xerces.jar;lib/soap.jar
➥-Dorg.xml.sax.parser=org.apache.xerces.parsers.SAXParser
➥com.mortbay.Jetty.Server etc/jetty.xml
```

CAUTION

Before you run the application, make sure that your classpath contains all the libraries. Most errors are due to improperly set classpaths or missing libraries.

We're two steps from running the actual application. The first of these steps is to deploy the SOAP merchant service. With the SOAP toolkit release 2.1, use the following command:

```
java -classpath lib/xerces.jar;lib/soap.jar;lib/mail.jar;
➥lib/activation.jar org.apache.soap.server.ServiceManagerClient
➥http://localhost:5401/soap/servlet/rpcrouter deploy
➥etc/ DeploymentDescriptor.xml
```

CAUTION

For some reason, the SOAP toolkit needs some time to "warm up." Depending on the speed of your processor, it may take up to three minutes for it to load. Be patient!

The last step before running the actual application is to create the database. Open your Web browser and enter the following URL:

```
http://localhost:5401/mall/console
```

Of course, if you run Jetty on a different port, you will need to update this URL. If everything goes well, the result should be similar to Figure 12.1.

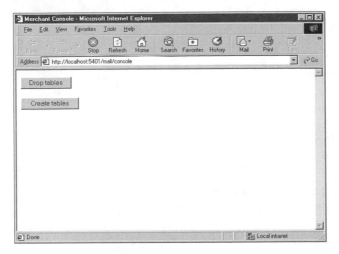

Figure 12.1: *The XCommerce console where you can configure the database.*

Click the Create Tables button to initialize the database. In the subsequent screen enter a few products as illustrated in Figure 12.2.

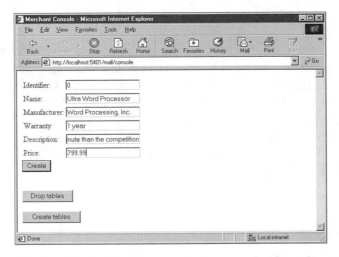

Figure 12.2: *Use the console to enter product description.*

CAUTION

When you enter products in the XCommerce console, make sure that you leave no fields blank. Indeed, to make the code more readable, there is little error-checking in XCommerce. Blank fields in product descriptions may crash the application.

You are finally ready to visit the mall, as illustrated in Figure 12.3. Direct your browser to the following address. Again, you may have to use a different URL if you have changed the Jetty configuration:

```
http://localhost:5401/mall/
```

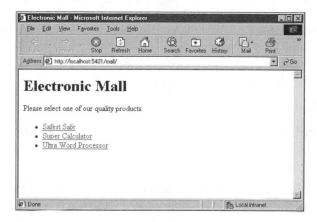

Figure 12.3: *The XCommerce mall simulates an online shop.*

A Simpler Alternative

The previous sections should have convinced you that installing XCommerce is more work than you want to do. Again, I urge you to download the XCommerce package from www.marchal.com or www.quepublishing.com. Note, however, that the JDK remains a separate download.

If you download the package, be sure to review the readme.html file for the latest updates. In particular, due to changes in licensing, you may have to download other libraries separately.

After downloading and installing the XCommerce package, you will find several Windows batch files designed to make your life easier. Open xcommerce.bat in a text editor. It should be similar to Listing 12.5.

Listing 12.5: xcommerce.bat

```
set JAVA_HOME=c:\jdk1.3
call jetty.bat
set JAVA_HOME=
```

The first line sets the path to your copy of the JDK. Update this to reflect the path on your machine. For example, if the JDK is in d:\java\jdk1.3, edit the first line from xcommerce.bat as follows:

```
set JAVA_HOME=d:\java\jdk1.3
```

Save your modifications. Double-click `xcommerce.bat`, and it should start the XCommerce server. You don't have to do anything else to set up the project, and you can directly visit the mall, as illustrated in Figure 12.3 by pointing your browser to

`http://localhost:5401/mall/`

First Tier: The Database

This section and the following two each present one tier. Recall from the discussion in Chapter 11 that XCommerce is organized around three tiers:

- A SQL database (the data tier) that provides permanent storage

- A SOAP service (the middle tier) that implements the business logic on top of the database: accessing product information and entering orders

- A servlet (the presentation tier) that manages the interaction with the shopper

Figure 12.4 illustrates the breakdown among the three tiers.

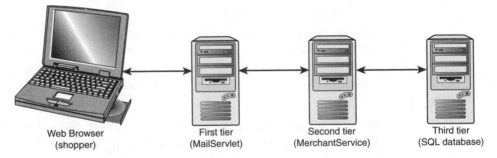

| Web Browser | First tier | Second tier | Third tier |
| (shopper) | (MailServlet) | (MerchantService) | (SQL database) |

Figure 12.4: *XCommerce is implemented over three tiers.*

EXAMPLE

Because this is not a full-blown shop, the database remains simple. It uses three tables to store product and order information:

- The `products` table stores product descriptions. The columns include an identifier (`id`), name (`name`), description (`description`), price (`price`), name of the product manufacturer (`manufacturer`), and a description of the warranty (`warranty`). Of course, it would be easy to add more columns—for example, for an image.

- The `orders` table contains basic information on orders. The fields are the customer's name (`name`), its company/enterprise name if any (company), its postal address (`street`, `region`, `postal_code`, `locality`, `country`), and its e-mail, too (`email`).

- The `lines` table is used to record the lines in the order. It has three columns for the order identifier (`orderid`), the product identifier (`productid`), and the quantity ordered (`quantity`).

As you can see, the `orders` and `lines` tables respect the academic example of an order database.

Although the user never accesses or manipulates these tables directly, the shop administrator needs an application to create and delete products as well as review orders.

This management application is implemented in the `MerchantConsole` servlet; see Listing 12.6. In addition to editing products, the servlet lets the shop administrator create and delete the database.

Listing 12.6: `MerchantConsole.java`

```java
package com.psol.xbe2;

import java.io.*;
import java.sql.*;
import javax.servlet.*;
import javax.servlet.http.*;

public class MerchantConsole
   extends HttpServlet
{
   protected void doGet(HttpServletRequest request,
                        HttpServletResponse response)
      throws ServletException, IOException
   {
      doProcess(request,response);
   }

   protected void doPost(HttpServletRequest request,
                         HttpServletResponse response)
      throws ServletException, IOException
   {
      doProcess(request,response);
   }

   protected void doProcess(HttpServletRequest request,
                            HttpServletResponse response)
      throws ServletException, IOException
```

Listing 12.6: continued

```
{
    try
    {
        Class.forName(MerchantService.driver);
        Connection connection =
            DriverManager.getConnection(MerchantService.url,
                                        MerchantService.user,
                                        MerchantService.password);
        try
        {
            String action = request.getParameter("action");
            if(null != action)
            {
                if(action.equalsIgnoreCase("create"))
                    doUpdates(request,connection,createStatements);
                else if(action.equalsIgnoreCase("drop"))
                    doUpdates(request,connection,dropStatements);
                else if(action.equalsIgnoreCase("delete"))
                    doDelete(request,connection);
                else if(action.equalsIgnoreCase("insert"))
                    doInsert(request,connection);
            }
            doPage(request,response,connection);
        }
        finally
        {
            connection.close();
        }
    }
    catch(Exception e)
    {
        e.printStackTrace();
        throw new ServletException(e);
    }
}

private static final String[] dropStatements =
{
    "drop table products",
    "drop table orders",
    "drop table lines",
};
```

Listing 12.6: continued

```java
private static final String[] createStatements =
    {
        "create table products (id integer not null primary key," +
        "name varchar(50), manufacturer varchar(50), price real," +
        "warranty varchar(20), description varchar(150))",
        "create table orders (id integer not null primary key, " +
        "name varchar(50), company varchar(50), " +
        "street varchar(100), region varchar(50), " +
        "postal_code varchar(15), locality varchar(50), " +
        "country varchar(25), email varchar(50))",
        "create table lines (orderid integer not null, " +
        "productid integer not null, quantity integer not null)"
    };

    protected void doUpdates(HttpServletRequest request,
                             Connection connection,
                             String[] statements)
        throws SQLException
    {
        Statement stmt = connection.createStatement();
        SQLException e = null;
        try
        {
            for(int i = 0;i < statements.length;i++)
              try
                  { stmt.executeUpdate(statements[i]); }
              catch(SQLException x)
                  { e = e != null ? e : x; }
            if(null != e)
            {
                throw e;
            }
        }
        finally
        {
            stmt.close();
        }
    }

    protected void doDelete(HttpServletRequest request,
                            Connection connection)
        throws SQLException
    {
        PreparedStatement stmt =
          connection.prepareStatement(
              "delete from products where id = ?");
```

Listing 12.6: continued

```java
    try
    {
        String id = request.getParameter("id");
        stmt.setInt(1,Integer.parseInt(id));
        stmt.executeUpdate();
    }
    finally
    {
        stmt.close();
    }
}

protected void doInsert(HttpServletRequest request,
                        Connection connection)
    throws SQLException, ServletException
{
    String id = request.getParameter("id"),
           name = request.getParameter("name"),
           manufacturer = request.getParameter("manufacturer"),
           warranty = request.getParameter("warranty"),
           description = request.getParameter("description"),
           price = request.getParameter("price");
    if(Util.isEmpty(id) || Util.isEmpty(name)
        || Util.isEmpty(manufacturer) || Util.isEmpty(warranty)
        || Util.isEmpty(description) || Util.isEmpty(price))
        throw new ServletException("Empty parameter disallowed");
    PreparedStatement stmt =
        connection.prepareStatement(
            "insert into products (id,name,manufacturer," +
            "warranty,description,price) values(?,?,?,?,?,?)");
    try
    {
        stmt.setString(1,id);
        stmt.setString(2,name);
        stmt.setString(3,manufacturer);
        stmt.setString(4,warranty);
        stmt.setString(5,description);
        stmt.setString(6,price);
        stmt.executeUpdate();
    }
    finally
    {
        stmt.close();
    }
}
```

Listing 12.6: continued

```java
protected boolean isSchemaCreated(Connection connection)
    throws SQLException
{
    // ask the name of all the tables in the database
    // check if one of them is "products"
    DatabaseMetaData meta = connection.getMetaData();
    ResultSet rs =
        meta.getTables(null,null,null,new String[] { "TABLE" });
    int found = 0;
    while(rs.next())
    {
        String tableName = rs.getString("TABLE_NAME");
        if(tableName.equalsIgnoreCase("products")
            || tableName.equalsIgnoreCase("orders")
            || tableName.equalsIgnoreCase("lines"))
            found++;
    }
    rs.close();
    return 3 == found;
}

protected void doPage(HttpServletRequest request,
                      HttpServletResponse response,
                      Connection connection)
    throws SQLException, IOException
{
    // tell the browser not to cache: otherwise it
    // may be difficult to reload the form
    response.setHeader("Cache-Control","no-cache");
    Writer writer = response.getWriter();
    writer.write("<html><head><title>Merchant Console");
    writer.write("</title></head><body>");
    Statement stmt = connection.createStatement();
    try
    {
        if(isSchemaCreated(connection))
        {
            writer.write("<p><form action='");
            writer.write(request.getRequestURI());
            writer.write("' method='post'><table>");
            writer.write("<tr><td>Identifier:</td>");
            writer.write("<td><input type='text'");
            writer.write(" name='id'></td></tr>");
            writer.write("<tr><td>Name:</td>");
            writer.write("<td><input type='text'");
```

Listing 12.6: continued

```
        writer.write(" name='name'></td></tr>");
        writer.write("<tr><td>Manufacturer:</td>");
        writer.write("<td><input type='text'");
        writer.write(" name='manufacturer'></td></tr>");
        writer.write("<tr><td>Warranty:</td>");
        writer.write("<td><input type='text'");
        writer.write(" name='warranty'></td></tr>");
        writer.write("<tr><td>Description:</td>");
        writer.write("<td><input type='text'");
        writer.write(" name='description'></td></tr>");
        writer.write("<tr><td>Price:</td>");
        writer.write("<td><input type='text'");
        writer.write(" name='price'></td></tr>");
        writer.write("</table><input type='submit'");
        writer.write(" value='Create'>");
        writer.write("<input type='hidden'");
        writer.write(" name='action' value='insert'>");
        writer.write("</form><p>");
        ResultSet rs =
           stmt.executeQuery("select id, name from products");
        writer.write("<table>");
        while(rs.next())
        {
           writer.write("<tr><td>");
           writer.write(rs.getString(2));
           writer.write("</td><td><form action='");
           writer.write(request.getRequestURI());
           writer.write("' method='post'>");
           writer.write(" <input type='submit'");
           writer.write(" value='Delete'>");
           writer.write("<input type='hidden'");
           writer.write(" name='action' value='delete'>");
           writer.write("<input type='HIDDEN'");
           writer.write(" name='id' value='");
           writer.write(rs.getString(1));
           writer.write("'>");
           writer.write("</form></td></tr>");
        }
        writer.write("</table>");
        rs = stmt.executeQuery("select id, name from orders");
        writer.write("<table>");
        while(rs.next())
        {
           int id = rs.getInt(1);
           writer.write("<tr><td valign='top'>");
```

Listing 12.6: continued

```
            writer.write(rs.getString(2));
            writer.write("</td><td>");
            PreparedStatement selectLines =
               connection.prepareStatement(
                  "select lines.quantity, products.name " +
                  "from lines, products where lines.productid" +
                  " = products.id and lines.orderid = ?");
            try
            {
               selectLines.setInt(1,id);
               ResultSet rsl = selectLines.executeQuery();
               boolean first = true;
               while(rsl.next())
               {
                  if(!first)
                     writer.write("<br>");
                  first = false;
                  writer.write(rsl.getString(1));
                  writer.write(" * ");
                  writer.write(rsl.getString(2));
               }
            }
            finally
            {
               selectLines.close();
            }
            writer.write(" </td></tr>");
         }
         writer.write("</table>");
      }
      writer.write("<p><form action='");
      writer.write(request.getRequestURI());
      writer.write("' method='post'>");
      writer.write("<input type='submit'");
      writer.write(" value='Drop tables'>");
      writer.write("<input type='hidden'");
      writer.write(" name='action' value='drop'>");
      writer.write("</form>");
      writer.write("<form action='");
      writer.write(request.getRequestURI());
      writer.write("' method='post'>");
      writer.write("<input type='submit'");
      writer.write(" value='Create tables'>");
      writer.write("<input type='hidden'");
      writer.write(" name='action' value='create'>");
```

Listing 12.6: continued

```
        writer.write("</form>");
      }
      finally
      {
        stmt.close();
      }
      writer.write("</body></html>");
      writer.flush();
    }
}
```

At first sight, this class appears complex because it does a lot of things. However, if you break it down into pieces, you'll find it's easy to understand.

When it receives a GET and POST request, the servlet forwards it to doProcess(). doProcess() has no special significance, but it lets you share code between doGet() and doPost().

```
protected void doGet(HttpServletRequest request,
                     HttpServletResponse response)
    throws ServletException, IOException
{
    doProcess(request,response);
}
```

TIP

It is easy to process GET and POST requests interchangeably, but, unfortunately, it is not always possible.

Indeed, using GET requests to update information on a server may pose a security threat. The MerchantConsole servlet works around this problem by carefully creating POST forms where appropriate.

However, that won't stop a determined hacker, so, before applying this technique, you have to decide whether the risk is acceptable. MerchantConsole is an internal tool and therefore trusted. MallServlet, the presentation tier, is more strict.

---

doProcess() routes the request to another method based on the value of the HTTP action parameter:

```
protected void doProcess(HttpServletRequest request,
                         HttpServletResponse response)
    throws ServletException, IOException
{
    try
    {
        Class.forName(MerchantService.driver);
        Connection connection =
```

```
                 DriverManager.getConnection(MerchantService.url,
                                      MerchantService.user,
                                      MerchantService.password);
        try
        {
           String action = request.getParameter("action");
           if(null != action)
           {
              if(action.equalsIgnoreCase("create"))
                 doUpdates(request,connection,createStatements);
              else if(action.equalsIgnoreCase("drop"))
                 doUpdates(request,connection,dropStatements);
              else if(action.equalsIgnoreCase("delete"))
                 doDelete(request,connection);
              else if(action.equalsIgnoreCase("insert"))
                 doInsert(request,connection);
           }
           doPage(request,response,connection);
        }
        finally
        {
           connection.close();
        }
     }
     catch(Exception e)
     {
        e.printStackTrace();
        throw new ServletException(e);
     }
  }
}
```

The doUpdates(), doDelete(), and doInsert() methods run the appropriate SQL statements. For example, doDelete() issues a SQL delete to remove a product from the database:

```
protected void doDelete(HttpServletRequest request,
                     Connection connection)
   throws SQLException
{
   PreparedStatement stmt =
      connection.prepareStatement(
         "delete from products where id = ?");
   try
   {
      String id = request.getParameter("id");
      stmt.setInt(1,Integer.parseInt(id));
      stmt.executeUpdate();
```

```
   }
   finally
   {
      stmt.close();
   }
}
```

CAUTION

It is unsafe to delete products that have been ordered because it breaks the relationship between the lines and orders tables.

However, for simplicity, the console does not check for this error. You have been warned.

The largest method is probably doPage(), which is called by doProcess() regardless of the value of the action parameter. It prints a rather large HTML page with several forms to create and drop the database tables, create and delete products, and print the list of orders. Notice that it sets the action parameter to a different value on every such form.

There's only one potential problem with doPage(). What happens when the shop manager invokes the servlet for the first time, before he has created the tables? Indeed, because the servlet is used to create the tables, there's a potential catch-22 situation here.

The trick is to test whether the tables have been created in the database before attempting to display products and orders. This is the role of isSchemaCreated(), a method that uses JDBC metadata to test the existence of the tables.

isSchemaCreated() simply loops over all the tables in the database until it finds products, orders, and lines.

```
protected boolean isSchemaCreated(Connection connection)
   throws SQLException
{
   // ask the name of all the tables in the database
   // check if one of them is "products"
   DatabaseMetaData meta = connection.getMetaData();
   ResultSet rs =
      meta.getTables(null,null,null,new String[] { "TABLE" });
   int found = 0;
   while(rs.next())
   {
      String tableName = rs.getString("TABLE_NAME");
      if(tableName.equalsIgnoreCase("products")
         || tableName.equalsIgnoreCase("orders")
         || tableName.equalsIgnoreCase("lines"))
```

```
        found++;
  }
  rs.close();
  return 3 == found;
}
```

The remainder of doPage() is a list of straightforward SQL select state-ments such as the following, that prints a list of products:

```
ResultSet rs =
  stmt.executeQuery("select id, name from products");
writer.write("<table>");
while(rs.next())
{
  writer.write("<tr><td>");
  writer.write(rs.getString(2));
  writer.write("</td><td><form action='");
  writer.write(request.getRequestURI());
  writer.write("' method='post'>");
  writer.write(" <input type='submit'");
  writer.write(" value='Delete'>");
  writer.write("<input type='hidden'");
  writer.write(" name='action' value='delete'>");
  writer.write("<input type='HIDDEN'");
  writer.write(" name='id' value='");
  writer.write(rs.getString(1));
  writer.write("'>");
  writer.write("</form></td></tr>");
}
```

Second Tier: The SOAP Service

EXAMPLE

As you know, the middle tier server is implemented as a SOAP service. It mediates between the database and the presentation tier.

As explained in Chapter 11, the benefits of this approach are to abstract the presentation layer from the specifics of the database. Among other things, it would make it easier to share the load over several servers.

In practice, the middle tier server is implemented as a Java class, MerchantService, that exports some of its methods as SOAP entry points. It offers three operations:

- getProductList returns the complete list of products sold in the shop. Because the list is large, it does not return much information per product.

- getProductDetails returns more details on a specific product.

- addOrder enters an order into the database.

As you will see in the next section, the presentation layer uses these three operations to retrieve product information and pass customers' orders. In most cases, the presentation layer can simply apply a style sheet to the result from the SOAP call to prepare the HTML page.

The middle tier server is in the MerchantService class, shown in Listing 12.7.

Listing 12.7: MerchantService.java

```java
package com.psol.xbe2;

import java.sql.*;
import java.util.*;

public class MerchantService
{
   public final static String driver = "org.hsql.jdbcDriver",
                              url = "jdbc:HypersonicSQL:db/merchant",
                              user = "sa",
                              password = null;

   public Product[] getProductList()
      throws SQLException
   {
   Vector vector = new Vector();
   try
   {
      Class.forName(driver);
      Connection connection =
         DriverManager.getConnection(url,
                                     user,
                                     password);
      try
      {
         Statement stmt = connection.createStatement();
         try
         {
            ResultSet rs =
               stmt.executeQuery(
               "select id, name from products order by name");
            while(rs.next())
            {
               Product product = new Product();
```

Listing 12.7: continued

```
                product.setId(rs.getInt(1));
                product.setName(rs.getString(2));
                vector.addElement(product);
            }
        }
        finally
        {
            stmt.close();
        }
    }
    finally
    {
        connection.close();
    }
}
catch(ClassNotFoundException e)
{
    e.printStackTrace();
}
Product[] productList = new Product[vector.size()];
vector.copyInto(productList);
return productList;
}

public ProductDetails getProductDetails(int id)
    throws SQLException
{
    ProductDetails productDetails = null;
    try
    {
        Class.forName(driver);
        Connection connection =
            DriverManager.getConnection(url,
                                        user,
                                        password);
        try
        {
            PreparedStatement stmt =
                connection.prepareStatement("select id, name, " +
                    "manufacturer, warranty, description," +
                    "price from products where id = ?");
            try
            {
                stmt.setInt(1,id);
                ResultSet rs = stmt.executeQuery();
```

Listing 12.7: continued

```
            if(rs.next())
            {
                productDetails = new ProductDetails();
                productDetails.setId(rs.getInt(1));
                productDetails.setName(rs.getString(2));
                productDetails.setManufacturer(rs.getString(3));
                productDetails.setWarranty(rs.getString(4));
                productDetails.setDescription(rs.getString(5));
                productDetails.setPrice(rs.getDouble(6));
            }
        }
        finally
        {
            stmt.close();
        }
    }
    finally
    {
        connection.close();
    }
}
catch(ClassNotFoundException e)
{
    e.printStackTrace();
}
return productDetails;
}

public boolean addOrder(String name,
                        String company,
                        String street,
                        String region,
                        String postalCode,
                        String locality,
                        String country,
                        String email,
                        OrderLine[] lines)
{
    try
    {
        Class.forName(driver);
        Connection connection =
            DriverManager.getConnection(url,
                                        user,
                                        password);
```

Listing 12.7: continued

```java
int maxId = 0;
try
{
   Statement stmt = connection.createStatement();
   try
   {
      // not good enough for a live system
      // but portable and safe enough in this context
      ResultSet rs = stmt.executeQuery(
                       "select max(id) from orders");
      if(rs.next())
         maxId = rs.getInt(1);
   }
   finally
   {
      stmt.close();
   }
   PreparedStatement insertOrder =
      connection.prepareStatement("insert into orders " +
            "(id, name, company, street, region, " +
            "postal_code, locality, country, email) " +
            "values (?,?,?,?,?,?,?,?,?)");
   try
   {
      insertOrder.setInt(1,maxId + 1);
      insertOrder.setString(2,name);
      insertOrder.setString(3,company);
      insertOrder.setString(4,street);
      insertOrder.setString(5,region);
      insertOrder.setString(6,postalCode);
      insertOrder.setString(7,locality);
      insertOrder.setString(8,country);
      insertOrder.setString(9,email);
      insertOrder.executeUpdate();
   }
   finally
   {
       insertOrder.close();
   }
   PreparedStatement insertLine =
      connection.prepareStatement("insert into lines " +
            "(orderid, productid, quantity) " +
            "values(?,?,?)");
   try
   {
```

Listing 12.7: continued

```
            for(int i = 0;i < lines.length;i++)
            {
                OrderLine line = lines[i];
                insertLine.setInt(1,maxId + 1);
                insertLine.setInt(2,line.getId());
                insertLine.setInt(3,line.getQuantity());
                insertLine.executeUpdate();
            }
        }
        finally
        {
            insertLine.close();
        }
    }
    finally
    {
        connection.close();
    }
}
catch(ClassNotFoundException e)
{
    System.out.println(e.getMessage());
    return false;
}
catch(SQLException e)
{
    System.out.println(e.getMessage());
    return false;
}
catch(Exception e)
{
    e.printStackTrace();
    return false;
}
return true;
    }
}
```

If you review this class in more detail, you will find that it mostly consists of code to retrieve or insert information to and from a database.

The getProductList() method is a good example. It builds an array of Product objects (introduced in the next section) by reading from the products table in the database.

The code in getProductList() takes care to handle exceptions properly. However, notice that getProductList() takes advantage of Hypersonic SQL by opening a new database connection for every request.

This is generally not a problem with Hypersonic SQL, but for most other databases, the cost of opening all these connections would be prohibitive. If you turn to another database, you might want to use a spool of database connections:

```
public Product[] getProductList()
   throws SQLException
{
   Vector vector = new Vector();
   try
   {
      Class.forName(driver);
      Connection connection =
         DriverManager.getConnection(url,
                                     user,
                                     password);
      try
      {
         Statement stmt = connection.createStatement();
         try
         {
            ResultSet rs =
               stmt.executeQuery(
               "select id, name from products order by name");
            while(rs.next())
            {
               Product product = new Product();
               product.setId(rs.getInt(1));
               product.setName(rs.getString(2));
               vector.addElement(product);
            }
         }
         finally
         {
             stmt.close();
         }
      }
      finally
      {
         connection.close();
      }
   }
   catch(ClassNotFoundException e)
```

```
    {
        e.printStackTrace();
    }
    Product[] productList = new Product[vector.size()];
    vector.copyInto(productList);
    return productList;
}
```

NOTE

Again the benefit of using a 3-tiered architecture is to abstract the presentation layer from the specifics of the database. This makes it easier to enhance each tier independently. For example, you could redo the middle-tier server to check incoming orders against product availability. However, as long as you stick to the interface defined by those three operations, it would not impact the presentation layer at all!

Product

EXAMPLE

The middle-tier server uses what I describe as "three data classes" to communicate with the presentation tier. Those are simple classes that group several variables. The data classes have few or no methods besides setters and getters (methods to set and get the values of properties).

TIP

You need "data classes" in Java because there are no other mechanisms, in the language, to manipulate several variables as a whole.

In C, you would have used `structs` instead. In Pascal, you would have used `records`.

One of these classes is `Product`, shown in Listing 12.8, which holds basic product information: the identifier and the name.

Listing 12.8: `Product.java`

```
package com.psol.xbe2;

public class Product
{
    protected int id = -1;
    protected String name = null;

    public Product()
    {
    }

    public Product(Product product)
    {
        this.id = product.id;
```

Listing 12.8: continued

```
      this.name = product.name;
   }

   public void setId(int id)
   {
      this.id = id;
   }

   public int getId()
   {
      return id;
   }

   public void setName(String name)
   {
      this.name = name;
   }

   public String getName()
   {
      return name;
   }
}
```

ProductDetails

EXAMPLE

The Product class offers very little product information and is suitable for the level of detail provided by getProductList().

The getProductDetails() method uses ProductDetails instead. It derives from Product but adds several fields for description, product manufacturer, warranty, and price. Note that this matches the columns in the products table. Like Product, ProductDetails consists essentially of a few properties and appropriate getters and setters, see Listing 12.9.

Listing 12.9: ProductDetails.java

```
package com.psol.xbe2;

public class ProductDetails
   extends Product
{
   protected String description = null,
                    manufacturer = null,
                    warranty = null;
   protected double price = 0.0;
```

Listing 12.9: continued

```
public ProductDetails()
{
}

public ProductDetails(ProductDetails product)
{
    super(product);
    this.description = product.description;
    this.manufacturer = product.manufacturer;
    this.warranty = product.warranty;
    this.price = product.price;
}

public void setDescription(String description)
{
    this.description = description;
}

public String getDescription()
{
    return description;
}

public void setManufacturer(String manufacturer)
{
    this.manufacturer = manufacturer;
}

public String getManufacturer()
{
    return manufacturer;
}

public void setWarranty(String warranty)
{
    this.warranty = warranty;
}

public String getWarranty()
{
    return warranty;
}

public void setPrice(double price)
{
```

Listing 12.9: continued

```
      this.price = price;
   }

   public double getPrice()
   {
      return price;
   }
}
```

OrderLine

EXAMPLE

The last of these "data" classes is OrderLine, which groups information on one order line. An OrderLine is essentially the combination of a product and the quantity ordered. For simplicity, it derives from ProductDetails, inheriting all the product properties and adding only the quantity; see Listing 12.10.

Listing 12.10: OrderLine.java

```
package com.psol.xbe2;

public class OrderLine
   extends ProductDetails
{
   protected int quantity;

   public OrderLine()
   {
   }

   public OrderLine(ProductDetails product,int quantity)
   {
      super(product);
      this.quantity = quantity;
   }

   public void setQuantity(int quantity)
   {
      this.quantity = quantity;
   }

   public int getQuantity()
   {
      return quantity;
   }
```

Listing 12.10: continued

```
public double getTotal()
{
   return quantity * price;
}
}
```

Third Tier: The Presentation Servlet

The database and the middle tier server are invisible to the end-user. They provide the infrastructure on which to build the mall, but the mall, as seen by the end-user, is implemented in the servlet from Listing 12.11.

EXAMPLE

Listing 12.11: MallServlet.java

```
package com.psol.xbe2;

import java.io.*;
import java.net.*;
import java.util.*;
import javax.mail.*;
import org.xml.sax.*;
import javax.servlet.*;
import org.apache.soap.*;
import javax.servlet.http.*;
import org.xml.sax.helpers.*;
import javax.xml.transform.*;
import org.apache.soap.rpc.*;
import org.apache.soap.encoding.*;
import org.apache.soap.util.xml.*;
import javax.xml.transform.stream.*;
import org.apache.soap.encoding.soapenc.*;

public class MallServlet
   extends HttpServlet
{
   protected Templates mallTemplates,
                       productTemplates;
   protected SOAPMappingRegistry registry;
   protected URL rpcRouter;

   public void init()
      throws ServletException
   {
      super.init();
      try
      {
```

Listing 12.11: continued

```
        // read the XSLT style sheets
        TransformerFactory factory =
            TransformerFactory.newInstance();
        ClassLoader classLoader = getClass().getClassLoader();
        URL url = classLoader.getResource("etc/mall.xsl");
        Source styleSheet = new StreamSource(url.openStream());
        mallTemplates = factory.newTemplates(styleSheet);
        url = classLoader.getResource("etc/product.xsl");
        styleSheet = new StreamSource(url.openStream());
        productTemplates = factory.newTemplates(styleSheet);
        // prepare the SOAP mapping registry
        BeanSerializer serializer = new BeanSerializer();
        registry = new SOAPMappingRegistry();
        registry.mapTypes(Constants.NS_URI_SOAP_ENC,
                          new QName(
                              "http://www.psol.com/xbe2/chapter12",
                              "Product"),
                          Product.class,serializer,serializer);
        registry.mapTypes(Constants.NS_URI_SOAP_ENC,
                          new QName(
                              "http://www.psol.com/xbe2/chapter12",
                              "ProductDetails"),
                          ProductDetails.class,serializer,serializer);
        registry.mapTypes(Constants.NS_URI_SOAP_ENC,
                          new QName(
                              "http://www.psol.com/xbe2/chapter12",
                              "OrderLine"),
                          OrderLine.class,serializer,serializer);
        // finally get the router's URL
        rpcRouter = new URL(getInitParameter("rpc.router"));
    }
    catch(Exception e)
    {
        throw new UnavailableException(e.getMessage());
    }
}

public void doGet(HttpServletRequest request,
                  HttpServletResponse response)
    throws ServletException, IOException
{
    try
    {
        int productId = getProductId(request);
        if(productId == -1)
```

Listing 12.11: continued

```
              doMall(request,response);
          else
              doProduct(request,response,productId);
      }
      catch(TransformerException e)
      {
          throw new ServletException(e);
      }
      catch(MessagingException e)
      {
          throw new ServletException(e);
      }
      catch(SOAPException e)
      {
          throw new ServletException(e);
      }
  }

  public void doPost(HttpServletRequest request,
                     HttpServletResponse response)
      throws ServletException, IOException
  {
      try
      {
          int productId = getProductId(request);
          if(!isAddressComplete(request))
              doCheckout(request,response,productId);
          else
              doTakeOrder(request,response,productId);
      }
      catch(MessagingException e)
      {
          throw new ServletException(e);
      }
      catch(SOAPException e)
      {
          throw new ServletException(e);
      }
  }

  protected int getProductId(HttpServletRequest request)
  {
      try
      {
          StringTokenizer tokenizer =
```

Listing 12.11: continued

```
            new StringTokenizer(request.getPathInfo(),"/",false);
        String productId = tokenizer.nextToken();
        return Integer.parseInt(productId);
    }
    catch(Exception e)
    {
        return -1;
    }
}


protected void doRpcAndStyle(HttpServletRequest request,
                            HttpServletResponse response,
                            String methodName,
                            Vector params,
                            Templates templates)
    throws IOException, TransformerException,
        MessagingException, SOAPException
{
    Call call = new Call();
    call.setSOAPMappingRegistry(registry);
    call.setTargetObjectURI("http://www.psol.com/xbe2/chapter12");
    call.setMethodName(methodName);
    call.setEncodingStyleURI(Constants.NS_URI_SOAP_ENC);
    if(params != null)
        call.setParams(params);
    Response resp =
        call.invoke(rpcRouter,
                    "http://www.psol.com/xbe2/soapaction");
    if(!resp.generatedFault())
    {
        Transformer transformer = templates.newTransformer();
        transformer.setParameter("context-path",
                                request.getContextPath());
        BodyPart bp = resp.getBodyPart(0);
        Source source = new StreamSource(bp.getInputStream());
        Result result =
            new StreamResult(response.getOutputStream());
        transformer.transform(source,result);
    }
    else
    {
        Fault fault = resp.getFault();
        throw new SOAPException(fault.getFaultCode(),
                                fault.getFaultString());
    }
```

Listing 12.11: continued

```
   }

   protected void doMall(HttpServletRequest request,
                            HttpServletResponse response)
      throws IOException, TransformerException,
            MessagingException, SOAPException
   {
      doRpcAndStyle(request,response,"getProductList",
                    null,mallTemplates);
   }

   protected void doProduct(HttpServletRequest request,
                             HttpServletResponse response,
                             int productId)
      throws IOException, TransformerException,
            MessagingException, SOAPException
   {
      Vector params = new Vector();
      params.addElement(new Parameter("id",Integer.class,
                                      new Integer(productId),
                                      null));
      doRpcAndStyle(request,response,"getProductDetails",
                    params,productTemplates);
   }

   protected boolean isAddressComplete(HttpServletRequest request)
   {
      // region is not mandatory (only used in the US & Canada)
      String[] fields =
      {
         "name", "street", "postal-code",
         "locality", "country", "email"
      };
      int found = 0;
      for(int i = 0;i < fields.length;i++)
      {
         String value = request.getParameter(fields[i]);
         if(!Util.isEmpty(value))
            found++;
      }
      return found == fields.length;
   }

   protected ProductDetails doGetProductDetails(int productId)
      throws SOAPException
```

Listing 12.11: continued

```
    {
      Call call = new Call();
      call.setSOAPMappingRegistry(registry);
      call.setTargetObjectURI("http://www.psol.com/xbe2/chapter12");
      call.setMethodName("getProductDetails");
      call.setEncodingStyleURI(Constants.NS_URI_SOAP_ENC);
      Vector params = new Vector();
      params.addElement(new Parameter("id",Integer.class,
                                      new Integer(productId),
                                      null));
      call.setParams(params);
      Response resp =
        call.invoke(rpcRouter,
                    "http://www.psol.com/xbe2/soapaction");
      if(!resp.generatedFault())
        return (ProductDetails)resp.getReturnValue().getValue();
      else
      {
        Fault fault = resp.getFault();
        throw new SOAPException(fault.getFaultCode(),
                                fault.getFaultString());
      }
    }


  protected void writeRow(String label,
                          String key,
                          HttpServletRequest request,
                          Writer writer)
    throws IOException
  {
    writer.write("<tr><td>");
    writer.write(label);
    writer.write("</td><td><input type='text' name='");
    writer.write(key);
    writer.write('\'');
    String value = request.getParameter(key);
    if(!Util.isEmpty(value))
    {
      writer.write(" value='");
      writer.write(value);
      writer.write('\'');
    }
    writer.write("></td></tr>");
  }
```

Listing 12.11: continued

```
protected void doCheckout(HttpServletRequest request,
                          HttpServletResponse response,
                          int productId)
    throws IOException, SOAPException
{
    HttpSession session = request.getSession();
    String qt = request.getParameter("quantity");
    if(productId != -1 && qt != null)
    {
        int quantity = Integer.parseInt(qt);
        OrderLine line = (OrderLine)session.getAttribute(
                                    String.valueOf(productId));

        if(line == null)
        {
            ProductDetails product =
                doGetProductDetails(productId);
            line = new OrderLine(product,quantity);
            session.setAttribute(String.valueOf(productId),
                                line);
        }
        else
            line.setQuantity(quantity);
    }
    PrintWriter writer = response.getWriter();
    writer.write("<html><head><title>Checkout</title></head>");
    writer.write("<body><a href='");
    writer.write(request.getContextPath());
    writer.write("'>Shop some more!</a><form action='");
    writer.write(request.getContextPath());
    writer.write("/' method='post'><table border='0'>");
    writer.write("<tr><td colspan='2'>Please enter your ");
    writer.write("name and address:</td></tr>");
    writeRow("Name *:","name",request,writer);
    writeRow("Company:","company",request,writer);
    writeRow("Street *:","street",request,writer);
    writeRow("Region:","region",request,writer);
    writeRow("ZIP or postal-code *:","postal-code",
            request,writer);
    writeRow("Locality *:","locality",request,writer);
    writeRow("Country *:","country",request,writer);
    writeRow("Email *:","email",request,writer);
    writer.write("</table>");
    writer.write("<table border='0'><tr><td colspan='7'>");
    writer.write("Your order:</td></tr>");
    double total = 0.0;
```

Listing 12.11: continued

```
    Enumeration enum = session.getAttributeNames();
    while(enum.hasMoreElements())
    {
      OrderLine line =
        (OrderLine)session.getAttribute(
                              (String)enum.nextElement());
      writer.write("<tr><td>");
      writer.write(String.valueOf(line.getQuantity()));
      writer.write("</td><td>*</td><td>");
      writer.write(line.getName());
      writer.write("</td><td>at</td><td>");
      writer.write(String.valueOf(line.getPrice()));
      writer.write("</td><td>=</td><td>");
      writer.write(String.valueOf(line.getTotal()));
      total += line.getTotal();
      writer.write("</td></tr>");
    }
    writer.write("<tr><td colspan='6'>Total:</td><td>");
    writer.write(String.valueOf(total));
    writer.write("</td></tr></table>");
    writer.write("<input type='submit' value='Order'>");
    writer.write("</form></html>");
    writer.flush();
  }

  protected void doTakeOrder(HttpServletRequest request,
                             HttpServletResponse response,
                             int merchantId)
    throws ServletException, IOException,
           MessagingException, SOAPException
  {
    HttpSession session = request.getSession();
    if(session.isNew())
      throw new ServletException("Error with session");
    Enumeration enum = session.getAttributeNames();
    Vector vector = new Vector();
    while(enum.hasMoreElements())
      vector.addElement(session.getAttribute(
                              (String)enum.nextElement()));
    OrderLine[] lines = new OrderLine[vector.size()];
    vector.copyInto(lines);
    Call call = new Call();
    call.setSOAPMappingRegistry(registry);
    call.setTargetObjectURI("http://www.psol.com/xbe2/chapter12");
    call.setMethodName("addOrder");
```

Listing 12.11: continued

```
call.setEncodingStyleURI(Constants.NS_URI_SOAP_ENC);
Vector params = new Vector();
params.addElement(
   new Parameter("name",String.class,
               request.getParameter("name"),null));
params.addElement(
   new Parameter("company",String.class,
               request.getParameter("company"),
               null));
params.addElement(
   new Parameter("street",String.class,
               request.getParameter("street"),null));
params.addElement(
   new Parameter("region",String.class,
               request.getParameter("region"),null));
params.addElement(
   new Parameter("postalCode",String.class,
               request.getParameter("postal-code"),null));
params.addElement(
   new Parameter("locality",String.class,
               request.getParameter("locality"),null));
params.addElement(
   new Parameter("country",String.class,
               request.getParameter("country"),null));
params.addElement(
   new Parameter("email",String.class,
               request.getParameter("email"),null));
params.addElement(
   new Parameter("lines",lines.getClass(),
               lines,null));
call.setParams(params);
Response resp =
   call.invoke(rpcRouter,
               "http://www.psol.com/xbe2/soapaction");
if(!resp.generatedFault())
{
   Parameter ret = resp.getReturnValue();
   boolean ok = ((Boolean)ret.getValue()).booleanValue();
   Writer writer = response.getWriter();
   if(ok)
   {
      writer.write("<html><head><title>Checkout</title>");
      writer.write("<body><p>Your order has been processed");
```

Listing 12.11: continued

```
            writer.write(" successfully. Thank you for shopping");
            writer.write(" with us.</html>");
        }
        else
        {
            writer.write("<html><head><title>Checkout</title>");
            writer.write("<body><p>Unfortunately your order could");
            writer.write(" not be processed.</html>");
        }
        writer.flush();
        session.invalidate();
    }
    else
    {
        Fault fault = resp.getFault();
        throw new SOAPException(fault.getFaultCode(),
                                fault.getFaultString());
    }
    }
}
```

This is a large servlet because it fully implements the mall. Obviously, it relies heavily on the middle-tier server. It offers four different screens to the user, implemented in four do*XXX*() methods:

- doMall() is the mall homepage. It displays a list of products inviting the user to select a particular product for more details.

- doProduct() zooms into product details. This page has all the details about one product as well as an order form.

- doCheckout() implements a simple shopping cart function. Through this screen, the user adds products to his card. Order details are recorded in a servlet session.

- doTakeOrder() passes the order to the middle-tier server where it is stored permanently.

Let's review these methods in more detail.

Initialization

During the servlet initialization in init(), it loads two style sheets (mall.xsl and product.xsl), the use of which will become clearer in a moment.

> **TIP**
>
> The servlet loads the style sheets from its own JAR file using `ClassLoader.getResource()`. This is a common Java trick to bundle files, such as images, configuration, and...stylesheets, in the JAR file alongside the class files.
>
> Why bother? It just makes it easier to distribute the servlet because everything (including the style sheet) is in one JAR file.

To load the style sheet, the servlet uses the TrAX (Transformation API for XML) API. TrAX is the official Java API for XSLT processors. It plays a role for XSLT processors similar to what SAX does for XML parsers.

First, the servlet creates a `TransformerFactory` with the `newInstance()` static method. Next, it creates a `StreamSource()` object passing it an `InputStream` to the style sheet. Finally, using the `TransformerFactory.newTemplates()` method, it creates a `Templates` object. This `Templates` object retains the loaded style sheet.

```
TransformerFactory factory = TransformerFactory.newInstance();
ClassLoader classLoader = getClass().getClassLoader();
URL url = classLoader.getResource("etc/mall.xsl");
Source styleSheet = new StreamSource(url.openStream());
mallTemplates = factory.newTemplates(styleSheet);
```

During initialization, the servlet also initializes SOAP. It creates a registry mapping for the various "data" classes introduced in the middle-tier section.

```
// prepare the SOAP mapping registry
BeanSerializer serializer = new BeanSerializer();
registry = new SOAPMappingRegistry();
registry.mapTypes(Constants.NS_URI_SOAP_ENC,
                  new QName(
                      "http://www.psol.com/xbe2/chapter12",
                      "Product"),
                  Product.class,serializer,serializer);
```

> **CAUTION**
>
> Notice that the registry contains the same mappings as introduced in the `DeploymentDescriptor.xml` in Listing 12.3. It is essential that the two match.

Request Routing

The servlet implements `doGet()` and `doPost()` to route HTTP GET and POST requests. In both cases, it attempts to extract a product identifier from the URL to determine which method to call:

```
int productId = getProductId(request);
if(productId == -1)
```

```
        doMall(request,response);
    else
        doProduct(request,response,productId);
```

URLs to the servlet are of the following form:

```
http://localhost:5401/mall/
http://localhost:5401/mall/1/
```

The first URL points to the mall home page; the second points to a specific product. As you can see, the product code (1 in this example) is passed to the server as part of the path. Our servlet needs to extract this parameter from the path.

Most servlets takes parameters from forms, and they use the getParameter() method for that purpose. Likewise, to extract a parameter from the path, the servlet uses getPathInfo().

However, getPathInfo() is risky: Depending on the servlet engine, the path may be returned as /1, /1/, or 1. The trick is to use a StringTokenizer to remove unwanted /:

```
protected int getProductId(HttpServletRequest request)
{
   try
   {
      StringTokenizer tokenizer =
         new StringTokenizer(request.getPathInfo(),"/",false);
      String productId = tokenizer.nextToken();
      return Integer.parseInt(productId);
   }
   catch(Exception e)
   {
      return -1;
   }
}
```

TIP

Why pass product identifier in the URL path? Most Web sites use form parameters instead that are returned after a ? as in the following:

http://localhost:5401/mall?product_id=1

Form parameters are easier to use; they are better supported by servlets. Unfortunately, they are not compatible with all search engines and are not so easy to use in e-mails.

Passing the product identifier in the URL path increases the shop compatibility with search engines, and, as you have seen, it is not much more work. Note that Amazon.com, the Web's largest store, does this.

doMall() and doProduct()

The doMall() and doProduct() methods are similar. They send a SOAP
request to the middle tier. They use a neat trick to decode the response.
Indeed because, thanks to SOAP, it comes as an XML document, it suffices
to apply an XSLT style sheet to obtain an HTML page. This is implemented
in doRpcAndStyle():

```
protected void doMall(HttpServletRequest request,
                      HttpServletResponse response)
   throws IOException, TransformerException,
          MessagingException, SOAPException
{
   doRpcAndStyle(request,response,"getProductList",
                 null,mallTemplates);
}
```

If you study doRpcAndStyle(), you'll find that it starts by making a regular
SOAP request:

```
Call call = new Call();
call.setSOAPMappingRegistry(registry);
call.setTargetObjectURI("http://www.psol.com/xbe2/chapter12");
call.setMethodName(methodName);
call.setEncodingStyleURI(Constants.NS_URI_SOAP_ENC);
if(params != null)
   call.setParams(params);
Response resp =
   call.invoke(rpcRouter,
               "http://www.psol.com/xbe2/soapaction");
```

Next it extracts the XML document from the response, and it applies a
style sheet to it. The XML document is accessible through
Response.getBodyPart(), which returns a BodyPart object. The
BodyPart.getInputStream() method returns the XML document:

```
Transformer transformer = templates.newTransformer();
transformer.setParameter("context-path",
                         request.getContextPath());
BodyPart bp = resp.getBodyPart(0);
Source source = new StreamSource(bp.getInputStream());
Result result =
        new StreamResult(response.getOutputStream());
transformer.transform(source,result);
```

The benefits of this solution are as follows:

- The XML document was generated automatically by the SOAP toolkit.
  The operative word here is "automatically": There's not a single line of

code in the middle-tier server that deals with XML directly. It uses objects, and SOAP serialized those to XML.

- Because an XSLT style sheet does the presentation, little programming is required. Indeed, if you look at this servlet, there's not much code.

- As you will see in the next sections, SOAP maximizes the flexibility. The servlet can either access the XML document directly, as doRpcAndStyle() does, or retrieve the Java objects, as illustrated by doTakeOrder(). SOAP buys you total flexibility.

Style Sheets

EXAMPLE

Two methods, doMall() and doProduct(), end up in calls to doRpcAndStyle() which, in turn, uses a style sheet. It stands to reason two style sheets are required: one for the mall home page (ultimately called by doMall()) and one for the product details (ultimately called by doProduct()).

Listing 12.12 is the style sheet for the mall home page. This is a regular XSLT style sheet, as introduced in Chapter 5, "XSL Transformations." Nonetheless, because the style sheet is applied to a SOAP-encoded result, it must take special care to bypass the SOAP envelope. The easiest solution is to select only elements in the http://www.psol.com/xbe2/chapter12 namespace through the following:

```
<xsl:apply-templates select="//xbe2:*"/>
```

Listing 12.12: mall.xsl

```
<?xml version="1.0" encoding="UTF-8"?>
<xsl:stylesheet version="1.0"
    xmlns:xsl="http://www.w3.org/1999/XSL/Transform"
    xmlns:xbe2="http://www.psol.com/xbe2/chapter12">

<xsl:output method="html"/>

<xsl:param name="context-path"/>

<xsl:template match="/">
    <html>
        <head><title>Electronic Mall</title></head>
        <body>
            <h1>Electronic Mall</h1>
            <p>Please select one of our quality products.</p>
```

Listing 12.12: continued

```
      <ul>
         <xsl:apply-templates select="//xbe2:*"/>
      </ul>
   </body>
 </html>
</xsl:template>

<xsl:template match="item">
   <li><a href="{$context-path}/{id}/">
      <xsl:value-of select="name"/>
   </a></li>
</xsl:template>

</xsl:stylesheet>
```

The style sheet takes one parameter: context-path, whose value is set by doRpcAndStyle() as the servlet context path. The parameter is used to reconstruct URLs in the style sheet:

```
transformer.setParameter("context-path",
                          request.getContextPath());
```

The style sheet for product details is shown in Listing 12.13.

Listing 12.13: product.xsl

```
<?xml version="1.0" encoding="UTF-8"?>
<xsl:stylesheet version="1.0"
   xmlns:xsl="http://www.w3.org/1999/XSL/Transform"
   xmlns:xbe2="http://www.psol.com/xbe2/chapter12">

<xsl:output method="html"/>

<xsl:param name="context-path"/>

<xsl:template match="/">
   <html>
      <head><title><xsl:value-of
         select="//xbe2:*//name"/></title></head>
      <body><xsl:apply-templates select="//xbe2:*"/></body>
   </html>
</xsl:template>

<xsl:template match="return">
   <form action="{$context-path}/{id}/" method="post">
      <b><xsl:value-of select="name"/></b><br/>
      <small>by </small><xsl:value-of select="manufacturer"/><br/>
      $ <xsl:value-of select="price"/><br/>
```

Listing 12.13: continued

```
      <i><xsl:value-of select="description"/></i><br/>
      <small>Warranty: </small><xsl:value-of
         select="warranty"/><br/>
      <small>Quantity: </small><input type="text" size="3"
                        value="1" name="quantity"/>
      <input type="submit" value="Buy"/>
   </form>
</xsl:template>

</xsl:stylesheet>
```

doCheckout()

The doCheckout() method is probably the most complex method because it is the only method that does not depend on the middle tier. In doCheckout(), the servlet does most of the work; it cannot defer it to the middle tier.

The method stores product orders in the HTTP session. A session is a useful concept introduced with the Java servlet API. A session associates Java objects to a visitor. The servlet API returns the objects with each request from the same visitor.

In practice, it requires a lot of work with cookies or another session tracking mechanism, but thanks to the servlet API, the programmer doesn't need to worry about the cookies. The server takes care of them for you.

In practice, doCheckout() stores an OrderLine object in the session for every product in the shopping cart:

```
HttpSession session = request.getSession();
String qt = request.getParameter("quantity");
if(productId != -1 && qt != null)
{
   int quantity = Integer.parseInt(qt);
   OrderLine line = (OrderLine)session.getAttribute(
                           String.valueOf(productId));
   if(line == null)
   {
      ProductDetails product = doGetProductDetails(productId);
      line = new OrderLine(product,quantity);
      session.setAttribute(String.valueOf(productId),line);
   }
   else
      line.setQuantity(quantity);
}
```

doTakeOrder()

The doTakeOrder() method retrieves the OrderLines from the session and uses them to build a SOAP request, passing the order to the middle-tier server:

```
Vector vector = new Vector();
while(enum.hasMoreElements())
   vector.addElement(session.getAttribute(
                     (String)enum.nextElement()));
OrderLine[] lines = new OrderLine[vector.size()];
vector.copyInto(lines);
Call call = new Call();
call.setSOAPMappingRegistry(registry);
call.setTargetObjectURI("http://www.psol.com/xbe2/chapter12");
call.setMethodName("addOrder");
call.setEncodingStyleURI(Constants.NS_URI_SOAP_ENC);
Vector params = new Vector();
params.addElement(
   new Parameter("name",String.class,
                 request.getParameter("name"),null));
params.addElement(
   new Parameter("company",String.class,
                 request.getParameter("company"),null));
// some parameters deleted
params.addElement(
   new Parameter("lines",lines.getClass(),lines,null));
call.setParams(params);
Response resp =
   call.invoke(rpcRouter,"http://www.psol.com/xbe2/soapaction");
```

Contrast this method with doRpcAndStyle() to fully appreciate the flexibility offered by SOAP. doTakeOrder() uses SOAP to make regular object calls: It passes OrderLine objects to the middle tier.

In contrast, doRpcAndStyle() uses the same SOAP service to access XML documents. The beauty of SOAP is that it gives you more options: You can mix-and-match regular object calls implemented by other RPC mechanisms with XML requests, as needed.

In fact, notice that nowhere in the SOAP request do we have to specify whether we need an RPC response or an XML response. We get both, and we can choose to use one or the other or even both.

Utility Class: Comparing Strings

EXAMPLE

Listing 12.14 is the `Util.java` class, provided for completeness. Several objects need to test whether a string is empty; `Util.isEmpty()` runs the test.

Listing 12.14: `Util.java`

```
package com.psol.xbe2;

public class Util
{
   protected static boolean isEmpty(String string)
   {
      if(null != string)
         return string.trim().length() == 0;
      else
         return true;
   }
}
```

What's Next

What's next? Your turn.

This chapter demonstrated that you can deliver solid applications by combining these techniques. As you have seen, XML is only a syntax for electronic documents. There are a dozen other syntaxes already, but what makes XML attractive is that it comes with an impressive toolbox. You've learned about the most useful ones: XSLT style sheets, XML models, parsers, and SOAP.

Like any good toolbox, you can use XML in many different ways, and I encourage you to try and test combinations that make sense. I hope XCommerce will prove inspiring.

After the first edition of this book was published, I received hundreds of e-mails from readers who had been inspired to deploy XML in their environment. The breadth and diversity of the solutions they built is truly impressive. It would appear that there are no limits to the XML toolbox besides those of your imagination.

Start small, but start today. Select simple projects where you can experiment with your new skills and grow from there. XML is versatile and flexible, so it is well suited for small projects with room to grow.

I hope you enjoyed reading this book as much as I enjoyed writing it. Pay a visit to www.marchal.com and use the feedback form to let me know what you think.

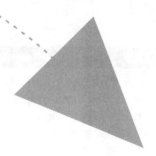

Appendix A

Crash Course on Java

If you are a JavaScript, Perl, or C++ programmer, this appendix is for you. Java is a natural companion to XML and this appendix teaches you just enough Java for XML. It assumes you already know another programming language.

In this appendix, you learn

- That Java is more than a programming language.

- Why Java is important for XML.

- How to install a Java Virtual Machine.

- Enough Java to read and write simple applications.

You don't have to become a Java guru, but some familiarity with Java is required for serious fun with XML. If anything, there are probably more XML tools written in Java than for any other platform.

✔ To learn how to run the Java package introduced in Chapter 3, "XML Namespaces," turn to the sections "Downloading Java Tools," on **page 445**, and "Understanding the Classpath," on **page 451**.

Java in Perspective

There are many comments on the relative importance of Java and XML. Some would like you to think that XML is everything you'll ever need, others say that only Java matters. In my experience, they are complementary. Admittedly, I am somewhat biased since I formed my company, Pineapplesoft, around Java development.

Before going any further, let me debunk a common misunderstanding: If you think of Java as just a programming language, you are wrong.

Yes, Java is a programming language but, more importantly, it is a development platform, known as the Java Virtual Machine (Java VM). Applications written for the Java VM are portable across platforms, running on Windows, Unix and Linux, Macintosh, PalmOS, IBM iSeries and zSeries (formerly known as AS/400 and S/390),and others.

Furthermore, Java, the language, is but one of the many programming languages available on the Java VM. The VM also supports C, JavaScript, Python, Tcl, Lisp, and many others. For a more comprehensive list, visit www.cs.tu-berlin.de/%7Etolk/vmlanguages.html.

Most Java applications are written for servers either as servlets or Enterprise JavaBeans. Java is also popular for writing components, such as the infamous JavaBeans.

Server-Side Applications

Java is very useful on servers because it combines a high-performance environment with portability.

Portability is vital for server development because that space has more diversity than the desktop. Windows clearly rules the desktop but there is no clear winner among servers: Unix and Linux, Windows 2000, and the IBM iSeries are some of the most important platforms.

A typical company runs several different servers (for example, Linux for the Web site and a mix of iSeries and Windows 2000 for the backoffice) and your application might have to run on all of them. It would be inefficient to port the application to all these platforms. Writing for Java VM is more efficient.

As an added bonus, portability brings scalability: When new hardware is introduced to boost performance, existing software can still run on it—not to mention that software can be developed on cheap machines and deployed on high-end servers.

JavaBeans

Increasingly, developers have access to a toolbox of components such as an XSL Processor or database access. Scripting languages—such as JavaScript, VBScript, Perl, Python, or ColdFusion—are used to glue the components together.

Scripting languages are popular because they are typeless and easier to use. You can code faster in scripting languages than in regular programming languages.

But, how do you write the components? Scripting languages are not appropriate for several reasons. Mainly, it is difficult to integrate different scripting languages and they are not as efficient as regular programming languages.

Java, the language, is well adapted for component programming because it is a compiled, low-level programming language. Most scripting languages can interface with Java components, and Java portability means that the components are available on a large number of platforms. In Java, components are called *JavaBeans*.

As you have seen throughout this book, XML is supported by many companion standards (DOM, SAX, XSL, CSS, XSDL, RDF, and so on), which are ideal candidates for components. In practice, XML is well adapted to this style of programming and the components are often written in Java.

Downloading Java Tools

This section lists the various components you need to run the examples in this book. When possible, I chose software that is available free of charges.

If you find yourself doing lots of Java development, however, you will want to buy or download an integrated development environment such as JBuilder (www.borland.com), Forte (www.sun.com/forte), VisualCafé (www.webgain.com), Visual Age (www.software.ibm.com), CodeWarrior (www.metrowerks.com), or Kawa (www.allaire.com).

TIP

Some of these environments have free, limited editions, which are ideal for beginners.

Java Environment

As I have already explained, the trick behind Java portability is the *Java Virtual Machine*. Java programs are compiled to a portable binary format, called the *class files*. The Java VM runs class files.

Because there is a Java VM on almost any platform, class files run almost everywhere. You can download a Java VM from `java.sun.com`. It comes in one of two versions:

- *Java Runtime Environment (JRE)* is a naked Java VM. It runs existing applications but lacks tools to develop new ones.

- *Java Development Kit (JDK)* offers everything in the JRE as well as development tools such as the compiler.

The book listings are available in source and compiled form at `www.marchal.com` and `www.quepublishing.com`. If you are only interested in testing the examples, a JRE is enough. If you want to modify the examples, you will need a JDK.

At the time of writing, there are two major generations of Java VMs:

- JDK 1.0 and JDK 1.1 are the original versions. They are seldom used anymore. JDK 1.0 was slow and limited, JDK 1.1 is the first mature version.

- Java 2 is the most commonly used version. There has been two versions so far: JDK 1.2 and the more recent JDK 1.3.

To confuse things further, Java 2 has been declined in several editions. For this book, you need the Java 2 Platform, Standard Edition (J2SE).

XML Components

The examples in this book have been tested with Apache's Xerces and Xalan. Xerces is an open-source parser that supports both the SAX and DOM interfaces. Xalan is an open-source implementation of XSLT.

The downloads from `www.marchal.com` and `www.quepublishing.com` include all the components you need to run the examples. If you want, you can download the latest version of Xerces and Xalan from `xml.apache.org`.

CAUTION

Beware if you download a more recent version of a component. Subtle changes may break existing code. The code on `www.marchal.com` and `www.quepublishing.com` has been tested at the time of writing. Although, components (such as Xerces) should be upward compatible and should run with existing code, I can make no such guarantee.

There are several other parsers and XSL processors for Java:

- Oracle parser is known as XDK and it supports both SAX and DOM. It is available from `technet.oracle.com`.

- Ælfred, originally from Microstar but currently maintained by David Brownell, is a SAX parser that boasts a very small memory footprint. The latest version is available from `home.pacbell.net/david-b/xml`. The original version is from `www.opentext.com/microstar`.

- Michael Kay wrote SAXON, an XSLT processor available from `users.iclway.co.uk/mhkay/saxon`.

- James Clark has written a SAX-compliant parser (XP) and an XSL processor (XT). They are available from `www.jclark.com` and `www.4xt.org`.

- Microsoft has a DOM and SAX parser available from `msdn.microsoft.com`. The Microsoft parser is also available as a COM component.

Servlet Engine

Servlets are Java's version of CGI scripts. Servlets are increasingly called *Web Applications* to stress that they are in fact applications running on Web servers. The e-commerce example in Chapter 12, "Putting It All Together: An e-Commerce Example," is based on servlets.

There are many servlet-enabled Web servers on the market. The most popular are

- Jetty, which I used throughout the book, is available from `www.mortbay.com`.

- Tomcat is the servlet engine for the popular Apache Web server. It is available from `jakarta.apache.org`. Tomcat is the reference implementation for servlets.

- Oracle 8i supports servlets. It is available from `www.oracle.com`.

- iPlanet, formerly Netscape, has full servlet support. It is available from `www.iplanet.com`.

- JRun is available from `www.allaire.com`. The developer edition is free.

- Enhydra is an open-source project. It is available from `www.enhydra.org`.

Some of these servers can run as add-ons for IIS. For a more comprehensive list, visit `www.servlets.com`.

I strongly recommend Jetty. It is an open source Web server with a small memory footprint. The examples in this book have been tested with Jetty 3.0.

> **NOTE**
>
> Open-source software means that the source code for the software is freely available. Developers are encouraged to modify the software (for example, fix bugs or add new features) and to contribute their changes to the community. This approach leads to the development of software by volunteers.
>
> The most famous open-source projects are Linux, GNU (various utilities), Apache (a Web server) and Mozilla (Netscape Web browser).

Database and JDBC

The standard Java API for databases is called JDBC and it resides in package `java.sql`. Through JDBC you can access any SQL database including Oracle, SQL Server, Informix, Sybase, and others.

The examples in Chapter 12 use Hypersonic SQL, an open-source database for Java. Hypersonic SQL boasts a small memory footprint, which makes it ideal for testing and prototyping. The latest version is available from `sourceforge.net/projects/hsql`.

Your First Java Application

Enough talk, let's code. This section shows you how to write, compile, and run your first Java application.

EXAMPLE

Unix uses an LF character to signal end of lines, the Mac uses the CR character, and Windows uses a combination of CR/LF. Needless to say, text files (and XML documents) saved on one platform are not easy to manipulate on another platform. Listing A.1 rewrites text files to your platform end-of-line convention.

Listing A.1: `src\com\psol\xbe2\FixEoL.jar`

```java
package com.psol.xbe2;

import java.io.*;

/**
 * Rewrite a text file with system-specific end of lines.<BR>
 * Useful for text files downloaded from the Net.
 *
 * @author Benoît Marchal
 * @version 21 November 2000
 */

public class FixEoL
{
```

Listing A.1: continued

```
/**
 * Entry-point for the program.<BR>
 * Expect two filenames on the command-line: input and output.
 *
 * @param args command-line parameters
 */
public static void main(String[] args)
{
    if(args.length < 2)
        System.err.println(
            "Usage is: java com.psol.xbe2.FixEoL input output");
    else if(new File(args[1]).exists())
        System.err.println("Error: output file already exists");
    else
        try
        {
            BufferedReader reader =
                new BufferedReader(new FileReader(args[0]));
            PrintWriter writer =
                new PrintWriter(new FileWriter(args[1]));
            try
            {
                for(String line = reader.readLine();
                    null != line;
                    line = reader.readLine())
                    writer.println(line);
            }
            finally
            {
                writer.close();
            }
        }
        catch(IOException e)
        {
            System.err.println("Error: " + e.getMessage());
        }
}
}
```

Save the listing in a file called src\com\psol\xbe2\FixEoL.java. Be careful, Java is picky about filenames. Double-check for upper and lower cases. To compile, issue the command:

```
mkdir classes
javac -d classes src\com\psol\xbe2\FixEoL.java
```

CAUTION

This assumes the Java compiler is in your path. If not, you will have to prefix the `javac` command with the path to the compiler, as in

`c:\jdk1.3\bin\javac -d classes src\com\psol\xbe2\FixEoL.java`

OUTPUT

Before we examine Listing A.1 in detail, let's run the application. Issue the following commands:

```
set classpath=classes
java com.psol.xbe2.FixEoL productlist.xml productlist_lel.xml
```

Figures A.1 and A.2 illustrate how the `FixEoL` program reorganizes the file. Notice that in Figure A.1 the lines are all wrong.

Figure A.1: *A Unix file under Windows.*

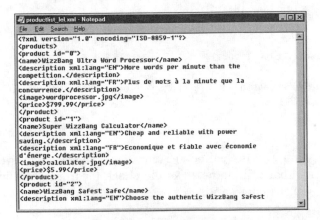

Figure A.2: *The same file after* `FixEoL` *rewrote it.*

NOTE

For large projects, having to compile the files manually is a major annoyance. Increasingly, Java programmers use Ant to automate compilation. Ant is similar to Make, a popular Unix utility, but it is optimized for Java.

A discussion of Ant is outside the scope of this book, suffice it to say that you can download Ant, and its documentation, from `jakarta.apache.org`.

When you download the listings from `www.marchal.com` or `www.quepublishing.com`, each project includes an Ant 1.2 build file.

Understanding the Classpath

One of the most confusing aspects of Java is the `classpath`. In my experience, most problems when running Java applications are related to the `classpath`.

The Java VM loads Java classes as needed. For example, because the application uses the `FixEoL` class, the Java VM will load it. However, it needs to know where the class is located and it uses the *classpath* for that purpose.

The `classpath` is a list of directories or JAR files (more on JAR files in the next section) that the Java VM searches. Essentially, it is similar to the DOS path but for class files.

EXAMPLE

If the Java VM cannot find a class in the `classpath`, it reports a `java.lang.ClassNotFoundException` error.

You can set the `classpath` for a given application with the `classpath` parameter, as in

```
java -classpath classes com.psol.xbe2.FixEoL productlist.xml
➥productlist_lel.xml
```

Alternatively, you can set a global `classpath` in an environment variable, as in

```
set classpath=classes
```

It is easy to type the `classpath` incorrectly. For example, in the following command, it is incorrect:

```
java -classpath class com.psol.xbe2.FixEoL productlist.xml
➥productlist_lel.xml
```

The Java VM reports the following error:

```
Exception in thread "main" java.lang.NoClassDefFoundError:
com/psol/xbe2/FixEoL
```

When the Java VM reports a `java.lang.NoClassDefFoundError`, it's a sure sign that the `classpath` is incorrect.

CAUTION

Neither the JavaVM nor the compiler issues a warning if there are invalid directories in the `classpath`.

Invalid directories are ignored but, of course, they cause problems because the Java VM cannot find your classes.

Flow of Control

Java has all the statements for tests and loops: `if/else`, `switch/case`, `for`, `while`, and `do/while`. I assume you are familiar with them from other programming languages. Multiple statements are grouped with the { and } characters. Java also supports exceptions to report error conditions (see the section titled "Exceptions").

As in C, each statement is terminated with the ; character. In practice, as long as you terminate most lines with a ;, it works.

The following excerpt from Listing A.1 loops through the lines in the input file and prints them in the output file:

EXAMPLE

```
for(String line = reader.readLine();
    null != line;
    line = reader.readLine())
    writer.println(line);
```

The following excerpt tests the value of `args.length` to print an error message:

EXAMPLE

```
if(args.length < 2)
    System.err.println(
        "Usage is: java com.psol.xbe2.FixEoL input output");
```

Variables

Variables in Java must be declared before being used. Furthermore, Java is a typed language, so every variable must have a type.

The following excerpt declares one variable, `line`. The declaration must include the type. The type precedes the name of the variable in the declaration. Variables can be initialized with the = operator.

EXAMPLE

```
String line = reader.readLine();
```

Java supports the following primitive types:

- `boolean`: `true` or `false`
- `char`: Unicode character
- `byte`: 8-bit signed integer

- `short`: 16-bit signed integer

- `int`: 32-bit signed integer

- `long`: 64-bit signed integer

- `float`: 32-bit floating-point

- `double`: 64-bit floating-point

It supports one more type: a reference to an object. In the previous example, `String` declares a variable `line` as a reference to a `String` object.

To declare arrays, append the `[]` characters to the type, as in

```
int[] arrayOfInteger = new int[6];
```

EXAMPLE

Class

Because Java is an object-oriented language, it supports the notions of classes and objects. An *object* is an instance of a class. A *class* is the type of a set of objects. In Java, with the exception of the primitive types (see previous section), everything is an object.

The following example declares a class `FixEoL`:

```
public class FixEoL
{
    // ...
}
```

EXAMPLE

Creating Objects

Every object in Java is allocated on the heap with the `new` operator.

EXAMPLE

The following example creates a `BufferedReader` object:

```
BufferedReader reader =
new BufferedReader(new FileReader(args[0]));
```

Objects are typically assigned to variables, but they need not be. It is common to create anonymous objects that are used and discarded in one sequence. The following example creates a `File` object, calls its `exists()` method, and then discards it. The object is immediately discarded because it is never assigned to a variable:

```
if(new File(args[1]).exists())
    System.err.println("Error: output file already exists!");
```

You don't explicitly destroy objects in Java. When an object is no longer in use, it is automatically reclaimed by the garbage collector.

Accessing Fields and Methods

A class has fields or data variables that are attached to objects. It also has methods with the executable code of the class.

To access a field or a method of an object, you separate its name from the object reference with a dot, as in

```
writer.close();
```

Static

By default, the variables or methods declared in a class are attached to objects of that class. However, it is possible to declare variables or methods attached to the class.

The following example declares a class with two fields: x and y. Every Point object has the two fields:

```
class Point
{
    public int x, y;
}
```

However, it is possible to attach methods or fields to the class itself. These are declared with the static modifier. This is useful, for example, for keeping track of how many Point objects have been created:

```
class Point
{
    public int x, y;
    public static int numberOfPoints = 0;
}
```

Method and Parameters

In Java, the code is contained in methods. Note that there are no stand-alone methods. Every method must be attached to a class.

The following example declares the main() method. A method accepts parameters declared between parentheses:

```
public static void main(String[] args)
{
    // ...
}
```

Methods may return a value. The type of the return value is declared before the method name. If the method returns no value, its type is void.

The static main() is a special method that serves as the entry point for the application.

Constructors

A class can have *constructors*. Constructors are special methods called during the objects' creation. Constructors typically initialize the fields. Constructors are methods whose name is the class name. They have no return value.

EXAMPLE

The Point class now has a constructor to initialize its fields (notice it has no return value):

```
public class Point
{
    public int x, y;
    public Point(int x1,int y1)
    {
        x = x1;
        y = y1;
    }
}
```

Package

Java programs are organized in packages. Packages play a role similar to XML namespaces: They prevent naming conflicts.

EXAMPLE

Packages are declared with the package statement, as in the following example:

```
package com.psol.xbe2;
```

A package is a logical unit to group related classes. In this case, the xbe2 package stands for XML by Example, 2nd Edition. Large applications may be split over several packages.

TIP

To avoid conflicts in package names, they should always start with a domain name in reverse order.

In the previous example, the package starts with com.psol derived for the psol.com domain name (notice the domain name is in reverse order).

Java packages map to filenames: The class for com.psol.xbe2.FixEoL must be in file com\psol\xbe2\FixEoL.class. In other words, a dot in a class name maps to a directory on the file system.

TIP

In large projects, things quickly get out of hand. I encourage you to install class files in a directory called classes. The option -d controls where the compiler copies the class files. The following command places class files in the classes directory:

```
javac -d classes src\com\psol\xbe2\FixEoL.java
```

For the same reason, I encourage you to place source code in a directory structure that mimics the package. Notice that in the preceding command line, the source file (FixEoL.java) is in the src\com\psol\xb2 directory.

JAR Files

The compiler automatically generates the directories and subdirectories to match the package name. There is one directory for every word in the package name. The com.psol.xbe2 package, for example, results in three directories: com, psol, and xbe2.

In practice, it is not always easy for users to install the files in the right directory. To simplify deployment, turn to Java Archive (JAR files). A JAR file is simply a ZIP file with a special .jar extension. Because there is only one file to copy, it is more comfortable for the user.

Because they are ZIP files, you can create JAR files with WinZIP. In practice, it is easier to use the JAR utility included in the JDK.

EXAMPLE

To create a JAR file, issue the following command:

```
jar cvf fixeol.jar -C classes com\psol\xbe2\FixEoL.class
```

If everything goes well, this command creates a new file fixeol.jar. You can use this file in a classpath instead of your application directory, as in

```
set classpath=fixeol.jar
```

CAUTION

Never attempt to uncompress or modify JAR files you obtained from third parties, such as Hypersonic SQL, Jetty, Xerces, or Xalan.

Indeed, Java beginners often mess around with JAR files when they encounter a java.lang.ClassNotFoundException error. Unless you're an expert, it is always a bad idea and it is guaranteed to aggravate the situation.

If you encounter such an error, the problem is the classpath. Reread the section "Understanding the Classpath" for a solution.

Imports

As you have seen, the name of a class is its package name followed by the class name: The name of the class FixEoL in the package com.psol.xbe2 is com.psol.xbe2.FixEoL.

EXAMPLE

Typing these long names quickly becomes annoying. Fortunately, to save some typing, you can import classes or packages with the import statement. This example imports classes from the java.io package. Thanks to the import, the class java.io.IOException can be referenced simply as IOException.

```
import java.io.*;
```

Which makes it possible to write

```
catch(IOException e)
```

instead of the tedious

```
catch(java.io.IOException e)
```

Packages whose names start with java or javax are part of the standard Java library.

Access Control

The visibility of classes, methods, and fields is limited by *access control*.

EXAMPLE

Classes can be either package or public. Fields and methods can be package, public, protected, or private. The required access is declared with a modifier. The following class is public but its fields are protected:

```
public class Length
{
    protected int length;
    protected String unit;
}
```

The options are defined as follows:

- public is accessible from any class in any package. Public access is declared with the public modifier.

- package is accessible from the current package only. Package access is declared with no modifier. It is the default.

- protected is accessible to the descendants only. Protected access is declared with the protected modifier.

- private is accessible to the class only (excluding its descendants). Private access is declared with the private modifier.

Comments and Javadoc

Java supports regular comments and documentation comments.

EXAMPLE

Like C++ or JavaScript, comments are enclosed in /* and */:

```
/*
 * Listings for XML by Example, 2nd Edition are
 * available from www.marchal.com or www.mcp.com.
 */
```

EXAMPLE

There is an alternative form for short comments, also derived from C++. Anything after the // characters until the end of the line is a comment, as in

```
// we don't want to overwrite a file by mistake
```

EXAMPLE

Javadoc comments are enclosed in /** and */:

```
/**
 * Rewrite a text file with system-specific end of lines.<BR>
 * Useful for text files downloaded from the Net.
 *
 * @author Benoît Marchal
 * @version 21 November 2000
 */
```

Javadoc comments should contain the class documentation. The javadoc program extracts these comments from the source code and automatically generates the documentation in HTML. Inserting documentation in the source code minimizes the risks of the documentation being out of date.

To generate the documentation, issue the following command. This creates several HTML files with the documentation. The documentation is very complete and includes index, table of contents, and more.

```
javadoc src/com/psol/xbe2/FixEoL.java
```

OUTPUT

Figure A.3 shows the documentation page that is being generated.

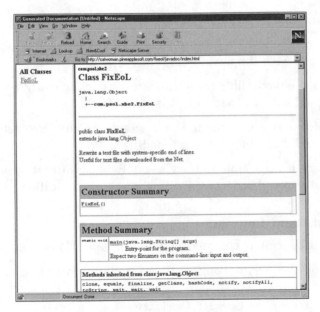

Figure A.3: *Javadoc documentation.*

Javadoc recognizes paragraphs starting with the @ character as special paragraphs. The most common ones are

- @version—States the application version.

- @author—States the name of the author (you can have multiple @author paragraphs).

- @param—Documents a method parameter (you can have multiple @param paragraphs).

- @return—Documents the value returned by a method.

- @exception—Documents the exception that a method can throw.

Exception

EXAMPLE

Like other object-oriented programming languages, Java uses exceptions (special objects) to signal errors.

The throw is used to throw exceptions:

```
throw new ServletException("Error: invalid parameter");
```

To report on exceptions, you must catch them with a try/catch statement. If an exception is thrown in the try statement, control goes to the catch statement, as in

```
try
{
    System.out.println("Before exception");
    throw new IllegalStateException("Test exception");
    System.out.println("After exception");
}
catch(IllegalStateException  e)
{
    System.out.println("Error: " + e.getMessage());
}
```

OUTPUT

The throw causes the catch statement to execute. It prints

```
Before exception
Error: Test exception
```

Notice that it never prints "After exception" because the exception moves control to the catch statement.

EXAMPLE

An optional finally statement can be attached to a try, where it is always executed, whether an exception is thrown or not. A finally statement is ideal for clean-up code that must always be executed, as in

```
try
{
    // can throw an exception
}
finally
{
    writer.close();
}
```

EXAMPLE

Exceptions that are not caught in a method must be declared in the throws statement of the method. The compiler won't let a method throw exceptions unless they are declared:

```
protected void doGet(HttpServletRequest request,
                         HttpServletResponse response)
    throws IOException
{
    // can throw an IOException
}
```

Servlets

Most modern Web sites rely heavily on server-side applications. They take many forms from the antique CGI scripts (still popular with some ISPs), to Microsoft ASP, and Java servlets.

Servlets are Java classes installed on the server to handle requests from the Web browser. Don't confuse servlets with applets. Applets execute on the Web browser, whereas servlets execute on the Web server.

Typically, the browser sends a special request (for example, the content of an HTML form) to the server. The server passes the request to the servlet, which prepares a response, most likely in HTML.

Figure A.4 illustrates the interaction between the various parts: The browser sends a form to the server and the servlet prepares an HTML page in response. Note that the servlet lives on the server.

> **NOTE**
>
> *Java Server Pages (JSP)* are an alternative to servlets. JSP are similar to Active Server Pages (ASP) from Microsoft in that they mix HTML and Java code.
>
> Because they are quick to develop, JSP are popular for prototyping.

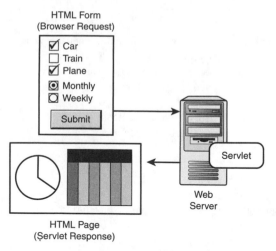

HTML Form
(Browser Request)

- ☑ Car
- ☐ Train
- ☑ Plane
- ◉ Monthly
- ◯ Weekly

Submit

Servlet

Web
Server

HTML Page
(Servlet Response)

Figure A.4: *Serving applications.*

Your First Servlet

Servlet development is easy. Let's illustrate it with a simple example.

Servlet Listing

EXAMPLE

Listing A.2 is the XMLGlossary servlet. It returns definitions of terms as entered in an HTML form.

Listing A.2: src\com\psol\xbe2\XMLGlossary.java

```java
package com.psol.xbe2;

import java.io.*;
import java.net.*;
import java.util.*;
import javax.servlet.*;
import javax.servlet.http.*;

/**
 * XMLGlossary is a simple servlet to return definitions.
 *
 * @version Nov 21, 2000
 * @author Benoît Marchal <bmarchal@pineapplesoft.com>
 */

public class XMLGlossary
    extends HttpServlet
{
```

Listing A.2: continued

```java
/**
 * handle GET method, HttpServlet forward GET request from
 * service() to this method
 * @param request the request received from the client
 * @param response interface to the client
 */
protected void doGet(HttpServletRequest request,
                     HttpServletResponse response)
  throws IOException
{
  response.setContentType("text/html");
  ResourceBundle definitions =
     ResourceBundle.getBundle("com.psol.xbe2.Definitions",
                              request.getLocale());
  Writer w = response.getWriter();
  w.write("<HTML>");
  w.write("<HEAD><TITLE>");
  w.write(getServletName());
  w.write("</TITLE></HEAD><BODY>");
  String word = request.getParameter("word");
  if(null != word)
  {
     w.write("<P><B>"); w.write(word); w.write(":</B> ");
     String lowerCaseWord = word.toLowerCase();
     try
     {
        w.write(definitions.getString(lowerCaseWord));
     }
     catch(MissingResourceException e)
     {
        w.write("unknown, sorry");
     }
     w.write("<HR>");
  }
  w.write("<FORM ACTION='");
  w.write(request.getRequestURI()); w.write("'>");
  w.write("<INPUT NAME='word'><INPUT TYPE='SUBMIT'>");
  w.write("</BODY></HTML>");
  w.flush();
  }
}
```

Compile the servlet with the following commands:

```
mkdir WEB-INF
mkdir WEB-INF\classes
set classpath=lib\javax.servlet.jar
javac -d WEB-INF\classes src\com\psol\xbe2\XMLGlossary.java
```

CAUTION

If there is an error message similar to "Package javax.servlet not found in import.", it's a classpath problem. Refer to the previous classpath section.

For reasons that will become clear in the next sections, the servlet needs the definitions in a text file similar to Listing A.3.

Listing A.3: WEB-INF\classes\com\psol\xbe2\Descriptions.properties

```
xml=eXtensible Markup Language
xsl=XML Stylesheet Language
xslt=XSL Transformation
fo=Formatting Objects
dtd=Document Type Definition
xsdl=XML Schema Definition Language
sax=Simple API for XML
dom=Document Object Model
css=Cascading Style Sheet
soap=Simple Object Access Protocol
api=Application Programming Interface
```

Servlet Descriptor

To register the servlet with a Web server, you must prepare a descriptor (see Listing A.4).

Listing A.4: WEB-INF\web.xml

```xml
<?xml version="1.0"?>

<!DOCTYPE web-app PUBLIC
    "-//Sun Microsystems, Inc.//DTD Web Application 2.2//EN"
    "http://java.sun.com/j2ee/dtds/web-app_2_2.dtd">

<web-app>
    <display-name>XML by Example, 2nd Edition</display-name>
    <servlet>
        <servlet-name>Glossary</servlet-name>
        <servlet-class>com.psol.xbe2.XMLGlossary</servlet-class>
    </servlet>
    <servlet-mapping>
        <servlet-name>Glossary</servlet-name>
        <url-pattern>/</url-pattern>
    </servlet-mapping>
</web-app>
```

The servlet descriptor is an XML document and, as the name implies, it describes the servlet for the Web server. The main elements in Listing A.4 are

- `display-name`: a human-readable name.
- `servlet-name`: the name of the servlet (there could be more than one servlet, the name serves as identifier).
- `servlet-class`: the Java class for the servlet. It is associated with a `servlet-name` in the servlet element.
- `url-pattern`: the Web server invokes the servlet for URLs that match its pattern.

  A single / character in a URL pattern matches the root of the Web server. A pattern can also include directories, as in `/xmlglossary/` that would match this URL: `http://hostname/xmlglossary/`.

  Finally, `*` is a wildcard. The `/xmlglossary/*` pattern will match `http://hostname/xmlglossary/` but also `http://hostname/xmlglossary/index.html`.

WAR File

The last step is to compress the servlet and its descriptor in a WAR file. *A WAR file* is a JAR file (see the previous "JAR File" section) with a special `.war` extension. WAR stands for Web Archive.

In the WAR file, the descriptor must be in the `WEB-INF` directory whereas the servlet class files must be in the `WEB-INF/classes` directory.

Issue the following command:

```
mkdir etc
jar cvf etc\xmlglossary.war WEB-INF
```

Running the Example

The last step is to install the servlet on the Web server. Unlike everything we've done so far, this last step is different with each Web server: some have graphical configuration screens, but Jetty uses a property file that is reproduced in Listing A.5.

Listing A.5: `etc\jetty.xml`

```
<?xml version="1.0" encoding="ISO-8859-1"?>


<!DOCTYPE Configure PUBLIC
    "-//Mort Bay Consulting//DTD Configure 1.0//EN"
    "http://jetty.mortbay.com/configure_1_0.dtd">


<Configure class="com.mortbay.HTTP.HttpServer">
```

Listing A.5: continued

```
   <Call name="addListener">
      <Arg>
         <New class="com.mortbay.HTTP.SocketListener">
            <Set name="Port">5401</Set>
            <Set name="MinThreads">5</Set>
            <Set name="MaxThreads">255</Set>
            <Set name="MaxIdleTimeMs">60000</Set>
            <Set name="MaxReadTimeMs">60000</Set>
         </New>
      </Arg>
   </Call>
   <Call name="addWebApplication">
      <Arg>/</Arg>
      <Arg>etc/xmlglossary.war</Arg>
      <Arg>etc/webdefault.xml/</Arg>
   </Call>
   <Set name="LogSink">
      <New class="com.mortbay.Util.RolloverFileLogSink">
         <Set name="LogDir">etc/logs</Set>
         <Set name="RetainDays">90</Set>
         <Set name="MultiDay">false</Set>
         <Set name="Append">true</Set>
      </New>
   </Set>
</Configure>
```

You don't need to know about most of Listing A.5. The servlet is registered through the following lines:

```
<Call name="addWebApplication">
   <Arg>/</Arg>
   <Arg>etc/xmlglossary.war</Arg>
   <Arg>etc/webdefault.xml/</Arg>
</Call>
```

The first argument is the url-pattern (granted, Jetty could read this from the servlet descriptor), the second argument is the WAR file, and the last argument points to a set of defaults.

You might also need to change the Web server port. In Listing A.5, the server listens on port 5401. If it's already in use on your computer, edit the following line:

```
<Set name="Port">5401</Set>
```

Issue the following commands to launch the server:

```
set classpath=lib\javax.servlet.jar;
➥lib\com.mortbay.Jetty.jar;lib\com.microstar.xml.jar
java com.mortbay.Jetty.Server etc\jetty.xml
```

OUTPUT

Point your browser to `http://localhost:5401/`. Figure A.5 shows the result in a browser. The servlet generates a page that contains the definition of the term and a form to issue another query.

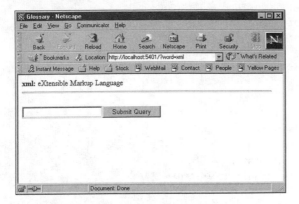

Figure A.5: The servlet in a Web browser.

Inheritance

The servlet introduces one new construct of the Java language: *inheritance*. Like other object-oriented language, Java enables new classes to inherit from existing ones. A class that inherits from another class is said to be a *descendant*. The class it inherits from is its *ancestor*.

The descendant has all the methods and fields defined in its ancestor, plus any new fields or method it decides to implement.

EXAMPLE

Inheritance is indicated with the `extends` keyword followed by the ancestor name. In Java, a class cannot inherit from more than one class (single inheritance). In the following example, `XMLGlossary` inherits from `HttpServlet`:

```
public class XMLGlossary
    extends HttpServlet
{
    // ...
}
```

doGet()

Java servlets are simply Java classes that inherit from `HttpServlet` and overwrite one or more methods among `doGet()`, `doPost()`, `doPut()` or `doDelete()`. Each of these methods corresponds to an HTTP command. In Listing A.2, the servlet overwrites `doGet()` to handle `GET` requests.

When the user presses the Submit Query button on the form, the browser issues a GET request to the server. Through the url-pattern in Listing A.4, the server maps the request to the servlet and calls its doGet() method. The servlet prepares its response as an HTML file.

If you are new to Web server programming, keep in mind that ultimately the servlet is invoked to serve requests from the browser.

EXAMPLE

The servlet accesses parameters sent by the browser through the HttpRequest object. For example, the method getParameter() returns the value of a form field:

```
String word = request.getParameter("word");
```

EXAMPLE

To generate an answer, the servlet uses the HttpResponse object. In the following example, the servlet sets the MIME type of the result to text/html (meaning HTML) and it starts writing the HTML page:

```
Writer w = response.getWriter();
w.write("<HTML>");
w.write("<HEAD><TITLE>");
w.write(getServletName());
w.write("</TITLE></HEAD><BODY>");
```

Locale and Multilingual Applications

EXAMPLE

The servlet stores the definitions in a ResourceBundle. In its simplest form, a ResourceBundle is a text file in which each line is key/value pair, as in Listing A.3. The servlet loads the values through the getBundle() method:

```
ResourceBundle definitions =
    ResourceBundle.getBundle("com.psol.xbe2.Definitions",
                             request.getLocale());
```

getBundle()'s first argument points to the text file. The second argument is a Locale. Each language (for example, French, German, or Italian) has a different Locale. request.getLocale() returns the language of the user, if available.

Java loads the definition in the requested language, if available. For example, Listing A.6 contains French definitions. The _fr suffix identifies the file as the French version. ResourceBundle are particularly convenient when writing multilingual Java applications.

Listing A.6: WEB-INF\classes\com\psol\xbe2\Descriptions_fr.properties

```
xml=Langage de balisage extensible
xsl=Langage de feuilles de style XML
xslt=XSL transformation
fo=Objets de mise en page
dtd=Definition du document
```

Listing A.6: continued

```
xsdl=Langage de définition de schémas
sax=API événementielle pour XML
dom=API objet pour XML
css=Feuilles de style
soap=Protocolle objet
api=Interface de programmation
```

The servlet looks up definitions with the getString() method:

```
w.write(definitions.getString(lowerCaseWord));
```

More Java Language Concepts

You have learned almost enough Java to read the examples in this book. There are, however, two important aspects of the Java language that have not been covered yet.

this and super

Java declares this and super as two special keywords. They replace variables. this refers to the current object whereas super refers to the ancestor of the current object.

EXAMPLE

In the following example, the object invokes a method on its ancestor:

```
super.init(config);
```

Interfaces and Multiple Inheritance

Java supports only single inheritance: A class cannot have more than one ancestor. Multiple inheritance in Java is based on interfaces.

An interface is the skeleton of a class; it declares the methods that a class supports but it does not provide the implementation.

EXAMPLE

Many Java APIs are defined in terms of interfaces. Listing A.7 is one of the interfaces defined by SAX, the API for parsers.

Listing A.7: A SAX Interface

```
package org.xml.sax;

public interface ContentHandler
{
  public abstract void setDocumentLocator(Locator locator);
  public abstract void startDocument()
    throws SAXException;
  public abstract void endDocument()
    throws SAXException;
```

Listing A.7: continued

```
  public abstract void startElement(String namespaceURI,
                                    String localName,
                                    String qName,
                                    Attributes atts)
    throws SAXException;
  public abstract void endElement(String namespaceURI,
                                  String localName,
                                  String qName)
    throws SAXException;
  public void startPrefixMapping(String prefix,
                                 String uri)
    throws SAXException;
  public void endPrefixMapping(String prefix)
    throws SAXException;
  public abstract void characters(char ch[],
                                  int start,
                                  int length)
    throws SAXException;
  public abstract void ignorableWhitespace(char ch[],
                                           int start,
                                           int length)
    throws SAXException;
  public void skippedEntity(String name)
    throws SAXException;
  public abstract void processingInstruction(String target,
                                             String data)
    throws SAXException;
}
```

EXAMPLE

A class can implement more than one interface—effectively enabling multiple inheritance. In the following example, SAXServlet inherits from HttpServlet and implements two interfaces: ContentHandler and EntityResolver.

```
public class SAXServlet
   extends HttpServlet
   implements ContentHandler, EntityResolver
{
   // ...
}
```

What's Next

Study the examples in Chapter 12, "Putting It All Together: An e-Commerce Example," to improve your mastery of Java. With the combination of Java and XML, you are limited only by your imagination.

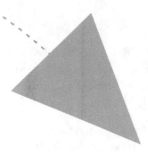

Appendix B

DTD and XML Schema Simple Types

This appendix summarizes the data types defined by DTDs and XML Schemas.

Simple Types Supported by DTD

Unlike XML Schemas, DTDs define few types. Also there is a difference in how they treat elements and attributes. In practice, DTDs give you almost no control over elements and little control over attributes.

Simple Types for Elements

DTDs recognize only one type for elements: #PCDATA, which stands for parsed character data, and, in practice, it means text. #PCDATA may contain CDATA sections.

Simple Types for Attributes

With DTDs, attribute types can take any of the following values:

- CDATA for string attributes.

- ID for identifier. An identifier is a name that is unique in the document.

- IDREF must be the value of an ID used elsewhere in the same document. IDREF is used to create links within a document.

- IDREFS is a list of IDREF separate by spaces.

- ENTITY must be the name of an external entity. This is how you assign an external entity to an attribute.

- ENTITIES is a list of ENTITY separated by spaces.

- NMTOKEN is essentially a word without spaces.

- NMTOKENS is a list of NMTOKEN separated by spaces.

- Enumerated type list is a closed list of NMTOKENS separated by |. The value has to be one of the nmtokens. The list of tokens can further be limited to NOTATIONs (introduced in the section "Parsed, Unparsed Entities, and Notation," in Chapter 4, "XML Models").

Optionally, the DTD can specify a default value for the attribute. If the attribute is not in the document, it is assumed to have the default value. The default value can take one of the four following values:

- #REQUIRED means that a value must appear in the document.

- #IMPLIED means that if no value is provided, the application must use its own default.

- #FIXED followed by a value means that the attribute must have the value declared in the DTD.

- A literal value means that the attribute will take this value if no value is given in the document.

Simple Types Supported by XML Schema

Supporting a rich data set was one of the goals of XML Schema, so it's not surprising that it offers numerous options.

Furthermore, unlike DTD, XML Schema makes no difference between attributes and elements when it comes to typing.

For more specifics on the simple types, you can turn to www.w3.org/TR/xmlschema-2.

Simple Types

XML Schema recognizes the following types:

- anyType—Any type, be it simple or complex.

- anySimpleType—Any simple type (to the exclusion of complex types).

- string—Character strings; for example, XML by Example.

- normalizedString—White space normalized strings. It does not contain carriage return, line feed, or tab characters; for example, XML by Example.

- token—A tokenized string. It does not contain line feed or tab characters, and it has no leading or trailing spaces and no internal sequences of two or more spaces.

- base64Binary—Base64-encoded arbitrary binary data.

- hexBinary—Arbitrary hex-encoded data; for example, (decimal 23590): 5C26.

- integer—Integer number; for example, 653.

- positiveInteger—Positive integer (excludes 0); for example, 653.

- negativeInteger—Negative integer (excludes 0); for example, -13.

- nonNegativeInteger—Non-negative integer (includes 0); for example, 653.

- nonPositiveInteger—Non-positive integer (includes 0); for example, -13.

- int—32-bits integer.

- unsignedInt—Non-negative integer.

- long—64-bits integer.

- unsignedLong—Non-negative long.

- short—16-bits integer.

- unsignedShort—Non-negative short.

- byte—8-bits integer.

- unsignedByte—Non-negative byte.

- decimal—Arbitrary precision decimal number, handy for amounts; for example, 27.93.

- float—IEEE single-precision 32-bit floating point type; for example, 11.87e-2.

- double—IEEE double-precision 64-bit floating point type; for example, 11.87e-2.

- boolean—Represents a boolean value (true or false); for example, true.

- dateTime—Specific instant of time, identified by its date and time; for example (11/8/1971, 10.00am): 1971-11-08T10:00:00.

- time—An instant of time that recurs every day; for example (1.20pm, GMT+1): 13:20:00+01:00.

- date—A calendar date; for example (11/8/1971): 1971-11-08.

- gYearMonth—A specific month of a given year in the Gregorian calendar; for example (November 1971): 1971-11.

- gMonth—A given month; for example, 11.

- gYear—A given year; for example, 1971.

- gDay—A day of the month; for example, 08.

- gMonthDay—A day of the year; for example (8th November): 11-08.

- duration—Duration of time; for example (100 days): P100D.

- Name—An XML name.

- QName—XML qualified XML name; for example, xbe2:name.

- NCName—Unqualified XML name; for example, name.

- anyURI—Uniform Resource Identifier; for example, http://www.marchal.com/.

- language—Language code as defined in RFC 1766.

- ID—ID as defined by DTD.

- IDREF—IDREF as defined by DTD.

- IDREFS—IDREFS as defined by DTD.

- ENTITY—ENTITY as defined by DTD.

- ENTITIES—ENTITIES as defined by DTD.

- NOTATION—NOTATION as defined by DTD.

- NMTOKEN—NMTOKEN as defined by DTD.

- NMTOKENS—NMTOKENS as defined by DTD.

Facets

XML Schema lets you restrict simple types with the restriction tag. The restrictions are called *facets*. The most commonly used facets are

- length—Forces a string to a specified length

```
<xsd:simpleType name="country-code">
  <xsd:restriction base="xsd:string"'>
    <xsd:length value="8"/>
  </xsd:restriction>
</xsd:simpleType>
```

EXAMPLE

- minLength—Sets the minimal length of a string

- maxLength—Sets the maximum length of a string

- pattern—Specifies a regular expression that the string must conform to

```
<xsd:simpleType name="us-zipcode">
  <xsd:restriction base="xsd:string">
    <xsd:pattern value="[0-9]{5}(-[0-9]{4})?"/>
  </xsd:restriction>
</xsd:simpleType>
```

EXAMPLE

- enumeration—Limits the set of values to those in the enumeration

- whiteSpace—Enforces the value of the xml:space attribute

- maxInclusive and maxExclusive—Set the upper limit, respectively, inclusively and exclusively

EXAMPLE

```
<xsd:simpleType name="cheap-items">
  <xsd:restriction base="xsd:decimal">
    <xsd:minInclusive value="10"/>
  </xsd:restriction>
</xsd:simpleType>
```

- minInclusive and minExclusive—Set the lower limit, respectively, inclusively and exclusively

- totalDigits—Sets maximum number of digits

- fractionDigits—Sets maximum number of digits in the fractional part of a number

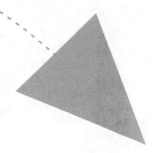

Index